I0885710

STORYTELLERS

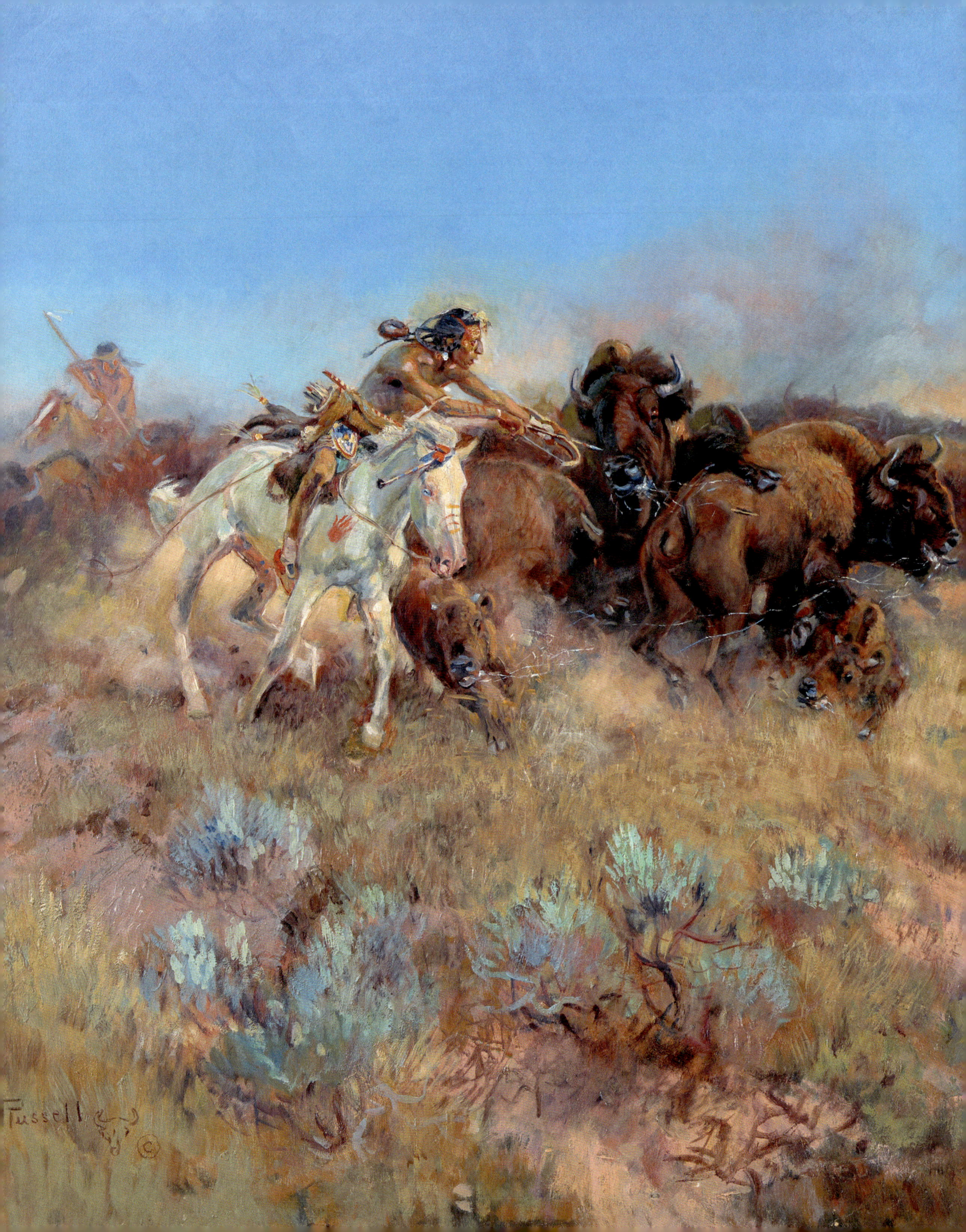

STORYTELLERS

THE BLACKFEET NATION AND CHARLES M. RUSSELL

DENVER ART MUSEUM

EDITED BY JR HENNEMAN

WITH A CONTRIBUTION BY EMILY C. BURNS

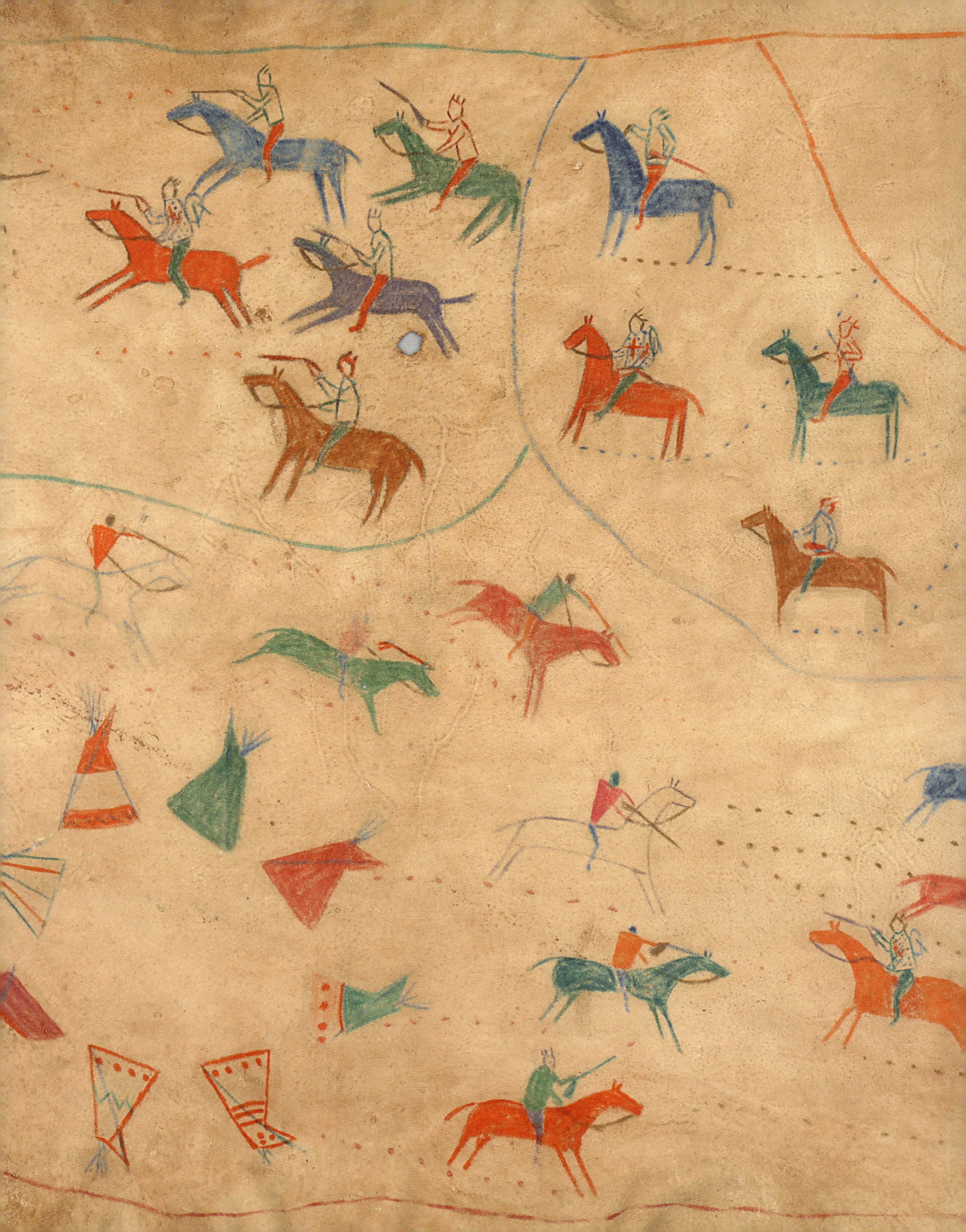

Contents

Director's Foreword

FOR OVER ONE HUNDRED YEARS, the Denver Art Museum has collected Indigenous art of North America, and the first object cataloged in our permanent collection in 1925 is the beaded *ah'kooyiinimaatsis* (tobacco bag) exhibited in *Storytellers: The Blackfeet Nation and Charles M. Russell* (cat. 2). For seventy of those years, the museum has also collected western American art, and since establishing a department for that collection in 2001 and the founding of the Petrie Institute of Western American Art in 2007, the collection has grown tremendously and is now one of the best in the country. In both areas, the museum has told important and compelling stories throughout the decades.

This long history makes us uniquely situated to present this first-of-its-kind exhibition that showcases the art and culture of the Nitsitapii, as the Blackfeet Nation and the larger Blackfoot Confederacy refer to themselves, alongside the work of Charles Marion Russell, the sine qua non of western art. The fine bead-, quill-, leather-, and featherwork in the Nitsitapii objects we care for in our collection are similar to that found on objects that inspired Russell to represent them in his paintings and sculptures. Seeing these works side by side offers a new perspective on Russell's art that is only now being fully explored and brings wider attention to the artistry of Nitsitapii makers and their histories.

Since its founding, the Petrie Institute has been at the forefront of art-historical scholarship, deepening our understanding of western art in its broader contexts of American art, modernism, and colonialism. And it has long been invested in the art of Charles Russell. In 2009, we presented a retrospective of Russell's paintings and sculptures, which was accompanied by an extensive catalog edited by Joan Carpenter Troccoli, the inaugural director and curator of what has become the Petrie Institute. We dedicated a volume of the *Western Passages* series to Russell in 2010, *Charlie Russell and Friends*, that explored Russell and the coterie of artists and illustrators who worked alongside him and were inspired by him and his example.

In 1991, the Magness family generously donated one of Russell's iconic paintings—*In the Enemy's Country*—that contributes an important part of the exhibition's narrative (cat. 83). Other Russell works have come into the collection over the years, and Thomas A. Petrie, a dedicated board member and generous supporter of the museum, has been an advocate for all things Russell during this time. Tom and his wife, Jane, who shares this passion for western American art, recently made a legacy gift of some of the most celebrated masterworks—both paintings and sculptures—by Russell. The gift of the Petrie Collection will further strengthen the breadth and caliber of the museum's comprehensive western American art collection.

Our commitment to Indigenous communities has strengthened our relationships locally but also those further afield and has informed the very heart of this project. I want to thank Director and Curator of the Petrie Institute of Western American Art JR Henneman for her thoughtful and careful approach to this project as well as her sharp presentation of the relation between Nitsitapii culture and Russell's work. I'd also like to extend my gratitude to our Nitsitapii advisers for their insights and contributions to the exhibition and the catalog and Emily C. Burns for her important essay.

I am pleased to acknowledge Tom and Jane Petrie as presenting sponsors of this exhibition. We are also grateful to Mary Pat and Richard McCormick for their contribution, the Wyeth Foundation for American Art for their grant to support the catalog, as well as the donors of the Annual Fund Leadership Campaign and the residents who support the Scientific and Cultural Facilities District (SCFD). Without this local support, the museum wouldn't be able to offer the engaging exhibitions and programs that our audiences so enjoy.

Christoph Heinrich
Frederick and Jan Mayer Director

PIWAA Director's Note

THE LITERATURE ON CHARLES MARION RUSSELL is vast. When asked to create an exhibition on the artist to celebrate the centenary of his death in 1926, I had doubts about how to make a new scholarly contribution, especially since the Petrie Institute of Western American art at the Denver Art Museum did *the* retrospective on Russell in 2009. Given the institute's unique situation within an encyclopedic museum and after consultations with scholars in the field—including Spencer Wigmore, Emily C. Burns, Heather Caverhill, Annika Johnson, Thomas Busciglio-Ritter, Michael Grauer, and Scott Winterrowd—it soon became clear that we had a significant opportunity to wed our western American art expertise with the museum's world-renowned collection of Indigenous arts of North America. This choice soon felt natural, given how closely it mirrors Russell's own interest in Indigenous art and culture. I am honored that the Petrie Institute is the first to present a project of this kind.

My approach has been guided by recent scholarship on Russell and Indigenous art, especially the multiauthored digital publication published in 2025 by the Amon Carter Museum of American Art (https://bulletin-v1.cartermuseum.org/) and recent interdisciplinary symposia sponsored by the Charles M. Russell Center for the Study of Art of the American West at the University of Oklahoma. I owe much to the extensive work being done by institutions across the Americas to reckon with colonial histories and meaningfully engage Indigenous communities, including groundbreaking reinstallations of American arts galleries, such as at the Joslyn Art Museum, and thoughtful community-focused projects that seek to indigenize histories of American art, such as *Connections: The Blackfeet and Winold Reiss* at the Museum of the Plains Indian in Browning, Montana. Indigenous scholars, artists, and activists continue to remind outsider scholars of our responsibilities; for this project, historian and ethnobotanist Rosalyn LaPier's work has been fundamental to helping us understand Nitsitapii lifeways while reminding us of our partial perspectives. The staff at the Charles M. Russell Museum has been generous in their time and attention to queries and requests to view Russell's personal collection of Indigenous art, called the studio collection. Visits to the Blackfeet Nation to consult with community members and institutional leaders, among them Cheryle "Cookie" Cobell Zwang (Niit si poo aki, Only Girl); Renee Bear Medicine, Curator at the Museum of the Plains Indian; and Aaron LaFromboise, Director of Library Services at Medicine Spring Library, Blackfeet Community College, convinced me that an exhibition celebrating the Indigenous people and influences in Russell's life is long overdue.

Project advisers from the Blackfeet Nation, Darnell (Niit Too Kim Mee) and Smokey (Ess Sta Kaawn) Rides At The Door, John Isaiah Pepion (Mahkoyi Sohkoo), Nit'koomii Jesse DesRosier, Tillie Keyonnie Torpey, Cheryle "Cookie" Cobell Zwang (Niit si poo aki,

Only Girl), Leon Rattler, M. A. T., and Aaron LaFromboise, dedicated significant time through onsite and virtual meetings. They weighed in and contributed to all aspects of the project, including the selection of exhibition objects, interpretation, catalog content, language, and exhibition and catalog design. We are proud to have produced this meaningful and beautiful project together.

We also conducted listening sessions at Blackfeet Community College in March 2025 and learned much from Rosalyn LaPier, Gheri Hall, Quanah Jackson, Natowakee Kipp, Melinda Kipp, George Kipp, Joyce Spoonhunter, Leon Rattler, and John Isaiah Pepion. Thanks also to John Murray and Gheri Hall at the Blackfeet Tribal Historic Preservation Office for fielding our inquiries.

A project of this complexity requires the contributions of many. Sincere thanks to the museum staff who helped make it possible: in the Native Arts Department, Andrew W. Mellon Curator of Native Arts John Lukavic, former Associate Curator of Native Arts (now Curator of Native Art at the National Gallery of Art) Dakota Hoska, Andrew W. Mellon Curatorial Fellow of Indigenous Arts of North America Jennie Trujillo, and Curatorial Assistant Caitlin O'Beirne; the entire exhibition and collection team, especially Associate Registrar and Project Manager Yvanne Vieuille, Manager of Traveling Exhibitions Caitlin Rumery, Assistant Preparator Manda Remmen, and the many others who worked on logistics, mounts, and installation; the conservation team, especially Associate Director of Conservation and Technical Studies Gina Lauren, Objects Conservator Aaron Burgess, and Senior Textile Conservator Allison McCloskey; photographers Christina Jackson, Eric Stephenson, and Bruce Fernandez; the provenance team, especially Provenance Research Fellow MacKenzie Coyle; graphic designers Tasso Stathopulos and Jenn Goodrich; Managing Editor Valerie Hellstein and Editor Leslie Murrell; Senior Interpretive Specialist Lauren Thompson; and the wonderful team at the Petrie Institute including Senior Curatorial Assistant Meg Selig, Denver Art Museum/University of Denver Chanzit Intern Chloe LeRoy, and Pathway Exploration Intern Neva Zamil.

Externally, we have been supported by exhibition designer Tomomi Itakura and her team at TSKP × IKD, especially Karen Kuo, and book designer Kevin Coochwytewa, in addition to the many generous lenders to the exhibition.

Finally, this project would not be possible without the support and enthusiasm of Thomas A. Petrie, a dedicated believer in the continued relevance of Russell's art and its expanding scholarship.

JR Henneman
Director and Curator, Petrie Institute of Western American Art

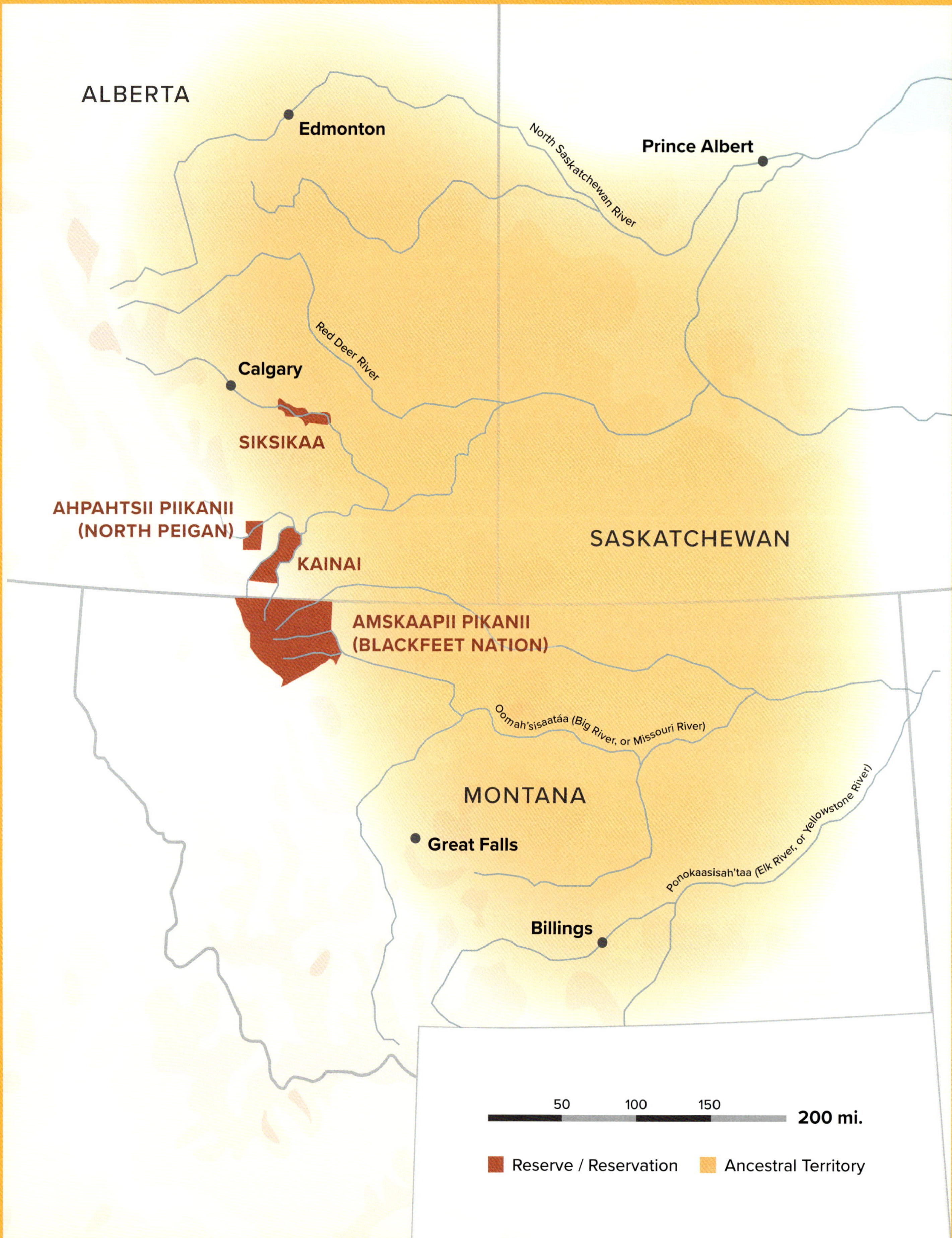
ALBERTA
Edmonton
Prince Albert
North Saskatchewan River
Red Deer River
Calgary
SIKSIKAA
AHPAHTSII PIIKANII
(NORTH PEIGAN)
KAINAI
SASKATCHEWAN
AMSKAAPII PIKANII
(BLACKFEET NATION)
Oomah'sisaatáa (Big River, or Missouri River)
MONTANA
Great Falls
Ponokaasisah'taa (Elk River, or Yellowstone River)
Billings
50
100
150
200 mi.
Reserve / Reservation
Ancestral Territory

Note on Language

WHAT IS OFTEN CALLED "RUSSELL COUNTRY" the Nitsitapii ("Real People," or Blackfoot Confederacy) call Nitawahsin ("our country") and have for millennia.[1] Ancestral Nitsitapii land spans what we now call the Great Plains from the North Saskatchewan River in Alberta, Canada, south to Ponokaasisah'taa (the Elk, or Yellowstone, River) in Montana (fig. 1).[2] Landforms within this vast territory, including the Maokakinistsii ("Backbone of the World," or Rocky Mountains), Ninastakoo (Chief Mountain), and the Katooyisiksi (Sweet Pine Hills, now known as Sweet Grass Hills), figure prominently in Nitsitapii creation stories and are "the source of bundles, pipes, songs, drums, and other ceremonial knowledge and objects."[3] While the Nitsitapii describe themselves as Saokitapiiksi ("Plains people"), the Maokakinistsii have always been central to their culture as a source of knowledge, power, and identity.[4]

A recent DNA study of ancestral and living members of the Nitsitapii reveals an ancient lineage going back at least eighteen thousand years.[5] Within the Blackfoot Confederacy, four distinct tribes share a common language and history: the Amskaapii Pikanii (Blackfeet Nation, or South Peigan) in Montana and the Kainai (Blood Tribe), Ahpahtsii Piikanii (North Peigan), and Siksikaa (Blackfoot) in Canada. Because he spent the majority of his life in Montana, Charles Russell primarily interacted with the Amskaapii Pikanii and regularly traversed the Blackfeet Indian Reservation during travels from his home in Great Falls to Glacier National Park and Canada. Because of this proximity, this exhibition largely features ancestral Nitsitapii objects that represent the Amskaapii Pikanii and Kainai tribes. When specific attributions are unknown to us, we attribute the works generally to the Nitsitapii.

There is no standard orthography for transliterating Nitsiipowah'sin ("Real People language") into English. While we have used consistent spelling of Nitsiipowah'sin words in this book, elsewhere different spellings abound. For example, we use "Pikanii," which is also written as Piikuni and Pikunni. Our Amskaapii Pikanii advisers emphasized their preference for spelling "Peigan" with "ei" when it is used, though it is common to see "Piegan," including in many of the titles of Russell's paintings. In the catalog and

Fig. 1.

Map of ancestral and current Nitsitapii lands. Courtesy Kevin Coochwytewa.

exhibition, we use Nitsiipowah'sin where appropriate to honor the first language and as recommended by our advisers. Because "Amskaapii Pikanii" and "Blackfeet" are often used interchangeably, we use both in this book. Where possible, we lead with the Nitsitapii names for objects, places, landforms, and rivers, followed by their English designations on first mention.

There is no word for "art" in Nitsiipowah'sin, at least as it is understood in English. Nitsitapii objects made explicitly for trade come closest to the Eurocentric idea of an object created for visual contemplation and whose value relies on the whims of a capitalist market. What we frequently refer to as "Nitsitapii artworks" are, according to our advisers, more correctly understood as "storytellers": objects intricately connected to community that represent ongoing histories and connections that are individual, collective, and spiritual.[6] They are active and alive, just as Nitsiipowah'sin is a dynamic language in which "the distinction between noun and verb entirely dissolves . . . as one cannot exist without the other."[7] To honor this understanding, and in allusion to Russell's reputation as a spinner of textual and visual yarns, we have titled this exhibition *Storytellers: The Blackfeet Nation and Charles M. Russell.*

NOTES

We would like to thank Leon Rattler and Nit'koomii Jesse DesRosier for their input and guidance on Nitsiipowah'sin terms and names used throughout this catalog and providing translations when appropriate.

1 Rosalyn LaPier, "Land as Text: Reading the Land," *Environmental History* 28, no. 1 (2023): 41.

2 Nitsitapii oral history relates that the Blackfeet traveled widely, including north to what is now Alaska and south to what is now Mexico.

3 Maria Nieves Zedeno, "Bison Hunters and the Rocky Mountains: An Evolving Partnership," *Quarternary International* 461 (July 2017): 96 and fig. 14 (map) on 97.

4 Ibid., 99. See also Rosalyn R. LaPier, *Invisible Reality: Storytellers, Storytakers, and the Supernatural World of the Blackfeet* (University of Nebraska Press and the American Philosophical Society, 2017).

5 Dorothy First Rider et al., "Genomic Analyses Correspond with Deep Persistence of Peoples of Blackfoot Confederacy from Glacial Times," *Science Advances* 10, no. 14 (2024), https://www.science.org/doi/10.1126/sciadv.adl6595. This is a correction of previous anthropological theories that indicated that the Nitsitapii had migrated west from the Great Lakes region and aligns with Nitsitapii knowledge and history. See, for example, John C. Ewers, *The Blackfeet: Raiders on the Northwestern Plains* (University of Oklahoma Press, 1958).

6 Recently, among art historians, the word "belongings" has gained currency as an identifier for Indigenous art objects to underscore their connection to community and agency. However, our advisers find the word "storytellers" more appropriate for this project. For more on belongings, see the essay by Emily C. Burns in this volume.

7 Leroy Little Bear and Ryan Heavy Head, "A Conceptual Anatomy of the Blackfoot World," *ReVision* 26, no. 3 (2004): 33. Little Bear and Heavy Head explain that Nitsiipowah'sin presents a reality that "emphasizes the flux dynamics of massive fluidity" in contrast to English, which targets a reality of "consistent composition and behavior of solids within solids" (32).

Nitsitapii Names and Terms Used in This Catalog

In the following essays, we italicize common nouns on the first mention and set all proper nouns in roman. Literal translations of Nitsiipowah'sin *are included in quotation marks when given. The English term or name follows.*

ah'kooyiinimaatsis: pipe bag, or tobacco bag
Ah'ktsistsii sissaat'taa: Shell Necklace River, or Mussellshell River
aistookiimaaksi: hand drum
akaitapiiks moh'sa'koo: Old North Trail, an ancient trade and travel route running from what is now Canada to Mexico
Amitoo's oomah'sikimii: Lake MacDonald
Amskaapii Pikanii: Blackfeet Nation, or South Peigan, in Montana
Ahpahtsii Piikanii: North Peigan in Canada
atapiimiiksi: "real dolls"

iinii: buffalo
iinyookskasiiksi: buffalo runners
Iitootooyiisii'wa Maatapiiksi: "time when people gather together"
iiniiskin: buffalo stone

Kainai: "Many Chiefs," Blood Tribe in Canada
kaniskinaitapiiksi: Mice People
Katooyisiksi: Sweet Pine Hills, now known as Sweet Grass Hills
kiipatapiisinoan: "our way of life"
Kipiitapooka: favored grandchild
kitawah'sinoan: "our food source," Blackfoot Territory
Ksistakii amaopisstaan: Beaver Bundle Society
ksistsiikoom: "thunder"
Kyiyo seet'-daa: Bear River, or Marias River

Maokakinistsii: "Backbone of the World," or the Rocky Mountains
Makoyi moosah'koo: "Wolf Tail," the Milky Way
Mataokiiksi: Buffalo Women Society
Miisinskiisah'taa: Badger Creek
Miistakiiksi: "reaches up," mountains

Naatoosii-sat'taa kao'koyi: Sun River Valley
Naattoosiseetáa: Medicine River, or Sun River
Napii: Trickster, Old Man
natoowaapinaa: medicine man
ninaipistsii: war robe
Ninastakoo: Chief Mountain
Nitsiipowah'sin: "Real People language"
Nitsitapii: "Real People," "First People," or the Blackfoot Confederacy
Nitsitapiiskaa'taksini: "Real peoples' knowledge"

O'kan: Sun Dance ritual
ookoonookists: sarvisberry, or serviceberry
Oomah'sisaatáa: Big River, or Missouri River
Oonikiisisaat'taa: Milk River
Ootakawananniitoomoo: Square Buttes
Oot'kiisisátaa: Yellow River, or Judith River

paaniikataanssii: chief's liner in a lodge
pisskaan: "deep blood-kettle," corral, or buffalo jump
Ponokaasisah'taa: Elk River, or Yellowstone River
pookitapiiksi: "Little People"

Saokitapiiksi: "Plains people"
Siksikaa: Blackfoot tribe in Canada
Siksikaasat'taa: Blackfoot River
Staamiksiiks: Buffalo Bull Society

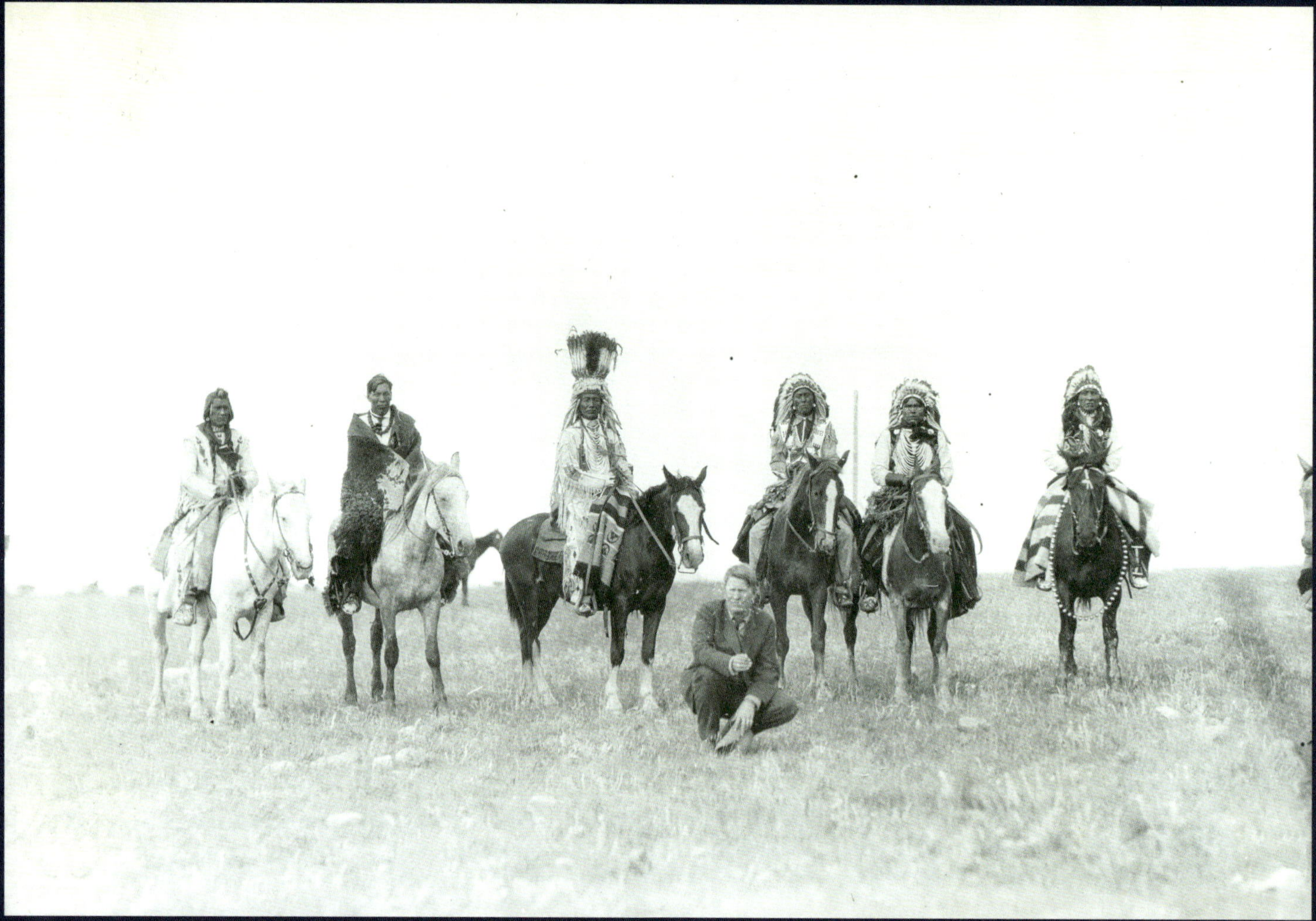

Russell in Pikanii Country

JR HENNEMAN

A PHOTOGRAPH HAS COME TO DEFINE this project for me (fig. 1). In it, Charles Marion Russell (1864–1926) sits on his haunches, hat in hand. He is literally foregrounded, both in the image and in its description: "Russell and men from the Blackfoot tribe." Yet, he is out of focus, fuzzy around the edges. Instead, six mounted Amskaapii Pikanii (Blackfeet, or South Peigan) men, with a seventh just out of view, are in focus. Arguably the most significant figures in this image, they are unnamed and unacknowledged.

Russell regularly traversed the Blackfeet Indian Reservation to and from his home in Great Falls, Montana, and his cabin, Bull Head Lodge, on Amitoo's oomah'sikimii (Lake MacDonald) in what became Glacier National Park. This photograph was probably taken in July 1912 when Russell stopped in Browning for the Fourth of July celebration on his way to the Calgary Stampede.[1] We know that Russell regularly socialized with and exchanged insight on art and culture with many Indigenous people. Arikara artist White Crow (also known as Myles, or Miles, Horn) met Russell in 1915 at the Roundup celebration in Miles City where Russell was staying at the on-site Indian camp. Over the years of their friendship, which lasted until Russell's death in 1926, Russell encouraged White Crow and gave him tips, such as "to always watch the sunset colors."[2] The relationship was mutually beneficial, as White Crow taught Russell about aspects of Plains Indian life that inevitably influenced Russell's artworks. Despite first-person accounts of intercultural exchange, the details, stories, and experiences of Russell's Indigenous neighbors and his own travels through reservations often go unexamined and unrecorded in the Russell scholarship, just as they do in the photograph of Russell and the mounted Amskaapii Pikanii men.

This project honors the reciprocity between Russell and the Indigenous people on whose land he lived and worked. For the sake of focus and clarity, it celebrates Nitsitapii ("Real, or First People," the Blackfoot Confederacy) art and culture, though there are many other Indigenous stories to tell. By presenting Nitsitapii objects, here called storytellers, from the Denver Art Museum's collection alongside Russell's paintings and sculptures, it offers new insight into this largely unexamined intercultural exchange. This project seeks to answer two questions: What can we learn about

Fig. 1.

Unknown photographer, Russell and men from the Blackfoot tribe. Courtesy C. M. Russell Museum.

Russell's life and work when we broaden our lens and redirect our focus to include Indigenous perspectives? And, how is our understanding of the art, history, and cultures of the Northern Great Plains and Rocky Mountain region enhanced when we follow Russell's example of being curious about other cultures and making space for conversation and storytelling?

A group of advisers from the Blackfeet Nation in Montana—Nit'koomii Jesse DesRosier, Aaron LaFromboise, John Isaiah Pepion (Mahkoyi Sohkoo), Leon Rattler, M. A. T., Darnell Rides At The Door (Niit Too Kim Mee), Smokey Rides At The Door (Ess Sta Kaawn), Tillie Keyonnie Torpey, and Cheryle "Cookie" Cobell Zwang (Niit si poo aki, Only Girl)—helped answer these questions and others. Thanks to them, the names of the riders in the 1912 photograph can be recorded. They are, from left to right, Fred Big Top, Rueben Black Boy, Yellow Kidney, Jim No Chief, James Big Top (no relation to Fred), and Black Weasel. Fred, Rueben, and Black Weasel were brothers. To members of the Blackfeet Nation, these are family members and ancestors, as are the Nitsitapii storytellers in this exhibition. With a project like this, which engages the complicated, imbalanced, and tense relationship between American and Indigenous art, we seek to expand our understanding of western art and history and reconnect Nitsitapii people with artworks from their community collected and maintained by the Denver Art Museum. We do so imperfectly, and we ask forgiveness for the many omissions a project of this scope must entail; may they inspire others to take up and continue similar work, moving us all forward in a good way.

This is the first known exhibition that gives Indigenous art and culture equal prominence alongside Russell's paintings and sculptures. As such, it is one step toward a broader assessment and intentional indigenization of Russell scholarship.[3] In the following pages, I explore the historical context of the period of relevance: the 1880s through the 1920s. I then consider two ways we might create a more expansive dialogue around Russell's life and work: first, by shifting attention to the Indigenous people and artworks that influenced him and, second, by broadening our frame of geographical and cultural reference from "Russell Country" to "Pikanii Country."

What Russell Knew ... and Didn't

Building on the work of many scholars who have considered Russell's historical and artistic inspirations, this exhibition reinforces that Russell studied Indigenous visual and material culture closely and that he maintained relationships with Indigenous people. Over the course of his career, Russell remained dedicated to close observation of his surroundings and subjects and indebted to Indigenous knowledge, which he translated through his unique artistic vision. Increasingly, his work took on the now-familiar hue of a romanticism expressed through a vibrant color palette and the timeless space of "The West That Has Passed."[4] Later in life, Russell said, "You've got to romance a lot to make money these days. If you don't do anything but tell the truth in stories and paintings, it's nothing but plain history, and nobody cares anything about buying history except a few old fellows like me."[5] His wife, Nancy, with her savvy business acumen and thumb on the pulse of art-market desire, often influenced the kind of work he produced. Tuned to an American art market driven primarily by wealthy patrons in major urban centers, they both recognized the importance of romance and the picturesque to sell paintings and sculptures. Understanding Russell's market helps bridge the gap between the realism of his works and their obvious romantic fantasy.[6] Amskaapii Pikanii advisers repeat similar observations, speaking enthusiastically about how Russell represented certain elements of their culture, history, and land while poking fun at the many times he exercised artistic license or revealed cultural ignorance to create more pleasing compositions, visually stirring stories, or market-ready works. Russell learned from his Indigenous neighbors and visually translated that teaching, but the bulk of his oeuvre was not made for them.[7]

As Emily C. Burns points out in her essay in this volume, it is difficult to clarify what exactly Russell knew—and didn't know—about Nitsitapii culture, though the fact remains that he was surrounded by Nitsitapii people and artworks that influenced his work. From a young age, Russell was fascinated with stories and representations of Native Americans that circulated in popular culture.[8] Even though his earliest imaginings were of Indians as enemies, he developed sympathy for diverse Indigenous people after moving to Montana Territory in 1880.[9] Upon arriving in Helena, he observed Native Americans waiting in line for government rations, a first encounter that was far from the high-adventure and fine-art representations of Indigenous people he had consumed in St. Louis.[10] Years later, Nancy wrote that Charlie was taken with the "picturesqueness" of this scene, but her retrospective articulation of a perceived "picturesque" says more about Nancy's interest in promoting Charlie's legacy than it does about the realities of Helena in the 1880s.[11] The truth is that violence and dispossession underpin this initial encounter. Its realities were far from picturesque.

Russell's representations of "the West that has passed" would not have been possible without the widespread impacts of American settler colonialism. The first career that he took up in Montana—night wrangling, or managing overnight herds of horses in the spring and cows in the fall so that the herd stayed together, settled, and fed in the morning—was predicated on the displacement and containment of Native peoples and the decimation of bison herds. While Russell sympathized with Indigenous nations and had strong opinions against any kind of modernization, he was nonetheless a product of the colonial machine that ended the so-called buffalo days. Some of his early work bore witness to the brutal devastation of Native cultures and economies, a product of which was the forced reliance on unreliable government rations that he had earlier witnessed in Helena. *Caught in the Act*, a grisaille oil painting created for reproduction in *Harper's Weekly* on May 12, 1888, presents a departure from the heroic scenes popular during the same period (fig. 2). Two cowboys approach an Indigenous family, possibly Apsáalooke (Crow), butchering a bovine, ostensibly from the cowboys' herd.

The gray hues underscore a tense scene and reinforce the biting cold against which the children tightly hold blankets around themselves. Two Indigenous men with guns stand in the center of the composition; the one on the left makes the Plains Indian Sign Language sign for "food," holding his fingers toward his mouth.[12] *Caught in the Act* points to the grim reality of starvation experienced by many Plains people at this time. Historian John Ewers explains that the Nitsitapii sometimes killed cattle from the Indian Agency's herd but also from ranches outside the reservation. The logic was simple: White men had killed the bison. Why couldn't the Nitsitapii kill a few of the White man's cattle?[13]

Just decades before, the Nitsitapii had been the primary military force in the region, made powerful by years of wealth and political capital accumulated from communal bison hunts, by access to goods and technology via an international trade market, and by deep rooted knowledge of the natural and supernatural worlds. Beginning in the late 1700s, they traded small game pelts, bison meat, and pemmican to White traders in exchange for tools, weapons, tobacco, alcohol, jewelry, paints, cloth, and beads.[14] In 1832, the American Fur Company established Fort McKenzie on the Oomah'sisaatáa (Big River, or Missouri River), and increasingly, the Nitsitapii traded bison robes in addition to other pelts.[15] The robe trade provided access to goods from a global market: "bells and mirrors from Leipzig, clay pipes from Cologne, beads from Venice, calico and other cloths from France, woolen goods and firearms from England, clothing and knives from New York and vicinity, shell ornaments from the Bahamas and the West Coast, guns from Pennsylvania, and powder and shot from St. Louis."[16] As they had for centuries, the Nitsitapii participated in complex trade markets and integrated new products and technologies into their everyday lives. Access to guns combined with their extraordinary equestrian prowess gave them enough advantage to push the Newe (Shoshone), Séliš (Flathead), and ʞupawiȼq̓nuk (Kutenai) west over the Maokakinistsii ("Backbone of the World," or the Rocky Mountains). By the mid-1800s, the height of their military power, the Nitsitapii commanded the Northern Plains from the North Saskatchewan River in Canada south to the Ponokaasisah'taa (Elk River, or Yellowstone River) in Montana (see fig. 1 on page 10).[17]

As historian Rosalyn LaPier writes, the Nitsitapii traveled strategically throughout their territory, going "to places where they knew animals to be or to places they created by altering the landscape."[18] The imposition of reservations changed this, drastically reducing their territory and curtailing the seasonal travel that made living on the Great Plains possible. With the 1855 Lame Bull Treaty, the Amskaapii Pikanii granted access to their lands.[19] In return, the treaty included annuities of goods paid to them in the fall. By the 1860s, these were distributed at Fort Benton.[20] Violence between the Pikanii and White settlers increased at this time, especially after settlers discovered gold in Montana in 1864. The Pikanii rejected the settlers' overharvesting of natural resources, including cottonwood trees, bison, and beavers.[21] Reservation boundaries were further reduced. By 1888, the current eastern, southern, and northern borders

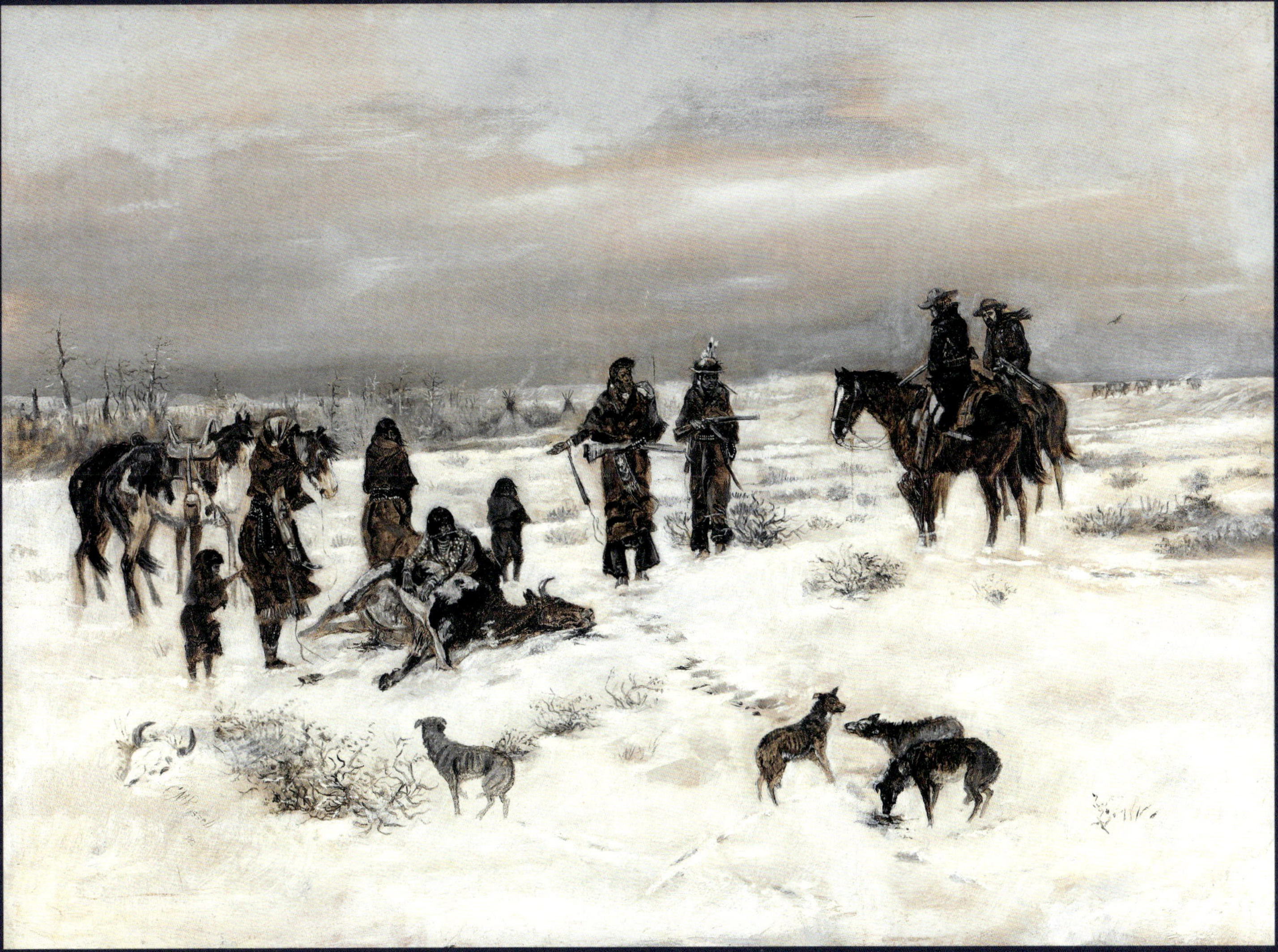

Fig. 2.

Charles Marion Russell, *Caught in the Act*, 1888. Oil on canvas. Montana Historical Society, Mackay Collection, X1952.03.03.

had been established, pushing the Pikanii, who referred to themselves as "Prairie people," up against the mountains.[22] In 1896, the US government carved out the westernmost part of the reservation, which would ultimately become Glacier National Park in 1910. An allotment system implemented on the reservation between 1907 and 1912 further fragmented Pikanii land inside reservation boundaries.

While the Amskaapii Pikanii maintained and continue to maintain knowledge of their traditional lands, their movement was drastically restricted by reservation policies. By the 1880s, bison had been pushed to near extinction primarily by Euro-American hunters supplying a market for bison robes. In 1879, the Siksikaaa (Blackfoot) in Canada recorded a starvation year, soon followed by the starvation winter of 1883–84. Amskaapii Pikanii artist Ni-tah-mah-kwi-i (also known as Lone Wolf, or Hart Merriam Schultz, c. 1882–1970) remembered that "burial boxes, piled two and three deep, lined the ridges. The trees along the river held many more [bodies].... The Blackfeet did not put their people in the ground and for many years those burials would remind us of that sad winter."[23] Hundreds of Nitsitapii perished.[24] (For more on Ni-tah-mah-kwi-i, see later in this volume.) Another extreme winter hit in 1886–87. Swathes of cattle herds died, to the detriment of East Coast and international investors. While wintering that year at the O-H Ranch near Utica, Montana, Russell made the first artwork that would bring him significant renown: a small watercolor *Last of the 5,000 (Waiting for a Chinook)* (1886; Collection of Montana Stockgrowers Association), in which a starving cow, represented with a raw economy of line, foreshadows the end of the open range era.[25] Plains people had been living this reality for years.

Between May and September 1888, Russell traveled to Canada with Phil Weinard and B. J. "Long Green" Stillwell. The summer he spent camping near High River, a small town on the Alberta prairie, left long legacies in Russell's work.[26] During the journey north, Weinard taught his companions Plains Indian Sign Language (PISL), which Russell often featured in his art.[27] They encountered Canadian Mounted Police taking Native prisoners, a theme that resurfaces in Russell's 1912 painting *Single-Handed* (cat. 7). Thousands of First Nations people lived in and passed through the High River area including Siksikaa, Tsuut'ina Nation (Sarcee), Nakoda (Stoney), Kainai (Blood Tribe), Ahpahtsii Piikanii (North Peigan), and Amskaapii Pikanii. While Russell did not assimilate (as many accounts would later claim), he spent time with Indigenous people as he moved around the area, including with Apskinas (born Kainai, adopted and raised Siksikaa, eventually enrolled with Tsuut'ina Nation). This unofficial chief of the district was, according to historian Hugh Dempsey, "everything the artist might hope for. He was from a strong warrior tradition, knowledgeable about the customs of his tribe, able to speak passable English, and living in the traditional way."[28] Russell's later bronze *Counting Coup* (modeled 1905; cat. 45) and oil painting *When Blackfeet and Sioux Meet* (1908; cat. 44) may have been inspired by Apskinas's stories.[29]

A few years after his Canadian summer, Russell painted *The Silk Robe* (1890; cat. 52), which depicts daily life in a summer camp. Based on similarities with Nitsitapii objects from the Denver Art Museum's collection, it is clear that Russell studied Nitsitapii art and material culture closely. In *The Silk Robe,* two men smoke and relax outside a lodge after a successful buffalo hunt. The man wearing a buckskin shirt (similar to cat. 12) makes a directional movement in PISL. Both men wear leggings and moccasins (similar to cats. 9 and 20). Two women process a bison hide using fleshing tools (such as cats. 53, 54, and 55). One wears beaded leggings and a belt studded with brass tacks (similar to cats. 29 and 28). A child wearing moccasins (similar to cat. 23) plays with the tail of the bison hide. Robes, beads, the metal pot hung over the fire, red trade blankets, and brass tacks point to longstanding trade. Amskaapii Pikanii advisers note the rolled-up lodge hide that Russell depicted would have allowed cooler air to pass through on a hot day. According to Russell scholar Frederic G. Renner, the "silk robe" of this painting's title refers to an especially prime and well-tanned bison hide.[30]

The winter scene *Indian Hunter's Return* also shows details of Amskaapii Pikanii daily life (1900; cat. 4). The man standing in the snow just to right of center wears a capote, or winter coat, made from wool trade blankets (similar to cat. 8). The mounted man carries a beaded medicine or tobacco bag (similar to cat. 43). Behind him, a white horse with saddle and travois sports a colorful crupper draped from the saddle to its tail (similar to cat. 73). Additional accessories—a knife scabbard studded with brass tacks and high-pommeled saddles—also resemble Amskaapii Pikanii objects in the exhibition (cats. 16 and 72). According to Ewers, Russell accurately captured the "method of transporting a butchered buffalo back to camp with the heavy burden of the dead animal's parts equally divided on each side of a pack horse."[31] Amskaapii Pikanii advisers tell us that horses were trained for specific tasks and thus highly specialized. This horse would have only been used to pack meat, an important and honorable role. Advisers also note that many different activities are compressed into this tight composition. Some figures—like the child running in from the right—seem dressed in their finest attire, yet the reason for such clothing rather than everyday wear is unclear. In this painting, Russell placed the lodges in a river bottom and painted trees selectively to convey depth and add visual interest to the upper right corner, which balances the activity in the lower left foreground. In reality, however, winter camp lodges—which were indeed set up in river bottoms—needed to be firmly situated *within* the trees, not along their outer edge, to avoid being blown away by regular and powerful winds.

According to Nancy's memoir of Charlie, he encountered Indigenous people numerous times while night wrangling in the 1880s and early 1890s around the Yellow (Judith), Musselshell, and Milk Rivers to the east of Great Falls. This area fell within the ancestral lands of the Nitsitapii, although numerous Native peoples including the A'aninin (Gros Ventre), Nakota (Assiniboine), Apsáalooke (Crow), and Nēhiyaw (Cree) traveled through it. According to Nancy, some of his earliest encounters were with Apsáalooke and

Amskaapii Pikanii men on horse raids. Charlie was equally frightened and awed by these men who traveled on campaigns to build wealth and establish status.[32]

Ksiks Unopachis (White Quiver; c.1850 or c.1860–1931) was one of the most notorious Amskaapii Pikanii warriors of the late buffalo days. His legendary activities included around forty horse raids, the last of which occurred in 1885 when he was about twenty-five years old, and twenty-two war trips.[33] Though he accumulated many horses, he gave the majority away. Our advisers explain that generosity is a primary cultural value, and the wealthiest Amskaapii Pikanii often have the fewest material possessions. It seems likely that Russell knew of this famous warrior's exploits, and some scholars claim that Ksiks Unopachis's story influenced Russell's artworks, including the bronze *Watcher of the Plains* (modeled 1901; cat. 85) and the oil painting from the same year *The Horse Thieves* (cat. 78).[34] Similarly, Russell may have been inspired by stories of other Nitsitapii leaders, such as Isapo-Muxika (Chief Crowfoot), whom he memorialized in a plaster bust in 1901.[35]

Many Indigenous peoples throughout Montana and into Canada contributed to Russell's creation of what he called "The West That Has Passed." Over the years, he reiterated themes, including buffalo hunting, counting coup, scouting, and women moving, based on stories he heard from Indigenous neighbors about the buffalo days. Over time, as he moved further away from a period he had arrived too late to witness, he transmuted his own sense of loss and mortality into increasingly romantic and nostalgic scenes aglow with burning sunsets, masculine valor, and feminine nobility. Even while his artistic vision changed, his work remained rooted in Indigenous sources.

Pikanii Country

Many of Russell's paintings depict Nitawahsin ("our country"). In his artworks, this land is a character all its own, one rooted in the climate and geography of Pikanii country south of the Canadian border. Consistently, recognizable landmarks show up in his work, including Ootakawananniitoomoo (the two Square Buttes, one to the east and one to the west of Great Falls), Round Butte, the Oomah'sisaatáa, the Naattoosiseetáa (Medicine River, or Sun River), multiple mountain ranges in the Judith Basin to the east, and the Maokakinistsii to the west. Amskaapii Pikanii advisers feel connected to the land Russell depicted, appreciating his sensitivity to its details, colors, and vast spaces. As someone from the same area, I wondered how my understanding of home would change if I broadened my perspective beyond the Russell framework—this region is frequently called "Russell Country"—to take a deeper look at the human history of Pikanii country. Here, I use the area around the western-most Square Butte (sometimes called Fort Mountain) that sits between Great Falls, the Maokakinistsii, the Oomah'sisaatáa, and the Naattoosiseetáa as a case study (fig. 3). Square Butte acts as a geographical anchor around which layers of human history coexist, layers not always acknowledged in the Russell scholarship.

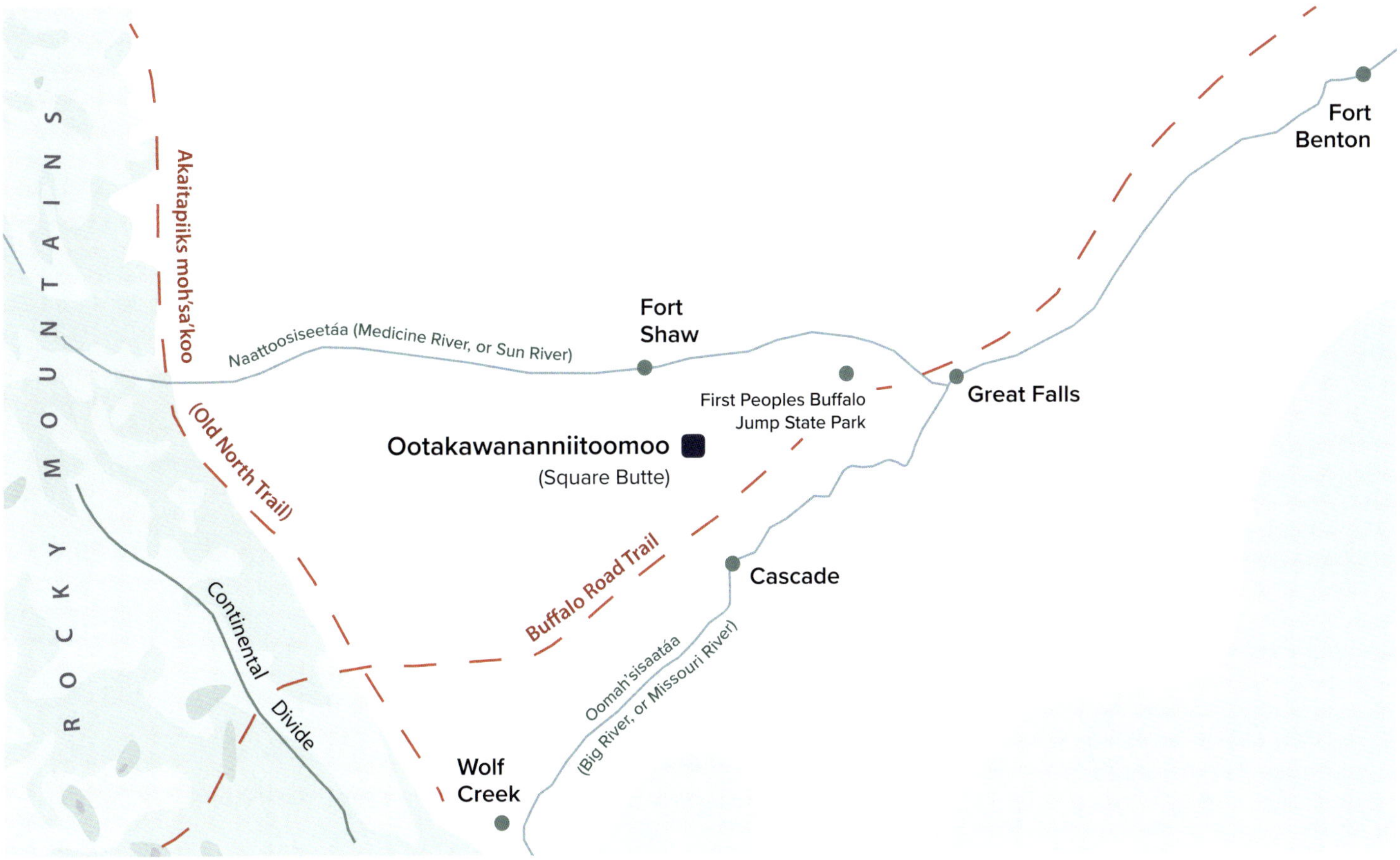

Fig. 3.

Map of western Square Butte and surrounding area. Courtesy Kevin Coochwytewa.

Russell frequently painted the two Square Buttes. While the eastern one in the Judith Basin rose over his early years in Montana working as a night wrangler, his adult life pivoted around the western-most one. Seen for miles in any direction, its striated towers shoot upward out of vast plains to its unmistakable flat top, which encompasses around two square miles. Its prominence makes it a geographical anchor: a landform used by people across time to situate themselves physically, geographically, culturally, and even psychologically. This was the case for Russell since it signaled his chosen home. Memorably, Russell placed this Square Butte in the middle of his 1922 painting *Charles M. Russell and His Friends,* a clear nod to the importance of this landscape (fig. 4). The town of Cascade lies just south of Square Butte along the Oomah'sisaatáa. There, in 1895 at the home of Ben and Lela Roberts, Charlie met Nancy Cooper and Josephine Wright, who was of Amskaapii Pikanii descent, when both women worked as domestic help for the family. Charlie and Nancy married in 1896, only a few years after Russell had decided to become a full-time artist, and they lived in a small cabin in Cascade before moving to Great Falls in 1897. Wright accompanied them, living in their home, helping with housework, and modeling for Russell. In her essay in this volume, Emily C. Burns explores in depth this relationship and Wright's importance to Russell's work.

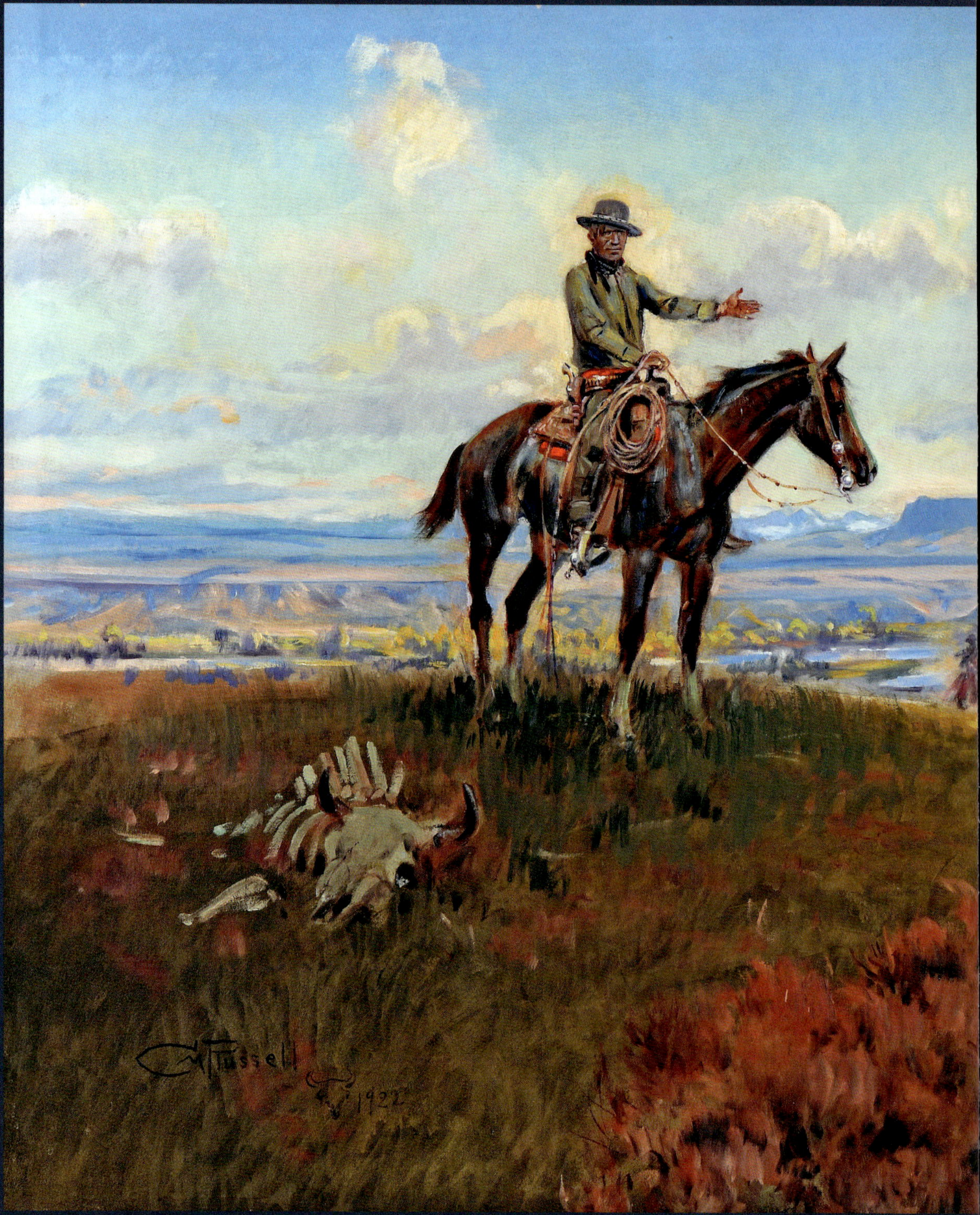
CM Russell
1922

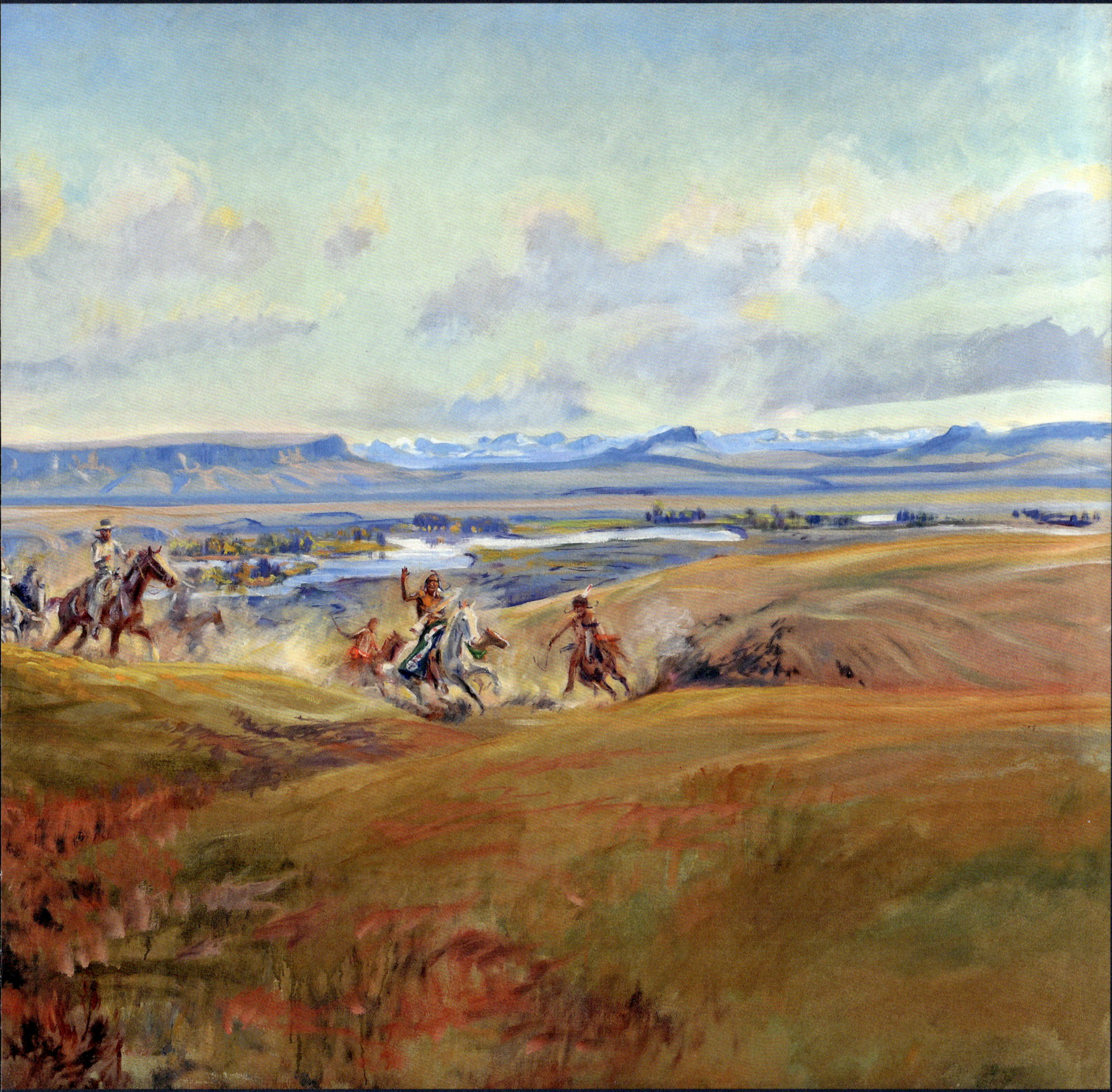

Square Butte has functioned as a geographical anchor for millennia, well before Russell painted it into works such as the c. 1918–20 watercolor *Watching the Enemy (Blackfeet Indians*) and the 1921 oil painting *In the Enemy's Country* (cats. 84 and 83). In the latter, Russell depicts ƙupawi¢q̓nuk hunters from the western side of the Maokakinistsii moving carefully through Amskaapii Pikanii territory on the eastern side of the mountains.[36] Dismounted, they have draped their horses with buffalo hides so that, from a distance, they resemble a small band of bull buffalo.[37] Archaeological evidence has shown that some bison wandered west of the Maokakinistsii, though the majority of the herds remained east of the mountains in Amskaapii Pikanii country, where these ƙupawi¢q̓nuk men journey.[38] Such travelers often took the Buffalo Road Trail, a major transit corridor used by Indigenous communities for centuries to cross the Continental Divide (see fig. 3).[39] The Buffalo Road Trail followed the Siksikaaasat'taa (Blackfoot River) on the western side of the mountains, crossing the Continental Divide east of the current town of Lincoln and descending along the Oomah'sisaatáa. On the eastern side of the Maokakinistsii, it bisected the Akaitapiiks moh'sa'koo (Old North Trail), an ancient trade and travel route running from what is now Canada to Mexico.[40] During the early 1800s, Meriwether Lewis, advised by Nimiipuu (Nez Perce) guides, used the Buffalo Road Trail to return eastward over the Maokakinistsii on his way to meet William Clark at the Great Falls of the Oomah'sisaatáa. On July 7, 1806, he stood atop the Continental Divide looking eastward over the plains. In the distance, he recognized the large flat-topped landform he had named "Fort Mountain" when heading west on July 14, 1805, now commonly known as Square Butte.[41] How many innumerable people had crossed this trail before him, seen Square Butte in the distance, and knew instantly their geographical and cultural location?

Square Butte lies a few miles west of a significant Indigenous historic site: First Peoples Buffalo Jump State Park and National Historic Landmark. This park contains Ulm Pishkun (from the Nitsiipowah'sin word *pisskaan*, or "deep blood-kettle"), a mile-long sandstone cliff used by Indigenous peoples including the Nitsitapii, Ql̓ispé (Kalispel or Pend d'Oreille), Séliš (Flathead), A'aninin, and Nakota for at least a thousand years before Lewis and Clark passed by.[42] Russell's many representations of buffalo hunts, including his *Buffalo Hunt* (1898; cat. 51), *Buffalo Hunt Number 40* (1919; cat. 56), and *Meat for Wild Men* (1924; cat. 57), focus on the dramatic and dangerous skills of mounted riders, though the seeds of this knowledge and practice "were sown centuries earlier, when," according to archaeologist María Nieves Zedeño and others, "the monumental, engineered landscape became a common sight along the northern Rocky Mountain foothills."[43] For millennia before the arrival of horses in the Northern Plains during the early 1700s, and even after the acquisition of horses, the Nitsitapii planned massive communal hunts that ensured the physical and social wellbeing of their communities.[44] Coordinating and executing communal hunts and maintaining communal hunting sites over time required extensive political and human capital.[45] Recent archaeological studies of communal hunting sites (pisskaan, or buffalo jumps) along the northern Maokakinistsii in Montana and Alberta, Canada, underscore the long-term presence of complex cultures and societies.

The basic steps of a communal hunt went something like this: Young men called *iinyookskasiiksi* ("buffalo runners") coaxed bison toward and between drive lanes. Composed of rocks, sticks, brush, bison dung, and/or clumps of sod placed at regular intervals, drive lanes acted as a funnel, guiding the animals toward a cliff or, at other times, into a corral with solid walls called a pound.[46] Men, women, and children along the drive lanes encouraged forward momentum. Bison moved ever more quickly through the lanes so that, by the time the first bison saw the edge of the cliff (or realized it was in a pound), it was too late. The entire herd tumbled over. Some might be killed on impact; others would be wounded and hunted at the base. In a pound, bison were hunted at close quarters. Afterward, women processed the meat and hides. Often, any remaining waste was burned, which accelerated decay and reduced the odor of the site, thereby eliminating any future giveaways to scent-sensitive bison.[47]

Locations for communal hunting sites were chosen carefully, and landscapes around these sites were purposefully engineered.[48] Landscape engineering refers to "the intentional modification of place and resource networks through sequences of actions and inscriptions. Such modification aimed to increase permanence, manage the flow of people and resources, and thus plan for the future."[49] Planning and construction of drive lanes responded to local topography, bison psychology, and sacred knowledge. In the words of archaeologist Jack Brink, planners "were ancient architects of the landscape ... detecting every little nuance of change in the roll and sway of the land, figuring out where each rock pile would have to go in order to control the animals."[50] Zedeño and her coauthors add that drive-line systems were "each uniquely suited to the local topography but all responding to the overarching principles that reified sacred knowledge."[51] Plains people also burned grasslands to attract bison to future hunts since grass grows back greener and more nutritious after a recent burn, and bison seek it out.[52] As Rosalyn LaPier writes, "The Blackfeet believed they could alter, change, and control nature to suit their needs.... [They] did not believe they had to adapt to nature; they made nature adapt to them."[53] Engineering drive lanes and burning grasslands are two examples of such modifications. "They made the bison come to them," writes LaPier, but could only do so with the assistance of the supernatural world.[54]

For the Nitsitapii, the visible world is only a small dimension of the universe. Because humans do not have supernatural power, they have to seek it out from those who do in parallel realms (the Above world, the Below world, and the Water world). Three powerful societies—the Mataokiiksi (Buffalo Women Society), Ksistakii amaopisstaan (Beaver Bundle Society), and Buffalo Chaser Society—held ritual knowledge and controlled the communal hunt.[55] Using supernatural relationships, ceremony, knowledge of the natural world, and *iiniiskin* (buffalo stones), the Amskaapii Pikanii called the buffalo and orchestrated communal hunts.[56] In addition to feeding the community, such hunts provided opportunities to build wealth, demonstrate leadership, exchange and integrate new technologies, and build relationships. These hunts reinforced the centrality of bison to all parts of Nitsitapii life for physical and spiritual sustenance.

Russell probably learned about buffalo hunting from repeated contact with Plains people and through the writing, art, and friendships of Euro-American observers including William Wesley Van Orsdel ("Brother Van"), Lieutenant John H. Beacom, George Bird Grinnell, James Willard Schultz (Apikuni), and Frank Bird Linderman, as well as from artists Carl Ferdinand Wimar, Karl Bodmer, George Catlin, and Titian Ramsay Peale, among others.[57] The Indigenous knowledge that Russell (and his peers and predecessors) relied on to create bison hunting scenes was millennia in the making, as was the landscape over which he rode his horse, Monte. Innumerable Indigenous peoples who lived with and engineered this landscape are unacknowledged contributors to Russell's paintings.

The Naattoosiseetáa flows eastward a short distance north of Square Butte. While Russell frequently took geographical license in his paintings, making topography fit his vision rather than representing it faithfully, *In the Enemy's Country* appears to represent the Naattoosiseetáa and the Maokakinistsii in the distance (cat. 83). This location had a long history before Russell painted it. Russell specialist Frederic Renner writes that the Blackfeet hunted in this river valley, the Naatoosii-sat'taa kao'koyi (Sun River Valley), during the summer.[58] Later, miners and settlers arriving in Fort Benton often traveled westward to Great Falls and along this river valley, passing in the shadow of Square Butte along the way, before dispersing into and along the Maokakinistsii.

In 1867, in large part to protect these new arrivals, the US military constructed Fort Shaw (originally named Camp Reynolds) in the shadow of Square Butte on the banks of the Naattoosiseetáa. Soldiers stationed at the fort participated in numerous acts of aggression against Native nations, including the horrific genocide of around two hundred peaceful Amskaapii Pikanii on the Kyiyo seet'-daa (Bear River, or Marias River) in 1870.[59] After the decimation of bison herds, smallpox epidemics, and increased settlement, Native communities became increasingly reliant on US government rations and forced onto reservations, leaving little work for the soldiers at Fort Shaw. Abandoned by the army in 1891, the site transferred to the Department of the Interior and became a Native American boarding school. The first Amskaapii Pikanii students arrived in January 1893.[60] For some students, Square Butte became the geographical anchor overlooking miserable experiences of cultural suppression, illness, and death; for others, it marked a place of opportunity, intercultural friendship, and personal triumph.

Between 1891 and 1910, the school lodged around two thousand students. At its peak capacity, 350 students represented many nations, though Nitsitapii students were most numerous.[61] Daily routines were strict, and only English was allowed to be spoken. In addition to academic studies and athletic teams, it also held gendered vocational training, including farming, sewing, woodwork, needle crafts, cooking, carpentry, blacksmithing, and animal husbandry. Life at Fort Shaw Indian Boarding School was strictly regimented, corporal punishment was commonly employed, and cultural assimilation was the goal. Amskaapii Pikanii artist Ni-tah-mah-kwi-i (Lone Wolf) had painful memories of the school, including loneliness, cultural suppression, and physical violence (see his remembrances in this volume).

A serious outbreak of measles followed by influenza, pneumonia, conjunctivitis, and dysentery in late 1898 through the summer of 1899 kept many students in the infirmary. During the years the school was open, twenty-nine Native children were buried in the Fort Shaw cemetery. Some of these included three Nitsitapii students who died during the 1898–99 outbreak: John New Robe (age 15, died November 17, 1898), Jessie Lemon (age 11, died November 18, 1898), and Robert Stone (age 8, died May 1, 1899).[62] Regular attempts by students to run away signal that many found the school's "civilizing" mission unbearable. Soon after their arrival in January 1893, three Amskaapii Pikanii boys—William Croff (age 18), Charles Powell (age 16), and Thomas Spotted Eagle (age unknown)—ran away. Caught in miserable winter weather, they ultimately retraced their steps to Fort Shaw. What must the sight of Square Butte have meant to them as, cold and defeated, they followed the Naattoosiseetáa back to a place that was not home?[63]

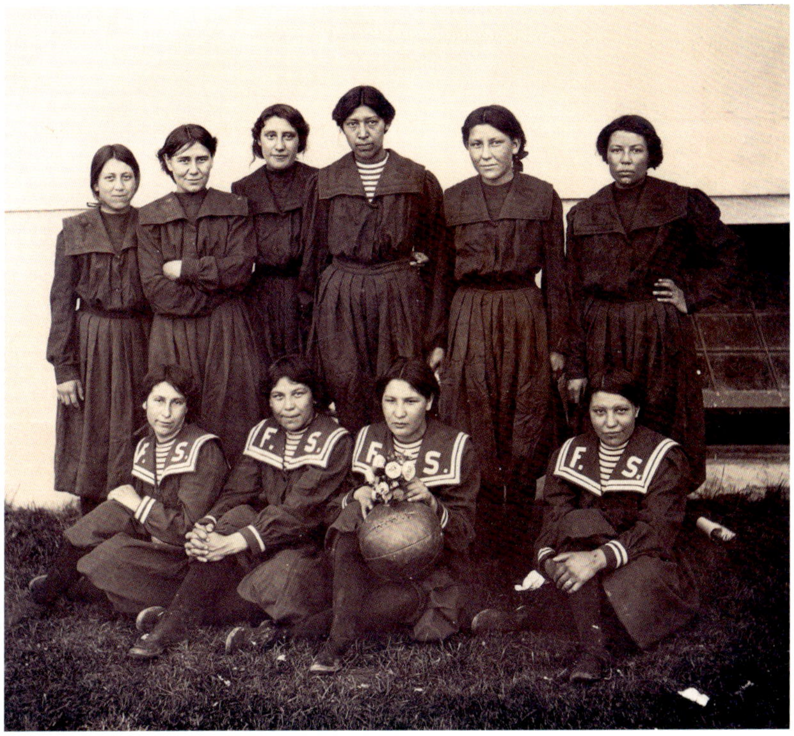

Fig. 5.

Indian girls dressed for a ball game, U.S. Government Indian exhibit (Fort Shaw Indian School basketball team), 1904. Pikanii team member Belle Johnson holds the basketball. St. Louis World's Fair. Missouri History Museum: St. Louis World's Fair Album, 1904, LPE (volume 11 of 11), N20703. Photo attributed to Jessie Tarbox Beals, courtesy Wikimedia Commons.

While many had painful memories of the school, some found opportunity and intertribal community there.[64] The women's basketball team became an important activity for a number of students, including Pikanii students Josephine Langley and Belle Johnson (fig. 5). Unlike in Victorian Europe and the US, Native women had long participated in physically competitive team sports. When basketball was still in its infancy, this team of Indigenous women played to packed houses in Great Falls and around the state before performing at the 1904 Louisiana Purchase Exposition in St. Louis, Missouri, where the team won the world championship basketball trophy. (Given the team's widespread fame, regular write-ups about their performances in the Great Falls press, and the fact that they performed to sold-out crowds at Luther Hall in downtown Great Falls—not far from the Charlie and Nancy's home—it is likely that Russell knew about them. There is even a possibility he might have seen them in St. Louis when he visited the 1904 exposition that October.[65]) Through basketball, these women chose their own path to victory. They responded and adapted to change, overcoming hardship through resourcefulness, community, and competition just as their ancestors had done.

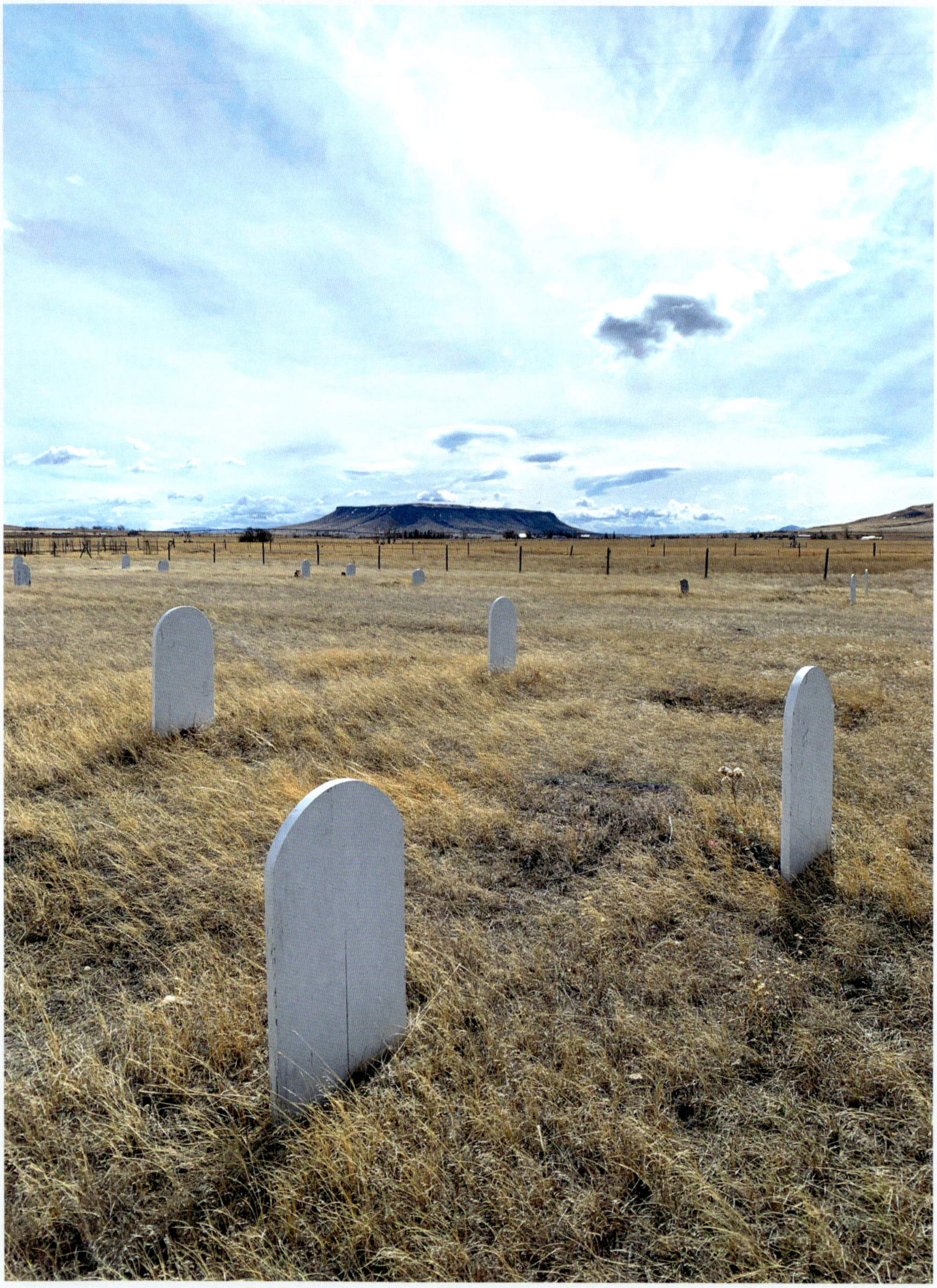

Today, Fort Shaw is on the National Register of Historic Places. Its windswept cemetery is well tended (fig. 6). Modern white headstones, many labeled with names and tribal affiliations and accompanied by small bouquets of fake flowers, stand in orderly rows. To the south, Square Butte sits low against the horizon, a looming guardian marking a home many students made the best of but did not necessarily choose. During the summers when Fort Shaw was open, teachers and students hiked up Square Butte to take in their surroundings, literally expanding their visual horizons.[66] I propose that taking an expanded and Indigenized view of "Russell Country" to encompass "Pikanii Country" reveals kaleidoscopic histories that enrich and enliven each other. Bringing into focus the Indigenous people who generously shared their space, knowledge, and art with Russell honors their culture, generosity, and presence—then, now, and into the future. Such an exercise is in keeping with Russell's own philosophy to make more room for curiosity and storytelling.

In the following essay, Emily C. Burns moves deeper into a consideration of how Amskaapii Pikanii art, people, and culture profoundly influenced Russell's practice and artistic vision. Through an analysis that shifts our perspective toward Indigenous epistemologies, Burns demonstrates the ongoing agency of Nitsitapii arts and people both outside of and within Russell's artworks.

Then, Amskaapii Pikanii artist Ni-tah-mah-kwi-i's reminiscences present insights into the challenging early Reservation Era in which familial warmth and stark cultural suppression coexisted. While Ni-tah-mah-kwi-i and Russell had much in common—they knew each other, spent time working the range, and competed in the same fine art market—Ni-tah-mah-kwi-i's story reveals aspects of Indigenous life that rarely show up in Russell's art, thereby providing a critical historical perspective.

Finally, additional content contributed by Pikanii advisers, in addition to content from sources available in Selected Readings, accompanies illustrations of works in the exhibition.

Fig. 6.

Fort Shaw cemetery, beneath Square Butte. Courtesy of the author.

NOTES

1 Another version of the photograph, along with this information, is in Larry Len Peterson, *Charles M. Russell: Photographing the Legend* (University of Oklahoma Press, 2014), 124.

2 Indian Arts and Crafts Board, *Contemporary Indian Artists: Montana, Wyoming, Idaho* (Tipi Shop, 1972), 24.

3 This project is inspired by the work of scholars, including Spencer Wigmore, Emily C. Burns, Annika Johnson, and others, who recently published new perspectives on Russell in *Carter Bulletin, vol. 1 (Charles M. Russell: New Perspectives)* (Amon Carter Museum of American Art, 2025), https://bulletin-v1.cartermuseum.org/, as well as to recent programs by the Sid Richardson Museum focusing on Plains Indian Sign Language in Russell's work, featuring Melanie McKay-Cody, who also contributed to the *Carter Bulletin*. Fundamentally, it is indebted to the work of Heather Caverhill, Cheryle "Cookie" Cobell Zwang (Niit si poo aki, Only Girl), Annabel Crop Eared Wolf, Ponokaakii (Elk Woman, Marjie Crop Eared Wolf), and many Nitsitapii community members who seek to indigenize the art of Winold Reiss (American, born in Germany, 1886–1953). See "Connections: The Blackfeet and Winold Reiss," Museum of the Plains Indian, accessed September 9, 2025, https://iacbmuseums-viewingroom.exhibit-e.art/viewing-room/connections-the-blackfeet-and-winold-reiss#tab:slideshow;tab-1:thumbnails; Heather Caverhill, "Mutable Modernisms: An Art Colony in Nitsitapii Territory and the Lives of its Works" (PhD diss., University of British Columbia, 2024); Cheryle "Cookie" Cobell Zwang (Niit si poo aki, Only Girl), Ponokaakii (Elk Woman, Marjie Crop Eared Wolf), and Heather Caverhill, "'We Know Who They Are': Connecting with the Nitsitapii in the Portraits of Winold Reiss," in *The BNSF Railway Art Collection* (forthcoming), 28–41.

4 The phrase was the title of a traveling exhibition of Russell's works that began in 1911 at the Folsom Gallery in New York City and well describes Russell's most consuming interest: his imagined "Old West."

5 Charles Russell, quoted in "'Just Kinda Natural to Draw Pictures, I Guess,' Says Cowboy Artist in Denver to Exhibit Work," *Rocky Mountain News*, November 27, 1921.

6 As art historian Brian Dippie has pointed out, we must acknowledge both sides of the Russell coin: his accuracy and his fantasy. In Dippie's words, "By focusing on Russell's authenticity at the expense of his artistry, his realism at the expense of his heartfelt romanticism, we distort his achievement." Brian W. Dippie, *Looking at Russell* (Amon Carter Museum, 1987), 5–6.

7 George P. Horse Capture Sr. (A'aninin) argues that Russell no doubt made many paintings of people on reservations in Montana, just as there is no doubt he visited and socialized with his Indigenous neighbors, though little evidence remains of these relationships and artworks created. George Horse Capture Sr., "Memories of Charles M. Russell Among My Indian Relatives," in *The Masterworks of Charles M. Russell: A Retrospective of Paintings and Sculpture*, ed. Joan Caprenter Troccoli (University of Oklahoma Press in cooperation with the Denver Art Museum, 2009), 121–27.

8 As kids, he and his brothers played "Indian," and his father read them the "Frank stories" by Harry Castlemon (Charles Austin Fosdick) and histories of Davy Crockett, Daniel Boone, and Kit Carson. Nancy Cooper Russell, *Back-Tracking in Memory: The Life of Charles M. Russell, Artist; Recollections, Reflections and Personal Perspectives*, ed. Thomas A. Petrie and Brian W. Dippie (C. M. Russell Museum and Sweetgrass Books, 2021), 5 and 9. His boyhood sketchbooks include copies of Swiss artist Karl Bodmer's representations of Native people. John C. Ewers, "Charlie Russell's Indians," *Montana The Magazine of Western History* 37, no. 3 (1987): 38.

9 Nancy records that, when young, Charlie would stand in front of a portrait of his father's first cousin William Bent, who founded Bent's Fort along the Santa Fe Trail, and dream of "fighting Indians and conquering the West," while he and his brothers played "massacre," stealing and "scalping" their sister's dolls before burning them at the stake, "just as they imagined their red-skinned brothers would do." Russell, *Back-Tracking*, 5. Bent's influence on Russell's attitudes and perceptions merits scholarly analysis.

10 As John Taliaferro writes, they were not "the noble savages he had expected." John Taliaferro, *Charles M. Russell: The Life and Legend of America's Cowboy Artist* (Little, Brown & Co., 1996), 31.

11 Later, Nancy wrote that at this encounter, Charlie "was filled with the picturesqueness of the whole scene." Russell, *Back-Tracking*, 31. Elsewhere, she specified that the "picturesque" nature was due to the skin leggings and bison robes worn by the waiting Indigenous people, writing, "They did not have civilized clothes." Nancy Russell, "Biographical Note," in Charles M. Russell, *Good Medicine* (1929 [1966]), 16. Homer Britzman writes differently, saying that Russell considered the Indigenous men he saw in Helena a disappointment because they were not wearing feather bonnets. According to Britzman, Russell saw men dressed in breechcloths, leggings, and trade blankets near Fort Hall, Idaho, along his route to Montana. Ramon F. Adams and Homer E. Britzman, *Charles M. Russell: The Cowboy Artist, a Biography* (Trail's End Publishing Co., 1948), 26 and 28.

12 See William Tomkins, *Universal Indian Sign Language of the Plains Indians of North America* (W. Tomkins, 1926), 22 and 25. John Taliaferro identifies the Native subjects as Apsáalooke (Crow). Taliaferro, *Charles M. Russell*, 76.

13 John C. Ewers, *The Blackfeet: Raiders on the Northwestern Plains* (University of Oklahoma Press, 1958), 303.

14 At this time, White traders were most interested in beaver pelts. The Nitsitapii generally did not hunt beaver, a sacred species. Instead, they traded the provisions that trappers needed to survive. Although the Nitsitapii traded for commercial tobacco, they had long grown their own, which they used in all rituals and daily prayer to communicate with the supernatural world. For more on the tradition of growing tobacco and its sacred uses, see LaPier, *Invisible Reality*, 49, 75–76.

15 Ewers writes that nine thousand robes left Fort McKenzie in the 1834–35 winter trade. By 1841, that number increased to about twenty-one thousand. Ewers, *The Blackfeet*, 64, 66.

16 Ewers, *The Blackfeet*, 69.

17 According to oral histories, the Nitsitapii traveled widely, including north to what is now Alaska and south to what is now Mexico.

18 LaPier, *Invisible Reality*, 49.

19 This treaty defined Blackfeet land as west of the Rocky Mountains and north of the Musselshell and Missouri Rivers up to 49th parallel, the US-Canada border.

20 See LaPier, *Invisible Reality*, 44–63.

21 LaPier explains that this overharvesting desecrated sacred species with "complex mythological origins and relationships with the Blackfeet peoples." LaPier, "Land as Text," 42.

22 LaPier, *Invisible Reality*, 11.

23 Lone Wolf, quoted in Paul Dyck, "Lone Wolf Returns to That Long Ago Time," *Montana The Magazine of Western History* 22, no. 1 (1972): 20.

24 Ewers explains that, with the bison nearly gone, increasing numbers of Blackfeet were dependent upon rations. In September 1883, a Montana delegation visited the reservation where weekly rations lasted only a few days. Three Suns told the delegation that, given the approaching winter, starvation was imminent without additional resources. The summer's crops had failed. Indian Agent Young was informed that Congress had already exhausted all appropriations. The starvation winter arrived. Probably around five hundred people died. Ewers, *The Blackfeet*, 294. Lone Wolf stated that six hundred died. Dyck, "Lone Wolf Returns," 20. That same winter, the secretary of the interior gave Indian agents permission to punish reservation communities by withholding rations for practicing their culture. LaPier, *Invisible Reality*, 17.

25 For more on the open range era, see Christopher Knowlton, *Cattle Kingdom: The Hidden History of the Cowboy West* (Houghton Mifflin Harcourt, 2017).

26 Hugh Dempsey provides a thorough account of this trip, which had reached legendary proportions in the Russell myth by the late twentieth century. Hugh A. Dempsey, "Tracking C. M. Russell in Canada, 1888–1889," *Montana The Magazine of Western History* 39, no. 3 (1989): 2–15. The group left Helena in May 1888. Russell and Stillwell left Canada in September.

27 For more on the history and use of Plains Indian Sign Language, especially by Russell, see Melanie McKay-Cody, "The Inclusive Work of Charles M. Russell and Hand Talk," *Carter Bulletin*.

28 Dempsey, "Tracking C. M. Russell in Canada," 13.

29 Russell attributed his inspiration to a man named Medicine Whip whom he met in Canada. See Rick Stewart, *Charles M. Russell: Sculptor* (Amon Carter Museum, 1994), 147. However, Dempsey has determined that Medicine Whip was probably not a real person; at least, there is no record or memory of a man by that name among the Nitsitapii. It is possible that Apskinas (or other Indigenous storytellers Russell met in 1888) may have been the original source. See Dempsey, "Tracking C. M. Russell," 14.

30 Frederic G. Renner, *Charles M. Russell: Paintings, Drawings, and Sculpture in the Amon Carter Museum* (Abradale Press/Harry N. Abrams, Inc., 1984), 45.

31 Ewers, "Charlie Russell's Indians," 42–43.

32 Russell, *Back-Tracking*, 57–59. Britzman supports some of Nancy's stories and writes that Russell, like others, feared the Blackfeet. See Adams and Britzman, *Charles M. Russell*, 30, 34–35, 59, and 62. On the importance of stealing horses to build wealth and status, see Ewers, "Raiding for Horses and Scalps," in *The Blackfeet*, 124–44. For a moving fictional account, see James Welch (Pikanii and A'aninin), *Fools Crow* (Viking, 1986).

33 As recounted by Ksiks Unopachis and quoted in Adolf Hungry-Wolf, *The Blackfoot Papers, Volume Four: Pikunni Biographies* (The Good Medicine Cultural Foundation, 2006), 1434–6. On Ksiks Unopachis, see also "The White Quiver Saga," in James Willard Schultz, *Blackfeet and Buffalo: Memories of Life Among the Indians* (University of Oklahoma Press, 1962), 210–24; Ewers, *The Horse in Blackfoot Culture*, 191–93; and Ewers, *The Blackfeet*, 302–3.

34 Unfortunately, these sources do not provide direct evidence. See Stewart, *Charles M. Russell*, 337–39; and Renner, *Charles M. Russell*, 159. Jennifer Bottomly-O'Looney and Kirby Lambert make a similar claim about the watercolor *Roping by Moonlight* (1900) in *Montana's Charlie Russell: Art in the Collection of the Montana Historical Society* (Montana Historical Society Press, 2014), 131.

35 Stewart, *Charles M. Russell*, 340–43.

36 The Kupawiǫ́q́nuk moved to the western side of the Maokakinistsii during the late 1700s after the horrific smallpox epidemic of 1781 and because of increased aggression by the Amskaapii Pikanii. They returned to the east side seasonally to hunt. Ted Binnema, *Common and Contested Ground: A Human and Environmental History of the Northwestern Plains* (University of Oklahoma Press, 2001), 128.

37 Reporter M. R. F. Valle explained in a 1921 *Rocky Mountain News* article: "Old bulls traveled in small bands, and no Indian cared for bull meat. Therefore they were not molested." Quoted in Brian W. Dippie, "In the Enemy's Country: Western Art's Uneasy Status," in *Redrawing Boundaries: Perspectives on Western American Art*, ed. Peter H. Hassrick, vol. 3, *Western Passages* (Denver Art Museum, 2007), 14.

38 Sara A. Scott notes that butchered bison bones dating to approximately 1000 CE have been excavated along the Siksikaaasat'taa (Blackfoot River) west of the Continental Divide. Additionally, when Meriwether Lewis passed through the same area on July 6, 1806, he noted bison dung. Sara A. Scott, "Ties That Bind on the Northwestern Plains: Contexts for Pheistoric Trade and Travel" (PhD diss., University of Montana, 2014), 74.

39 According to Scott, Indigenous communities located on the western side of the northern Maokakinistsii "traveled over the Continental Divide and onto the Plains of central and eastern Montana as many as three times a year to hunt bison. These excursions were generally made during the summer and fall." Scott, "Ties that Bind," 98. For references to historic use of the Buffalo Trail, see ibid., 7, 68. See also "Road to the Buffalo-Alice Creed," National Park Service, accessed April 14, 2025, https://www.nps.gov/places/road-to-the-buffalo-alice-creek.htm.

40 For a map, see Scott, "Ties that Bind," 70. For a late-nineteenth-century anthropologist's perspective on Amskaapii Pikanii history and culture, see Walter McClintock, *The Old North Trail: or, Life, Legends and Religion of the Blackfeet Indian* (Macmillan Co., 1910).

41 Scott, "Ties that Bind," 76. See also "Square Butte," National Park Service, accessed April 14, 2025, https://www.nps.gov/places/square-butte.htm. On the naming and geology of this landform, see Joseph A. Musseulman, "Square Butte: Lewis's Fort Mountain," Discover Lewis & Clark, accessed April 14, 2025, https://lewis-clark.org/the-trail/falls-of-the-missouri/square-butte/.

42 Krys Holmes, "Ulm Pishkun: World of the Early Plains Bison," *Montana The Magazine of Western History*. 49, no. 2 (1999): 87. On *pisskaan*, see George Bird Grinnell, *Blackfoot Lodge Tales: The Story of a Prairie People* (1892; repr. University of Nebraska Press, 1962), 228–30. Grinnell explains that this referred to the corral or enclosure—the deep-blood-kettle—built at the bottom of a cliff or bluff into which bison fell after being herded over the cliff and where they were harvested.

43 Maria Nieves Zedeno et al., "Landscape Engineering and Organizational Complexity Among Late Prehistoric Bison Hunters of the Northwest Plains," *Current Anthropology* 55, no. 1 (2014): 28.

44 Ibid., 23.

45 Such communal hunts required the "ability to organize and integrate labor under a shared worldview that sanctified order and compliance while helping to retain the hunting ground." To execute successfully, coordinators would have needed wealth, influence, and control of land. Ibid., 41.

46 Maximilan, Prince of Wied, witnessed a communal hunt and wrote that "scarecrows, made of stones, branches of trees, etc." lined the tract through which the bison were driven into a narrow gorge. Maximilian, quoted in Jack Brink, *Imagining Head-Smashed-In: Aboriginal Buffalo Hunting on the Northern Plains* (Athabasca University Press, 2008), 96.

47 For more on communal hunts, see Brink, *Imagining Head-Smashed-In*; Zedeno et al., "Landscape Engineering"; LaPier, *Invisible Reality*; and Binnema, *Common and Contested Ground*.

48 Consider the site of Head-Smashed-In in Alberta, Canada, which is situated in an area just east of the Maokakinistsii where bison could probably be found most of the year. Near the "jump," or cliff, a large natural depression acted as a kind of collecting area where bison would naturally congregate. There is a slight decline at the end of the drive just before the cliff, which would have made it harder for the front-heavy animals to stop. Additionally, this decline creates an optical illusion: From this angle, the cliff visually disappears into the prairie landscape. The bison literally would not have seen what was coming. Brink, *Imagining Head-Smashed-In*, 144.

49 Zedeno et al., "Landscape Engineering," 24.

50 Brink, *Imagining Head-Smashed-In*, 79.

51 Zedeno et al., "Landscape Engineering," 41.

52 Brink, *Imagining Head-Smashed-In*, 117–19.

53 LaPier, *Invisible Reality*, xxxvii.

54 Ibid., xxxvi.

55 Zedeno et al., "Landscape Engineering," 28. As the authors articulate: "The right to own knowledge of the hunt was worn as a badge of honor, as indicated in men's ceremonial shirts that depict bison drive lines and corrals, in the possession and transfer of bison-calling bundles, and in the ownership of buffalo painted lodges and ceremonies, among other manifestations."

56 According to Brink, "Native groups *orchestrated* every aspect of the communal bison kill, including choosing the seasons in which they were held." Brink, *Imagining Head-Smashed-In*, 60. Brink writes that they planned hunts according to bison behavior and quality. Cows and bulls are better for harvesting at different times of the year based on the fat and hormone content of their meat. See ibid., chapters 2 and 3. *Iniiskin* are marine fossils that are associated with sacred bundles and important rituals and ceremonies. See Zedeno, "Bison Hunters," 82, and Grinnell, *Blackfoot Lodge Tales*, 126.

57 Ewers, "Charlie Russell's Indians," 36; Dippie, *Looking at Russell*, 53–61; Ann Morand, "Charles M. Russell: Creative Sources of a Young Artist Painting the Old West," in *The Masterworks of Charles M. Russell*, 129–51.

58 Renner, *Charles M. Russell*, 61.

59 Darrell Kipp provides the number of Amskaapii Pikanii massacred. Darrell Kipp, "Introduction to the New Bison Books Edition," in Clark Wissler and D. C. Duvall, *Mythology of the Blackfoot Indians* (University of Nebraska Press, 2007), v. Known as the Bear River Winter Massacre, it is also sometimes called the Baker Massacre after the leader, Colonel Baker, from the 2nd Cavalry stationed at Fort Ellis in Bozeman. Mounted infantry from Fort Shaw supplemented the 2nd Cavalry in the attack. For more, see Andrew R. Graybill, *The Red and the White: A Family Saga of the American West* (Liveright Publishing Corporation, 2013); and Paul R. Wylie, *Blood on the Marias: The Baker Massacre* (University of Oklahoma Press, 2016).

60 The Fort Shaw Government Industrial Indian Boarding School was modeled on the Carlisle Indian Industrial School in Carlisle, Pennsylvania, to which the first Amskaapii Pikanii students had been sent in 1890. See "Student Records," Carlisle Indian School Digital Resource Center, accessed May 2, 2025, https://carlisleindian.dickinson.edu/student_records. For Fort Shaw–related information, see Linda Peavy and Ursula Smith, *Full-Court Quest: The Girls from Fort Shaw Indian School, Basketball Champions of the World* (University of Oklahoma Press, 2008); and "World Champions: The 1904 Girls' Basketball Team from Fort Shaw Indian Boarding School," *Montana The Magazine of Western History* 51, no. 4 (2001): 2–25.

61 "Fort Shaw Indian School," Lost Colleges, accessed May 2, 2025, https://www.lostcolleges.com/fort-shaw-indian-school.

62 See Peavy and Smith, *Full-Court Quest*, 96–97 and 397n18. Additional Nitsitapii students buried there include: Joseph Sienback (age unknown, died April 18, 1894), Charles Middlecalf (age 10, died January 9, 1898), and James Rutherford (about age 15, died March 6, 1901).

63 Ibid., 38–39 and 382n4. The boys ran away again in March and were expelled from the school. Ibid., 383n7. Runaways were extremely common at all Indian boarding schools. For more on student resistance, see David Wallace Adams, *Education for Extinction: American Indians and the Boarding School Experience, 1875–1928* (University Press of Kansas, 1995, rev. 2020).

64 For example, the Johnson children (Amskaapii Pikanii) had very mixed experiences, with Willie describing the "harsh discipline, the senseless routine, and the bad food," while Mary and Charlie "had nothing but praise for the school." Peavy and Smith, *Full-Court Quest*, 76.

65 The Russells traveled to the St. Louis Exposition, where Charlie had three watercolors (in the Montana Building) and an oil painting (in the Palace of Fine Arts) on display, the first week of October and stayed for several more. The Fort Shaw team played on Saturday, October 8, in addition to their twice-daily performances of Henry Wadsworth Longfellow's "The Famine" from *Hiawatha* as part of the Model Indian School program. See Stewart, *Sculptor*, 30 and 37; Peavy and Smith, *Full-Court Quest*, 329, 334; and Taliaferro, *Charles M. Russell*, 155–56. Peavy and Smith write that over the course of the Expo (June 1 to November 1), three million people toured the Model Indian School, or around twenty thousand people per day. In comparison, around five hundred people per day visited the Montana Building, where Russell's watercolors were on display, leading the authors to write that "The Fort Shaw girls were, indeed, Montana's most visible ambassadors." Peavey and Smith, "World Champions," 9fn22.

66 Peavy and Smith, *Full-Court Quest*, 50.

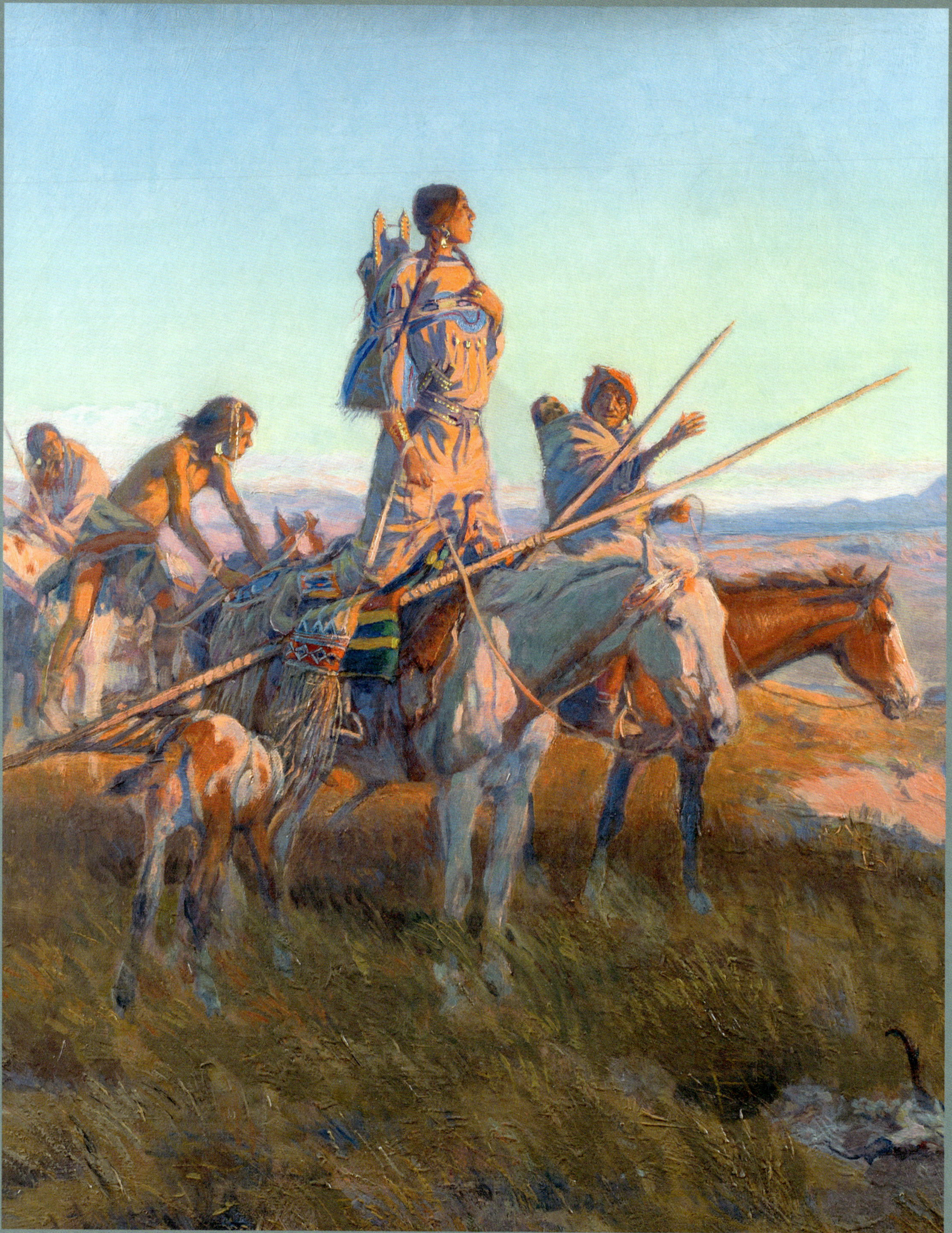

In the Wake of Nitsitapii Art: Charles Marion Russell, Belongings, and Native American Knowledge Systems

EMILY C. BURNS

IN CHARLES MARION RUSSELL'S 1911 PAINTING *In the Wake of the Buffalo Runners,* an Amskaapii Pikanii (Blackfeet, or South Peigan) woman on the back of a horse sits up tall on her knees, craning to look in the distance over a butte warmed by the sun's glow (cat. 33 and facing page). Wearing a buckskin dress with a beaded yoke, she prepares to enter a space of plenty, following an unseen bison hunt below in the transitional light of dawn or dusk. The painting's ambivalent time of day produces a sense of timelessness in which the figure is suspended in anticipation, in a liminal space on the precipice. She forms the pinnacle of a triangle shaped by a multigenerational group, with a boy balancing on the travois behind her, a cradleboard on her back, and an Elder woman who gestures toward the unseen landscape with another baby on her back. The foal suckling beneath the central white horse, its back to the viewer, reinforces this intergenerational relationship. Behind this group, a row of figures on horseback and dogs await the cue to descend once the dust settles.

Euro-American viewers who consumed pictures like this one imagined they had entered an old West that preceded Indigenous dispossession, cultural repression, and the reservation system which bounded Native American lands across the continent, limited access to resources, enforced assimilation, and imposed privatized land ownership.[1] The sense of having privileged access to the cultural world of *In the Wake of the Buffalo Runners* results, in part, from the veritable museum of Indigenous artistry that Russell depicts from tribal nations along the so-called Hi-Line region that surrounds and cloaks the central figure.[2] The principal woman's gesture, clasping her left hand to her chest, draws the viewer's attention to her jewelry, her beaded dress, her studded belt and knife sheath, and the band that affixes a beaded cradleboard to her back. Below her, more riches abound: a Hudson's Bay striped trade blanket and an adorned saddle bag, its tendrils of hide fringe fluttering in the breeze. The brightest pops of saturated color across the painting, they affirm the figures' Native American identities to the viewer.

Charles Marion Russell
In the Wake of the Buffalo Runners
(detail; cat. 33).

Scholarship on Russell has tried to divine what Russell understood about Native Americans and to secure the validity of longstanding claims that the artist had lived with Native Americans.[3] However, it is difficult to ascertain the extent of his knowledge of these cultures or his investments in critiquing settler colonialism. What we can know for certain is that the Amskaapii Pikanii community, and the larger Nitsitapii world operating adjacent to Russell, was culturally independent from settler society, despite land expropriation and insistence on assimilation.[4] *In the Wake of the Buffalo Runners* offers a point of entry into a relational world, one that operated beyond Russell's articulated awareness. As a non-Native observer invested in producing sellable images of the American West, Russell's view of Nitsitapii society could only have been incomplete. He engaged with Native Americans throughout his career, benefited from the privilege of land access, and occasionally participated in critical conversations around the theft of Indigenous lands and cultural suppression. His knowledge was partial, as is that of this non-Native author. Instead of focusing on what Russell understood, this essay brings to the foreground the Nitsitapii knowledge system that exists alongside Russell's imaginary and that is inherently articulated through the Indigenous people and material belongings he painted. *In the Wake of the Buffalo Runners* depends on the Native American artworks, in this essay referred to as belongings, he represented. These belongings have their own lives and roles in societies fundamentally different from Russell's and spur transnational dialogues between Russell's painting and Nitsitapii making.

Analyzing these belongings as animate beings with their own agency, this essay interprets the painting as a contest of knowledge systems, or epistemologies, between settler, Nitsitapii, and other Indigenous worlds. By tracing belongings—and privileging Native American voices as well as scholars from Native American and Indigenous studies on multigenerational practices of making—new stories emerge that show how material forms perpetuated Native American voices even during an oppressive period of erasure. Just as an Amskaapii Pikanii woman peers over the precipice to the lost past Russell imagined for her, the painter craned to see and collect Native American art. As she tracks the bison run in the painting, Russell tracked Native American art. His dependence on it casts him perpetually in its wake, even as he acted as a key historical figure translating Nitsitapii culture for non-Native viewers.[5]

To begin, it's important to introduce key aspects of Nitsitapii culture and contextualize the settler incursions on Indigenous communities in and near Montana during the early Reservation Era in which Russell worked. This allows me to then chart some of the distinctions between how art functioned for Russell's audience and for Native American societies broadly, and Nitsitapii culture specifically, to show art and knowledge systems that are concurrent and equivalent but incommensurable. Drawing on anthropology and literary studies, I propose models for interpreting the movements of belongings into settler spaces like Russell's paintings. Finally, I consider how Josephine Wright (1883–1938), an Amskaapii Pikanii model who posed for many of his artworks (including *In the Wake of the Buffalo Runners*), and Russell's own collection of Native American material translated Nitsitapii culture. What happens when we recenter these belongings not as "props" indexing Russell's American West but as Native American, mainly Nitsitapii, belongings with their own stories, ontologies, and epistemologies? Alongside Wright's story, the history of contemporary Amskaapii Pikanii quillworker Holds Together Woman (Gretchen Duvall; born 1870s) points to the complex transnational interactions between settler and Nitsitapii worlds. Both women self-consciously participated in translating Amskaapii Pikanii culture for non-Native audiences. Focusing on the central figure's dress, which was made by a Nitsitapii woman, and other belongings in *In the Wake of the Buffalo Runners* and other paintings, I show Russell's dependence on Nitsitapii knowledge and make space for seeing the enduring presence of Nitsitapii and other Native American cultural systems in his paintings.

Nitsitapii Ways of Knowing: *Nitsitapiiskaa'taksini* and Threats to the "Backbone of the World"

The Nitsitapii's deep ties to an expansive region and migration route have existed for millennia. With epistemologies imbuing places and objects with animacy, spiritual practices that connect with *kiipatapiisinoan* ("our way of life") inform daily life and seasonal movements.[6] Stories and the connective tissue between spirit and human worlds are braided into Nitsitapiiskaa'taksini ("Real peoples', or Nitsitapii, knowledge").[7] Here, humans have entwined relationships with place, spiritual beings, and with nonhuman kin—distinct from the worldview of settler colonial societies. Amskaapii Pikanii and Métis historian Rosalyn LaPier describes "a multi-layered reality" in which humans ally with spirit beings, connecting visible and invisible worlds, the supernatural and the natural.[8] As anthropologist Gerald A. Oetelaar explains, the Nitsitapii's "world ... is made up of a complex web of relations between animate and inanimate entities ... mediated by the spirits who respond to the prayers and actions of the Blackfoot people."[9] After separating seasonally, Nitsitapii bands join in summer for the O'kan (Sun Dance ritual) and to renew kinship ties during Iitootooyiisii'wa Maatapiiksi, or the "time when people gather together."[10] Giveaways at the O'kan, which demonstrate generosity and relationality, balance the universe. As historian Blanca Tovías summarizes, "The Blackfoot must strive to exercise the principles of sacrifice, generosity, and reciprocity with all their relations, both from the animate and the inanimate world."[11]

Russell worked in northern Montana, which became a US state in 1889 after a series of land cessations by Nitsitapii bands on both sides of the US-Canada border. Russell arrived in the early 1880s, during the US and Canadian governments' longstanding attempts to quell nomadic practices to make way for settlement. This history bears tremendous violence, notably the Bear (Marias) River Massacre of 1870, in which the US military killed approximately 217 peacefully encamped Amskaapii Pikanii people.[12] Furthermore, LaPier describes the winter of 1883–84 as a "starvation winter," due to lack of resources and access to food staples when the US government abandoned its agreements to provide resources in exchange for land.[13] Decimation of bison herds and smallpox epidemics ruptured ancestral practices and devastated the population.[14] Cultural violence shaped settler policies; through missionization, laws banning O'kan, and the construction of agencies, settlers sought to assimilate Nitsitapii people. Severe depletion of reservation lands between 1873 and 1896 challenged Nitsitapii cultural continuity and disrupted migratory patterns, interrupting Nitsitapii spiritual practices tied to land as "an archive or repository of traditional knowledge" and a space where ritual migrations "fulfill spiritual obligations."[15]

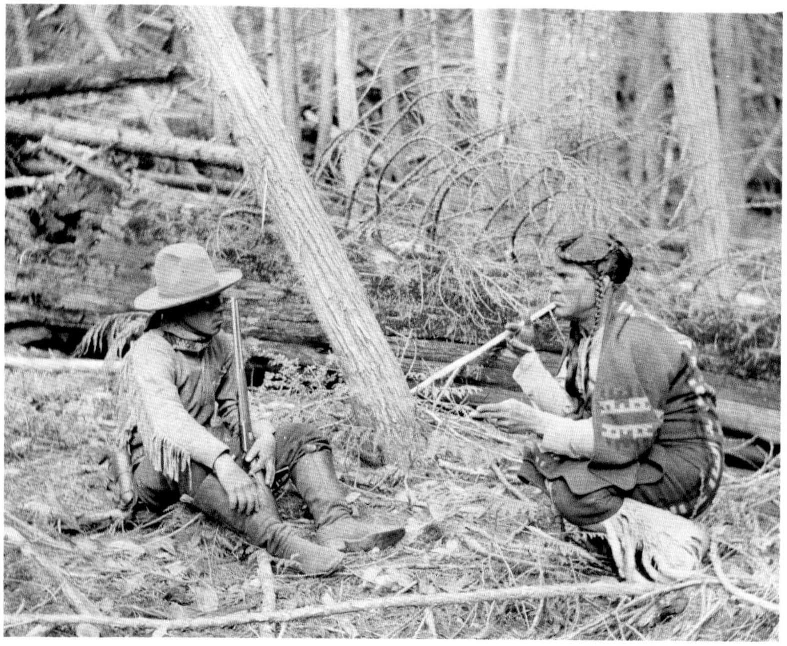

Russell lived nearest to the Amskaapii Pikanii Tribe, which abuts the east side of Glacier National Park. Longstanding agreements promised the Amskaapii Pikanii continued access, mobility, and hunting and fishing rights in the park, but the act founding the park in 1910 did not mention these rights, thus curtailing access.[16] The Great Northern Railway conveyed hordes of settlers and tourists to the park, which put further pressure on ancestral practices. Many Native American artists adapted to the new markets brought by the railroad, especially as a settler market emerged for beadwork, painting, and carving.[17] Amskaapii Pikanii society evolved to perpetuate culture as much as possible with the repressions of settler society. Women continued to make belongings following ancestral practices, though at least one government agent, Lorenzo Cook, "threatened to jail women who did beadwork."[18] After reservations were formalized, the O'kan continued in more localized contexts and was scheduled earlier to coincide with Fourth of July events, at least one of which Russell attended.[19] Essentially, the continued practice of ancestral Nitsitapii ritual and syncretic faith were open secrets.[20]

In the 1890s, in the midst of Nitsitapii adaptation, Russell purchased land near Amitoo's oomah'sikimii (Lake Macdonald) from a White homesteader in what would become the park. In 1905–6, he built a studio and cabin that he called Bull Head Lodge. When the park was formed, he and other White landowners retained permits to live and hunt there.[21] Rugged nature became a backdrop to Russell's frequent act of redface; in one photograph taken near the cabin in 1907, he and artist Philip R. Goodwin (1881–1935) pose, both in redface, and Russell, wearing a braided headpiece and blanket wrapped around his body, signs toward his friend (fig. 1). As scholars working on redface have observed, playing Indian enacts an appropriation, a "self-indigenization," that absorbs Nativeness into Whiteness.[22]

Fig. 1.

Unknown photographer, Charles Marion Russell and Philip R. Goodwin in costume, c. 1907. Charles M. Russell Research Collection, Britzman, Gilcrease Museum, University of Tulsa (TU2009.39.7651.130).

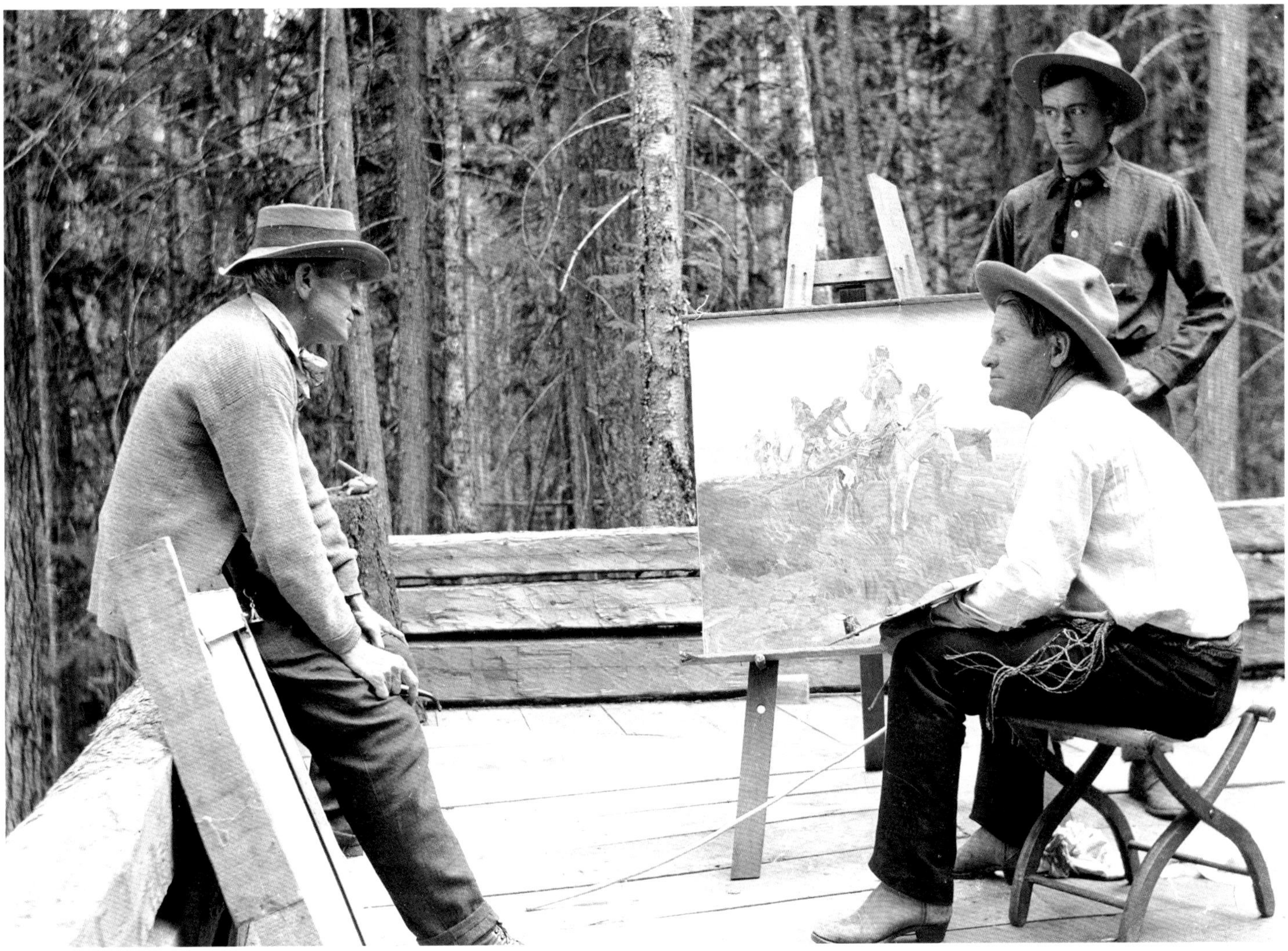

Access to the landscape around Bull Head Lodge further inscribed settler placemaking in Russell's art. A 1911 photograph shows Russell pausing from work on *In the Wake of the Buffalo Runners* while two other men, Fergus Mead and the painter's nephew, Austin Russell, look on (fig. 2). The painting is partially complete, with the main composition and underlayers fully sketched out. Russell often began his paintings in the park, completing them in his Great Falls studio. The presence of Russell and his coterie of guests in this landscape contributed to the displacement of the peoples he often nostalgically romanticized in paintings like this one.

Fig. 2.

Unknown photographer, Charles Marion Russell, Fergus Mead, and Austin Russell at Bull Head Lodge, 1911. Charles M. Russell Research Collection, Britzman, Gilcrease Museum, University of Tulsa (TU2009.39.5748b-c).

Russell did, though, occasionally lament the incursions of settler society into Nitsitapii territories.[23] A few of his artworks explicitly critique Native American suppression, forced removal, and racism, including *Caught in the Act*, discussed by JR Henneman in this volume (see fig. 2, page 17ff). Others, like depictions of Nitsitapii people selling belongings at trading posts in exchange for alcohol, are ambivalent. Russell's advocacy can been seen in conversations around the formation of Rocky Boy's Indian Reservation, established in 1916, for a band of displaced Ojibwe (Chippewa).[24] He inscribed a copy of anthropologist George Bird Grinnell's *The Fighting Cheyennes* (1915) for fellow artist Joe De Yong (1894–1975): "The Red Man was the true American They have almost all gon. but will never be forgotten The history of how they fought for their country is written in blood a stain that time cannot grind out" (fig. 3).[25] On the frontispiece, Russell painted a watercolor of a wistful seated Native man, looking to an uncertain future from a precipice, his horse beside him. Witness to the change after the railway came to Glacier National Park, Russell may have been invested in Native American, and specifically Nitsitapii, continuity with his romanticization of the past, yet imperialist nostalgia drove the market for his paintings.

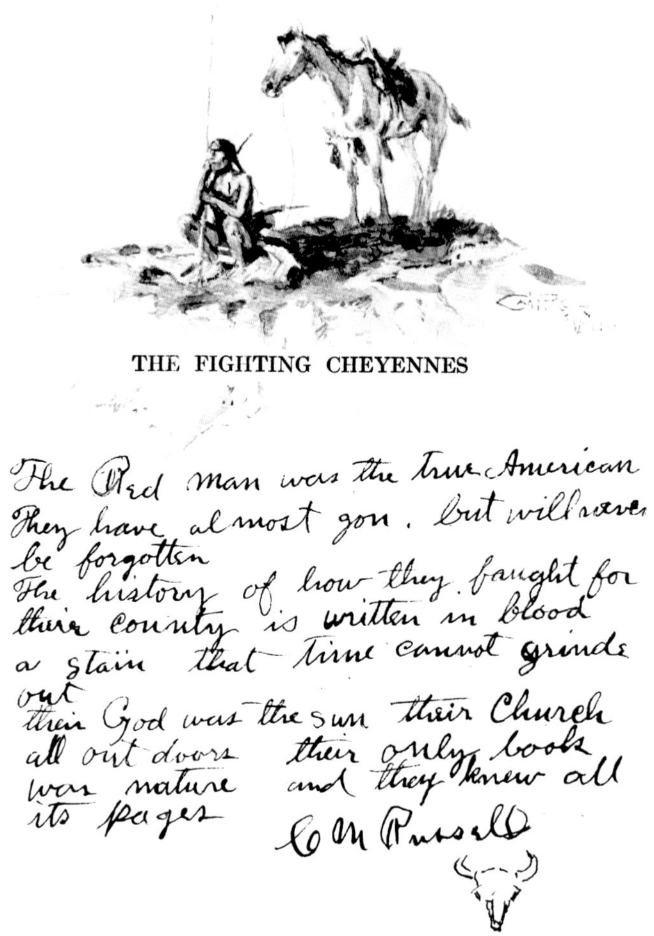

Fig. 3.

Reproduction from George Bird Grinnell, *The Fighting Cheyenne* (1916), signed by Charles M. Russell. Private collection. Photograph courtesy Amon Carter Museum of American Art.

Russell built his career on producing imagery that responded to US society's interest in depictions of Native Americans. His success was tied to the reproducibility of his representations, which often traveled as illustrations in popular periodicals and books, such as "A Meeting in a Blizzard" in Emerson Hough's *The Story of the Cowboy* (1898; cat. 82). To affirm the contexts he imagined in his paintings, Russell collected at least one hundred works by Native American artists by gift, trade, or purchase through friends, acquaintances, models, and at trading posts.[26] His interest in Nitsitapii material culture is evident in multiple paintings depicting vibrant trading posts, including *Joe Kipp's Trading Post* (1898; cat. 10) and *Robe Traders of Fort Benton* (1901; cat. 11). He filled his studios with these belongings, as seen in a 1914 studio photograph with Nitsitapii beadwork, a Hi-Line warrior shirt, and a Nitsitapii dress hanging on the wall (fig. 4).[27] This installation produced an immersive effect that many collectors sought in what became popularly known as an "Indian corner."[28] As early as 1892, a review of this "cowboy" artist set the stage for readers: "[Russell] has with him a collection of Indian relics, collected by himself at different trading posts, and they form an interesting study. In this assortment can be found the tomahawk and scalping knife of the bloodthirsty savage, and the rudely fashioned pipe of the nomad; gaily beaded pouches, war clubs and other paraphernalia dear to the wandering tribes who once roamed unmolested through these regions."[29] The commentary suggests that the belongings represented a precontact past, a narrative that continued throughout his career, though Russell often acquired more recently made materials.[30] Viewers often uphold Russell's rendering of these belongings as proof of insider knowledge of ancestral Native American life. Painted largely for non-Native audiences, they materially authenticated his paintings as indexes of the American West and intimated his access to Nitsitapii culture; as art historian Alexander Nemerov put it, such material form produced "the reality of the historical world of which it is a fragment."[31]

Following the painter and his contemporary critics, scholars make similar claims.[32] In publications about his studio and in the studio museum, belongings have not been understood as works of art but as "props," "mementos," "materials," "artifacts," and "Indian gear."[33] This vocabulary produces a hierarchy in which Russell's painting operates as art and the Native American belongings are sidelined as subservient to the paintings' legitimacy. Curator Peter H. Hassrick wrote, for instance, that "apparel and artifacts" enabled Russell's figures to be "appreciated as authentic as well as emotionally provocative."[34] Such comments privilege Russell's own vision for his art and suppress the complicated transnational exchange between Native Americans' making and Russell's acquisition and translation of belongings.

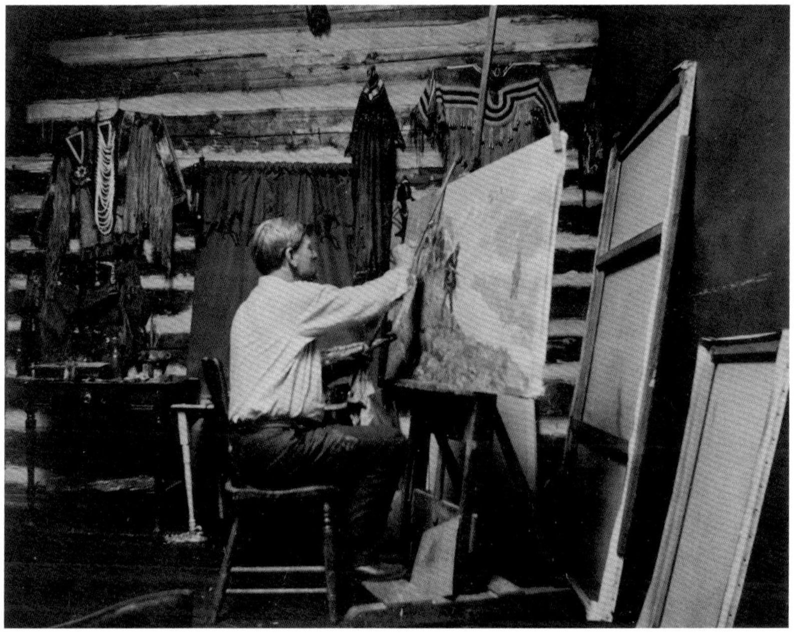

While Russell acquired belongings via a variety of means, lack of resources within communities and a need for access to cash often resulted in imbalanced pricing. His use of belongings to imagine an old West recontextualized them within his own stories and perspectives. As scholars Alyssa Mt. Pleasant, Caroline Wigginton, and Kelly Wisecup observe, "Native materials that are now archival objects ... were frequently obtained in contexts of duress or without permission ... [and] were nearly always enfolded into colonialist narratives that aimed to determine the meaning of Indigenous writing and actions."[35] Inupiaq artist Stephen Foster and Snohomish leader Mike Evans similarly observe that settler artists' depictions of Native Americans "had the ontological impact of defining Indigenous peoples within particular and racialized categories (a kind of ontological violence that continues to this day)."[36] As with the act of "playing Indian," such depictions reinforce settler colonial authority by subsuming Native American cultures into non-Native framing. Viewers today risk reasserting that colonializing perspective by continuing to read belongings as mere props. This tendency forecloses the agency, art practices, and politics of Native American artists and belongings by implying that they yield and bend to settler intentions, metaphorically flattened as they are translated by artists like Russell into two dimensions. Concurrently, however, the agency in the belongings that Russell painted is apparent when we understand them from Native American perspectives.

Fig. 4.

Unknown photographer, Russell working on *Whose Meat?* in his studio, 1914. Charles M. Russell Research Collection, Britzman, Gilcrease Museum, University of Tulsa (TU2009.39.273.35a-b).

Reinscribing "Relational Reality"

In a broad discussion of Indigenous aesthetics, Chickasaw and Choctaw scholar and curator heather ahtone explains, "Each Indigenous culture globally has an aesthetic system that represents the total of its epistemology and philosophies, its history and its knowledge."[37] Art, in other words, weaves cultural understandings and community knowledge into the fabric of material form. For Native American nations, the idea of "expressive culture" offers a more expansive system of aesthetic practice than Western art history's focus on painting and sculpture; as Kiowa scholar Jenny Tone-Pah-Hote describes, "regalia, adornment, figural art, and dance" mingle together in expressions enacted through bodily engagement.[38]

The concept of expressive culture underscores the animacy of material forms. Natural materials, like hide and porcupine quills, retain the animacy of animal and plant lifeways and connect humans with animals. Relationality is fundamental to Nitsitapii society, not only in community networks among humans but in kinships that affirm material animacy. In curator Jill Ahlberg Yohe and Kiowa artist Teri Greeves's terms, "We are related to it, and it relates back."[39] Mohegan playwright Madeline Sayet refers to such forms as "sacred relations" that "hold space on their own" even exceeding their material properties.[40] Scholars increasingly use the term "belongings" to describe Native Americans' relationally made material forms because it inflects interconnected animate ties among place, people, and material forms, even across time.[41] Given this ontology, then, the vocabulary that dominates the scholarly literature on Russell's Native American collection, like "prop," "artifact," or even "object," does not align with this Native definition of material form.

When belongings are drawn into settler contexts and spaces, they become objectified, or "artifacted" as I call it. As Foster and Evans note, this movement transforms them into a context of "surveying" rather than of "relationships." Belongings become resituated into a "fiction of non-relational reality."[42] One might think of Russell's paintings as producing fictions that, as they narrate stories of an imagined past Nitsitapii life, do not recognize the belongings' relational reality. Yet, as this essay suggests, community-dictated values are intrinsic and inhere even when belongings are removed from their contexts; in mobility or re-presentation, relational animacy becomes itinerant. Even in the non-Native spaces of Russell's paintings, which were and are widely reproduced, Native American belongings are mobilized. Anthropologists Rosemary A. Joyce and Susan D. Gillespie have proposed the phrase "object itinerary" to consider how layers of "spatial and temporal" existences emerge and focus attention on "the relationality of things."[43] Here, I refine their phrase to "belonging itinerary." This model of relational ontology and enmeshed meanings aligns with how Nitsitapii and other Native American belongings travel in Russell's paintings and how their stories expand.[44]

As a result of this transnational dialogue between Russell and Native American makers, Native American aesthetics become fundamental to the art of the American West in underacknowledged ways. Literary scholar Caroline Wigginton has argued that Native American "craftwork"—the belongings that Indigenous makers labored to craft—shapes American literature, broadly defined. Her argument that "one cannot fully understand American literature and textual cultures without Native craftwork and aesthetics" can be extended to the art of the American West.[45] Wigginton coins the term "Indigenuity" to emphasize the "dynamic creativity, abundant skill, intentional design, and multisensory materiality of Native making and using."[46] Similarly, Nitsitapii and other Indigenous meanings shape Russell's paintings of the American West through the belongings that he collected and rendered.

The continued circulation of Native American belongings during a period of cultural repression creates something of a paradox. As Wigginton observes, settler society "sought to supplant Native practices and peoples through appropriation, denigration, and obsolescence while also propagating Indigenous aesthetics, often unwittingly, as they wove them into colonialist archives."[47] Because belongings embed "aesthetic knowledge," recognizing Indigenous perspectives in Russell's paintings articulates "enduring presences ... thereby exceeding these settler colonial narratives" and enacts the possibility to reconsider how Indigenous voices and agencies operate through Russell's pictures.[48]

The belongings express and embody Nitsitapii worldviews, and tending to them underscores Nitsitapii layers of knowing. Methodologically resituating these belongings in their relations—as this essay seeks to do—combats the imposition of settler possession. To show the constructed nature of Russell's imaginary and the operations of Indigenous belongings within it disrupts and decenters Western epistemology. From Indigenous perspectives, instead of authenticating the paintings that Russell produces, these belongings trouble his narratives' assumptions of erasure and pastness.

Josephine Wright, Holds Together Woman, and Belongings: Safeguarding Amskaapii Pikanii Futures

Russell met Josephine Wright and Nancy Cooper in 1895 at the home of Ben and Lela Roberts in Cascade, Montana, where both women worked as live-in help.[49] On her mother's side, Wright was the granddaughter of Mary Ethata Ahkahtah (Amskaapii Pikanii; 1847–1889).[50] Abandoned around the time of the death of her father, Dorus Edward Wright (1851–1890), and the remarriage of her mother, Angeline F. Gobert (1864–1932), in 1891, Wright found housing and work as a housekeeper and caring for children.[51] Russell married Cooper in 1896. By 1900, if not before, Wright was boarding with the couple while attending school.[52] *The Great Falls Leader* charted Wright's camping jaunts and other social activities with the Russells in 1901.[53]

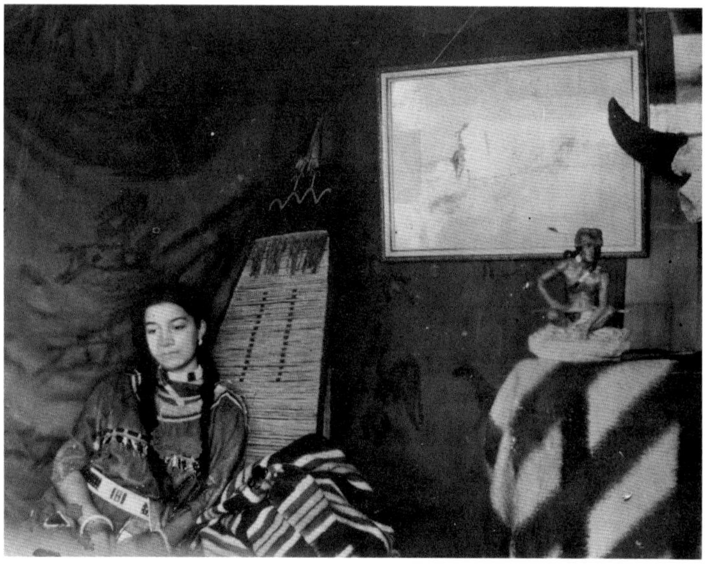

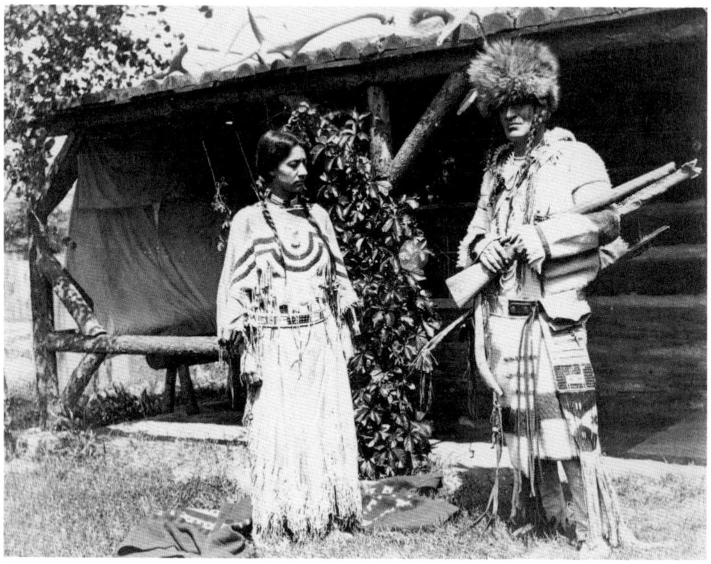

Wright posed for Russell's paintings and lived with the Russells until her marriage in 1903 to George Frederick ("Fred") Tharp (1875–1947) of the Great Northern Railway and relocation to Polson, Montana, on the Flathead Indian Reservation.[54] She appears to have been the primary model for Russell's paintings of Native American women. A photograph from about 1901 depicts Wright wearing a beaded hide dress with a beaded or quilled belt and necklace, her hair in braids, looking pensive as she leans against a backrest (similar to cats. 40 and 41) and striped Hudson's Bay blanket (fig. 5). She sits in front of two painted hides hanging on the walls, one of which is visible in Russell's painting *The Kindergarten* (cat. 62). A painted version of Russell's 1901 sculpture *Watcher of the Plains* sits on a nearby pedestal (cat. 85). In this "Indian corner" in the Great Falls house, Russell cultivated a space to install his growing collection of belongings and his own creations, which became entwined.

Coming of age in a household funded by depictions of an imagined precontact Nitsitapii life likely shaped Wright's life and posing. Later photographs outside Russell's log-cabin studio, built in 1903, depict Wright wearing a Nitsitapii beaded hide dress (cat. 34) next to Russell, who plays Indian, wearing a fur cap of his own devising and a capote (similar to cat. 8) made from a Hudson's Bay blanket (fig. 6).[55] Each photograph presents Wright's face with slightly different profiles, likely to be used as studio tools. Within a period of repression of Nitsitapii culture and lifeways, what did it mean to Wright to wear Nitsitapii and other Native American belongings in the context of the artist's studio?

Both Wright's and Russell's depictions in these photographs invite analysis of masquerade. Russell also occasionally rendered himself in the guise of a Native American man and artist in his artworks. In *The Picture Robe* (fig. 7), the female figure who also appears in *Waiting and Mad* (1899; cat. 36) sits alongside what appears to

Fig. 5.

Josephine Wright, Posing, c. 1901. C. M. Russell Museum, Great Falls, MT, Gift of Les Peters, 989.5.3.

Fig. 6.

Unknown photographer, Josephine Wright with Charles M. Russell, c. 1907. Gelatin silver print. Charles M. Russell Research Collection, Britzman, Gilcrease Museum, University of Tulsa (TU2009.39.5851a).

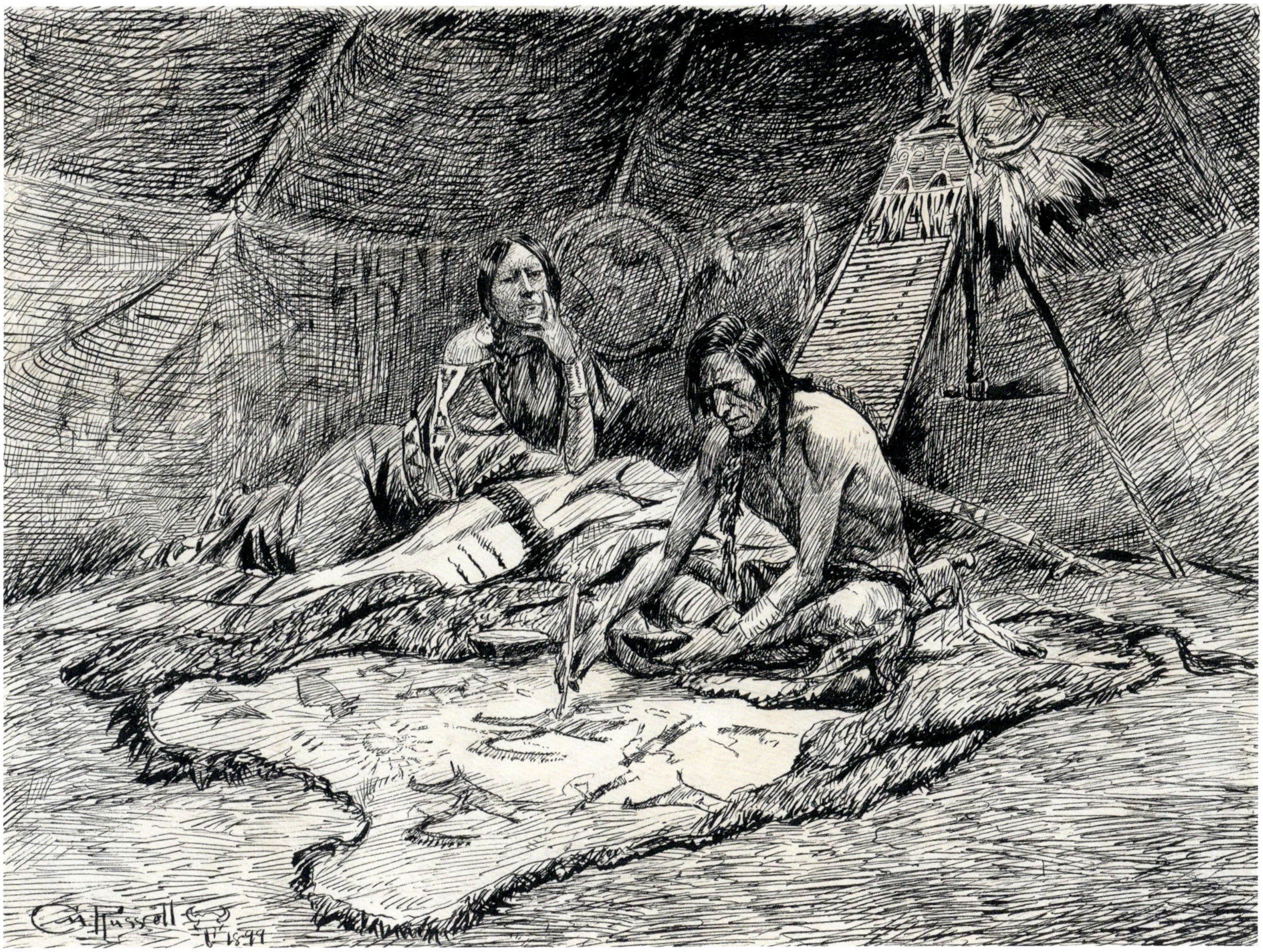

be a self-portrait of Russell as a Nitsitapii artist, intently drawing warrior histories on a hide. The backrest and warrior paintings draw from the "Indian corner" in Russell's studio, here translated into the imagined interior of a Nitsitapii lodge. Russell invested in these stories and constructions, wanting to embody an Indigenous maker. In the process, he acknowledged the powerful importance of making and storytelling in Nitsitapii culture.

Fig. 7.

Charles Marion Russell, *The Picture Robe*, 1899. Ink and graphite on paper, 10¾ × 14⅝ in. Amon Carter Museum of American Art, Fort Worth, Texas, Amon G. Carter Collection, 1961.143.

Wright became tied to Russell's performative artistic persona through the photographs and artworks. Yet, as Laura Peers, who studies living Native Americans performing as ancestral Native American figures at historic sites, shows, "Representations always have multiple interpretations; nor are they ever finalized, either in their creation or in their reception. These sites are always works in progress, continually revised through contestation, negotiation, and compromise."[56] As Peers observes, in the context of reenactment, which could be used to frame Wright's posing, multiple temporalities emerge from self-fashioning in which posers both inhabit past and present, expressing agency as they "articulate Native identity to themselves and to visitors" and "challenge established social structure."[57] Peers concludes that "playing ourselves" marks a crucial assertion of cultural identity, self-determination, and pride in the face of settler colonial insistence on assimilation.[58] For Wright, posing likely operated to build or reinforce identity, connecting her with self and with her culture.

Once Wright's visage is recognized, one sees versions of her face throughout Russell's work. In this exhibition alone, she is visible in *In the Wake of the Buffalo Runners* (1911; cat. 33), *Indian Women Moving* (1898; cat. 71), *When White Men Turn Red* (1922; cat. 79), and potentially *Waiting and Mad*.[59] Whether we invoke her presence depends on whether we interpret the figure as a type standing in for any and all Native American women (as Russell's initial audience did) or as an individual portrait of an Amskaapii Pikanii woman. Whether she serves as a metonym or a specific individual, we can understand Wright's role translating Amskaapii Pikanii culture not only for Russell but also for those who viewed his paintings.

Wright is often excluded from the scholarship on Russell. Photographs of her with Russell in the Gilcrease collection name her as "a friend."[60] In an article about the "ladies" in Russell's life, Wright is a model in almost every painting reproduced, but the author does not name her in a discussion of how "Indian women ... offered him infinite variety for his creative moods" and Russell's "straightforward, documentary manner" of depicting them.[61] Wright is scarcely mentioned in *Charles M. Russell: The Women in His Life and Art* (2018), which focuses on specific White women in Russell's career but anonymizes Native American makers and sitters related to his paintings.[62] While art historian Brian W. Dippie suggests that "Russell's West belonged to Native women," it might be more accurate to say that, given Russell's dependence not only on Wright but also the belongings largely made by Nitsitapii women and others, the labor and artistry of Native American women *shaped* Russell's West.[63]

Another Amskaapii Pikanii woman contemporaneous to Wright and about ten to thirteen years her senior, Holds Together Woman (Gretchen Duvall), has also been omitted from the record, except for the recovery and foregrounding of her story by Rosalyn LaPier. Her grandfather's aunt, whom she calls "Grandma Gretchen," Holds Together Woman was born in the 1870s and married David C. Duvall (Amskaapii Pikanii; b. 1878), son of Louise Yellow Bird, who worked with and translated for anthropologist Clark Wissler.[64] Holds Together Woman knew from her husband that Wissler coveted specific Nitsitapii artworks for the anthropology collections at New York's American Museum of Natural History. Among Wissler's desired artworks was a quillwork blanket band—a narrow, long strip sewn along the spine of painted buffalo robe or trade blanket worn by Nitsitapii men and later often affixed to blankets draped across horses (visible in Russell's *The Scout* [1915; cat. 86] and *Red Man's Wireless* [1916; cat. 13]).

In their form, materials, placement, and role within expressive culture, such belongings highlight Nitsitapii epistemology, kinship networks, and connections with an invisible reality. As LaPier recounts, Holds Together Woman spent five hours a day over four months during the winter of 1906–7 developing a quilled blanket band to sell to the museum (fig. 8).[65] As she harvested quills, dyed them using natural plant dyes, and developed the design, Holds Together Woman not only expressed connections with the animal realm but also affirmed her connection to place.[66] In this four-foot-long band, Holds Together Woman articulated continuity with the longstanding practice of porcupine quillwork, knowledge transferred to Nitsitapii women by Ksistsiikoom (Thunder).[67]

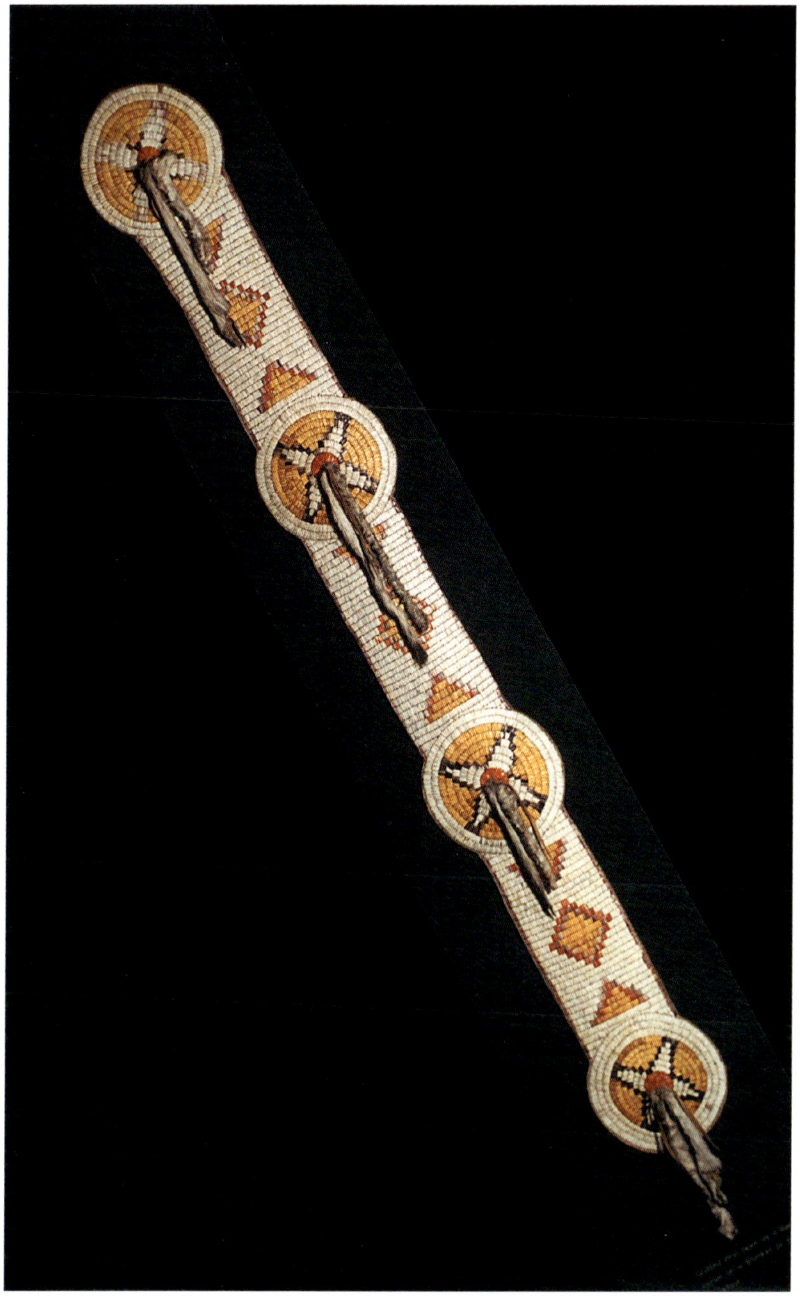

Fig. 8.

Holds Together Woman (Gretchen Duvall), *Blanket Band*, 1906–7. Hide, porcupine quills, and fur, 4 ft. American National Museum of Natural History, New York, 50/6787.

As LaPier details, Holds Together Woman would have understood the Nitsitapii ritual associated with developing such a band, which included painting designs on the maker's face during production that aligned with the beliefs embedded in the band.[68] LaPier shares that the "disks on a blanket band represented from left to right the four major deities in the Blackfeet worldview: the Sun, the Moon, the Mistaken Morning Star, and the Morning Star."[69] As LaPier describes, Morning Star is the son of the Sun and Moon, and Mistaken Morning Star a human turned divine named Paie (Scar Face).[70] Powerfully, the symbols relate the convergence between spirit and human worlds and affirm the blanket user's connection with Nitsitapii identities. As LaPier explains, "When Holds Together Woman created a blanket band it was not just a pretty object for a museum. It was also a visible mnemonic device that told the story of a history of relationships with the invisible realm ... a blanket band was a visible reminder of the Blackfeet cosmology."[71] Drawing on ancestral making and knowledge, Holds Together Woman constructed a belonging to serve as a symbol of her community, an ambassador entering a settler space, and as an articulation for the future. She made additional belongings to sell to the museum, including a quilled cradleboard and possibly a beaded belt.[72]

Paralleling the erasure of Wright's name from the historical record, Holds Together Woman's name is not recorded in the museum's ledger or registration catalog, and while half of the blanket band illustrates Wissler's 1910 article on Nitsitapii material culture, she is unnamed.[73] Yet, Wright and Holds Together Woman were knowledge sharers who perpetuated Nitsitapii culture explicitly in non-Native contexts. Both women were raised amid the tremendous pressures their community faced from settler society. Wright and Holds Together Woman knew they were reiterating Nitsitapii culture and communicating between past and future. They also knew their representations would circulate not only in Nitsitapii spaces but also communicate to Nitsitapii descendants and non-Native people alike. Both sought employment and security by engaging with the settler culture industry around Native Americans. Both participated in the new economies developing in the early twentieth century; Wright would have found security by posing for Russell, and the $60 paid to Holds Together Woman for the blanket band, about $2,000 today, would have been crucial funding in the limited cash economy on the reservation.[74] In their awareness of speaking to settler audiences through pictures or quillwork as they facilitated belonging itineraries, both women imagined and participated in bridging Nitsitapii continuity and futures.

As Wright and Holds Together Woman engaged with the telling of Nitsitapii culture in material form across settler and Native American worlds, the belongings that Russell replicated within his paintings also center women as cultural producers of Nitsitapii knowledge.[75] The spirit world conveyed making practices; Elk Woman taught Nitsitapii women how to transform animal materials into connective kinship tissue to strengthen bonds among communities.[76] Women remain central in Nitsitapii society as participants in ceremony, during times of war and negotiation, and in the crucial practice of making belongings to affirm kinship relations. What happens if we interpret Nitsitapii women artists as coauthors of Russell's paintings? Can we recenter these new stories by focusing on the belongings' itineraries in Russell's paintings?

The painting I began with, *In the Wake of the Buffalo Runners*, depicts women and community members following the buffalo hunters, preparing to transport, butcher, and prepare the carcasses for communal use. Beverly Hungry Wolf (Sikski-Aki; Black-faced Woman, b. 1950) has described the long and meticulous process of preparing hide for robes and other belongings, which includes scraping, tanning, and smoking to ensure that the fabric remains soft even after being wet, that connects the maker with the animal realm (see also the entry for cat. 53).[77]

In the Wake of the Buffalo Runners is replete with Native American belongings, all of which express their own context and network of relations beyond Russell's goals and viewers' expectations. Neither period reviews nor subsequent scholarship has addressed the ontologies of these belongings, which express Indigenous knowledge in their every fiber. Though Russell's collecting and painting of Native American belongings takes them out of circulation in explicitly Native contexts, rooted meanings and makings inhere in them. For example, the cradleboard in *In the Wake of the Buffalo Runners* appears akin to Cáuigù: (Kiowa) and Tsistsistas (Southern Cheyenne) cradleboards of the Southern Plains (fig. 9).[78] Oglála-Sičhą́ǧu Lakȟóta artist Colleen Cutschall (Sister Wolf, b. 1951) describes, "Considered gifts from the Creator, ... the

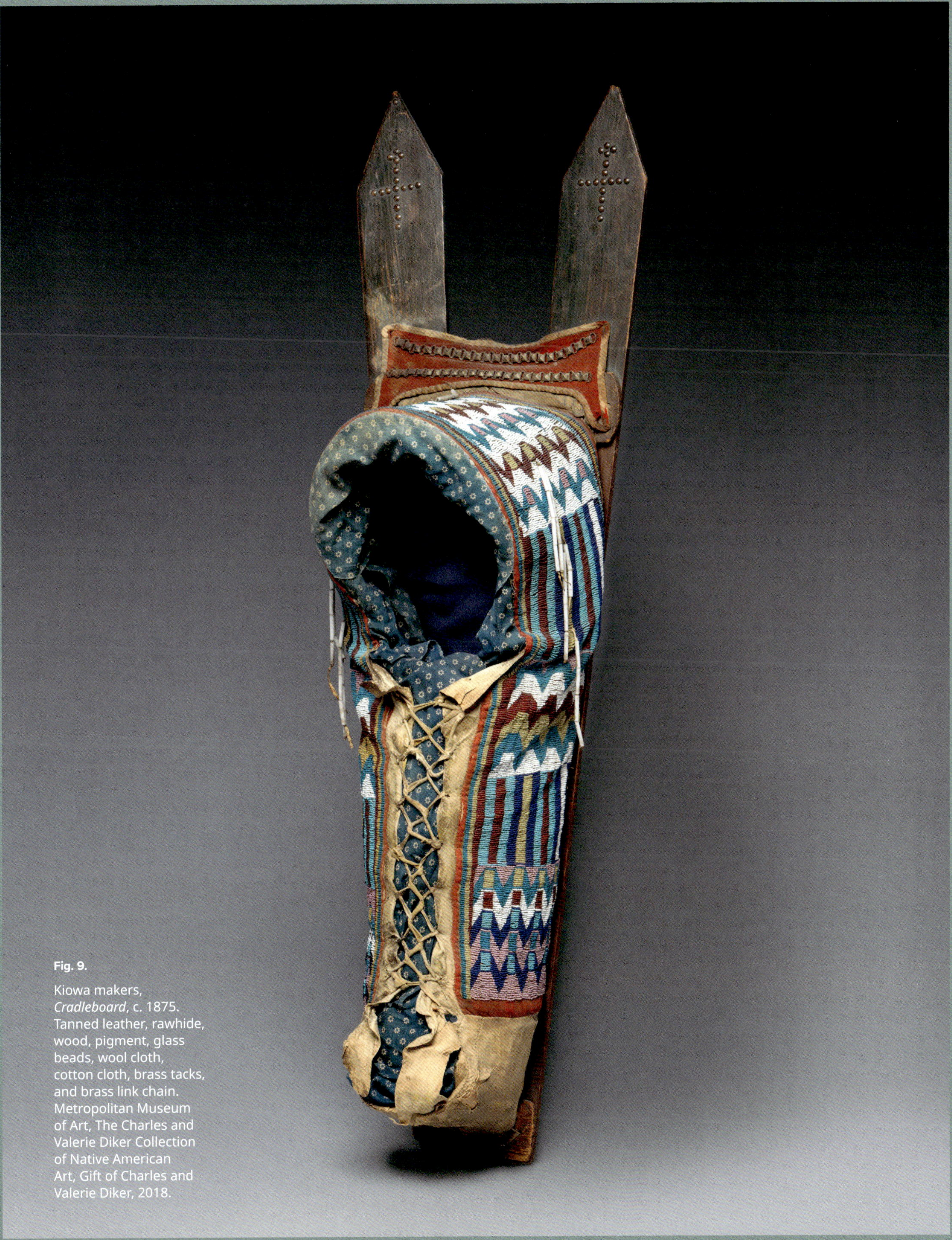

Fig. 9.

Kiowa makers, *Cradleboard*, c. 1875. Tanned leather, rawhide, wood, pigment, glass beads, wool cloth, cotton cloth, brass tacks, and brass link chain. Metropolitan Museum of Art, The Charles and Valerie Diker Collection of Native American Art, Gift of Charles and Valerie Diker, 2018.

construction, beading technique, designs, and colors on … cradleboards are meant to physically and spiritually protect a child."[79] Cáuigù: cradleboards have a wooden frame, as in Russell's painting, which is made by the father. The mother and/or other close women in the community produce the beading, in Yohe and Greeves's terms, "imbuing it with meaning and protective ornaments. They work together, with the baby in mind and in heart, to create an exquisite and durable first earthly bed for their beloved child, their *ah-day*."[80] Representations of multigenerational and community relations form the materials and design. They retain their signification and significance even in the context of Russell's painting.

The Nitsitapii dress Wright wears in *In the Wake of the Buffalo Runners* circulates in many paintings and remains in Russell's studio collection (see fig. 6 and cat. 34). In the painting, her upper body is elongated, adding visual attention to the dress. As Ron Clark, husband of Wright's granddaughter Nancy Josephine Clark, observes, "Each piece she wore … was steeped in history, telling stories of her ancestors and their way of life."[81] Cutschall notes that Native American women's dresses "are canvases for the expression of tribal culture and personal identity," and they foster relationality and connect human and spirit worlds.[82] These ontologies are embedded in the Nitsitapii dress, which is a two-hide dress with beaded lane stitching (also referred to as line stitching) in blue and emerald pony beads. Deer hides for the dress were tanned and smoked for softness and protection from the rain.[83] In the angled light of the painting, the green beads register as red. As Hungry Wolf shares, these beads were called "real beads," paralleling elders' descriptions of "real stories" to signify the spiritual understandings of Nitsitapii people of the "'real' world that was full of supernatural beings, animals, rocks, trees and other elements."[84] A row of thimbles affixed with strips of hide further adorn the center of the dress, catching the sun's glint in the painting. When worn, these would have enhanced the dynamism of the dress and produced sound to let others know the woman was entering the space, reinforcing propriety and, in the terms of Nakon (Assiniboine) beadwork artist Juanita Growing Thunder Fogarty, "the feeling that the dress is alive."[85] Amskaapii Pikanii designer Jackie Parsons also articulated how wearing such dresses render her "so very connected to everything around me."[86] Here, deer tails are affixed to the dress at the top center on both sides, further embedding the animal spirit into the belonging. It was sewn using animal sinew, a tendon that comes from the backbone of the animal and that represents the embodied animacy of the animal and its backbone's strength.[87] The dress is further adorned with a buckskin fringe and additional rows of seed beads running along the base. When wearing the dress, Wright participated in a constellation of Nitsitapii reciprocity and relationality that becomes muted but not erased within the painting.

The belongings in the painting and their materiality also highlight Nitsitapii connections with wider worlds through trade. The central figure's horse has a vibrant striped Hudson's Bay blanket across its back.[88] Wool point blankets have a long history in the region, from the beginning of the fur trade, and they were widely incorporated into Nitsitapii cultural practices as their warmth and protection made them desirable for coats, shawls, and leggings (similar to cats. 8 and 9).[89] The absorption of trade goods into Nitsitapii society demonstrates makers' active adaptation of new materials. Indigenous scholars have convincingly argued that glass beads, such as the pony and seed beads in the Nitsitapii dress, became a favored medium because they were used to make designs akin to porcupine quilling.[90] The indigenization of glass beads imbued them with the quills' signification of human-nonhuman relations. Métis, Algonquin, and Irish scholar Sherry Farrell-Racette describes such indigenization as a process of translating material forms from outside the community into the Indigenous culture, whether trade blankets made in England or glass beads made in Venice and the Czech Republic.[91] She writes, "Whether a woman worked with hide, cloth, beads, or quills, she continued to work with animate media on living surfaces, and used many of the same stitches and techniques. Women literally stitched new goods into daily and ceremonial life."[92] In the process of adapting new materials, Farrell-Racette argues that instead of indicating cultural decline, it showcases women's creative practice and expression of Indigenous epistemologies.[93] As Wigginton also articulates, "What was once foreign is grafted to Native place through Native forms and materials."[94] In other words, cultural meanings are continuous, even in fluid material contexts.

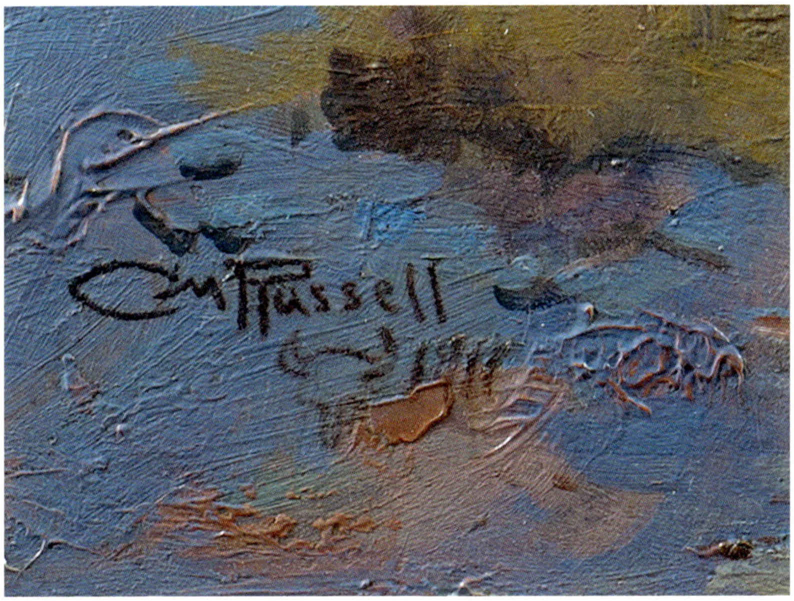

The designs from the belongings, replicated in Russell's painting, similarly retained cultural meanings in their itinerancy. Above the trade blanket, part of a geometric beaded saddle bag hangs (similar to cat. 75). Nitsitapii designs may appear abstract, such as the geometries on the saddle bag and two pipe bags (cats. 2 and 43), but these designs often signify stories about the connections between humans and the supernatural world, as in the case of the quilled blanket band discussed above (see fig. 8). Belongings linked the multidimensional universe; as LaPier describes, "The Blackfeet surrounded themselves with and relied on objects that served as mnemonic devices to remind them of their stories ... of these supernatural beings and the relationships that humans formed with them."[95] Belongings were necessary storytellers and infused with significance.[96] The belongings' influence on Russell's painting may be more than iconographic. Some of the colors of the belongings—especially the blanket's teal, red, and yellow stripes, and the red, white, and blue of the saddle bag—inform the colors in the palette, especially in the landscape. In these nonnarrative passages, the naturalist painter plays with texture, building up mounds of medium and stippling (fig. 10). Might the beaded abstractions surrounding Russell have informed his experiments with texture, extending these transnational aesthetic dialogues further?

Fig. 10.

Charles Marion Russell, *In the Wake of the Buffalo Runners* (detail; cat. 33).

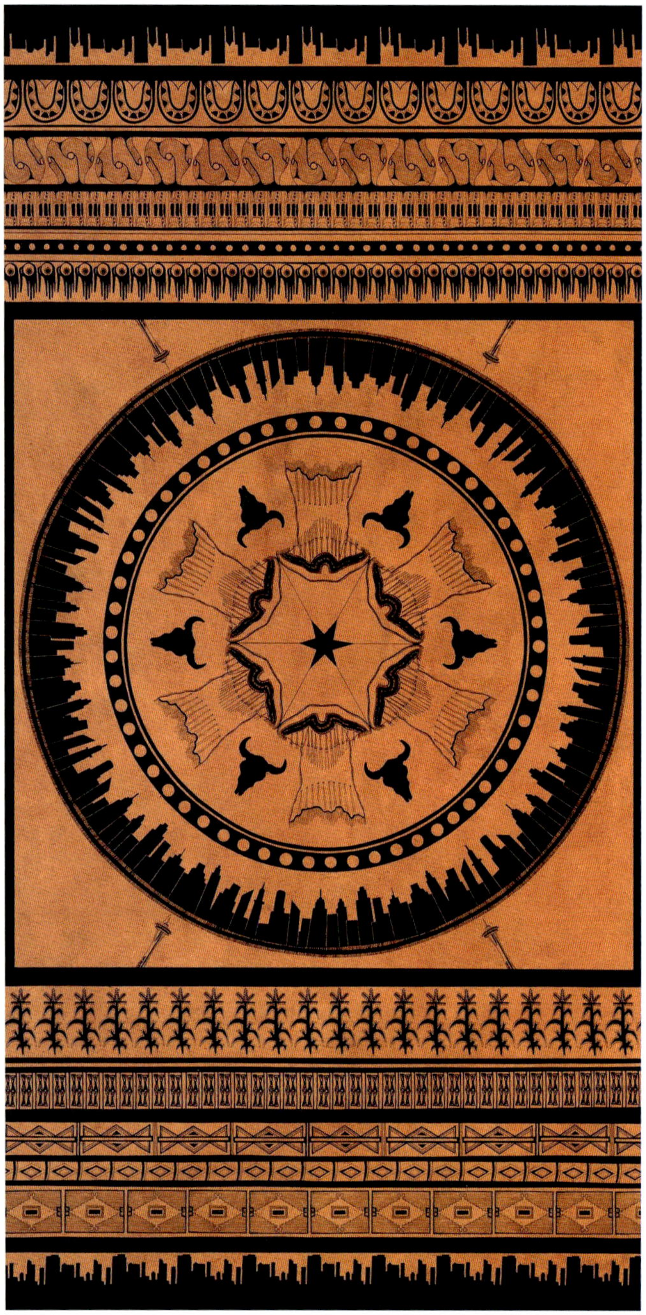

Fig. 11.

Nancy Josephine Clark, *Reinvention: Renewal*, 2019. Pen and ink on archival print, 72 × 36 in. Montana Museum of Art and Culture, University of Montana, Missoula.

Links to Native American and, in particular, Northern Plains belongings in Russell's paintings achieve more than simply affirming the settler painter's access to the American West. In the mediation of repainting these material forms, we might think about how the belongings' itineraries, and their entanglements with Native Americans, expand and complicate our understanding of settler appropriation. Within Russell's paintings, the belongings become, in Métis scholar Gloria Jane Bell's terms, "willing and unwilling" Indigenous travelers who gain new stories in their metamorphosis and transit and who circulate in new ways through the mobilities of Russell's art.[97] Paintings such as these, and the belongings they depict, are aspirational and incipient, full of a wistful longing for a possession that could never be total because of the incommensurable cultural gap that did not communicate the complexities of how belongings articulate Nitsitapii epistemology. They remain perpetually in the shadow of, in the wake of, Native American and, particularly, Nitsitapii art.

This perspective is enabled by reading archives and objects against the grain of settler colonial possession and histories of repression to honor emic interventions of these belongings and their makers' agency. These Native American belongings offer embedded knowledge and truths beyond Russell's awareness or grasp, which are not effaced in their re-presentation; rather, Russell becomes the medium for new layers in their stories, propelling their itineraries. His paintings depend on the belongings as "objects" to substantiate their own claims, but that relationship is not reciprocal. The belongings supersede the painting, and the painting becomes only a stopover on their larger journeys.

Wright's granddaughter Nancy Josephine Clark (Amskaapii Pikanii), named after both Nancy Russell and Josephine Wright and presently living in Seattle, often makes artwork that affirms the power of such belongings to facilitate intergenerational connection. Clark honors her family history and the artistic collaborations between Russell and Wright in her art practice. Clark is the daughter of Russell Tharp, Josephine and Fred's son born in 1917. The Russells adopted a son, Jack, in 1916, and family photographs depict the two boys at Bull Head Lodge, suggesting kinship entwinements exceeding Wright's earlier posing.[98]

In 2014, Clark made a series of archival prints titled *Russell Series*, in which renderings of the Nitsitapii dress worn by Wright repeat as a design motif.[99] Clark's work reminds us that the dress was always more than a "prop." In *Reinvention: Renewal*, Clark depicts the dress at the core of the patterned scene as a belonging (fig. 11). Using a tan paper matching the color of hide and black ink, Clark renders the dress multiple times alongside other forms from Nitsitapii and other Native American artistic practices. Repeating motifs recall the building of symbolism through abstract beading. Like a saddle blanket with symmetrical designs, the drawing follows careful symmetry. Surrounding a star at the center is a circular form reminiscent of circles on beaded and quilled warrior shirts and of the view as if looking upward inside a Nitsitapii lodge. Clark pairs the Nitsitapii dress with Russell's signature bison skull, which becomes refigured from its omen of a so-called dying West into a diagram of relations that include icons from Nitsitapii visual culture, southwest Tohono O'odham (Papago) pottery vessels, Northern Plains beaded saddle blanket designs, as well as corn stalks, the urban skyline, and Seattle's Space Needle.[100] In this vein, Clark shows her urban identity to be compatible with her Amskaapii Pikanii identity, resituating the dress in the context of yet another realm of intergenerational and cross-temporal relations and connections and highlighting how cosmological meaning is both material and spatial.

This essay challenges assumptions that Indigenous aesthetic and knowledge systems embedded in belongings collected and painted by Russell, which were mostly made by Nitsitapii women, were erased when they are rendered as "props." This work seeks to intellectually return—in Wigginton's terms, enact "Indigenous aesthetic repatriation"—of Native American belongings by centering their stories and layered itineraries.[101] As Wigginton concludes, we can attend to "how writing and objects seemingly distant from their origins in Native craftwork are in fact also part of a Native archive that offers points of entry for Indigenous communal expression, creation, and regeneration."[102] These belongings, in other words, can be re-storied.[103] This case study of *In the Wake of the Buffalo Runners* offers just one example of how Russell's paintings embed complex stories and significations far beyond the story easily gleaned by the non-Native viewer. Understanding Nitsitapii knowledge and this settler system of representation as fundamentally distinct, but often entwined, and making space to consider the continued operations of Nitsitapii and Indigenous meanings and cultural identity speaking through the agentic belongings in Russell's paintings honors the knowledge producers who embedded, beaded, wove, and quilled culture as a multi-generational conversation.

NOTES

Thanks to JR Henneman, Spencer Wigmore, Will Gillham, Alicia Harris, and Valerie Hellstein for feedback on this research. I am grateful to Cheryle "Cookie" Cobell Zwang (Niit si poo aki, Only Girl), Aaron LaFromboise, Nancy Clark, Ron Clark, John Pepion, Renee Bear Medicine, Jackie Larson Bread, and Heather Caverhill for conversations about Nitsitapii culture and relationships between Nitsitapii models and settler painters. Thanks to Kim Wilson for investigating Josephine Wright's genealogy, and to Sharon Burchett and Valentine Karrer for research support. Lastly, I thank the C. M. Russell Museum staff, especially Sarah Adcock, Olivia Cotterman, and Geoff Stocking, and Karina Ceron from the American Museum of Natural History, for research assistance.

1 Roxanne Dunbar-Ortiz, *An Indigenous Peoples' History of the United States* (Beacon Press, 2014); Ned Blackhawk, *The Rediscovery of America: Native Peoples and the Unmaking of U.S. History* (Yale University Press, 2023).

2 Jessa Rae Growing Thunder, "Hi-Line Treasures: Bold Colors and Geometric Designs Exemplify Beadwork from Montana's Northern Plains," *Native American Art Magazine* (April/May 2022): 92–97.

3 For period claims, see "Cowboy Artist, St. Louis' Lion," *Daily Independent* (Helena), May 13, 1901, 5; Arthur Hoeber, "The Painter of the West That Has Passed," *The World's Work* 22, no. 3 (1911): 14626, 14629; "Cowboy Vividly Paints the Passing Life of the Plains," *New York Times*, March 19, 1911, SM5; and "Smart Set Lionizing a Cowboy Artist," *New York Press*, January 31, 1904. For scholarly discussion, see Spencer Wigmore, "Charles M. Russell: New Perspectives," *Carter Bulletin* 1 *(Charles M. Russell: New Perspectives)* (Amon Carter Museum of American Art, 2025), https://bulletin-v1.cartermuseum.org/wigmore/; Hugh Dempsey, "Tracking C. M. Russell in Canada, 1888–1889," *Montana The Magazine of Western History* 39, no. 3 (1989): 2–15; John C. Ewers, "Charlie Russell's Indians," *Montana The Magazine of Western History* 37, no. 3 (1987): 36; and George P. Horse Capture Sr., "Memories of Charles M. Russell Among My Indian Relatives," in *The Masterworks of Charles M. Russell: Retrospective of Paintings and Sculpture*, ed. Joan Carpenter Troccoli (University of Oklahoma Press in cooperation with the Denver Art Museum, 2009), 121–27.

4 Rosalyn R. LaPier, *Invisible Reality: Storytellers, Storytakers, and the Supernatural World of the Blackfeet* (University of Nebraska Press and the American Philosophical Society, 2017).

5 Nitsitapii artists have engaged with and responded to Russell's art practice from his lifetime into the present, an important topic not considered here.

6 Betty Bastien, *Blackfoot Ways of Knowing: the Worldview of the Siksikaaitsitapi* (University of Calgary Press, 2004); *Nitsitapiisini: The Story of the Blackfoot People* (Glenbow Museum, 2001), https://www.glenbow.org/blackfoot/EN/html/index.htm; Audrey Weasel Traveller, "A Shining Trail to the Sun's Lodge: Renewal Through Blackfoot Ways of Knowing" (master's thesis, University of Lethbridge, 1997); Gerald A. Oetelaar, "Entanglements of the Blackfoot: Relationships with the Spiritual and Material Worlds," in *Tracing the Relational: The Archaeology of Worlds, Spirits, and Temporalities*, ed. Meghan E. Buchanan and B. Jacob Skousen (University of Utah Press, 2015), 131–45; and Ryan Hall, *Beneath the Backbone of the World: Blackfoot People and the North American Borderlands, 1720–1877* (University of North Carolina Press, 2020).

7 Nimachia Hernandez, "Mokakssini: A Blackfoot Theory of Knowledge" (PhD diss., Harvard University, 1999); and Blanca Tovías, *Colonialism on the Prairies: Blackfoot Settlement and Cultural Transformation, 1870–1920* (Sussex Academic Press, 2011), 131.

8 LaPier, *Invisible Reality*, 25. See also, ibid., 26–29.

9 Oetelaar, "Entanglements of the Blackfoot," 131.

10 Tovías, *Colonialism on the Prairies*, 2. See also, ibid., 15–23.

11 Tovías, *Colonialism on the Prairies*, 160, as well as 17, 19–20, 22, 71–72.

12 Paul R. Wylie, *Blood on the Marias: The Baker Massacre* (University of Oklahoma Press, 2016); Roger C. Henderson, "The Pikanii and the U.S. Army's Piegan Expedition: Competing Narratives of the 1870 Massacre on the Marias River," *Montana The Magazine of Western History* 68, no. 1 (2018): 48–70; and Tristan Scott, "Remembering the Marias Massacre," *Flathead Beacon*, January 15, 2020, https://flatheadbeacon.com/2020/01/15/remembering-marias-massacre/.

13 LaPier, *Invisible Reality*, 11, 14, 19.

14 Tovías, *Colonialism on the Plains*, 25, 34.

15 Oetelaar, "Entanglement of the Blackfoot," 132. See also Gerald A. Oetelaar and D. Joy Oetelaar, "The Structured World of the *Nitsitapii*: The Landscape as Historical Archive Among Hunter-Gatherers of the Northern Plains," in *Structured Worlds: The Archaeology of Hunter-Gatherer Thought and Action,* ed. Aubrey Cannon (Equinox Pub., 2011), 69–94.

16 Mark David Spence, "Crown of the Continent, Backbone of the World: The American Wilderness Ideal and Blackfeet Exclusion from Glacier National Park," *Environmental History* 1, no. 3 (1996): 29–49; David R. Craig et al., "'Blackfeet Belong to the Mountains': Hope, Loss, and Blackfeet Claims to Glacier National Park, Montana," *Conservation & Society* 10, no. 3 (2012): 232–42.

17 Heather Caverhill, "Mutable Moderns: An Art Colony in Blackfoot Territory and the Lives of Its Works" (PhD diss., University of British Columbia, 2024); and Tovías, *Colonialism on the Prairies*, 109.

18 John C. Ewers, *The Blackfeet: Raiders on the Northwest Plains* (University of Oklahoma Press, 1958), 311.

19 LaPier, *Invisible Reality*, 3–4; Tovías, *Colonialism on the Plains*, 44; Ewers, *The Blackfeet*, 311; and Mary Eggermont-Molenaar, ed., *Montana 1911: A Professor and His Wife Among the Blackfeet* (University of Calgary Press, 2005), 79–93, 254–56.

20 LaPier, *Invisible Reality*, 3–4, 22.

21 On Bull Head Lodge, see Brian W. Dippie, "'It is a Real Business': The Shaping and Selling of Charles M. Russell's Art," in *Charles M. Russell: A Catalogue Raisonné*, ed. B. Byron Price (University of Oklahoma Press, 2007), 32; and Nancy Cooper Russell, *Back-Tracking in Memory: The Life of Charles M. Russell, Artist: Recollections, Reflections and Personal Perspectives*, ed. Thomas A. Petrie and Brian W. Dippie (C. M. Russell Museum, 2021), 98, 124–31.

22 Caroline Wigginton, *Indigenuity: Native Craftwork and the Art of American Literature* (University of North Carolina Press, 2022), 10. See also Bethany Hughes, *Redface: Race, Indigeneity, Performance* (New York University Press, 2024); and Kevin Bruyneel, *Settler Memory: The Disavowal of Indigeneity and the Politics of Race in the United States* (University of North Carolina Press, 2021).

23 Richard B. Roeder, "Charles M. Russell and Modern Times," *Montana The Magazine of Western History* 34, no. 3 (1984): 7; and Brian W. Dippie, ed., *"Paper Talk": Charlie Russell's American West* (Alfred A. Knopf, 1979), 139.

24 Frank Bird Linderman, *Recollections of Charley Russell* (University of Oklahoma Press, 1988), xvi–xviii, 129–30; and Ewers, "Charlie Russell's Indians," 49.

25 Original punctuation and spelling retained.

26 *The Log Cabin Studio of Charles M. Russell: Montana's Cowboy Artist* (The Committee, 1931; repr. C. M. Russell Museum, nd), 15–29; and Elizabeth A. Dear, *C. M. Russell's Log Studio* (C. M. Russell Museum, 1995), 23–51.

27 Larry Len Peterson, *Charles M. Russell: Photographing the Legend: A Biography in Words and Pictures* (University of Oklahoma Press, 2014), 66–68, 72–75; and Dear, *C. M. Russell's Log Studio*, 8–10.

28 Elizabeth Hutchinson, *The Indian Craze: Primitivism, Modernism, and Transculturation in American Art, 1890–1915* (Duke University Press, 2009), 11–50.

29 "Indian Relics: An Interesting Collection in the Possession of the Cowboy Artist," *Great Falls Tribune*, November 27, 1892, 5.

30 Annika Johnson, "Cultural Intersections in Charles M. Russell's Studio Collection," *Carter Bulletin* 1, https://bulletin-v1.cartermuseum.org/johnson/; "Smart Set Lionizing a Cowboy Artist."

31 Alexander Nemerov, "Doing the 'Old America': The Image of the American West, 1880–1922," in *The West as America: Reinterpreting Images of the Frontier*, ed. William H. Truettner (Smithsonian Institution Press, 1991), 290. On settler use of Native American material culture, see Ramey Mize, "Battle Grounds: Painting, War, and Witness in the Americas, 1861–1902" (PhD diss., University of Pennsylvania, 2023), 125–30.

32 Frederic G. Renner, *Charles M. Russell: Paintings, Drawings, and Sculpture in the Amon Carter Museum* (Abradale Press/Harry N. Abrams, Inc., 1974), 179; Peter H. Hassrick, *Charles M. Russell* (Harry N. Abrams Inc., Publishers and National Museum of American Art, Smithsonian Institution, 1989), 87; and Frederic G. Renner, "Charlie's Log Cabin Studio," in *C. M. Russell's Log Cabin Studio*, by Dan Cushman, Frederic G. Renner, and Terry Melton (C. M. Russell Museum, nd).

33 Dear, *C. M. Russell's Log Studio*, 3, 19, 21, 22, 34.

34 Hassrick, *Charles Russell*, 87.

35 Alyssa Mt. Pleasant, Caroline Wigginton, and Kelly Wisecup, "Materials and Methods in Native American and Indigenous Studies: Completing the Turn," *William & Mary Quarterly* 75, no. 2 (2018): 217.

36 Stephen Foster and Mike Evans, "Decolonizing Representation: Ontological Transformations Through Re-Mediation of Indigenous Representation in Popular Culture and Indigenous Interventions," in *The Routledge Companion to Indigenous Art Histories in the United States and Canada*, ed. Heather Igloliorte and Carla Taunton (Routledge, 2022), 275.

37 heather ahtone, "Shifting the Paradigm of Art History: A Multi-Sited Indigenous Approach," in ibid., 42.

38 Jenny Tone-Pah-Hote, *Crafting an Indigenous Nation: Kiowa Expressive Culture in the Progressive Era* (University of North Carolina Press, 2019), 5.

39 Jill Ahlberg Yohe and Teri Greeves, "Introduction," in *Hearts of Our People: Native Women Artists*, ed. Jill Ahlberg Yohe and Teri Greeves (Minneapolis Institute of Art and University of Washington Press, 2019), 22. See also Colleen Cutschall, "Dresses, Designers, and the Dance of Life," in *Identity by Design: Tradition, Change, and Celebration in Native Women's Dresses*, ed. Emil Her Many Horses (Smithsonian Institution Press, 2007), 65.

40 Madeline Sayet, *Where We Belong* (Methuen Drama, Bloomsbury Publishing, Plc., 2022), 41.

41 Lorén Spears and Amanda Thompson, "'As We Have Always Done': Decolonizing the Tomaquag Museum's Collection Management Policy," *Collections: A Journal*

for Museum and Archives Professionals 18, no. 1 (2022): 37. See also Carolyn Smith, "Northwestern California Baskets and Weaving the Roots of Home," presentation at Native American Art Studies Association, October 12, 2023; Clementine Bordeaux, "Wówayupike: Relational Practices Between Art, Land, and Culture" (PhD diss., University of California—Los Angeles, 2024); Maureen Matthews, *Naamiwan's Drum: the Story of a Contested Repatriation of Anishinaabe Artefacts* (University of Toronto Press, 2016), 20–21, 49–79, 103–38; and Mary Deleary, "A Place for Us to Sit: Making and Remembering Visual and Material Histories of Deshkan Ziibiing" (PhD diss., University of Oklahoma, 2023). The 2025 symposium, "Belonging: Native American Art in Settler Contexts," at the Charles M. Russell Center for the Study of Art of the American West at the University of Oklahoma also analyzed this concept. YouTube, accessed December 6, 2025, https://www.youtube.com/live/q5h-ml-EpiU.

42 Foster and Evans, "Decolonizing Representation," 276.

43 Rosemary A. Joyce and Susan D. Gillespie, "Making Things out of Objects that Move," in *Things in Motion: Object Itineraries in Anthropological Practice,* ed. Rosemary A. Joyce and Susan D. Gillespie (School for Advanced Research Press, 2015), 3, 5. Thanks to Carolyn Smith for suggesting this crucial model.

44 Ibid., 7.

45 Wigginton, *Indigenuity*, 15.

46 Ibid., 2.

47 Ibid.

48 Ibid., 14, 10–11.

49 Nancy Josephine Clark, "Josie: the Blackfeet Woman in Charles M. Russell's Life," lecture, C. M. Russell Museum, June 15, 2018, YouTube, accessed December 12, 2025, https://www.youtube.com/watch?v=hYdR0w0N6iU; Joan Stauffer, *Behind Every Man: The Story of Nancy Cooper Russell* (Daljo Publishing, 1990), 54–56, 74; Dippie, "'It Is a Real Business'," 6–7; and Ronald H. Clark, *Charles M. Russell Legacies: Amazing Tales of Charles and Nancy Russell, Josephine Wright, and Nancy Josephine Clark* (pub. by author, 2025), 6–7, 19–21, 24–25, 34–36.

50 "Mary Ahkahtah," The Blackfeet Genealogy, accessed November 14, 2025, http://www.blackfeetgenealogy.com/pafg249.htm#10509; see also Clark, *Charles M. Russell Legacies,* 6; and Montana, US, County Marriages, 1856–1987, Certificate Number 2626.

51 The 1880 census lists Gobert as half Blackfeet. See Saint Peters Mission, Lewis and Clark County, Montana, USA, 1880 United States Federal Census. On her marriage, see "City and County News," *Great Falls Leader*, October 6, 1891, 5.

52 Great Falls, Cascade County, Montana, 1900 United States Federal Census.

53 "Great Falls and Vicinity," *Great Falls Leader*, August 20 and 27, 1901, 5; "Society," *Great Falls Leader*, November 30, 1901, 9; "The Week in Society," *Great Falls Leader*, December 1, 1901, 11.

54 Clark, *Charles M. Russell Legacies*, 36.

55 Dear, *C. M. Russell's Log Studio*, 4. On Russell's garments, see Johnson, "Cultural Intersections in Charles M. Russell's Studio Collection."

56 Laura Peers, *Playing Ourselves: Interpreting Native Histories at Historic Reconstructions* (Altamira Press, 2007), xxiii.

57 Ibid., 1, 45.

58 Ibid., 64.

59 Scholars suggest that Nancy Russell modeled for *Waiting and Mad* or that it could be a composite of both women. Jennifer Bottomly-O'Looney and Kirby Lambert, *Montana's Charlie Russell: Art in the Collection of the Montana Historical Society* (Montana Historical Society Press, 2014), 67.

60 For one example, see *Charles M. Russell and Friend*. TU2009.39.5849a. Charles M. Russell Research Collection (Britzman), late 19th century–early 20th century. Gilcrease Museum, accessed November 14, 2025, https://live-gmcd.pantheonsite.io/object/tu2009395849a.

61 Ginger K. Renner, "Charlie and the Ladies in His Life," *Montana The Magazine of Western History* 34, no. 3 (1984): 55.

62 Joan Carpenter Troccoli, ed., *Charles M. Russell: The Women in His Life and Art* (C. M. Russell Museum, 2018).

63 Dippie, "Introduction," in ibid., 4.

64 LaPier, *Invisible Reality*, 99, 110–11. See "Louise 459641G32 Yellow Bird Duvall," Blackfeet Geneaology, accessed January 5, 2026, http://blackfeetgenealogy.com/pafg374.htm#13878.

65 LaPier, *Invisible Reality*, 99–100. Letter from David C. Duvall to Clark Wissler, May 9, 1907, American Museum of Natural History, Division of Anthropology Archives, New York.

66 Carmen Robertson, "Land and Beaded Identity: Shaping Art Histories of Indigenous Women of the Flatland," *RACAR: Revue d'art Canadienne/Canadian Art Review* 42, no. 2 (2017): 16.

67 Beverly Hungry Wolf, *The Ways of My Grandmothers* (Quill, 1982), 241.

68 Elk Horn interview with Clark Wissler, 1903–4, cited in LaPier, *Invisible Reality*, 117.

69 LaPier, *Invisible Reality*, 117.

70 Ibid., 34. See also Weasel Traveller, "A Shining Trail to the Sun's Lodge," vi.

71 LaPier, *Invisible Reality*, 117.

72 These are belongings 50/6164 and 50/6181, American Museum of Natural History. On the cradleboard, which Wissler admired, see Letter from David C. Duvall to Clark Wissler, November 2, 1905, and Clark Wissler to David C. Duvall, December 28, 1905, American Museum of Natural History, Division of Anthropology Archives, New York.

73 Clark Wissler, "Material Culture of Blackfoot Indians," *Anthropological Papers of the American Museum of Natural History* 5, pt. 1 (1910): 123.

74 LaPier, *Invisible Reality*, 100.

75 On Native American women makers, see Yohe and Greeves, *Hearts of Our People*; Sherry Farrell-Racette, Michelle LaVallee, and Cathy Mathes, *Radical Stitch* (National Gallery of Canada, 2024); Carmen Robertson et al., ed., *Bead Talk: Indigenous Knowledge and Aesthetics from the Flatlands* (University of Manitoba Press, 2024); Colette A. Hyman, *Dakota Women's Work: Creativity, Culture and Exile* (Minnesota Historical Society Press, 2012); and Meagan Smetzer, *Painful Beauty: Tlingit Women, Beadwork, and the Art of Resilience* (University of Washington Press, 2021).

76 Tovías, *Colonialism on the Prairies*, 17, 73–74; Weasel Traveller, "A Shining Trail," 94. See also Rebecca Many Grey Horses, "Blackfoot Women: Keepers of the Ways and Pillars of the Nation," lecture, Galt Museum & Archives, June 22, 2020, YouTube, accessed December 13, 2025, https://www.youtube.com/watch?v=rNynWfPr5I8.

77 Hungry Wolf, *Ways of My Grandmothers*, 231–39.

78 Nancy Russell brought some belongings to California after the painter's death, which were dispersed (Dear, *C. M. Russell's Log Studio*, 9, 22).

79 Cutschall, "Dresses, Designers and the Dance of Life," in Her Many Horses, *Identity by Design*, 79. See also MaryAnn Guoladdle Parker, "Vessels that Carried Us: Kiowa Cradleboards," First Americans Museum, accessed January 13, 2025, https://tinyurl.com/ydv2fd3f; Deanna Tidwell Broughton, *Hide, Wood, and Willow: Cradles of the Great Plains Indians* (University of Oklahoma Press, 2019), 4–6, 21–23; and Greeves, "In Focus: Kiowa Cradleboard," in Yohe and Greeves, *Hearts of Our People*, 198–99.

80 Yohe and Greeves, "Introduction," in Yohe and Greeves, *Hearts of Our People*, 25.

81 Clark, *Charles M. Russell Legacies*, 20.

82 Cutschall, "Dresses, Designers, and the Dance of Life," 90; Janet Berlo, "Creativity and Cosmopolitanism: Women's Enduring Traditions," in Her Many Horses, *Identity by Design*, 97.

83 Hungry Wolf, *Ways of My Grandmother*, 238.

84 Ibid., 230; and LaPier, *Invisible Reality*, 24.

85 Her Many Horses, "Portraits of Native Women and Their Dresses," 62. On the dress, see Emily C. Burns, "Charles M. Russell's *Sun Worship in Montana*: Painting Blackfeet People, Artistry and *Mokakssini*," *Carter Bulletin*, https://bulletin-v1.cartermuseum.org/burns/.

86 Her Many Horses, "Portraits of Native Women and Their Dresses," 33.

87 Hungry Wolf, *Ways of My Grandmothers*, 240.

88 Ann M. Carlos and Frank D. Lewis, *Commerce on a Frozen Sea: Native Americans and the European Fur Trade* (University of Pennsylvania Press, 2010), 69–105, especially 104.

89 Robert W. Kapoun with Charles J. Lohrmann, "The Blanket in the Fur Trade," in *Language of the Robe: American Indian Trade Blankets* (Peregrine Smith Books, 1992), 21–29; and Laura Peers and Alison K. Brown, *Visiting with the Ancestors: Blackfoot Shirts in Museum Spaces* (AU Press, Athabasca University, 2015), 32, 37, 38, 70, 167.

90 Carmen Robertson, "Beading Back and Forth: Upending Temporality through Knowledge Transmission," *21: Inquiries into Art, History and the Visual* 5, no. 1 (2024): 65; Hungry Wolf, *Ways of My Grandmothers*, 245–47; and Robertson, "Land and Beaded Identity," 16.

91 Sherry Farrell-Racette, "My Grandmothers Loved to Trade: The Indigenization of European Trade Goods in Historic and Contemporary Canada," *Journal of Museum Ethnography*, no. 20 (March 2008): 69–81. See also Marsha Clift Bol, *The Art and Tradition of Beadwork* (Gibbs Smith, 2018); 8, 18; and Elliott H. Blair, "Glass Beads and Global Itineraries," in Joyce and Gillespie, *Things in Motion*, 81–88.

92 Farrell Racette, "My Grandmothers Loved to Trade," 72.

93 Ibid., 77.

94 Wigginton, *Indigenuity*, 4.

95 LaPier, *Invisible Reality*, 29.

96 Ibid., 116.

97 Gloria Bell, "Competing Sovereignties: Indigeneity and the Visual Culture of Catholic Colonization at the 1925 Pontifical Missionary Exhibition," *Journal of Global Catholicism* 3, no. 2 (2019): 20. See also Gloria Jane Bell, *Eternal Sovereigns: Indigenous Artists, Activists, and Travelers Reframing Rome* (Duke University Press, 2024), 130–31, 156–58.

98 Clark, *Charles M. Russell Legacies*, 40.

99 Ibid., 104. The dress also appears in Clark's *Empty Dress* series (2023) to draw attention to the pandemic of Missing and Murdered Indigenous Women and Relatives. Ibid., 114–17.

100 Clark, *Charles M. Russell Legacies*, 81.

101 Wigginton, *Indigenuity*, 2.

102 Ibid., 16.

103 On storywork, see Robertson, "Beading Back and Forth," 55–56; Jo-Ann Archibald, *Indigenous Storywork: Educating the Heart, Mind, Body and Spirit* (University of British Columbia Press, 2008).

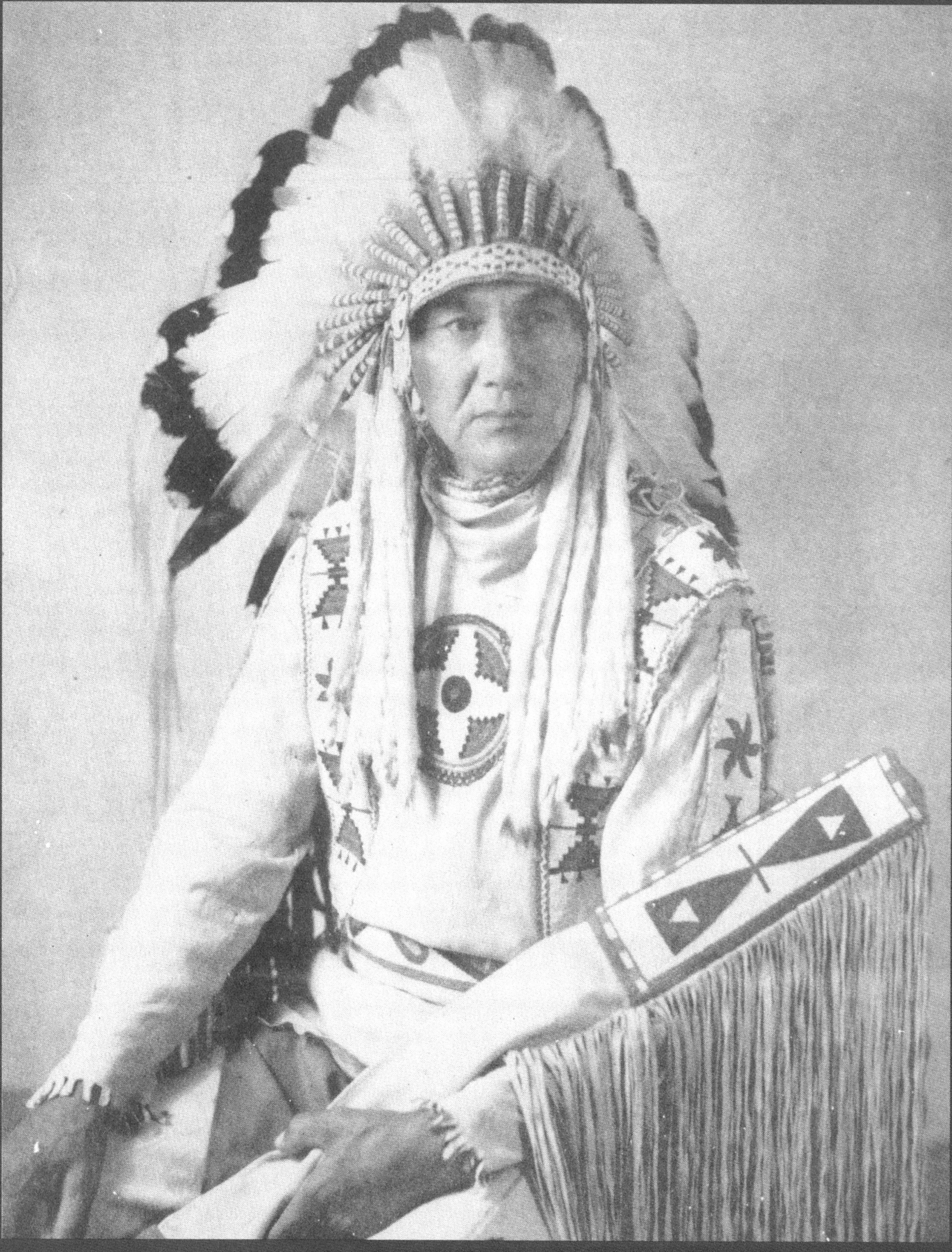

Remembrances of Lone Wolf, Amskaapii Pikanii Artist

NI-TAH-MAH-KWI-I, best known as Lone Wolf (also Hart Merriam Schultz; c. 1882–1970), belonged to the Inuck'siks (Small Robes) band of the Nitsitapii (fig. 1). His father was White settler James Willard Schultz (1859–1947), and his mother was Fine Shield Woman (Amskaapii Pikanii; c. 1860/65–1903), whose nickname was Na-tah-ki ("Pretty Girl"). Born around the same time that Charles Russell arrived in Montana Territory, Lone Wolf grew up on the Blackfeet Indian Reservation, and his accounts of his life provide a perspective that differs markedly from Russell's experience during the same era in many of the same locations. Throughout his life, Lone Wolf navigated cultural suppression and transformation. He negotiated two different value systems, ultimately leaving the reservation and forging a career as a painter and sculptor. Cursory comparisons between his sculpture and painting, such as *The Scout* (date unknown; fig. 2), and those of Russell, Frederic Remington (1861–1909), and Charles Schreyvogel (1861–1912)—all of whom he met—reveal his indebtedness to the romantic interpretation of Old West imagery they established.[1]

Lone Wolf's story, as represented here, is stitched together from an oral interview conducted in 1965 by Milo Wiltbank in Greer, Arizona, and a 1972 article published by Lone Wolf's adopted son, Paul Dyck.[2] Additional content provides context and resources.

Lone Wolf's grandmother Pah-ta-ki had two husbands. With the first, Black Eagle, she had Fine Shield Woman, who became Lone Wolf's mother. In Lone Wolf's words, his biological grandfather, Black Eagle, "was killed by his own tribesmen because he was too powerful and had too much success on the war path."[3] After Black Eagle's death, Pah-ta-ki married his brother Yellow Wolf. According to Lone Wolf, Yellow Wolf was one of his earliest artistic mentors: "An old warrior, always good to me and a good artist, too. I used to watch him paint his war history on a buffalo robe. Often while he was painting, I would ask him, 'Grandfather, how do you do that?' He'd find a buffalo shoulder-blade bone and show me how to put some color on it.... Yellow Wolf taught me how to use natural colors, colors found in the country. He showed me how to prepare them and how to draw animals and people. Most important, he told me that

Fig. 1.

Unknown photographer, Portrait of Hart Merriam Schultz (Lone Wolf), son of James Willard Schultz, date not known. Image number 301; collection number 0010. Montana State University, Bozeman: Merrill G. Burlingame Special Collections.

I should, when painting a picture, have the picture tell a story."[4] This description recalls the centuries-old tradition of Nitsitapii pictographs to record personal and collective stories. In the exhibition, a *ninaipistsii* (war robe) possibly painted by Percy (Two Gun) Plain Woman (Kainai; 1895–1961) illustrates this tradition (cat. 3).

Lone Wolf remembered learning how to prepare materials, paint, and sculpt from his elders. "When I was a boy, we were taught by our older people.... They were all the time drawing historical pictures.... So, we tried to imitate them.... Paints were all made of vegetable and mineral dyes, and our brushes were made of bone.... We got rawhide or buckskin stretchers, and we'd draw pictures of horses or buffalo or whatever, or teepees and so forth, and the old folks would correct our drawings."[5] Additionally, he remembered, "We'd all go down to the bank and there's a certain clay we used. We'd model horses and buffalo, animals, human beings, and all that sort of thing."[6] And "on sunny days, Grandfather would take me to the riverbank. There he could find good clay and we would sit by a flat rock and he would show me how to make real-looking horses and buffalo. He always had time to tell me stories or teach me the ways of the Old Ones."[7] Such lessons would inform Lone Wolf's career when he turned to art as an adult. Additionally, he passed along lessons about his culture to other artists. According to Dyck, after Lone Wolf had established himself as an artist and set up a summer studio at St. Mary's outside Glacier National Park, "Charles Russell, together with Olaf Seltzer, made several summer visits ... seeking facts on ethnological details. He would have Lone Wolf ask old warriors like Bear Head to help solve the problems."[8] Lone Wolf, too, is an underrecognized contributor to Russell's work, just as it is clear from his work that Lone Wolf learned from Russell.

Lone Wolf's father, James Willard Schultz, was a White man who came West in the 1870s and became a popular writer. Although from a wealthy family, Schultz craved western adventure. He and a friend took a steamer from St. Louis up the Missouri River to Fort Benton, Montana. There, Schultz met and started working for Joseph Kipp, a trader. As Lone Wolf stated, Kipp "had a trading post right on the Missouri River, and thousands of Indians would come in to trade, the Crees and the Blackfeet and the Assiniboines and some of the Flatheads. [My father] wanted to know the language ... and after a while, he could talk just like one of the Natives. And sometime in the '70s, he met my mother, who was a daughter of a chief, and they got married [in] 1879."[9]

According to Lone Wolf, his father "was named Apikuni by Chief Running Crane, a great warrior of the Blackfeet whose name had also been Apikuni."[10] Na-tah-ki "was a wise woman and a happy one. All who came near her carried away some of her sunshine. She saw beauty around her and passed it onto others. No wonder my father loved her so much. She could sew beautiful things, too, and made all our clothes and our mocassins [*sic*]. This was very hard for her because she had one hand that was badly crippled. In 1870, when she was a little girl, she and my grandmother, Pah-ta-ki, were caught in the Baker Massacre on the Marias. Grandmother was not hurt but

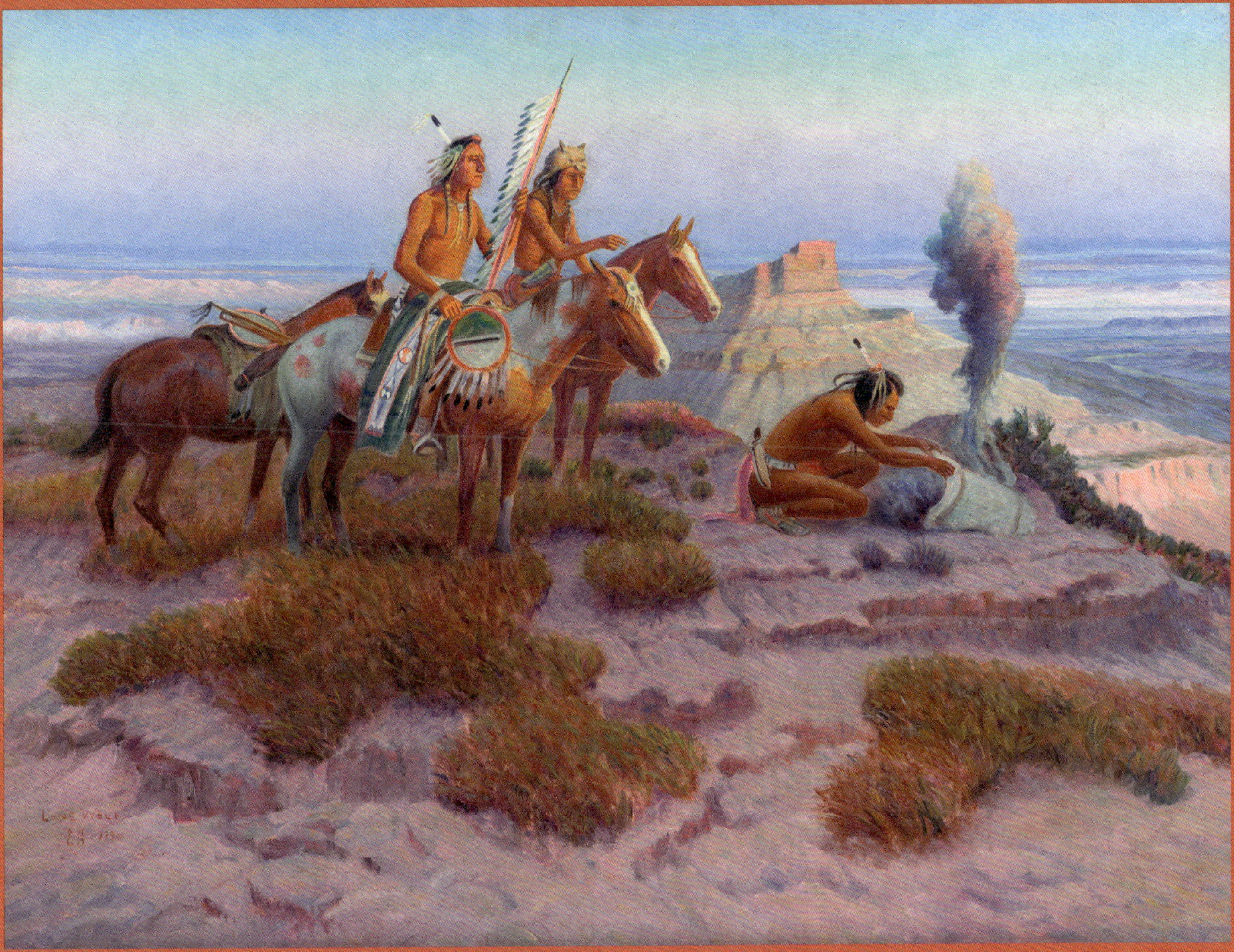

Fig. 2.

Lone Wolf, *The Scout*, date not known. Oil on canvas. Petrie Collection, Denver, Colorado.

my mother was shot in the hand."[11] Having survived this gruesome violence against her people, Na-tah-ki nonetheless "carried sunshine," in the words of her son, and made beautiful clothing for those she loved. Moccasins and other beadwork in the exhibition present examples of the kind of fine artistry produced during this period (see cats. 20–25).

Lone Wolf was born on Birch Creek in a lodge near James Kipp's Trading Post at Robare Crossing in 1882 or 1883 (fig. 3).[12] He grew up on a ranch at Two Medicine. His father was away most of the time, "acting as a guide for wealthy hunters and sportsmen from the East and West," so the chores fell to Lone Wolf, who "had to learn how to run the ranch and depended upon his uncle Last Rider for advice and help.... He looked upon [his uncle] as a second father."[13] Lone Wolf was closest to Nah-ta-ki's people, even though she told him, "You will have to follow the White Man's way so it is best to learn how to make a living right here [on the ranch]."[14] Although ranch chores kept him busy as a young man, he nonetheless sold his first watercolor painting in 1894, when he was twelve, to a clerk at Kipp's store in Browning.[15]

As a child, Lone Wolf moved between White and Amskaapii Pikanii worlds in rapid transition. He remembered panning for gold with his father and his father's friend Baker in the Katooyisiksi (Sweet Pine Hills, now known as Sweet Grass Hills) when he was about four years old.[16] Lone Wolf sat near Baker, watching him use his pan. "Now and then," he recounted, Baker "would pick out a small yellow stone and put it on the flat rock beside him. He had quite a few of these stones and I wondered why he chose only those of one color. They didn't look very interesting. I wanted to be helpful so I got busy and found a lot of small rocks of different colors. They looked much better to me." Baker "couldn't understand my Indian talk," and Lone Wolf couldn't understand Baker's interest in the boring yellow rocks. When Baker was busy, Lone Wolf threw the yellow stones back into the creek. "Baker sure was mad," he remembered, and yelled at his father in English.[17] His father had to explain that the yellow rocks—gold—were "what the White man makes money out of."[18]

During this same trip to the Katooyisiksi, "a war party of Cree horse raiders rode up on the hill overlooking our camp and soon spotting our grazing horses."[19] Although reservation agents forbade horse raiding parties, the Nitsitapii, Nēhiyaw (Cree), and Apsáalooke (Crow) continued to raid when possible. As Lone Wolf explained, "This was still proof of their manhood."[20] Na-tah-ki saw the Nēhiyaw raiders and pulled her son inside their lodge while Lone Wolf's uncle New Robe guarded them. "Suddenly," he remembered, "down the hill they came! They raced to our horses, unhobbled them, and away they went in a cloud of dust."[21] A few days later, New Robe and his brother, Boy Chief, headed to Canada in search of the raiders, armed with Apikuni's telescope and Nah-ta-ki's pemmican. "As I watched them ride away," remembered Lone Wolf, "ho, how I wished I was old enough to go along with them." Boy Chief and New Robe were gone for many days before they "came into camp trailing a good bunch of horses.

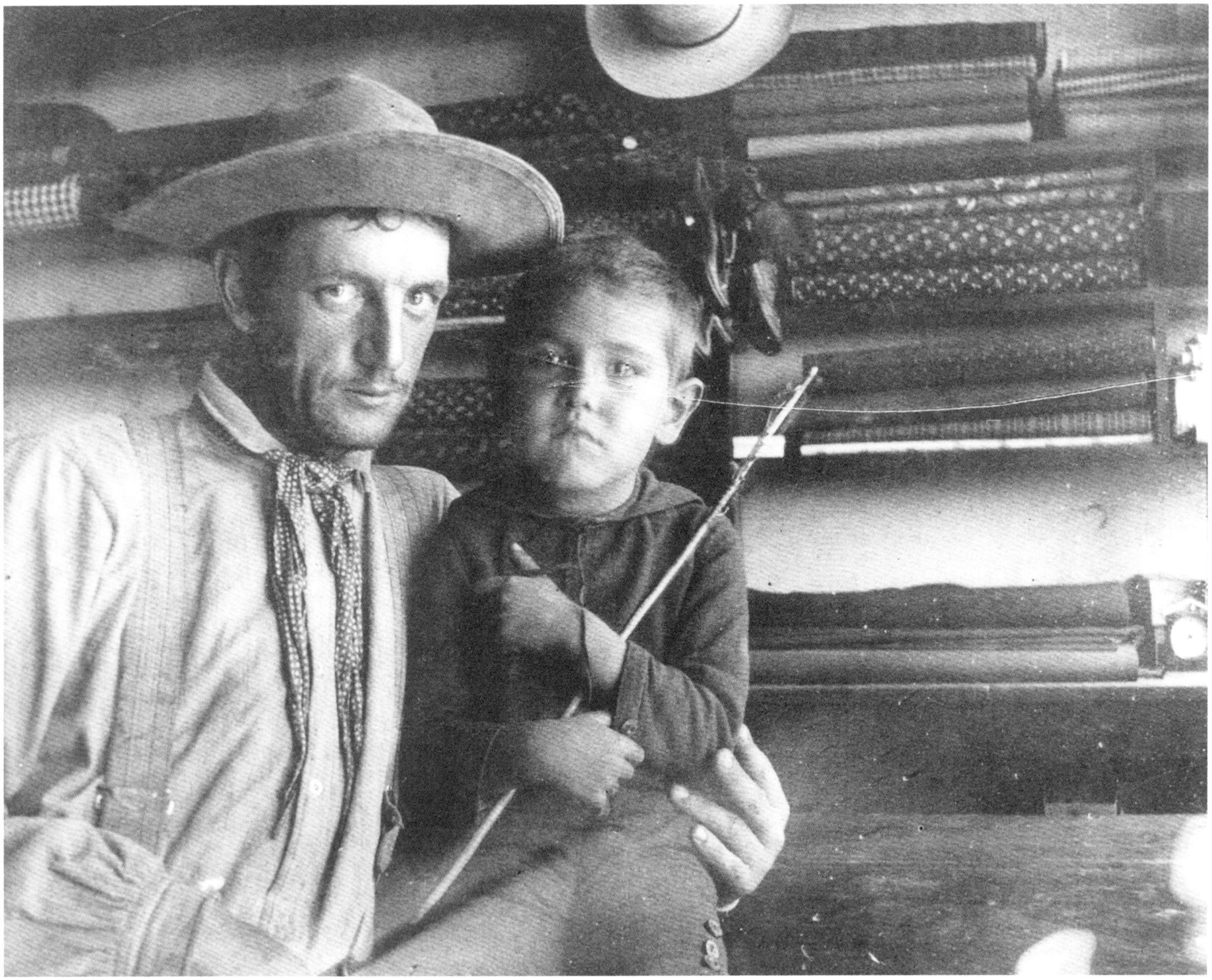

Among them were our stolen ponies.... They had found the Cree camp and while the Crees were holding their Medicine Lodge Ceremony, they slipped in and got the horses. Upon discovering their horses were gone, four Cree warriors took out after them and forced Boy Chief and New Robe to make a stand. Boy Chief killed two as he had a repeating rifle and the other two Crees high-tailed it back. Boy Chief scalped the dead Crees" and added these to his war shirt.[22] Boy Chief later gave this war shirt to Lone Wolf.

Fig. 3.

Unknown photographer, James Willard Schultz and Lone Wolf (Hart Merriam Schultz), 1884. Image number 303; collection number 0010. Montana State University, Bozeman: Merrill G. Burlingame Special Collections.

This adventure to the Katooyisiksi with his family left a mark in Lone Wolf's memory, perhaps because it so clearly illustrated the two different value systems he had to learn to negotiate: the world of the Pikanii warrior, who established his reputation by stealing horses, counting coup, and demonstrating extreme physical stamina and valor, and the world of the White man, who built status through the accumulation of gold.

Lone Wolf's childhood stories provide glimpses into early Reservation-Era life. Some are warm memories of family and friends, such as a humorous moment during the 1880s when his grandmother needed to travel to the Indian Agency on Miisinskiisah'taa (Badger Creek) to retrieve rations. He recalled:

> When the old horse was saddled and the travois hitched up, Grandmother fixed a place on the platform for me. I asked to take the puppy along. "Alright," said Grandmother and she tossed him up to me. Mother wrapped a blanket around us. It was nice and warm sitting there in the sunshine with the puppy beside me, the travois slowly bouncing along.
>
> I must have gone to sleep, for the next thing I knew Grandmother was shaking me. She was laughing, "Wake up, wake up."
>
> "'Are we at the Agency?" I asked.
>
> "No," said Grandmother. "You fell off the travois and have been sleeping here in the tall grass while I rode on down the trail. I didn't know you were gone until I turned around to point out the antelope on the hill. It took me a long time to find you. You and the puppy must have been dreaming a big medicine dream." I climbed back on the platform and wrapped my arms around the puppy. This time Grandmother tied us on to the travois with her rope. "Now, my Grandson, I will get you to the Agency without losing you."[23]

Lone Wolf also recalled games played with other children:

> In the wintertime, us kids, we'd all go out hunting with bows and arrows. Older people would make arrows, bows and arrows for us, and we'd go out hunting prairie chickens and cottontail rabbits. And once in a while, we'd run a rabbit into some buck brush, and one fella would get in there, and we'd surround it. And when the rabbit came out, everybody took a shot at the thing. Sometimes we got him. Sometimes we didn't.... And we also made the game where we stripped bark off a certain kind of bush that grew there.... We stripped the bark and braided it, and we set nice round stones for tops, and we'd go on the ice and whip them. And we'd whip them so they would just keep spinning and just hum. One boy would bring his top close to mine, and when the two stones come together, sometimes both of them would bust, or maybe one would bust.... We would take these rawhides and go way up on a high hill with the hair down and maybe two or three would ride it ... and one of the boys would shove us down this hill, something like a toboggan. And sometimes the thing wouldn't glide

> right.... It would throw us all over the hillside. Well, then in the spring, you practice bow and arrow. You pulled up the grass in an oblong shape and tie it in the middle, and you'd have your bow and your arrow ... and you'd throw ... the grass up in the air, and as it goes up in the air, you're supposed to hit that. Sometimes you hit it, and sometimes you don't.[24]

These stories of play and family love contrast sharply with other memories of abuse, cultural suppression, and forced reliance on a federal government that did not fulfill its promises. Multiple "starvation winters" marked the 1880s, the first around the time Lone Wolf was born, the winter of 1883–84, and another in 1886–87. By this time, the bison were gone.[25] Lone Wolf remembered that, during one hard winter, "600 persons died from starvation. Burial boxes, piled two and three deep, lined the ridges. The trees along the river held many more. You know that at that time the Blackfeet did not put their people in the ground and for many years those burials would remind us of that sad winter."[26]

Lone Wolf also remembered an Indian agent, Captain Cooke [*sic*], "who was going to make White Men out of the Blackfeet in a hurry. He prohibited all the Indian religious ceremonies and the wearing of Indian costumes. He even threatened to jail women who did beadwork."[27] The Code of Indian Offenses, a body of legislation written into law in 1883, gave Indian agents permission to punish residents for participating in the O'kan (Sun Dance), polygamy, or for being a *natoowaapinaa* (medicine man). They enacted punishment with fines, imprisonment, hard labor, or by withholding rations.[28]

Lone Wolf's memories of school also reflect deep unhappiness and injustice. He detailed his experiences at length:

> School wasn't for me when I was a kid. I tried three of them and they were all bad. The first time was when I was about 8 years old. The soldiers came and rounded up as many of the Blackfeet children as they could. The government had decided we were to get White Man's education by force.
>
> It was very cold that day when we were loaded into the wagons. None of us wanted to go and our parents didn't want to let us go. Oh, we cried for this was the first time we were separated from our parents. I remember looking back at Na-tah-ki and she was crying too. Nobody waved as the wagons, escorted by the soldiers, took us toward the school at Fort Shaw. Once there our belongings were taken from us, even the little medicine bags our mothers had given us to protect us from harm. Everything was placed in a heap and set afire.
>
> Next was the long hair, the pride of all the Indians. The boys, one by one, would break down and cry when they saw their braids on the floor. All of the buckskin clothes had to go and we had to put on the clothes of the White Man.

> If we thought that the days were bad, the nights were much worse. This was the time when real loneliness set in, for it was then we knew that we were all alone. Many boys ran away from the school because the treatment was so bad but most of them were caught and brought back by the police. We were told never to talk Indian and if we were caught, we got a strapping with a leather belt.
>
> I remember one evening when we were all lined up in a room and one of the boys said something in Indian to another boy. The man in charge of us pounced on the boy, caught him by the shirt, and threw him across the room. Later we found out that his collar-bone was broken.[29]

He continued:

> In the summer of 1889, bull trains began hauling building material for the new Catholic mission and school on Two Medicine River. This was to be our new school. But let me tell you how I got out of that one.
>
> It was in the New Grass Time and we all knew in a month or so the school would close for the summer and we could go home on a vacation. As it happened, though, I got out before the school officially closed.
>
> In our schoolroom there were two students to every desk. My desk mate was a boy older than I whose name was Chief Coward. We were reading in a McGuffey's Third Reader and had stopped to whisper about a word we couldn't understand. All of a sudden, whack! There was the teacher, banging us with a heavy wooden ruler. "I said there would be no talking in school."
>
> Well we both jumped up and piled on that teacher. We were beating him up good when the superintendent ran in and pulled us off of him. "Come to my office, you boys," he said. So we went with him. He sat down and, taking up a big book, he opened it and pointed to my name. "See your name here. I'm going to cross it out. Now you are expelled from this school. Go to the dormitory and get your clothes and take the trail to your home."
>
> My friend, Chief Coward, said to the superintendent, "I want to be expelled too."
>
> "No," said the superintendent, "you stay. We'll let this boy go and there won't be any more trouble."
>
> How glad I was to be headed for home with my small sack of clothes on my shoulder! When I reached my grandfather Yellow Wolf's house, they were very much surprised to see me and wanted to know all that had happened. When I told them, Grandmother said, "My Grandson, it is better that you know about horses and cows. Books are all right for the White Man but I don't think they

are good for Indians." That settled it for me as far as government schools were concerned....

During the winter of 1894, however, my father enrolled me in the Willow Creek School on the Reservation. Mother wasn't happy to see me go but Apikuni wanted me to be educated. I stayed at this school only a short time and hated every minute of it.[30]

When he was at the Willow Creek School, Lone Wolf remembered further abuses:

We didn't get much schooling, only two and a half hours each day, as the rest of the time was spent doing odd jobs around the school. Some of the boys would saw and split wood for the schoolrooms and the employees' houses while others had to work in the barns and cow sheds.

We were supposed to get overshoes and gloves as well as regular clothes and shoes. But these were seldom issued to us, even though the storerooms were filled with children's clothes. The weather stood around 30 to 40 degrees below zero and it was tough for us boys to work outside without gloves and overshoes. We did it but it didn't help our tempers.

One day I was chosen to go to our Agency in the town called Browning to get the mail for the school. The cold made me hurry but I took time to stop at the trader's store to buy some gum. I had been saving that nickel for a long time and this was my chance to spend it. As I wanted to make my purchase, I walked over to the side of the store where the dry goods were kept. There, hanging on the racks, were some of the clothes I had seen in the storeroom at the school. Now I knew why we were not getting the things we needed; they were being sold to the trader. Who sold them, nobody knew.

The meanest man at Willow Creek School was the disciplinarian. He had long gray whiskers and he liked to send us boys out to split wood, especially when the weather was bad. He would shout, "Rick up that split wood 3 feet high, 2 feet wide and 4 feet long and don't fool around. Finish it by noon or you'll go without your dinner."

The blocks of wood were tough to split and the axes were always dull. It was hard work and often some of us went without our food. One day as we were hurrying to finish before dinnertime, this fellow came out and when one of the boys didn't move fast enough he hit him with his fist and gave the boy a black eye. That evening us boys had a war council. I told the boys, "The next time that man hits one of us, let's jump him and beat the stuffin's [*sic*] out of him. We have been kicked around long enough."

> A few days later, this man had about eight of us boys cleaning the barns and cow sheds. Sure enough, he banged one of the boys with the handle of a pitchfork. I grabbed a rope that was handy and while Mr. Disciplinarian was cussing the boy out I made a loop, caught both his hind legs, and throwed him. Before he could get up the rest of the boys piled on him. When we got through with him he could barely walk.
>
> We were put in the Agency jail for that. After I got out of there Apikuni decided that his son and schools didn't mix and it was time for me to come home for good.[31]

After his father sold the ranch at Two Medicine, Lone Wolf worked as a cowboy on nearby properties. But, in 1903, tragedy struck: Nah-ta-ki died, and Apikuni left Montana. Soon after, Lone Wolf also left the reservation. He recalled:

> I found the reservation had got so miserable. We were still, then, prisoners of war, and the reservation was fenced. We were all fenced in.... No matter what you wanted to do, you had to go and ask the agent if you can do this or that.... And you couldn't leave the reservation without a pass. And this big fence around us had gates, and you had to have a written permit to show at the gate, and they'd let you out. And that paper says if you're going to be gone three days, it's marked on there you'll be absent for three days, and when you come back you have to go to the agent and present that to the agent. And if you fail, and you didn't show up and you failed to return back, or whatever you didn't do, why that was just about ninety days in jail.
>
> So, I figured, well, the best thing I can do is get out of there. And I wanted to—there was no jobs.... And I knew I could get a job off the reservation. I was offered a job, a good job. And I asked the agent about it, and he said, "No, you're not going." Well, yes, I'm going anyhow. He says, "Alright, if you go," he says, "when I catch you, I'll give you a year." Well, I kept going.... I came to California at the San Joaquin Valley, and I hired out to Miller and Lux, one of the biggest cow outfits in the West. And there I punched cows, and the wages were $20 a month and board. And I stuck there for quite a while, and then I drifted over to southern California at a place called Point Conception and worked for another cow outfit. Then I drifted down to Los Angeles and got a job here and there, over there on the ranches or dressing horses. And then my father says, "Why don't you go to Arizona?"[32]

His father had settled in Greer, Arizona, in 1913. Lone Wolf followed, working as a guide at the Grand Canyon in the northern part of the state and visiting his father in eastern Arizona.

Lone Wolf recounted that "when at the Canyon, during down times, I would paint, and I was selling my pictures. And finally, they gave me a studio at the Hopi House at the Grand Canyon. The Santa Fe Railroad gave me a studio there, and they were selling my pictures."[33] He started working seriously as an artist while at the Grand Canyon. "There … I met the great artist, Thomas Moran. He took a liking to me for he was a very kind and helpful man and had a deep interest in anyone who was Indian. When he found out that I was a Blackfeet from the North he became very much interested in what I was trying to do. I am sure that Grandfather Yellow Wolf would have been surprised that such a man as Thomas Moran would befriend his grandson and encourage him to make his way in art in the White Man's world."[34] Thomas Moran (1837–1926) was not the only significant artist with whom Lone Wolf interacted. In addition to Russell and Olaf Seltzer (1877–1957) in Glacier National Park, Lone Wolf met a number of other famous artists through his father's connections: "Charles Schreyvogel gave me the first oil colors I had ever seen."[35] Frederic Remington was among the "interesting men" his father introduced him to, in addition to Teddy Roosevelt, Owen Wister, William "Buffalo Bill" Cody, and George Bird Grinnell.[36]

Lone Wolf credited Yellow Wolf and early exposure to books as inspiration for his artistic career.[37] After this, and his meeting with Moran, he recalled, "I first went to Los Angeles, the Art Students League in Los Angeles. And then from there I went to the Art Institute of Chicago, and then from Chicago I went to New York and studied the pictures at the museums and so forth, and I studied under a sculptor, an Italian sculptor."[38] Lone Wolf thought highly of his teacher and remembered that when sculpting a large nine-foot statue of an American Indian, he requested Lone Wolf's help. After being asked to review the clay sculpture, Lone Wolf told him, "The figure's fine, but your regalia is wrong. That pipe that man is holding in his hand is a Chinese pipe. They don't have pipes like that. The moccasins he got on is wrong." He then proceeded to show him his moccasins and pipe and said, "Copy these, and it'll be right." The teacher did as instructed.[39] Afterward, some people visited the studio to see the sculpture. Lone Wolf recalled, "Well, they come in and asked me about what I felt about it, and I says, 'It's correct. It's a very good one.' So, [the sculptor] got $30,000 for it, and he taught me free for helping him."[40] Lone Wolf's contributions helped settler artists achieve ethnographic accuracy that perpetuated a sense of authority and authenticity in their, often romanticized, work. In this case, it also enabled him to wed his traditional Nitsitapii knowledge with European-influenced training as he developed as an artist.

Sometime around the mid-1910s, Lone Wolf established a studio at St. Mary's Lake in Glacier National Park. He spent the summers in Montana and the winters in Arizona.[41] While in Montana in 1916, Lone Wolf did some work on a friend's ranch near the Canadian border. There, he met Naomah Tracy.[42] In Naomah's words, her brother had told her about "a young cowboy named Lone Wolf who could ride anything on four feet and afterwards make a picture of it."[43] She remembered love at first sight. "Five months later," she continued, "we eloped. We had to slip out … and ride sixty-five miles on horseback across country. When we reached Lone Wolf's uncle's place, we spent the remainder of the night and early the next day rode on to Cut Bank where we were married by the justice of the peace. Our honeymoon was spent with the Last Rider family on their ranch at Blackfoot."[44] In Lone Wolf's words, they "got acquainted ... and ... took a liking to one another, and we decided to get married, and then we did, and that's all there was to it."[45] They were married for fifty-four years, until Lone Wolf's death.

Also around this time, Lone Wolf showed at the Babcock Galleries in New York and at the Kanst Galleries in Los Angeles, venues in which Russell also had exhibitions.[46] One of Lone Wolf's patrons, New York–based August Hecksher, helped the artist arrange exhibitions on the East Coast.[47] In his article, Dyck quotes a variety of news reports from New York, Brooklyn, New Jersey, San Francisco, Tucson, and Los Angeles from 1921 to 1925 in which the authors praise Lone Wolf's "genius" and call him a "sensation."[48] Collectors included Mrs. Calvin Coolidge, Herbert Hoover, Owen Wister, Burton Holmes, Robert Colgate, August Hecksher, H. B. Duryea, J. C. Kinney, and Dr. Phillip G. Cole, the latter of whom also collected works by Russell.[49] Lone Wolf said that once he started getting commissions, "I quit having exhibitions. It got so where I was well known. I had notices in all the leading papers in the United States and some abroad.... And I became famous in painting and in sculpture.... And at my old age now, I just began to find out that when a man gets around about seventy, he just begins to know something about art. But when I first started doing it, I thought I knew all about it. You couldn't tell me anything about it. But I realize now you have to work at it many, many years to really understand it."[50]

Lone Wolf lived a long life, dying in 1970 in Arizona. He lived through extreme cultural changes, first negotiating life during the early Reservation Era and ultimately extracting himself from an environment he found repressive. He used his cowboying and ranching skills to support himself until he established a national profile as a fine artist, working in the same competitive art world as Russell. While they had much in common, Lone Wolf's story acts as an important historical counterpart to Russell's, pulling back the curtain on any romantic fantasy of Plains Indian life to reveal the lived realities, hardships, and triumphs of this dedicated artist.

NOTES

1 The influence of settler artists on Nitsitapii easel painters and sculptors, including Lone Wolf, John L. Clarke (or Cutapuis; 1881–1970), Gerald Tailfeathers (Kanai; 1925–1975), and others during the twentieth century, merits further examination though falls outside the scope of this project.

2 Oral History Interview with Lone Wolf, 1956 (audio recording), Arizona Historical Society, Library and Archives; and Paul Dyck, "Lone Wolf Returns to That Long Ago Time," *Montana The Magazine of Western History* 22, no. 1 (1972): 18–41. Most recently, Tricia Loscher completed a dissertation on Lone Wolf, though this scholarship has not yet been published. Tricia Loscher, "Lone Wolf (Hart M. Schultz): Cowboy, Actor, and Artist" (PhD diss., University of Arizona, 2016).

3 Dyck, "Lone Wolf Returns," 19. Later, Lone Wolf was given the name Black Eagle in honor of his grandfather, but he "felt it was too honored and precious." He chose to keep "the name given to him by his Grandfather Yellow Wolf and throughout his life was known as Lone Wolf." Ibid., 27.

4 Ibid., 19.

5 Oral History Interview, part 1.

6 Ibid.

7 Dyck, "Lone Wolf Returns," 19.

8 Ibid., 32.

9 Oral History Interview, part 1. Joseph Kipp (1849–1913) was known to the Nitsitapii as Mastúnopachis (Raven Quiver). He was the son of James Kipp (1788–1880) and Sahkwi Ahki (Earth Woman; Nueta [Mandan], c. 1818–1910). While working for the American Fur Company, his father helped establish multiple forts on the Oomah'sisaatáa (Big, or Missouri River). Joseph continued after his father and built forts and trading posts in Montana and Canada. Schultz worked for him at Fort Conrad, located on the Kyiyo seet'-daa (Bear River, or Marias River). See James Willard Schultz, *Blackfeet and Buffalo: Memories of Life Among the Indians* (University of Oklahoma Press, 1962); and *Friends of My Life as an Indian* (Houghton Mifflin Co., 1923). For Schultz's version of his journey west, see James Willard Schultz, *My Life As An Indian: The Story of a Red Woman and a White Man in the Lodges of the Blackfeet* (Doubleday, Page & Co., 1907).

10 Dyck, "Lone Wolf Returns," 20.

11 Ibid.

12 In the Oral History Interview, Lone Wolf gives his birth year as 1883 but as 1882 in the Dyck article.

13 Dyck, "Lone Wolf Returns," 27.

14 Ibid.

15 Ibid. He sold the watercolor to Jack Carberry, who later returned the painting to the family. This watercolor is illustrated on page 35 in Dyck's article.

16 For his age, see Oral History Interview, part 1. In 1885, illegal miners began trespassing on the Katooyisiksi, part of Nitsitapii ancestral land. Given dates provided by Lone Wolf, it seems Baker and Schultz may have counted among this group. In 1888, the US government purchased this area, creating the current eastern boundary of the Blackfeet Indian Reservation. For additional context, see Rosalyn R. LaPier, *Invisible Reality: Storytellers, Storytakers, and the Supernatural World of the Blackfeet* (University of Nebraska Press and the American Philosophical Society, 2017).

17 Dyck, "Lone Wolf Returns," 22.

18 Oral History Interview, part 1.

19 Dyck, "Lone Wolf Returns," 22.

20 Ibid.

21 Ibid.

22 Ibid., 23.

23 Ibid.

24 Oral History Interview, part 1.

25 In 1884, the Blackfeet killed the last four wild buffalo in Katooyisiksi. LaPier, *Invisible Reality*, 14.

26 Dyck, "Lone Wolf Returns," 20. Indeed, after the winter of 1882–83, one ridge behind Old Agency was called Ghost Ridge because of so many burials. Sally Thompson, Kootenai Culture Committee, and Pikunni Traditional Association, *People Before the Park: The Kootenai and Blackfeet Before Glacier National Park* (Montana Historical Society Press, 2015), 26.

27 Dyck, "Lone Wolf Returns," 21. Lone Wolf referred to Captain Lorenzo Cook, whom John C. Ewers identified as a "strict disciplinarian" who punished traditional mourning, clothing, and games with jail time. Ewers confirmed that he threatened to jail women who did beadwork. John C. Ewers, *The Blackfeet: Raiders on the Northwestern Plains* (University of Oklahoma Press, 1958), 310–11.

28 LaPier, *Invisible Reality*, 17.

29 Dyck, "Lone Wolf Returns," 24.

30 Ibid., 24–25.

31 Ibid., 26–27.

32 Oral History Interview, part 1.

33 Ibid. Located on the south rim of the Grand Canyon, Hopi House (built 1905) was designed by Mary Colter for the Fred Harvey Company, which, in conjunction with the Santa Fe Railway, marketed Indigenous arts and crafts to tourists.

34 Dyck, "Lone Wolf Returns," 28.

35 Ibid., 27.

36 Ibid.

37 In his oral history, he recalled, "I never thought that someday that I would take [art] up as a profession.... When I went to school [and] got ahold of the books, and we saw pictures in there. And I said right there and then, 'That's just what I want to do.' I saw those beautiful drawings and paintings there in these books." Oral History Interview, part 1.

38 Ibid. The Italian sculptor has not yet been identified.

39 Ibid.

40 Ibid.

41 Dyck, "Lone Wolf Returns," 32.

42 Naomah remembers them meeting on the Jack Galbraith ranch. Ibid., 31. Naomah was born in Rock Springs, Wyoming, in 1898, to parents Eli Tracy and Mary Ellen Holmes. The family moved to Montana weeks after Naomah's birth. Oral History Interview, part 2. She died around 1971.

43 Ibid.

44 Ibid.

45 Oral History Interview, part 1.

46 Ibid. According to Dyck, Lone Wolf had his first show in Los Angeles in 1917. Dyck, "Lone Wolf Returns," 32. Lone Wolf had an exhibition at Babcock Galleries April 9–21, 1922. See the exhibition brochure, *Exhibition of Paintings by Lone Wolf, Blackfeet Indian*, available on The Internet Archive, accessed October 30, 2025, https://archive.org/details/frick-31072001486945/mode/2up?view=theater. The brochure indicates he had an earlier exhibition in the city, after which he developed the work for the 1922 show. Russell exhibited at Babcock Galleries in January 1920 and January 1921 and at the Kanst Galleries, also called Kanst Art Galleries, in Los Angeles in 1918, March 1921, and March 1922. B. Byron Price, ed. *Charles M. Russell: A Catalogue Raisonné* (University of Oklahoma Press, 2007), 328.

47 According to Dyck, Hecksher introduced Lone Wolf to the Babcock Galleries, "which handled his work for years." Dyck, "Lone Wolf Returns," 32.

48 Ibid., 33.

49 Ibid. Cole's collection was purchased by Thomas Gilcrease in 1944. B. Byron Price, "Charles M. Russell: Icon of the Old West," in *Charles M. Russell*, 214.

50 Oral History Interview, part 1.

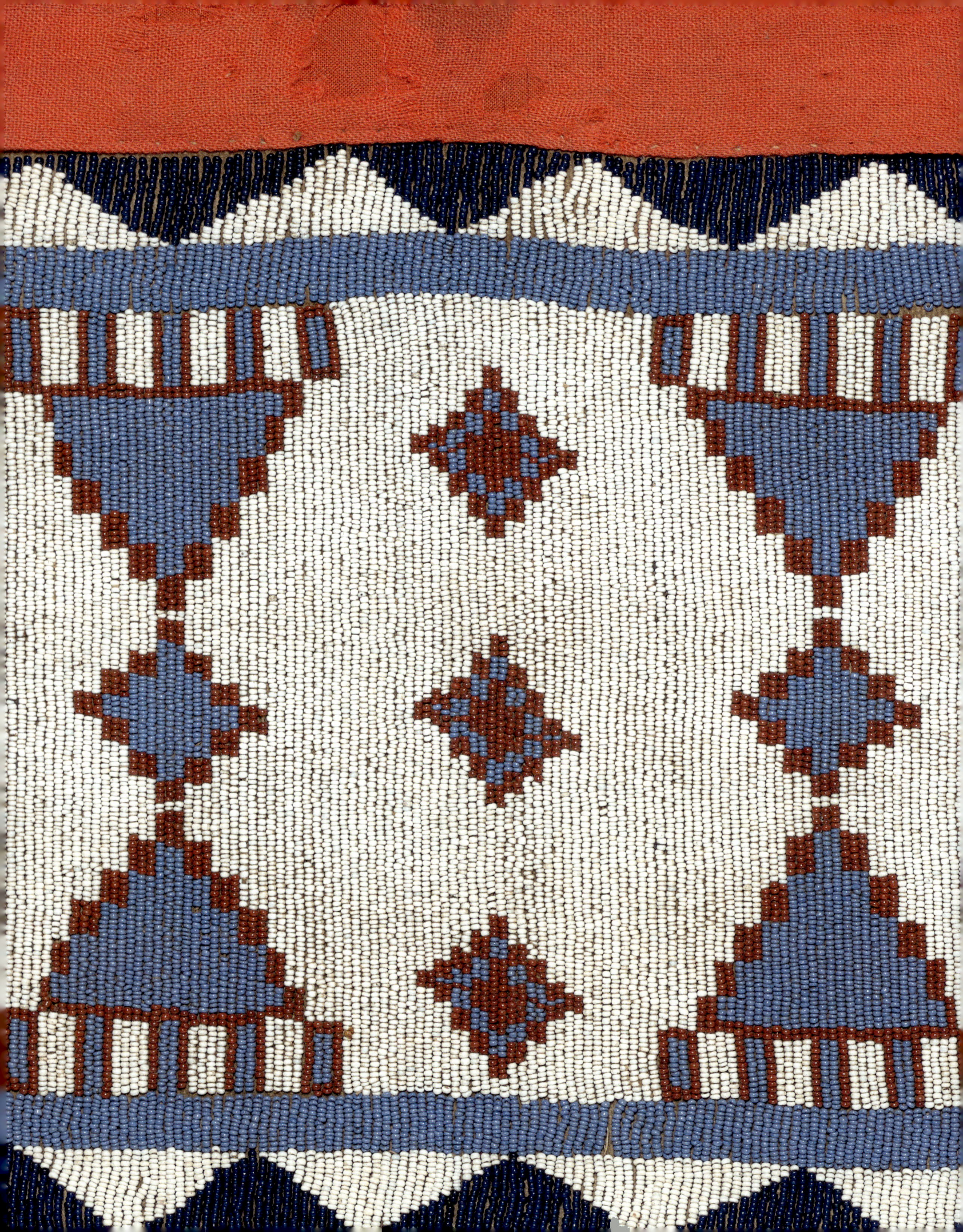

PLATES

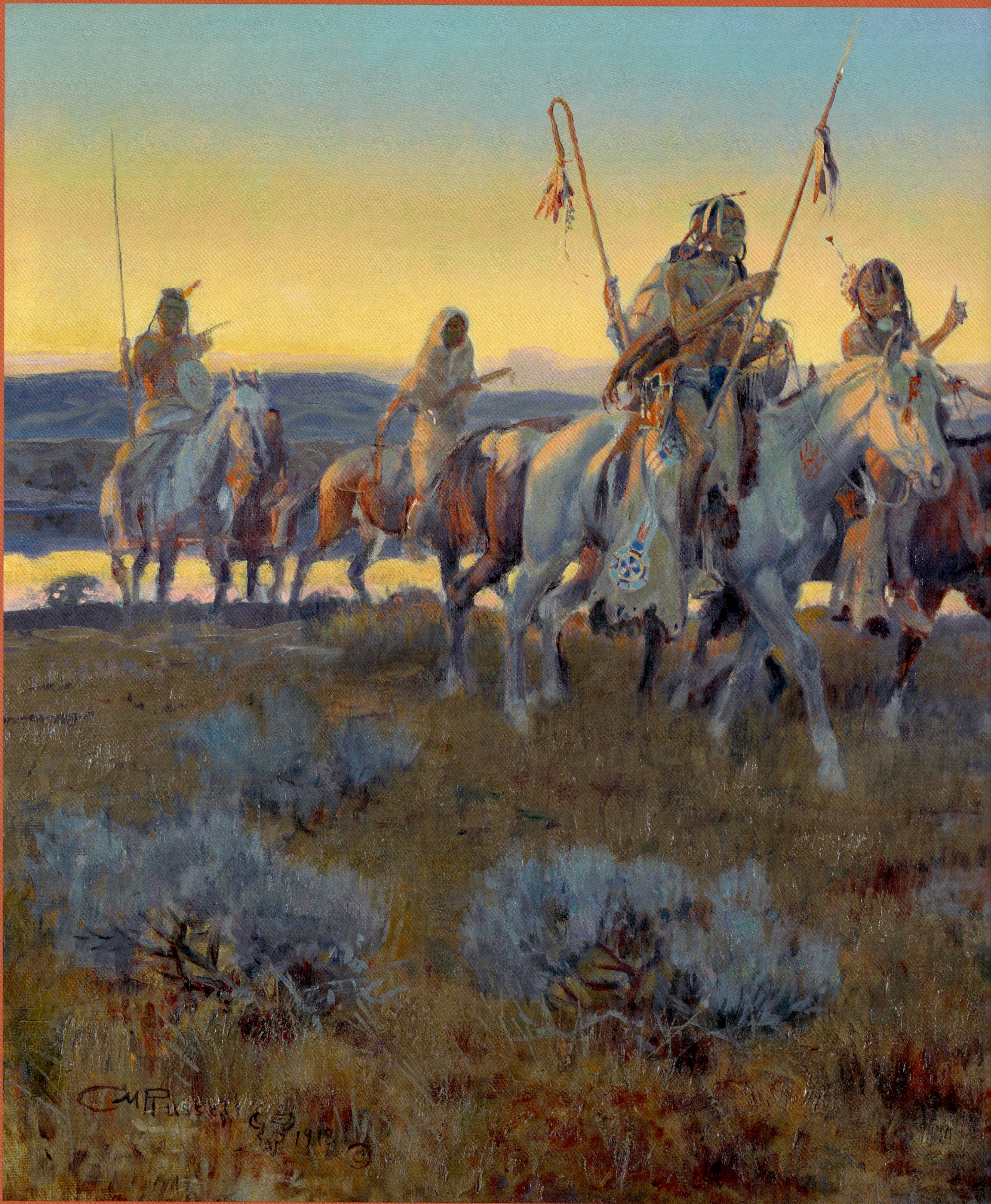

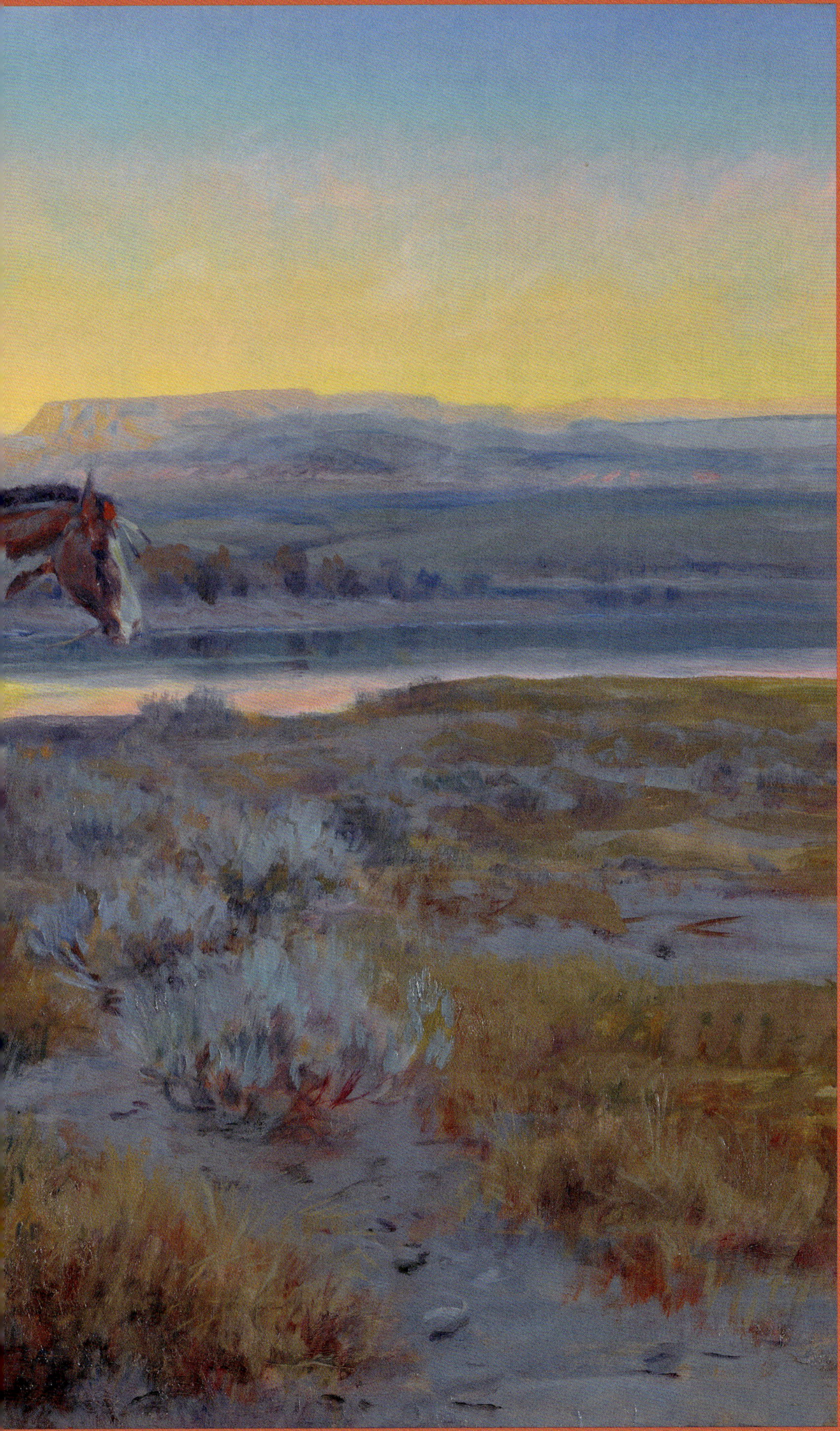

Cat. 1

Charles Marion Russell
Piegans
1918
Oil on canvas
34 × 46 × 2 ¼ in.
Petrie Collection, Denver, Colorado

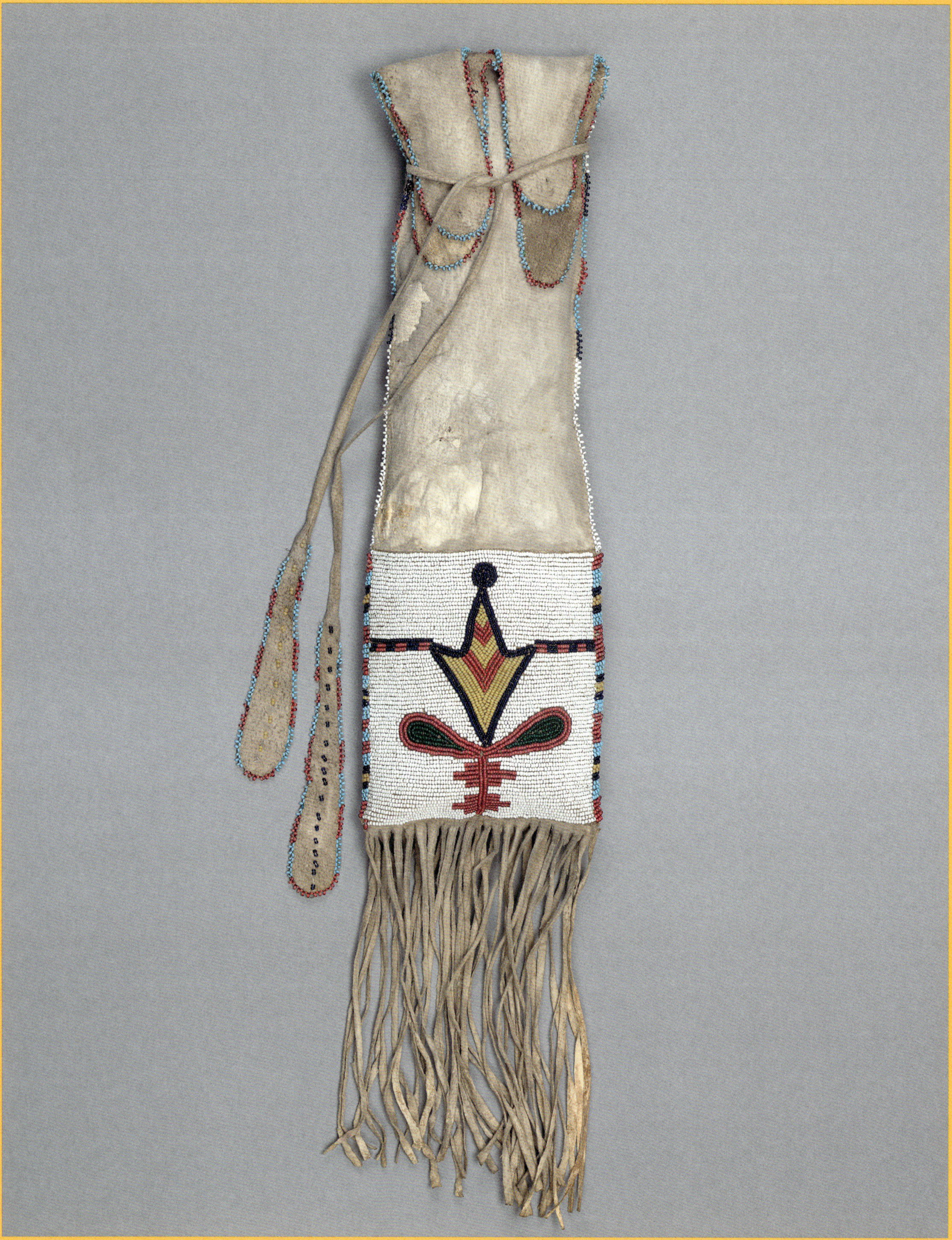

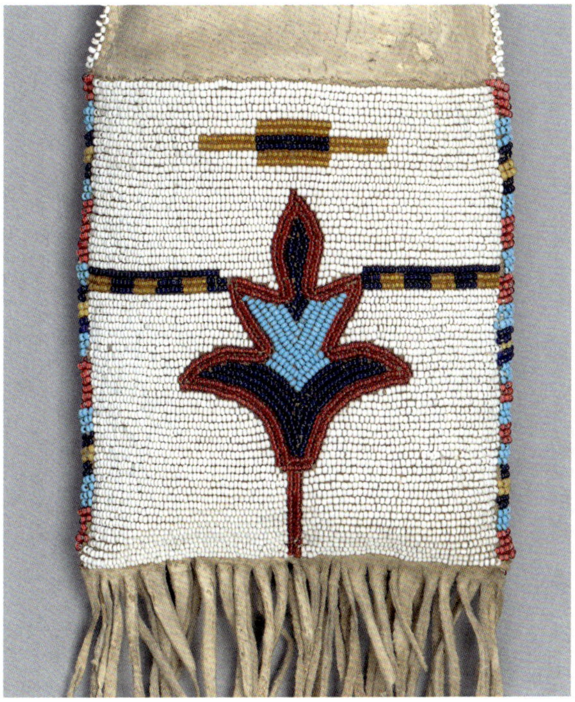

This *ah'kooyiinimaatsis* (pipe bag, also called a tobacco bag) features beaded designs on both sides and intricately beaded "thumbs," the teardrop shapes at the end of the ties, that echo beadwork along the top edge of the bag. Virtually nothing is known about the Amskaapii Pikanii woman who made the bag or its original owner or how it came to be the very first object cataloged in the Denver Art Museum's permanent collection.

During the late 1800s and early 1900s, collectors found new opportunities among communities deeply impacted by the loss of their traditional lifeways. Nitsitapii objects found their way to the museum through gifts and purchases from White collectors over time, who likely acquired them by a variety of means, including outright theft, trade under duress and coercion, and sale through new economic relationships and networks. We have included what provenance information we have for all of these objects in the catalog. While they were typically collected for their aesthetic or anthropological value, for the Nitsitapii, they are integral to daily life and the maintenance of ancestral, contemporary, and future relationships (see "Note on Language" in this volume).

The majority of Nitsitapii objects in this exhibition come from the museum's permanent collection, and we hope this project helps reconnect these storytellers with their communities.

Cat. 2

Amskaapii Pikanii artist
Ah'kooyiinimaatsis (Pipe Bag)
(front and back detail)
Before 1925
Beads, hide, thread, and sinew
25⅜ × 4¾ × 1¾ in.
Denver Art Museum:
Source unknown, 1925.1

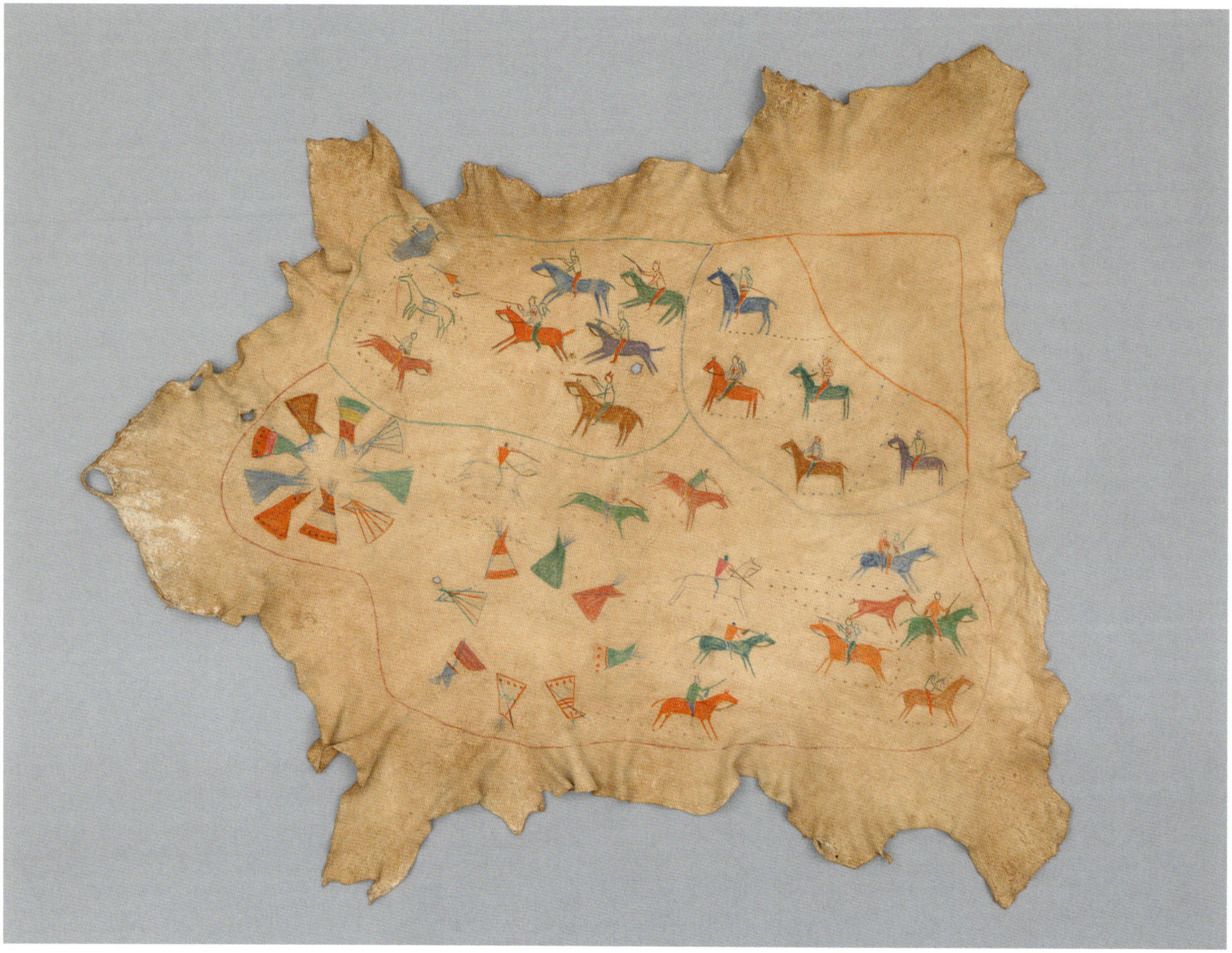

Cat. 3

Attributed to Percy (Two Gun) Plain Woman
(Kainai, 1895–1961)
War Robe
c. 1930s
Painted hide
56 × 45 × 1½ in.
Denver Art Museum: Native Arts acquisition funds, 1938.260

This *ninaipistsii* (war robe) is attributed to rodeo performer and painter Percy Plain Woman (Kainai), also known as Two Gun, who lived during the early Reservation Era (1850–87). Traditionally, warriors painted their own stories, but government restrictions denied young men the opportunity to prove their bravery through war or counting coup. Artists preserved the pictograph tradition, however, by recording experiences of past warriors.

Here, Plain Woman detailed the exploits of the Kainai warrior Aikstsiikinaa (Scratching Chief). The upper left section depicts five riders confronting two rival riders killing a buffalo. To the right, five riders parade across the prairie. Across the bottom, five riders dash away from adjacent camps with a stolen steed in tow. With warriors in hot pursuit, one horse thief turns back to stand against them. Dotted brown lines mark the forward motion of the mounted horses, and red dotted lines capture the arc of flying bullets.

Ninaipistsii document warriors' triumphs and serve as visual proclamations of bravery and masculinity. These evocative pictographs are both a record of the past and a living language. Nitsitapii pictographs encompass a wide range of styles and techniques. Here, the painter delineated humanoid figures using both compounded triangles and squares and horses vary in size, shape, and color, demonstrating a range of creativity and style.

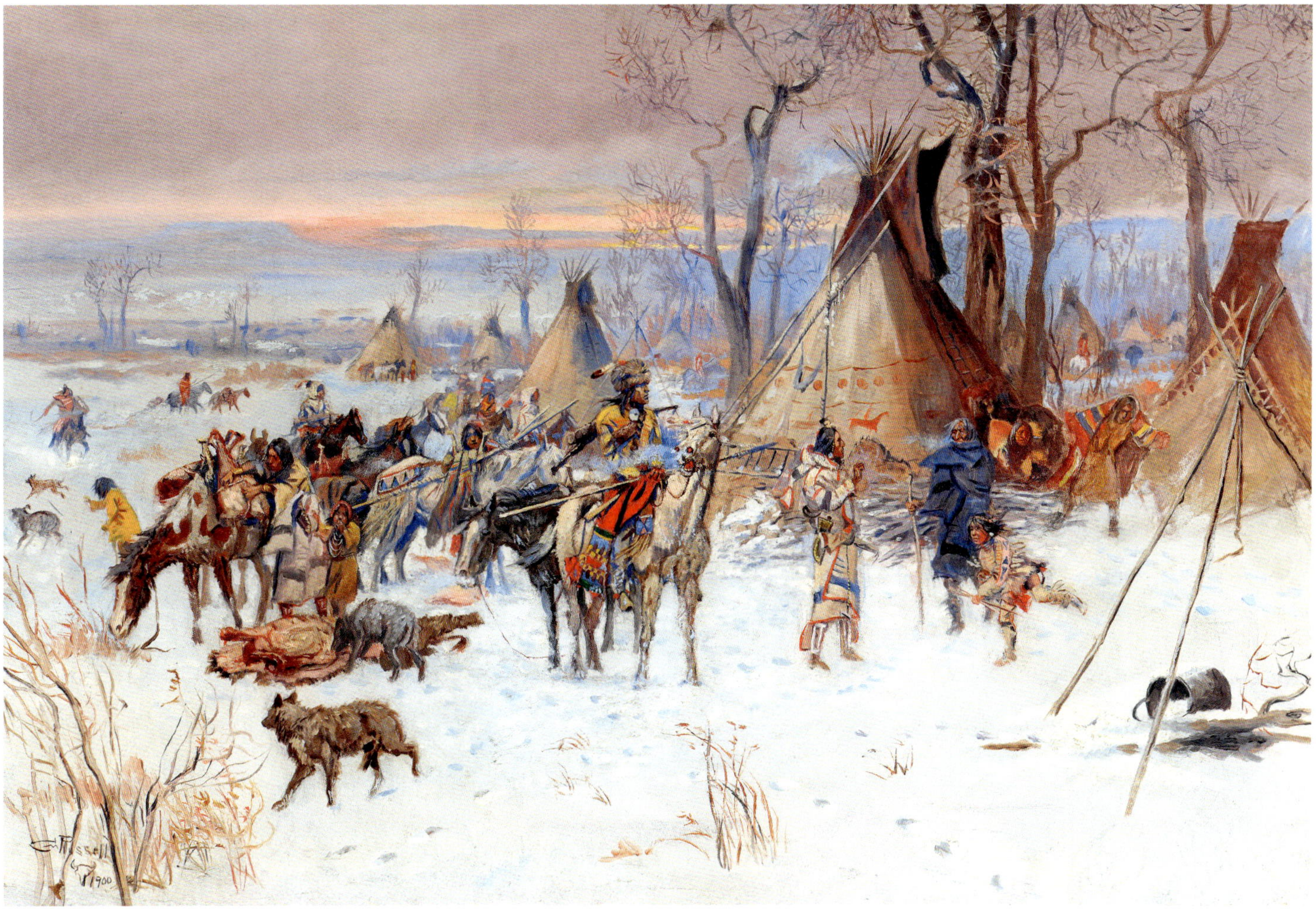

Cat. 4

Charles Marion Russell
Indian Hunters' Return
1900
Oil on canvas
33⅝ × 45½ in.
Montana Historical Society,
Mackay Collection, x1954.02.01

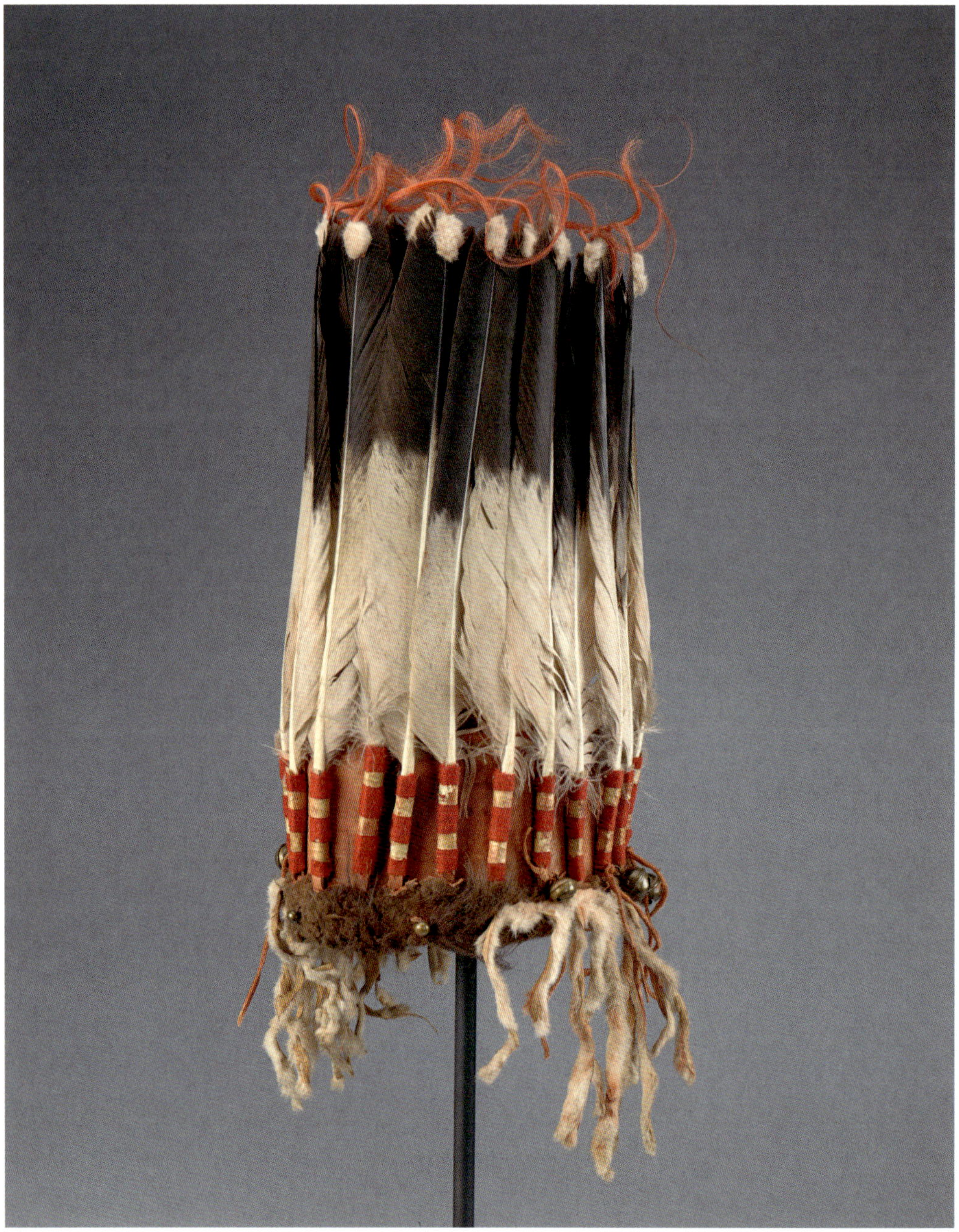

Cat. 5

Kainai artist
Headdress
c. 1880
Ermine fur, golden eagle feathers, leather, fabric, bells, pigment, horsehair, resin, and rawhide
23½ × 12½ × 6 in.
Denver Art Museum: Native Arts acquisition funds, 1939.125.2

The stand-up headdress style is unique to the Nitsitapii. It originated with the Staamiksiiks (Buffalo Bull Society), a group of male Elders who keep knowledge and share stories. Its straight-up style might be a reference to, and in honor of, the Creator. Women sometimes wear stand-up headdresses but only in special and sacred circumstances and sometimes during celebrations of veterans as part of the War Mothers Society. As with medicine bundles, stand-up headdresses come with great responsibility.

Each feather represents a deed accomplished by the intended wearer. This headdress features twenty golden eagle tail feathers tipped with small patches of weasel fur and red-dyed horsehair. The end quills of the feathers are wrapped in red stroud (wool trade cloth) and pericardium. The inside is lined with buffalo fur folded over the outer bottom edge, to which short strips of weasel fur are attached.

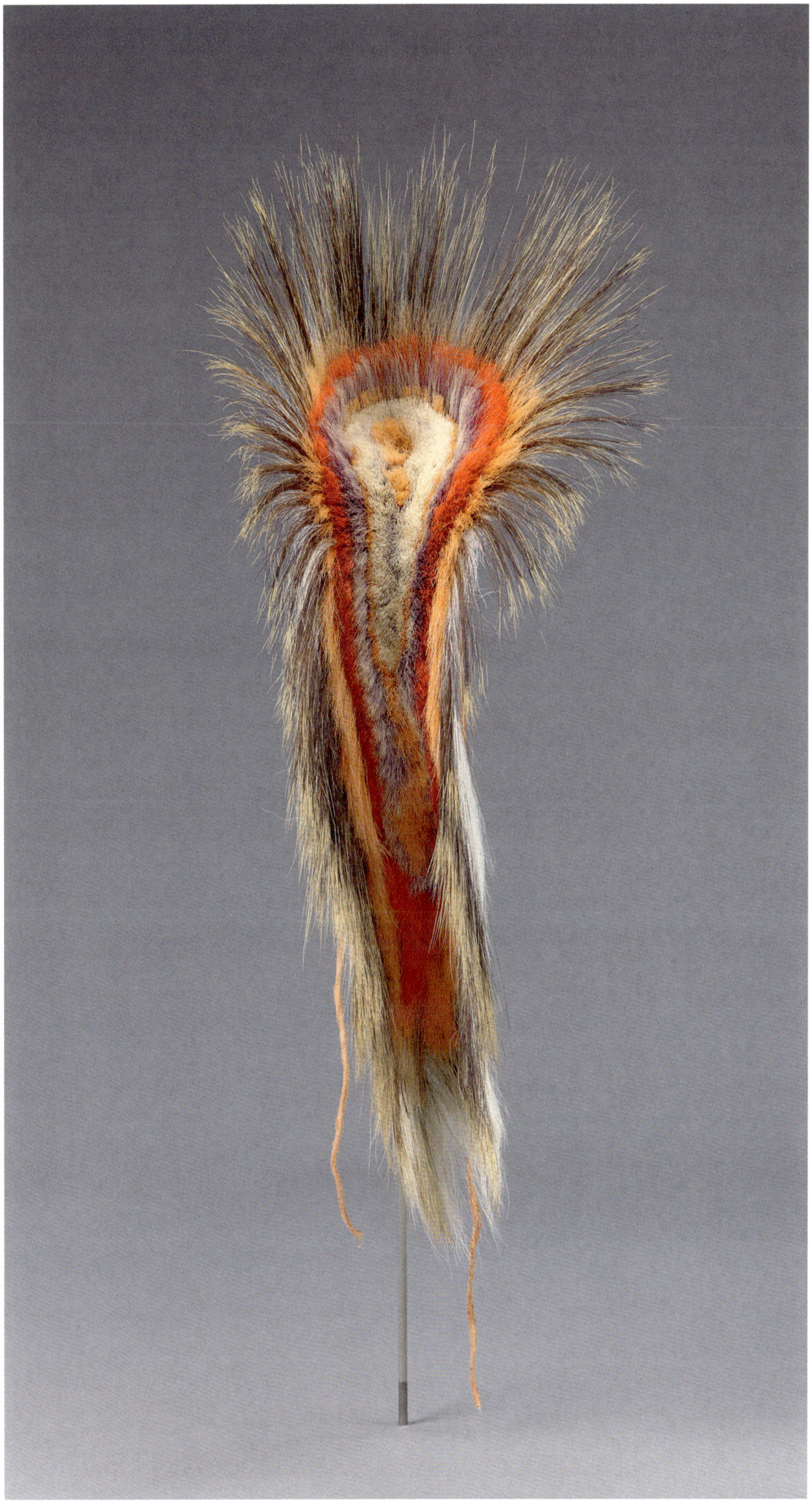

Cat. 6

Amskaapii Pikanii artist
Roach
Early 1900s
Porcupine and deer hair
17 × 4 × 6 in.
The L. D. and Ruth Bax Collection at the Denver Art Museum, 1985.146

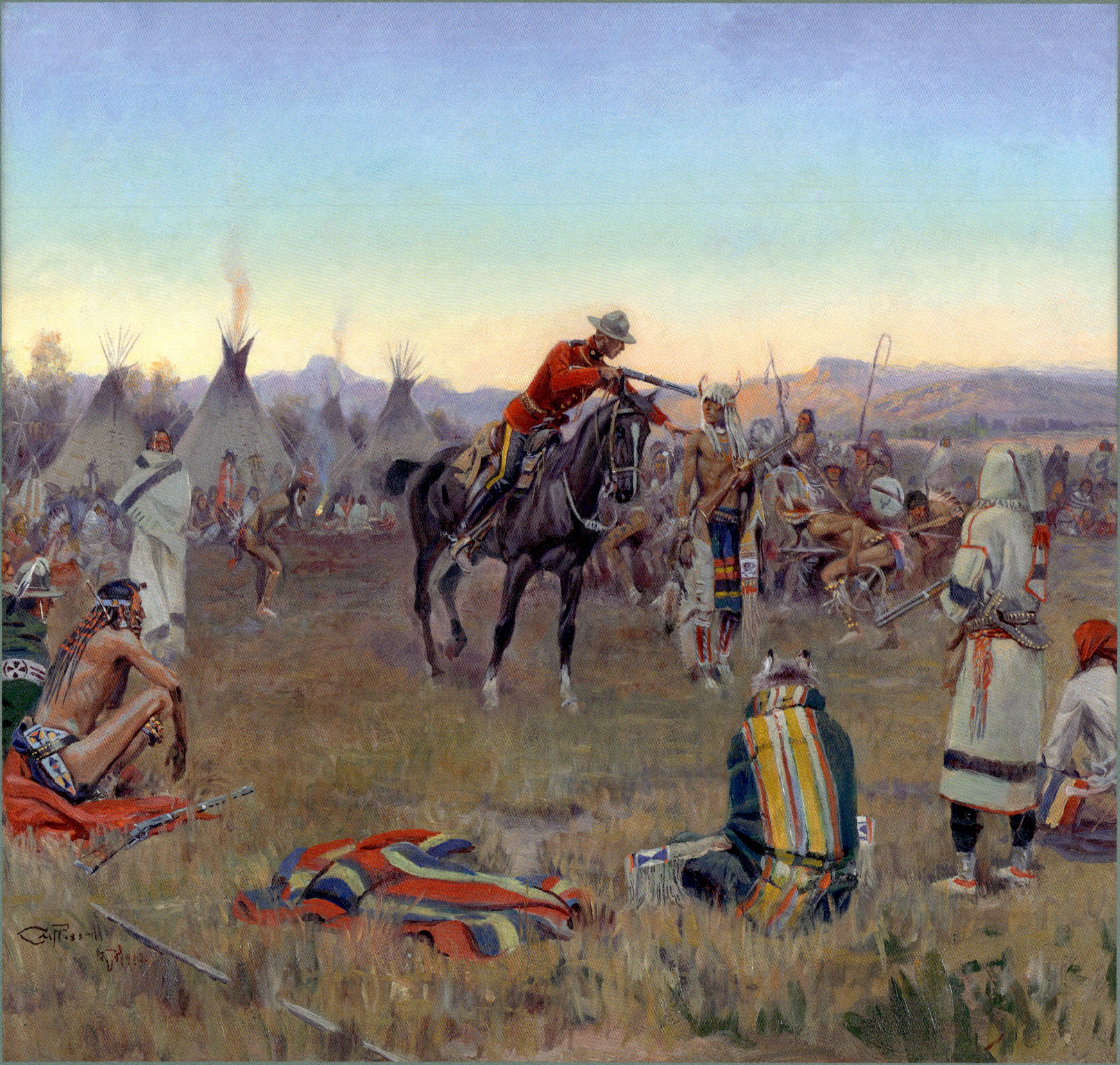

In *Single-Handed*, Russell packed a lot of detail into a small space. A member of the Royal Canadian Mounted Police, called a Mountie, apprehends a Nitsitapii warrior in the middle of camp. Even though the Mountie holds a rifle to the warrior's head, camp life continues around them: Chicken dancers move in the background while community members sit around the periphery and smoke rises from lodges. The painting is full of visual detail, including goods obtained through trade—striped blankets from the Southwest, Hudson's Bay blankets, capotes, guns, felt flat-brimmed hats, beads, and brass tacks—as well as more traditional objects such as rifle and tobacco bags, leggings, the central warrior's split horn bonnet, the dancers' head roaches (similar to cat. 6), spears, and shields. The man seated on the left wears locks of human hair held by a beaded headband. This array of visual and material culture underscores the sense that the camp could quickly overwhelm and outman the Mountie.

Cat. 7

Charles Marion Russell
Single-Handed
1912
Oil on canvas
Framed: 40½ × 43½ × 3 in.
Petrie Collection, Denver, Colorado

As they had for centuries, the Nitsitapii leveraged political power between and against imposing empires for their economic benefit, even after the US-Canada border cut through their ancestral land. For example, horses stolen in the US could be driven up to Canada for safe keeping, thereby building individual and community wealth. By the end of the 1800s, however, the US and Canadian governments worked together to enforce restrictions against traditional ways of life, to police interactions between Indigenous nations, and to ensure increased reliance on government assistance.

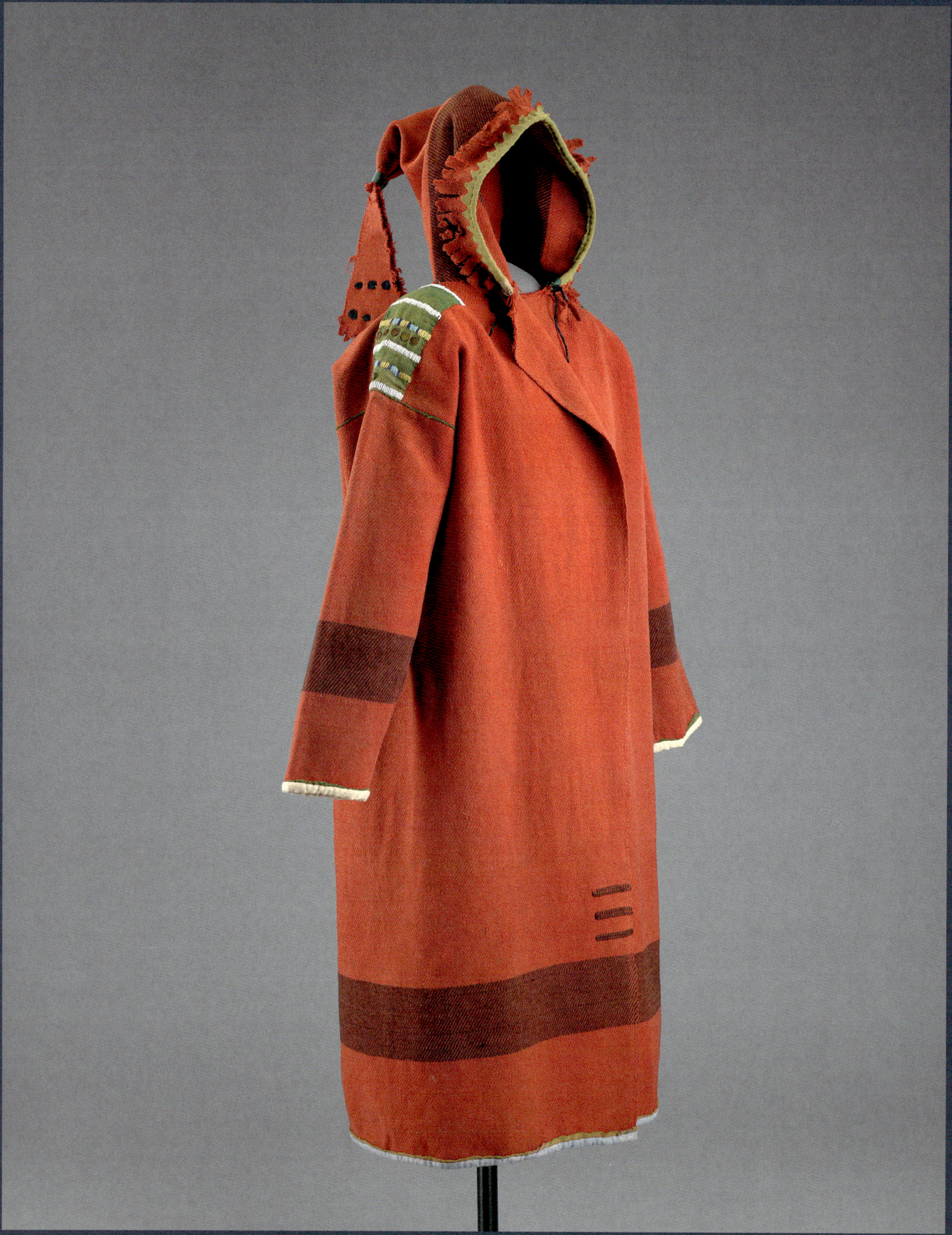

From the beginning of contact, Europeans traded woolen blankets, guns, tobacco, and whiskey with Indigenous peoples, typically for furs. By the mid-1600s, the British had established the Hudson's Bay Company in what is now Canada and, by the later 1700s, were exchanging their trademark design: point blankets. They came in several colors—red, as seen in this capote, blue, green, and white—and featured simple designs of broad bands. "Points" refer to the small stripes along the border that originally served as markers to identify the size of a blanket and that later often became indications of how many beaver pelts the blanket cost.

Indigenous people made use of these blankets in myriad ways, including as capotes. Adapted from European front-opening coats, they were popular in northern territories with both Native peoples and European fur traders for their warmth and ease of movement. Highly sought after, they were later considered ceremonial items. This capote features unique olive-green fabric and beadwork on the shoulders, mimicking military epaulettes.

Blankets were used to make other clothing items, such as leggings (cat. 9). In Russell's watercolor *Joe Kipp's Trading Post*, an Indigenous man uses Plains Indian Sign Language to barter a bison robe for a four-point blanket (cat. 10).

Cat. 8

Nitsitapii artist
Blanket Capote
1860s
Wool, beads, and brass
71¼ × 67½ × 12 in.
Denver Art Museum: Museum exchange with Jon Holstein, 1970.557

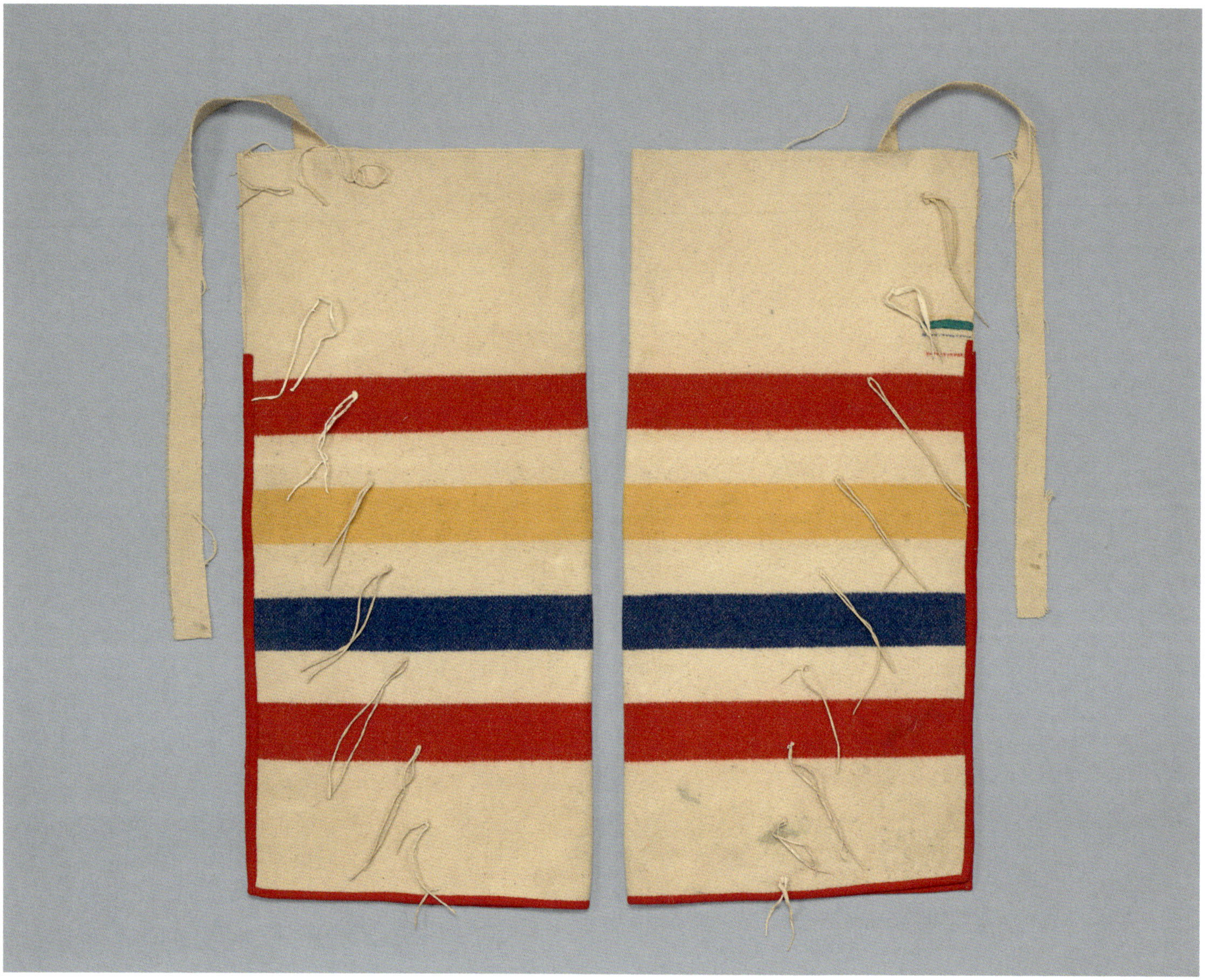

Cat. 9

Amskaapii Pikanii artist
Man's Leggings
c. 1890
Wool and leather
Each approx. 32 × 15 × 2 in.
Denver Art Museum: Native Arts acquisition funds, 1948.426

Cat. 10

Charles Marion Russell
Joe Kipp's Trading Post
1898
Watercolor on paper
Framed: 20¼ × 26¼ × 2 in.
Buffalo Bill Center of the West, Cody, Wyoming. Gift of Charles Ulrick and Josephine Bay Foundation, Inc. 1.85

Cat. 11

Charles Marion Russell
Robe Traders of Fort Benton
1901
Watercolor on paper
Framed: 27¾ × 37¾ × 1¼ in.
Gilcrease Museum, Tulsa, Oklahoma

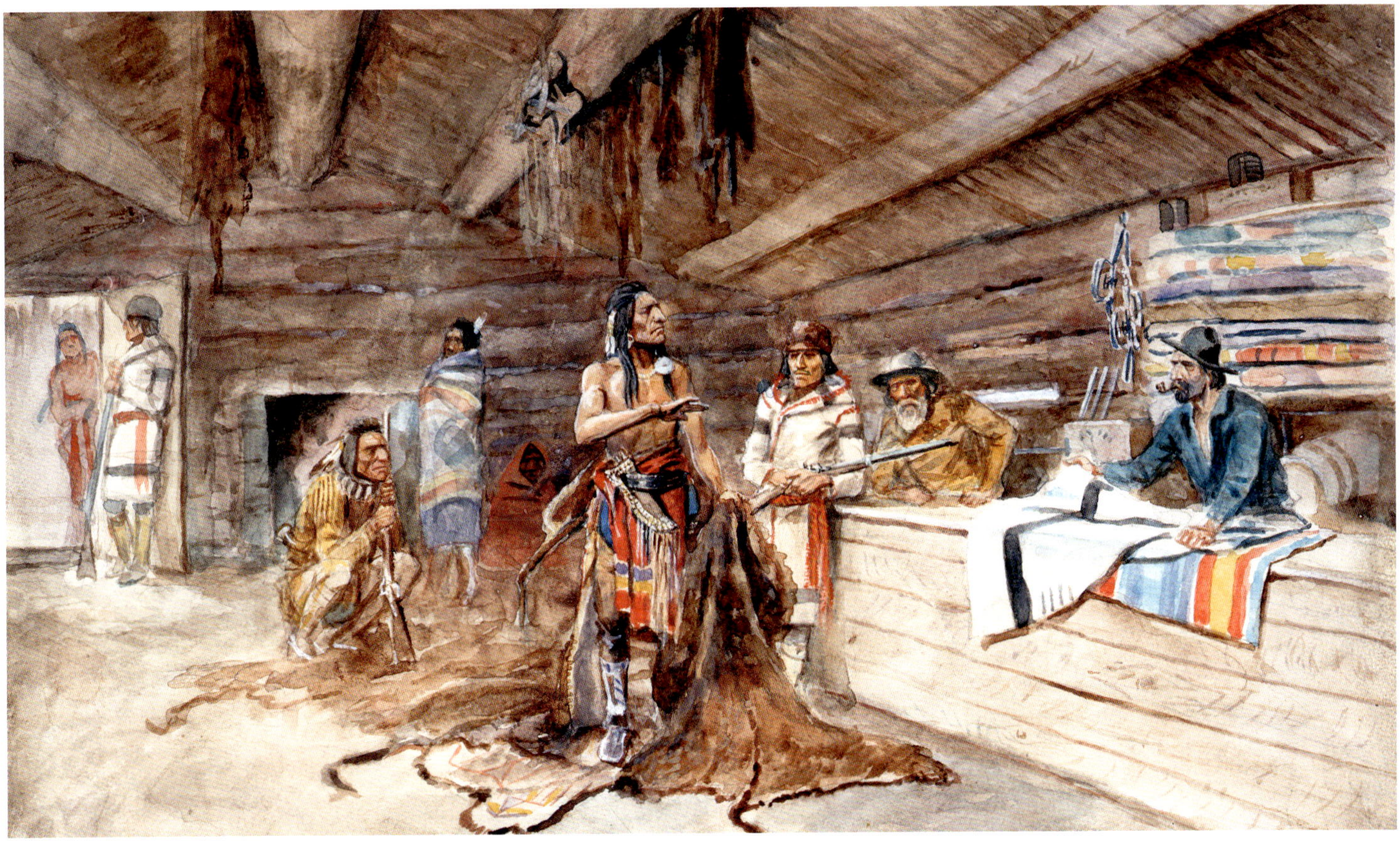

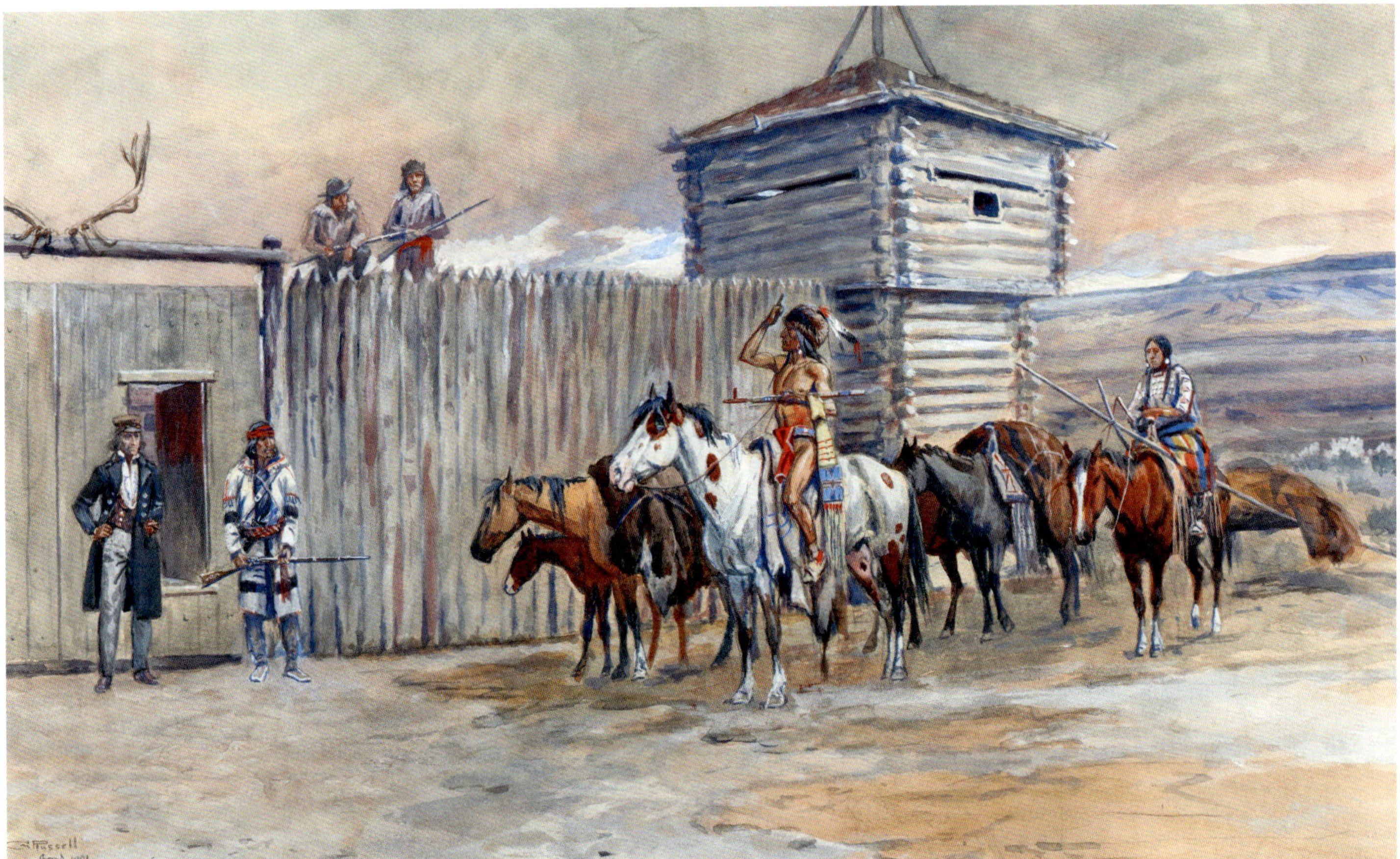

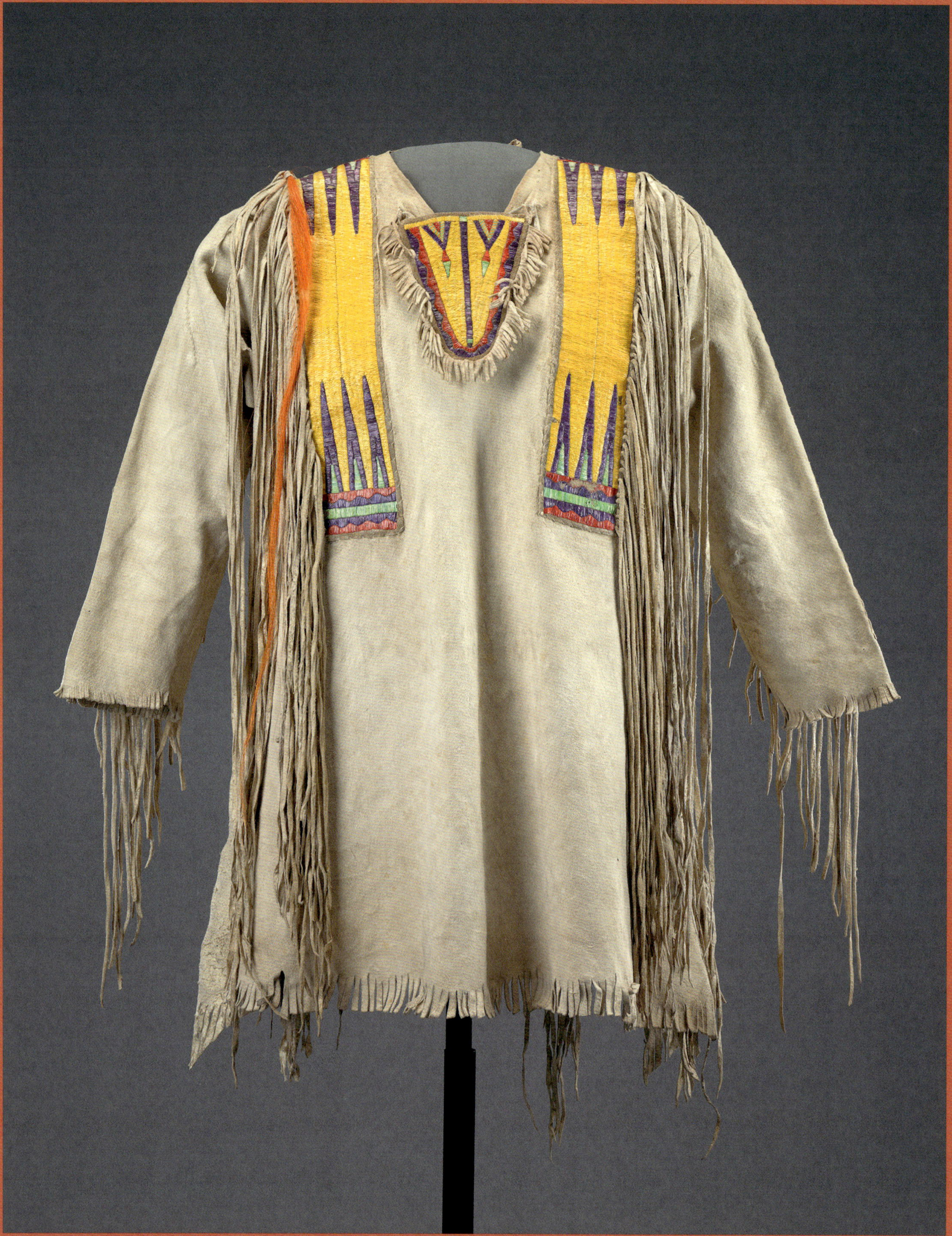

This special occasion shirt belonged to Running Crane, a fierce warrior whose war record boasted over thirty coups and who was a noted spiritual leader and pipe maker. One of his pipes, made from a rough sandstone mixed with feldspar, cost an entire horse. He attained the power of fearlessness from a supernatural vision, perhaps indicated here by the bear claw triangles dividing the yellow ornamentation of the shirt.

These exquisite designs are executed using quillwork, a sacred process restricted to initiated women who, in tandem with the intended wearer, created designs imbued with highly personalized meaning from the wearer's life. This meticulous process involved hooking the colorless quills from a live porcupine, then etching them to create an irregular surface that natural dyes could adhere to. Quillworkers then flattened the quills between their teeth and carefully sewed them into a tight sheath that could be removed if the shirt was damaged.

Cat. 12

Amskaapii Pikanii artist
Man's Shirt
Late 1800s
Leather, quills, horse hair, and commercial dye
34¼ × 55½ × 12 in.
The L. D. and Ruth Bax Collection at the Denver Art Museum, 1985.71

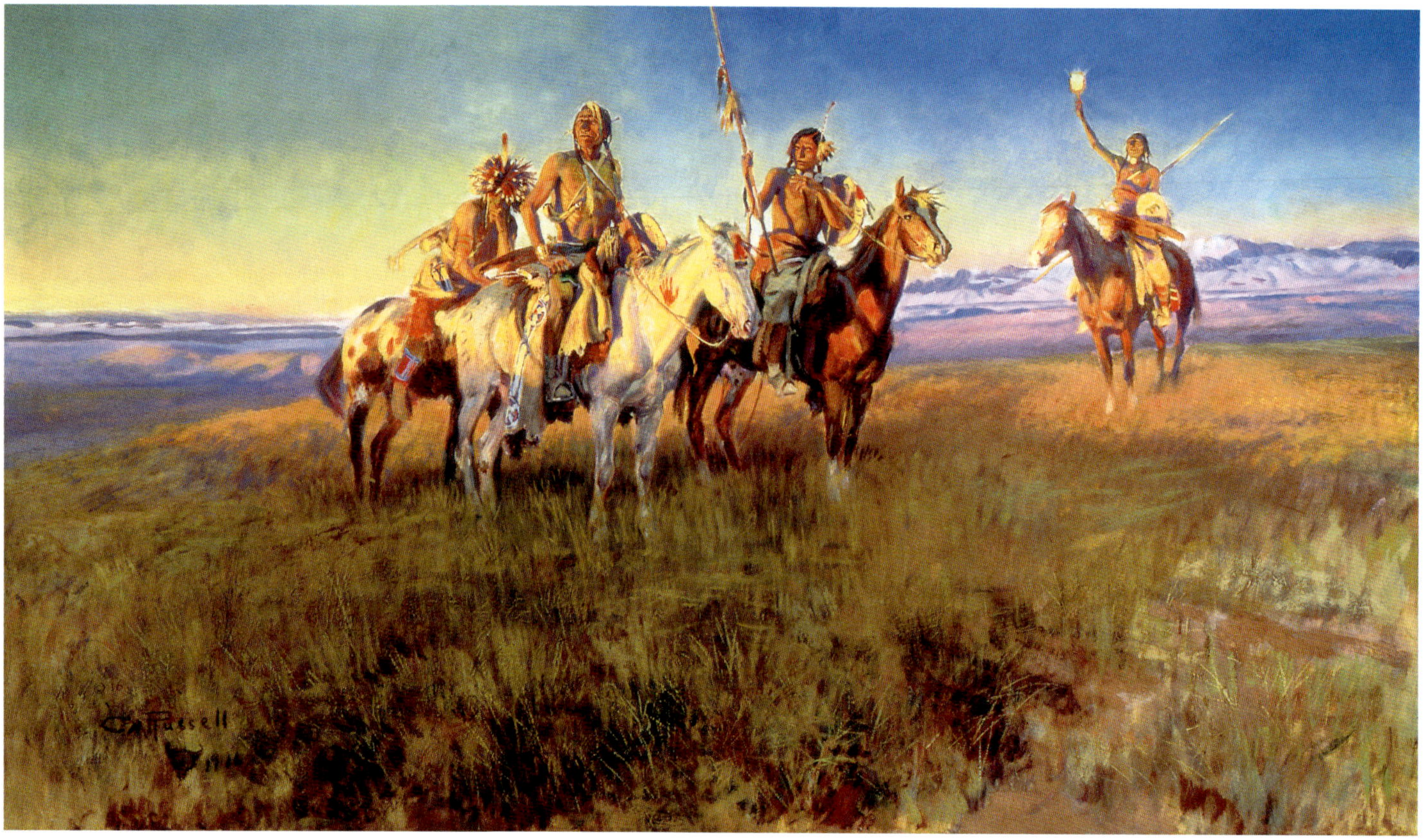

Cat. 13

Charles Marion Russell
Red Man's Wireless
1916
Oil on canvas
42 × 72 in.
National Cowboy & Western Heritage Museum, Charles S. Jones Collection, museum purchase with funding provided by Joel McCrea

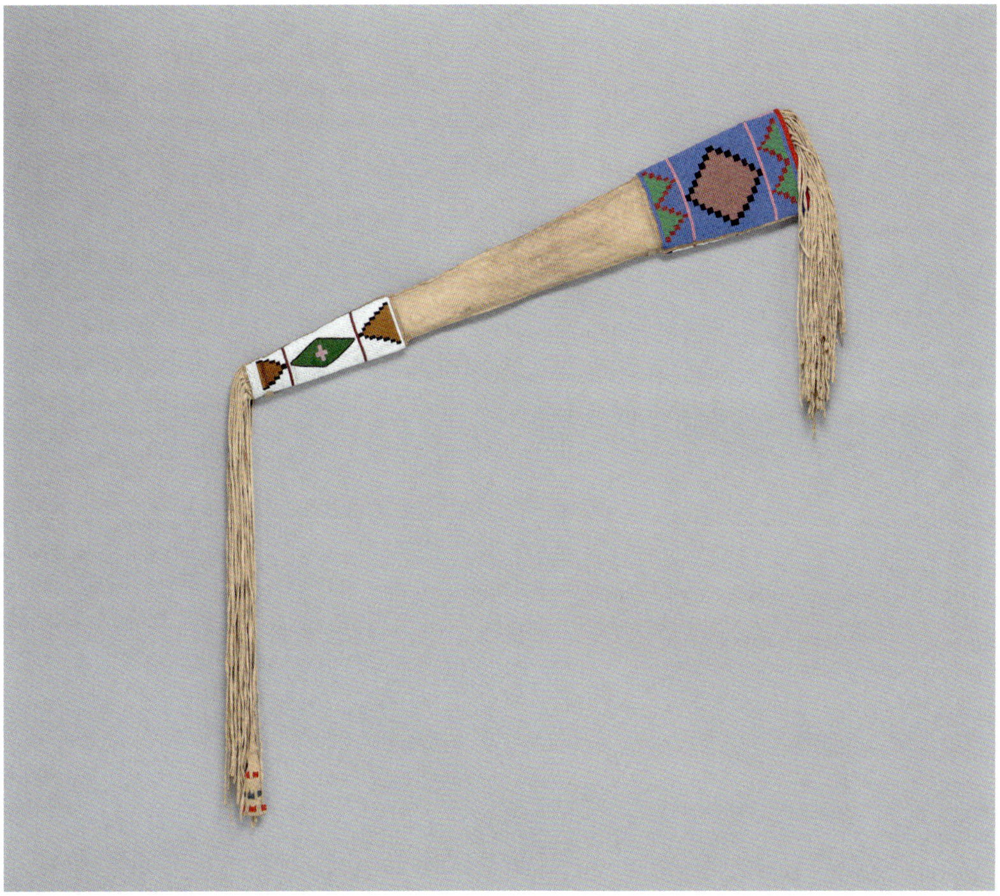

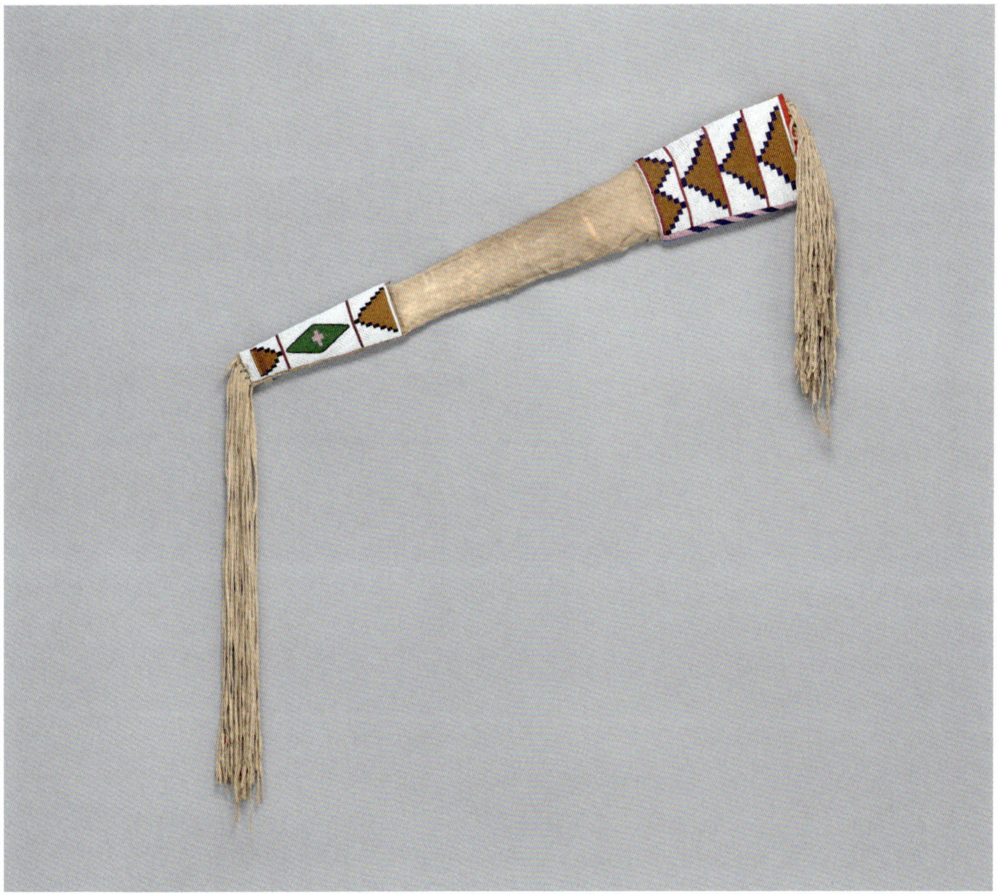

Cat. 14

Amskaapii Pikanii artist
Gun Case (front and back)
Late 1800s
Beads and leather
80 × 6¾ × 1½ in.
The L. D. and Ruth Bax Collection at the Denver Art Museum, 1985.88

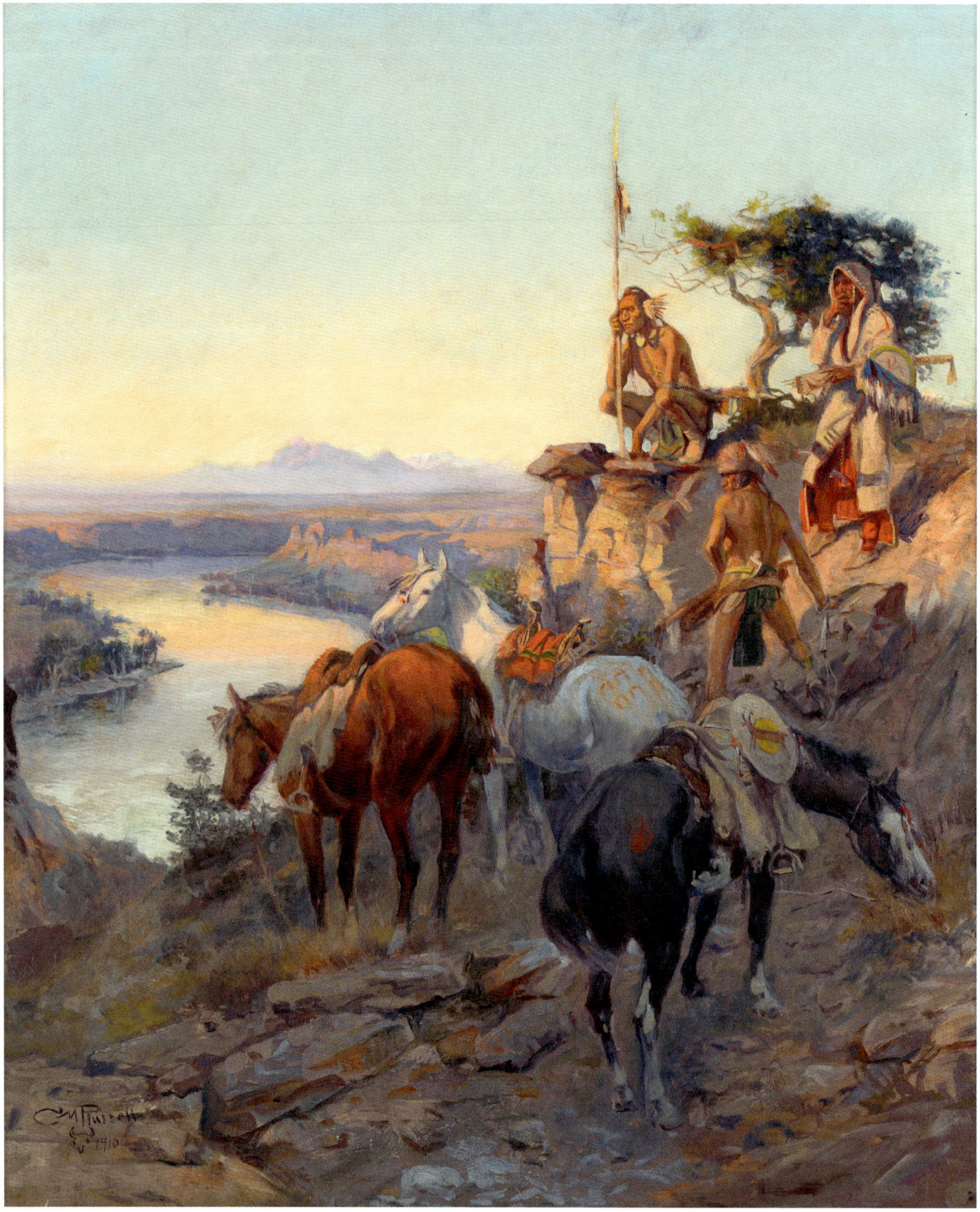

Cat. 15

Charles Marion Russell
Trouble Hunters
1910
Oil on canvas
Framed: 48 × 42 × 2½ in.
Petrie Collection, Denver, Colorado

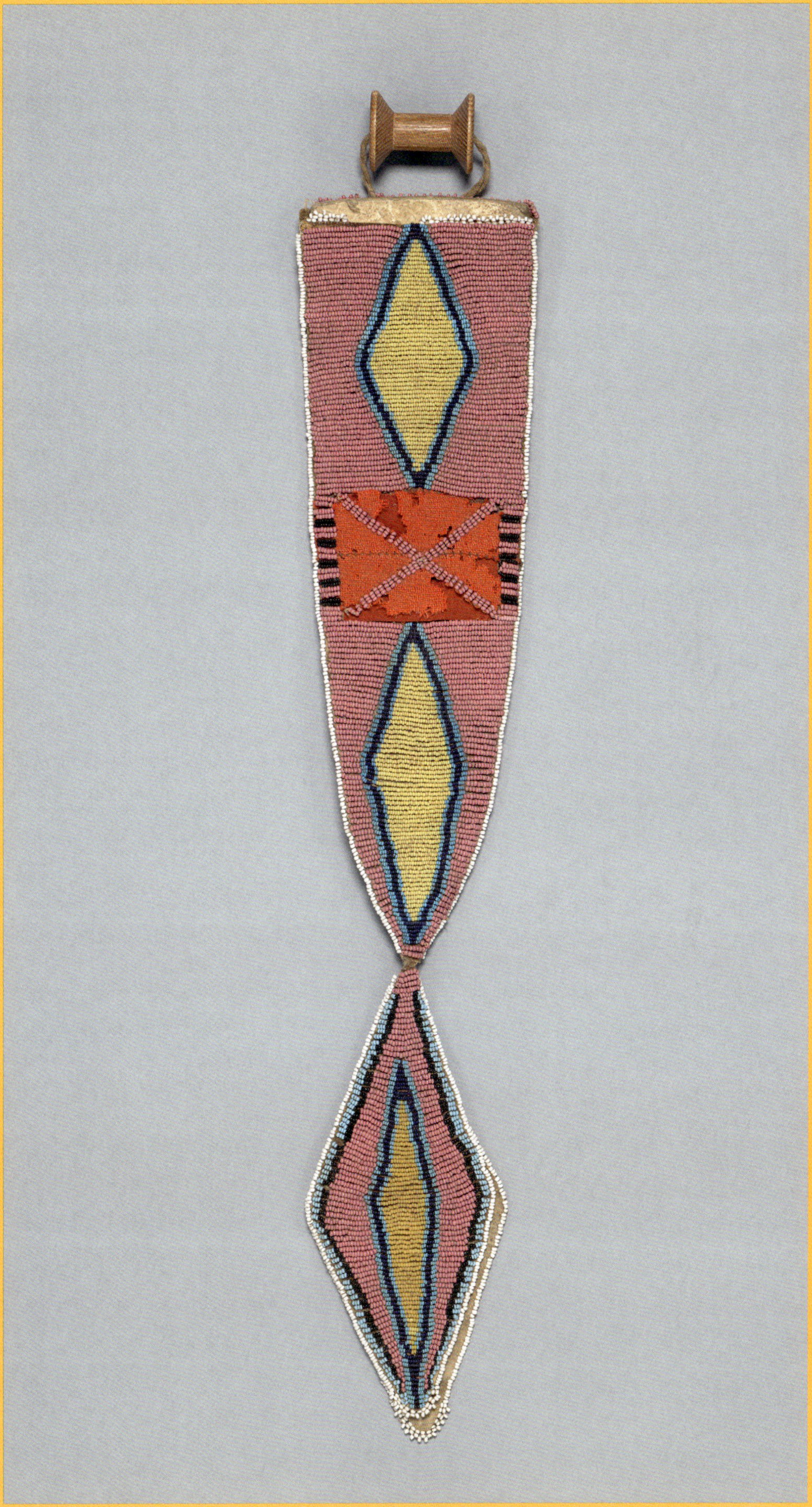

Cat. 16

Nitsitapii Pikanii artist
Knife Case
Before 1964
Leather, cloth, wood, and beads
24 × 4½ × 1½ in.
Denver Art Museum: Museum exchange with George Terasaki, 1964.123

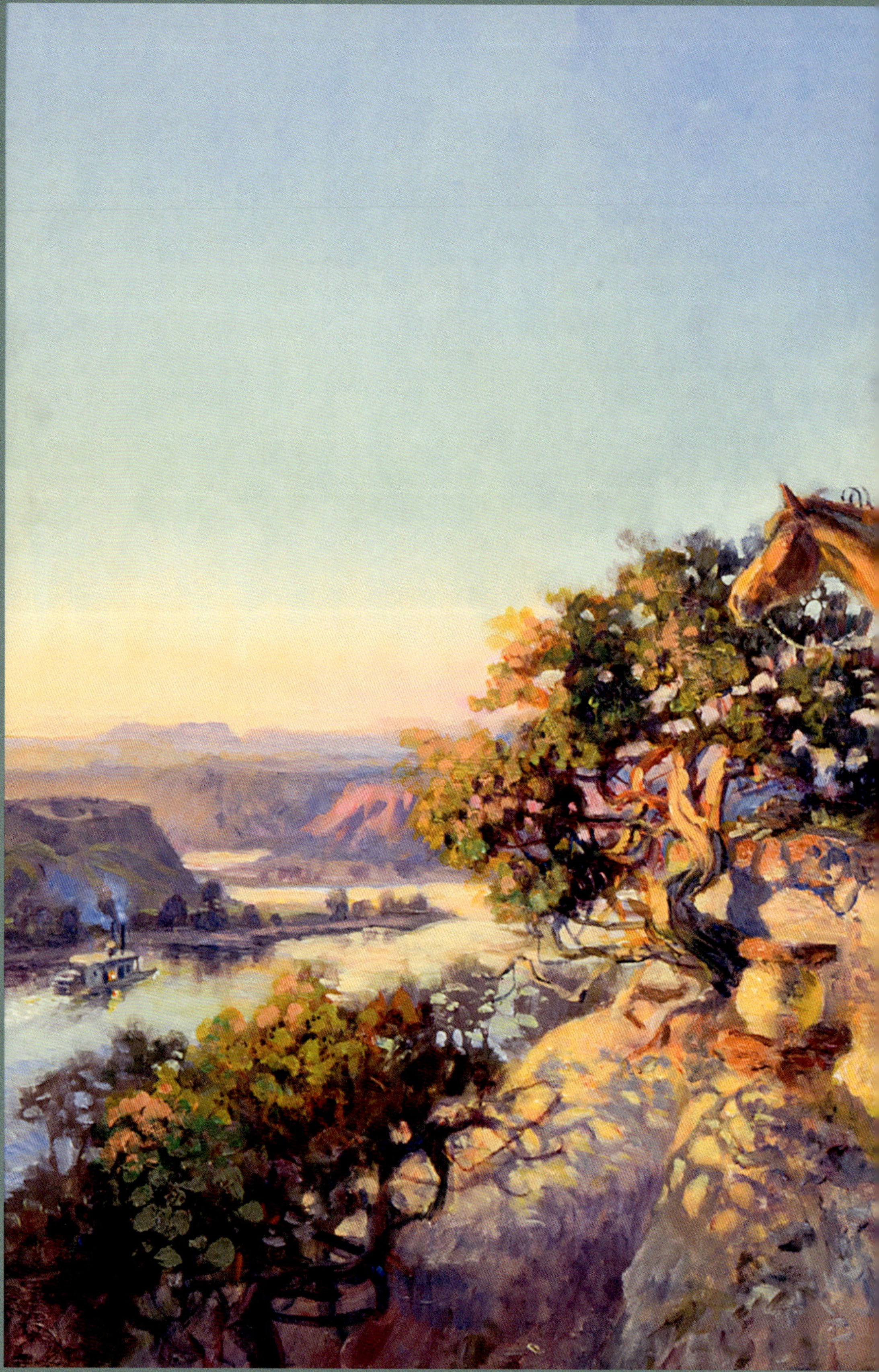

Cat. 17

Charles Marion Russell
The Fireboat
1918
Oil on board
Framed: 23 × 32 × 2½ in.
C. M. Russell Museum, Great Falls, Montana

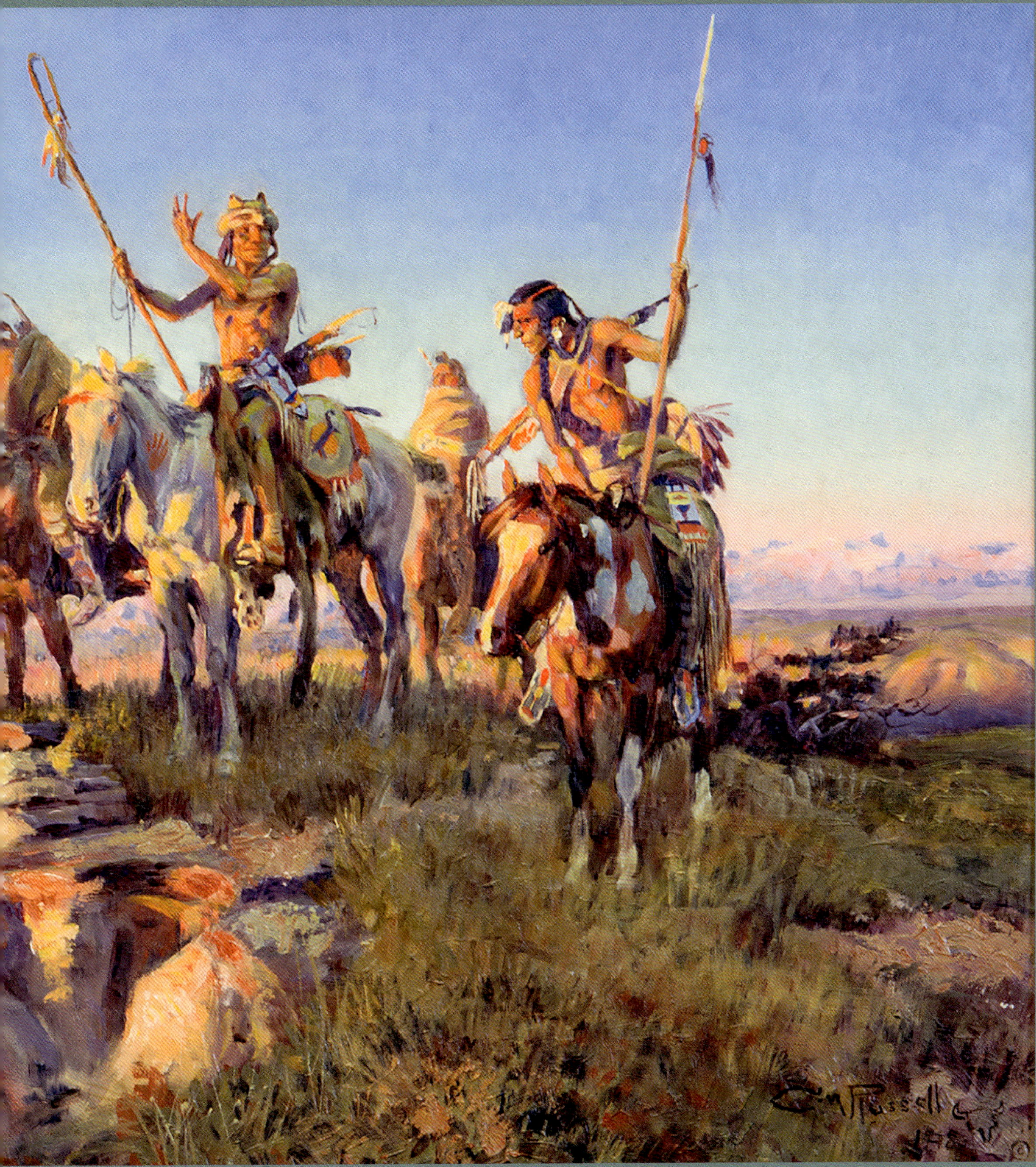
CM Russell

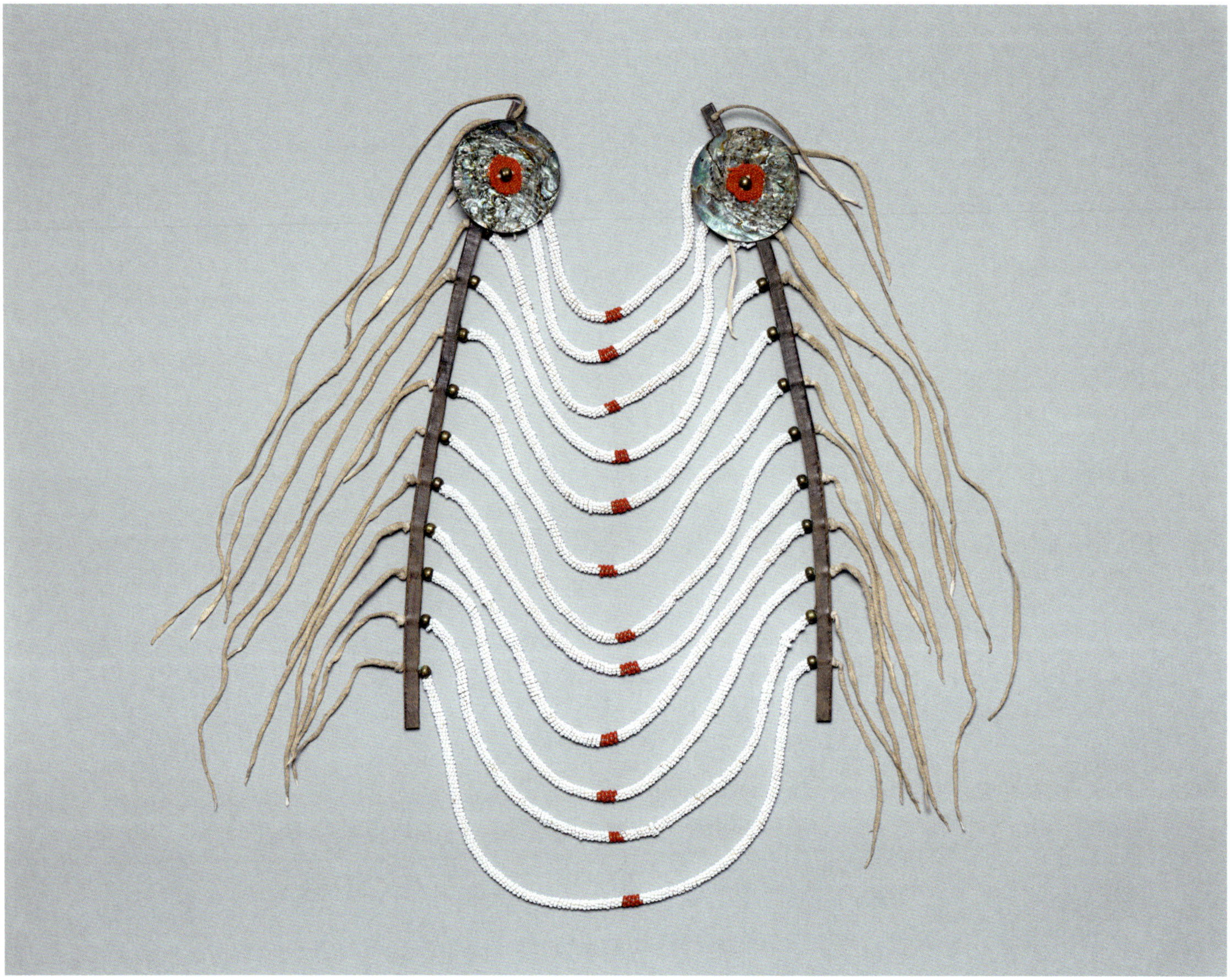

Cat. 18

Amskaapii Pikanii artist
Loop Necklace
After 1880
Leather, beads, and abalone shells
18¼ × 15½ × 1 in.
Denver Art Museum: Gift of Dr. Charles J. Norton, 1981.344

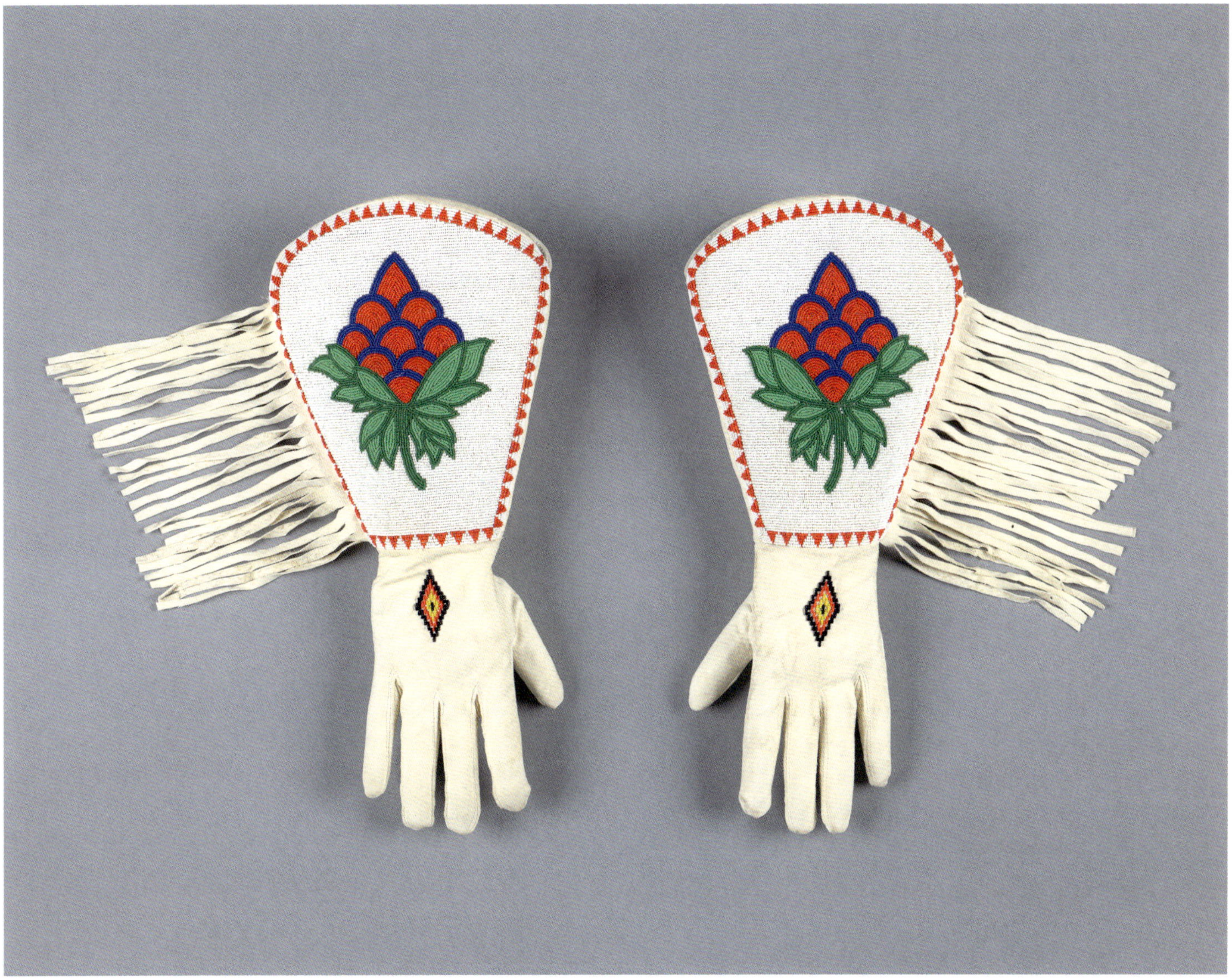

Cat. 19

Nora Spanish (Amskaapii Pikanii, 1898–1990)
Gloves
1940s
Leather and beads
Each approx. 18 × 8⅛ × 4¼ in.
Denver Art Museum: Bequest of the Estate of Gerald E. Welsh, 1981.240

"My maternal grandmother, Nora Spanish, was a leader in the Blackfeet Crafts Association. When they gathered to do beadwork, I sometimes tagged along. One day, I saw Mrs. Little Bull include a black bead among her navy beads and was going to mention it. My grandma explained that intentionally incorporating an imperfection in crafts reflects our understanding of the natural world and that we and it are imperfect. In one of the gloves, Grandma used two white beads in the green leaves of the berry design to create a slight imperfection ... a difference in the design. Like nature's imperfections, it is subtle but present; for me, it is her signature. Oki', Grandma!"—Cheryle "Cookie" Cobell Zwang (Niit si poo aki, Only Girl) (Amskaapii Pikanii)

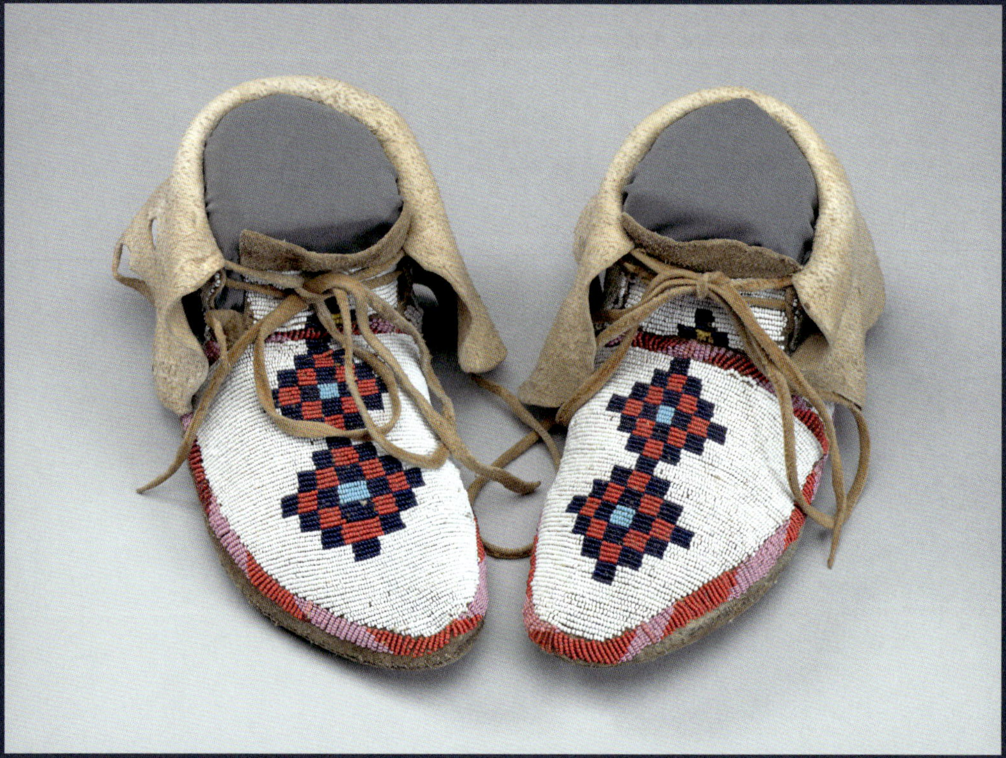

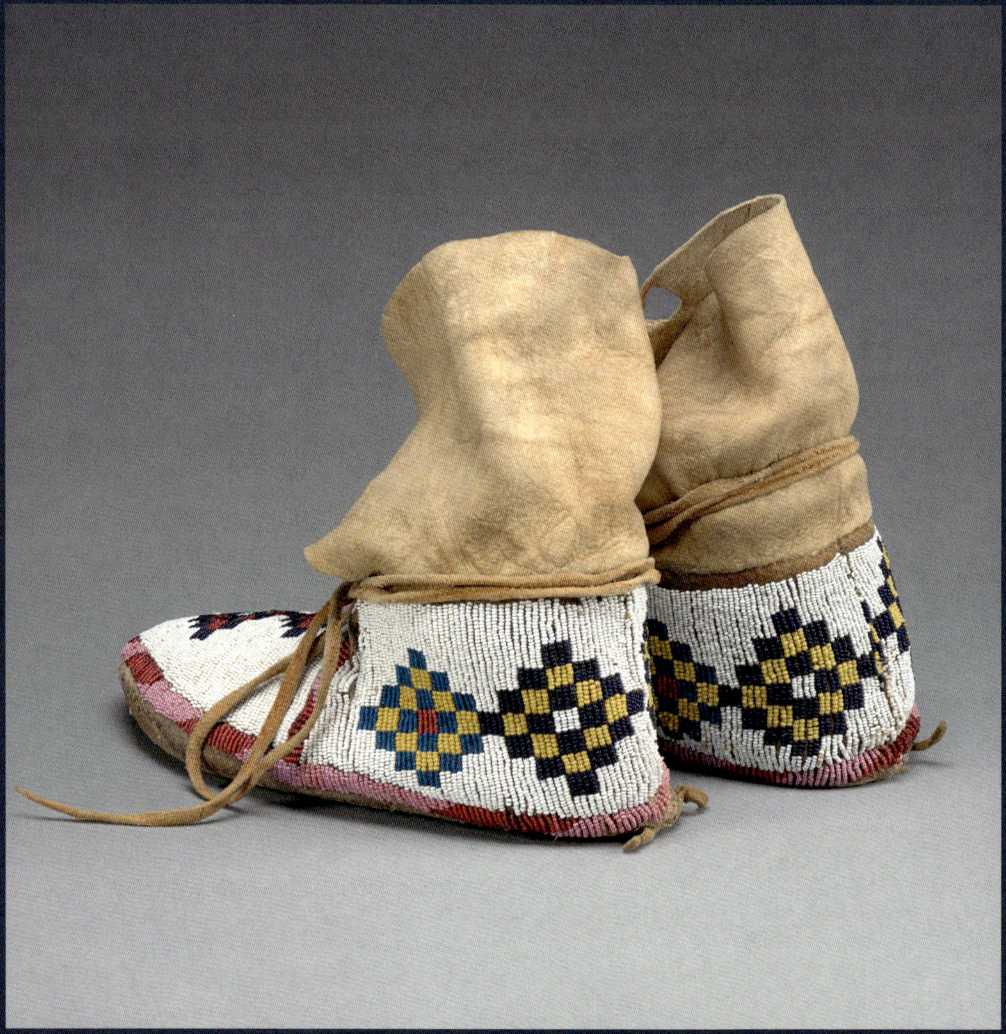

Cat. 20

Amskaapii Pikanii artist
Hard-Sole Moccasins (top and heels)
Late 1800s
Leather and beads
Each approx. 4⅝ ×4¾ × 10 in.
Denver Art Museum: Native Arts acquisition funds, 1947.91

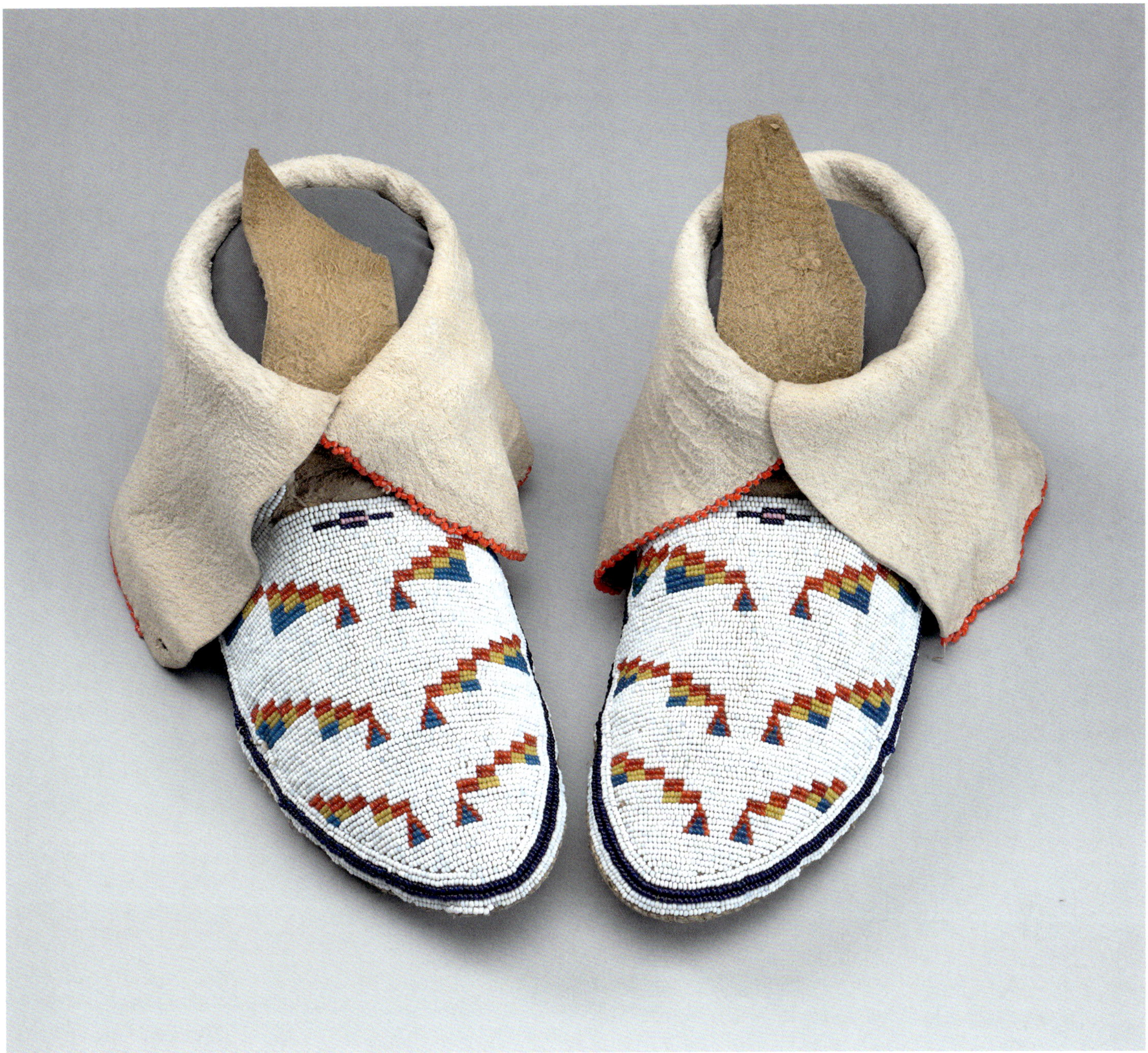

Cat. 21

Nitsitapii artist
Moccasins
c. 1930
Beads and hide
Each approx. 4½ × 5 × 10 in.
Denver Art Museum: Native Arts acquisition funds, 1937.18

In Nitsitapii culture, women traditionally make all clothing and beadwork, including the moccasins and leggings in this exhibition. These moccasins have a cuff that would have been raised and tied above the ankle. Some elements of the design are distinctly Nitsitapii, such as the mountain design of stacked rectangles and triangles. The trim of red beads along the edges of the cuffs was probably a trademark of the maker. Yet, the design does not seem strictly Blackfeet and may be a product of trade, gift, or intermarriage among neighboring nations including the Nakota (Assiniboine) or Nêhiyawak (Plains Cree).

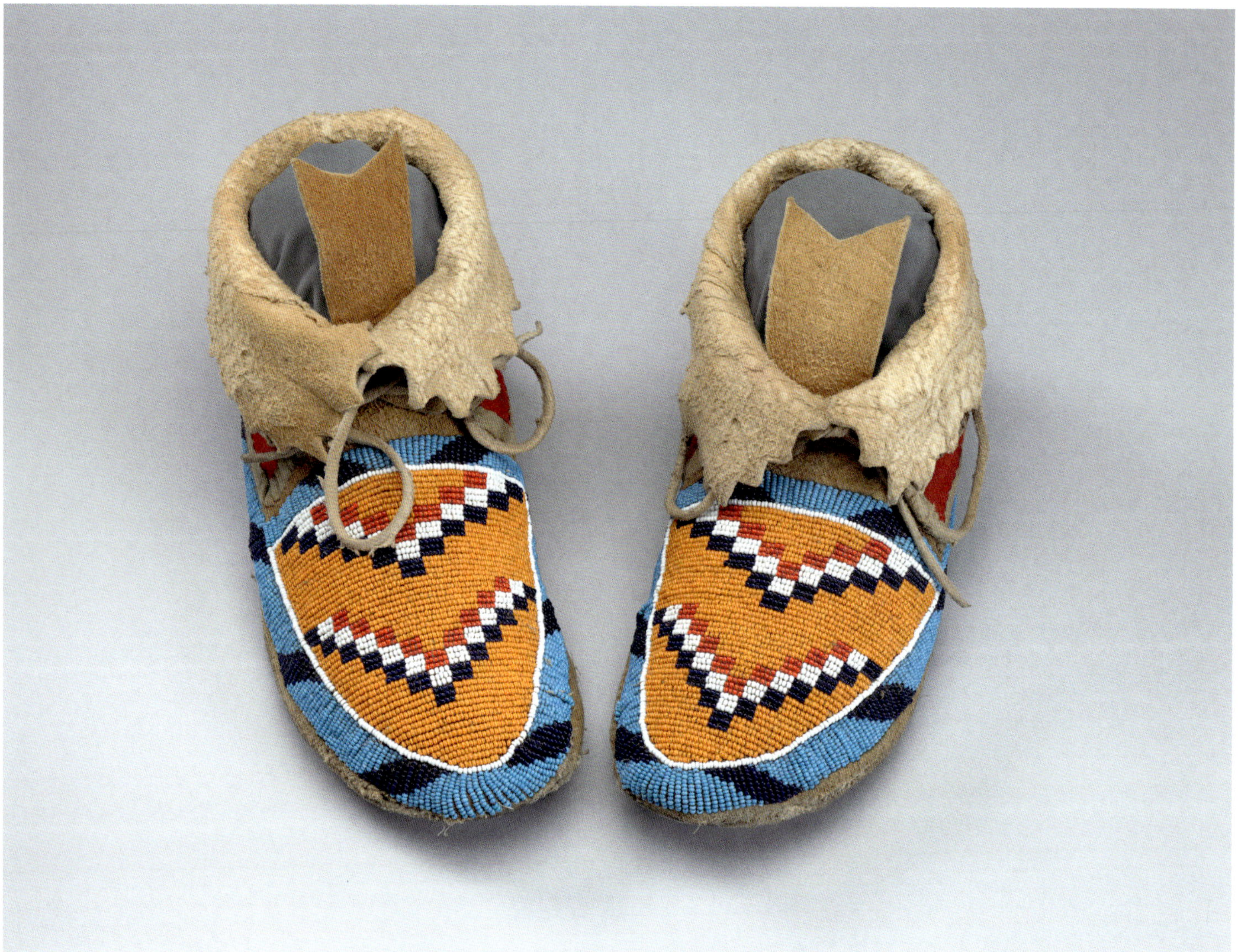

Cat. 22

Nitsitapii artist
Moccasins
Before 1938
Beads, hide, cloth, thread, and sinew
Each approx. 4½ × 4⅛ × 10½ in.
Denver Art Museum: Native Arts acquisition funds, 1938.38

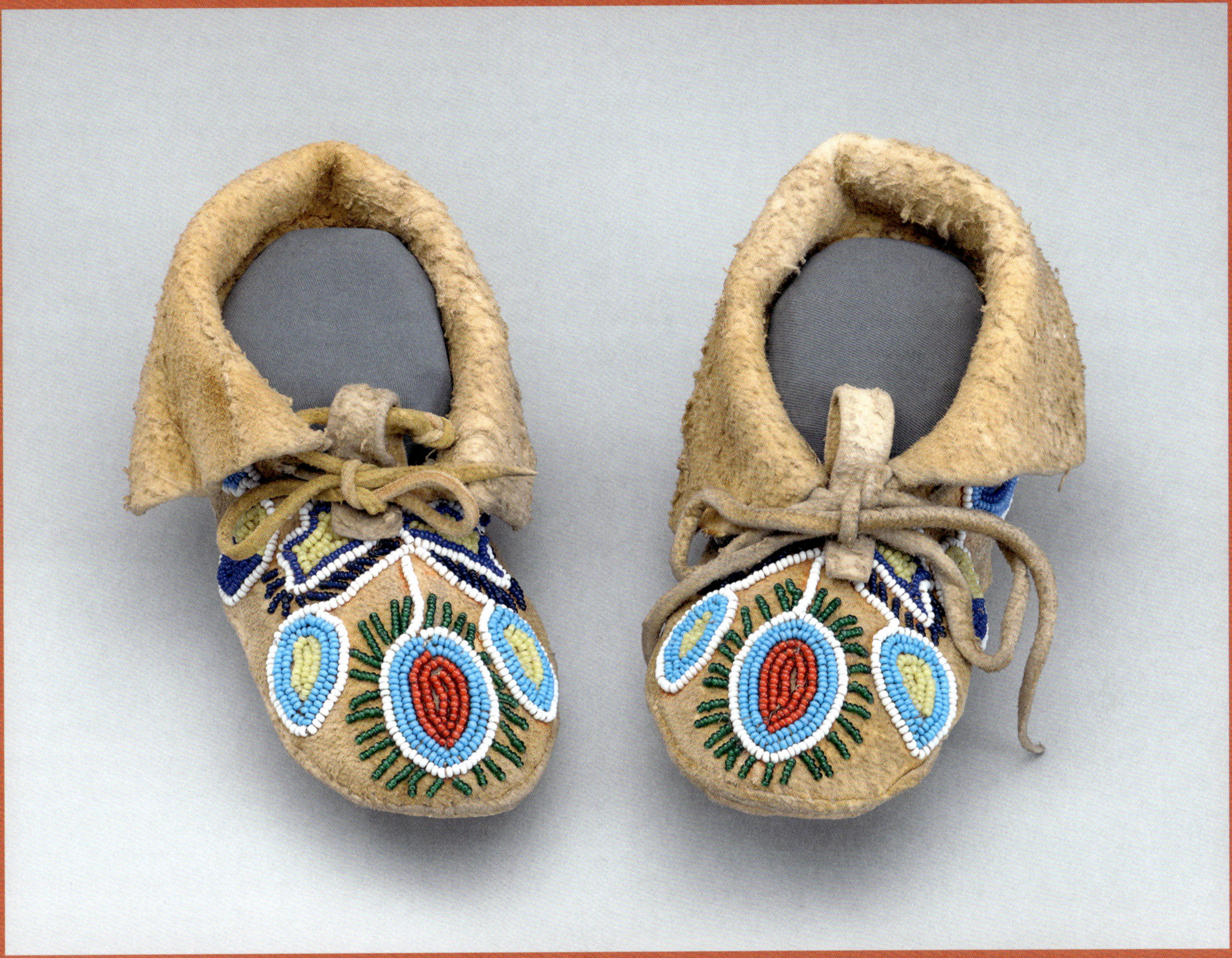

Cat. 23

Nitsitapii artist
Child's Moccasins
Before 1890
Hide and beads
Each approx. 3⅛ × 3⅛ × 5¾ in.
Denver Art Museum: Gift of Maude Steidley, 1935.27

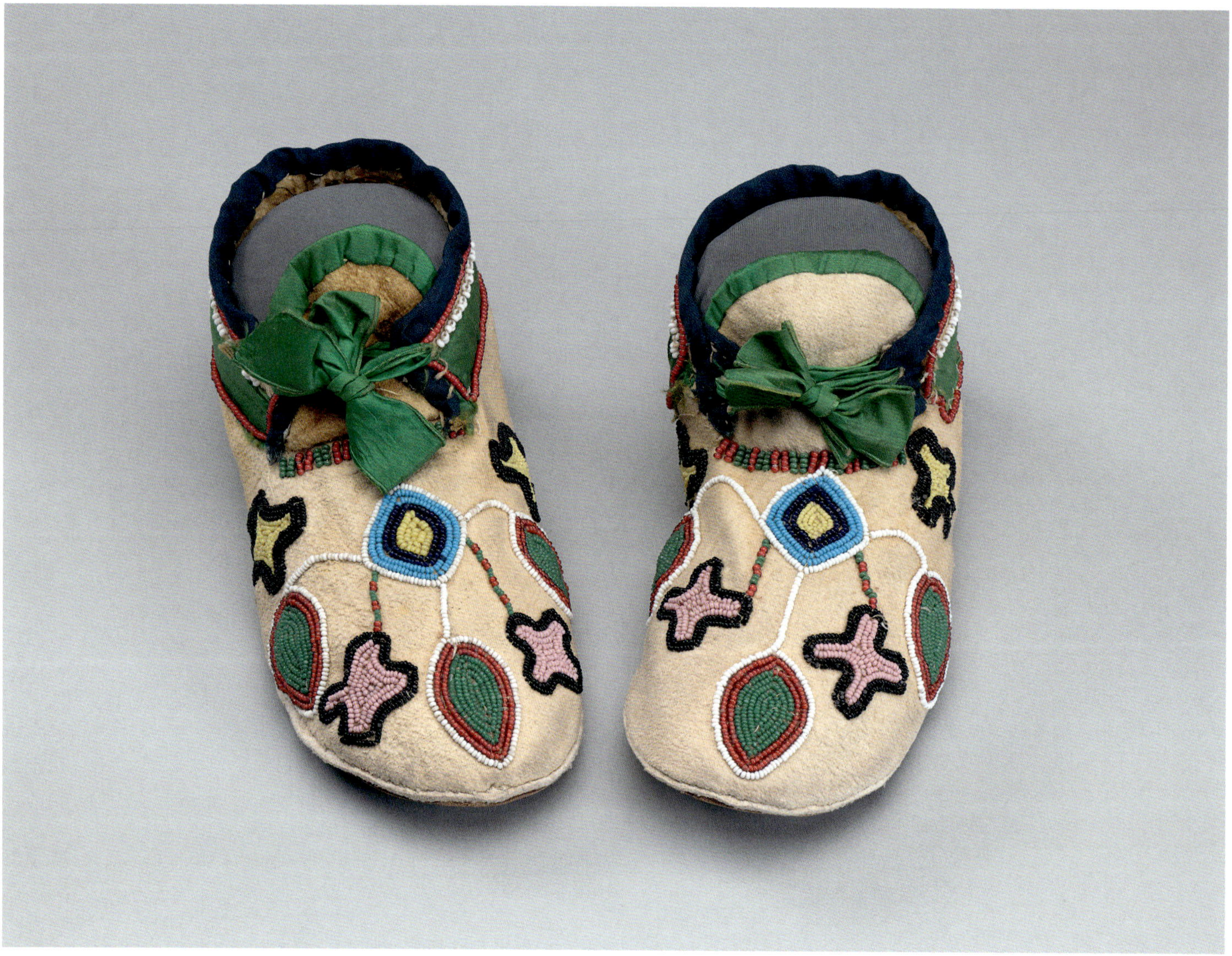

Cat. 24

Nitsitapii artist
Moccasins
Before 1942
Leather, beads, and silk
Each approx. 3¼ × 3 × 6½ in.
Denver Art Museum: Gift of Mrs. J. P. Dowden, 1942.47

This Nitsitapii moccasin style utilizes blue trade cloth and a decorative green silk ankle tie alongside beaded floral imagery inspired by regional plants like the *ookoonookists* (sarvisberry, or service berry). These petite moccasins would have belonged to a Kipiitapooka, a favored first grandchild and the primary recipient of their grandparents' wisdom. Both the design and material point to the prevalence of cross-cultural exchange. Floral designs spread from Eastern tribes across the Plains, largely as a result of tribal displacement due to forced removal, where they were incorporated into traditional Nitsitapii geometric patterns. Glass beads and vibrantly dyed trade cloth were valuable commodities that European traders supplied in exchange for fur. As evidenced by these moccasins, Amskaapii Pikanii styles adapted alongside a rapidly evolving geopolitical landscape.

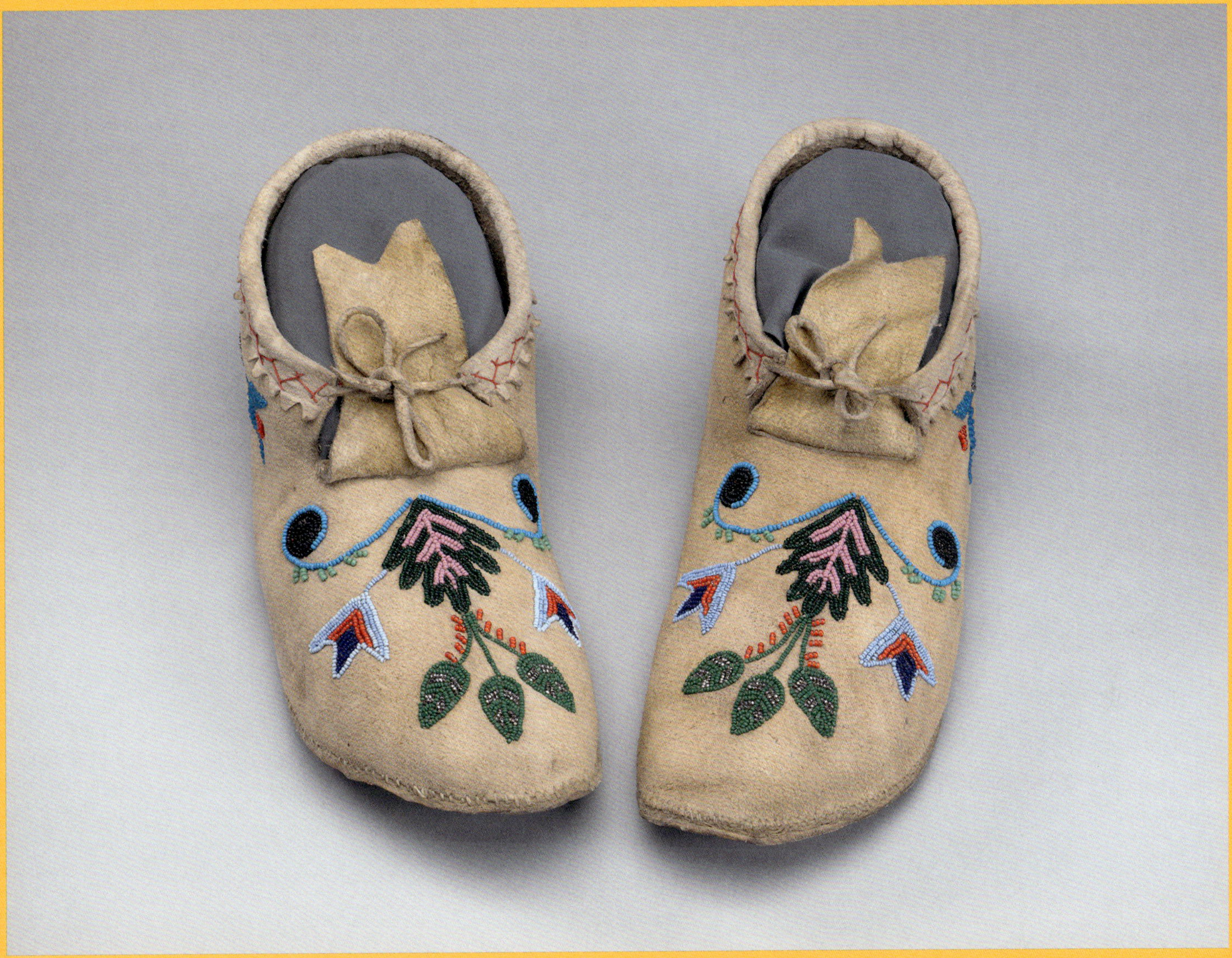

Cat. 25

Nitsitapii artist
Moccasins
Before 1846
Beads, thread, rawhide, and sinew
Each approx. 3¼ × 3⅞ ×10¼ in.
Denver Art Museum: Native Arts acquisition funds, 1934.16

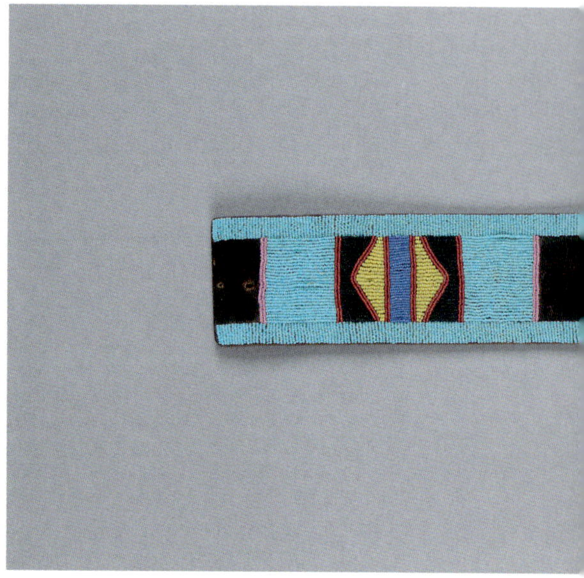

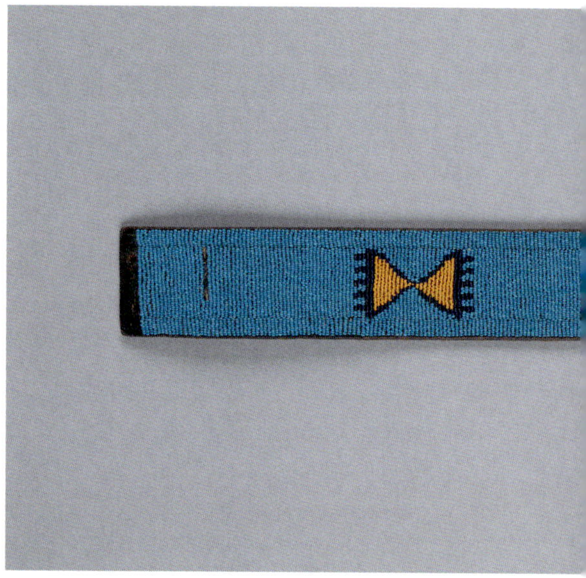

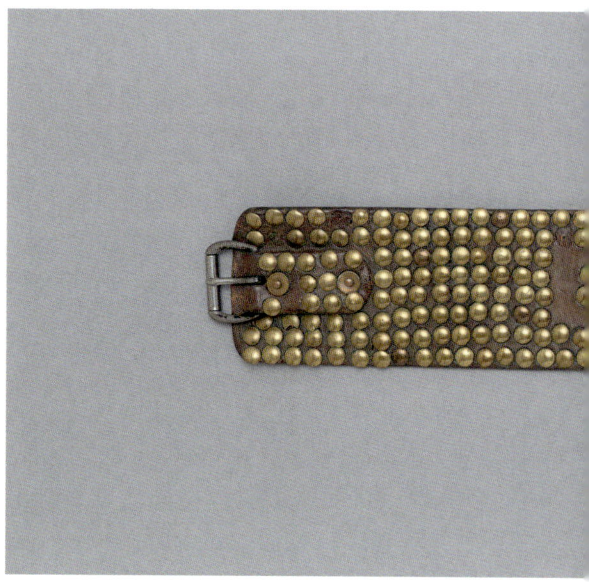

Cat. 26

Nitsitapii artist
Belt
c. 1900
Leather, beads, and silk
39 × 3 × ½ in.
Denver Art Museum: Bequest of Charles J. Norton, 1999.251

Cat. 27

Amskaapii Pikanii artist
Belt
Before 1936
Leather, beads, and cotton thread
43¼ × 2½ × ⅝ in.
Denver Art Museum: Gift of Thomas Dines, Quigg Newton Sr., and John Burnett, 1949.54

Cat. 28

Nitsitapii artist
Belt
c. 1875
Leather, brass, steel, sinew, and thread
40 × 3½ × ¾ in.
Denver Art Museum: Native Arts acquisition funds, 1939.98

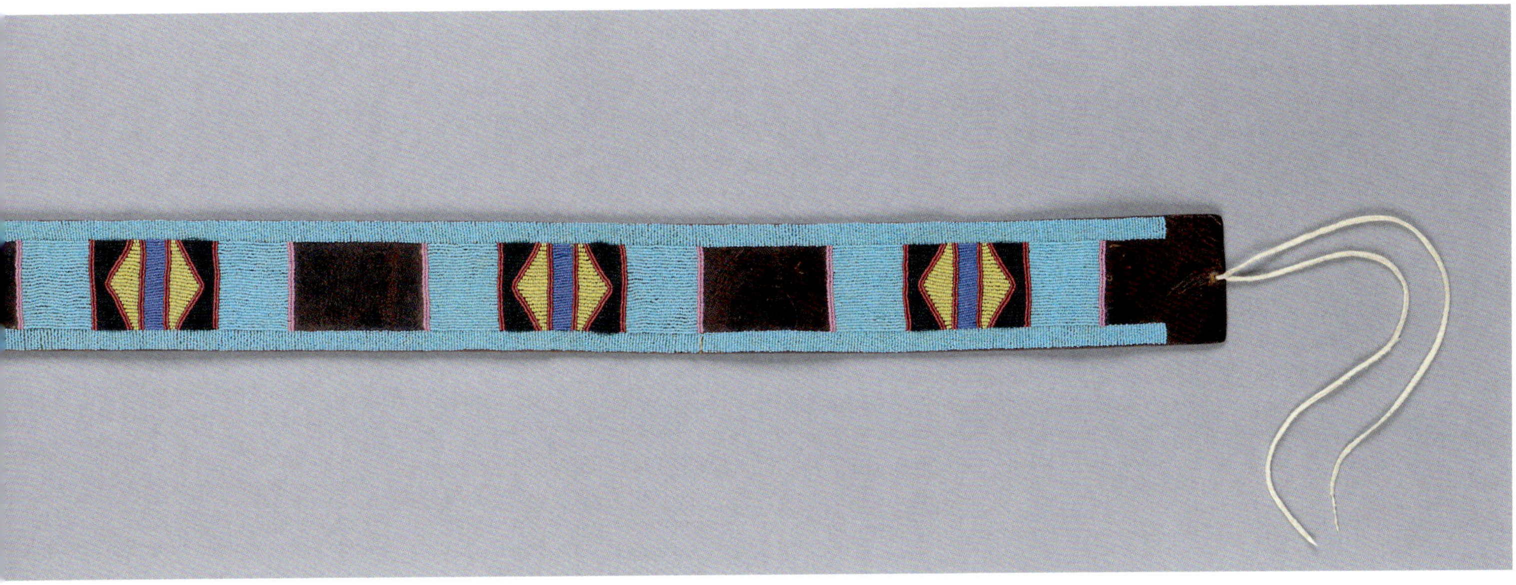
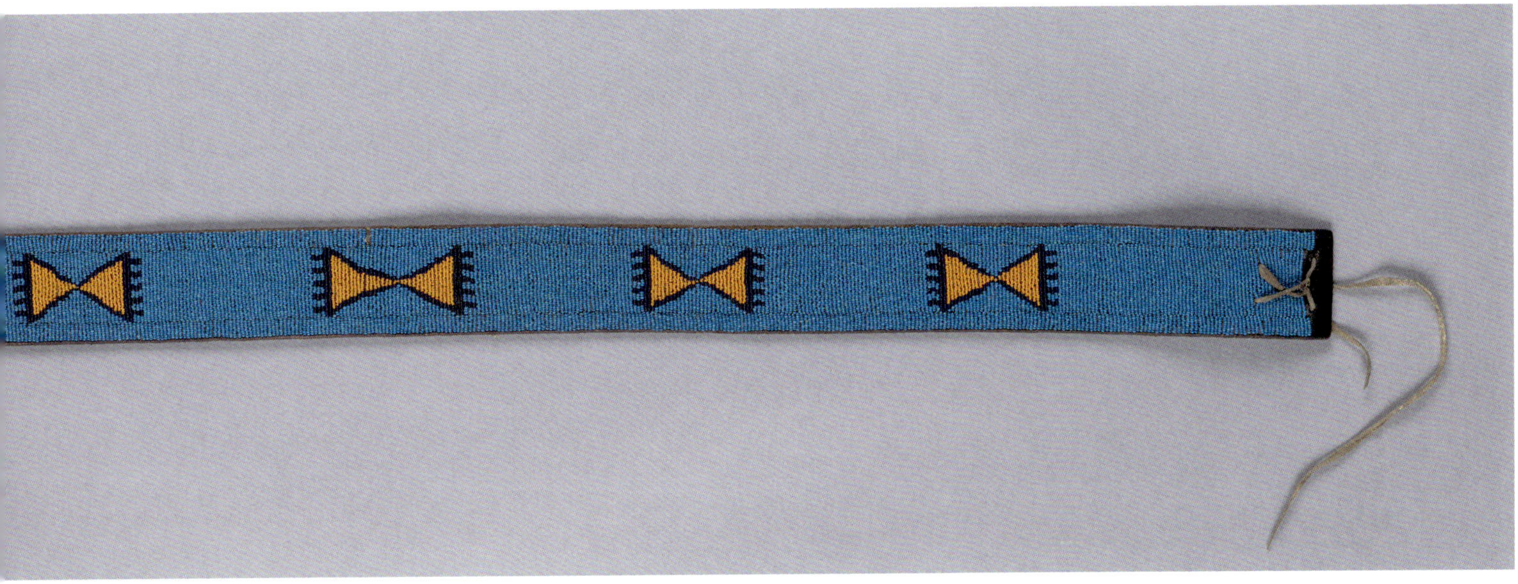
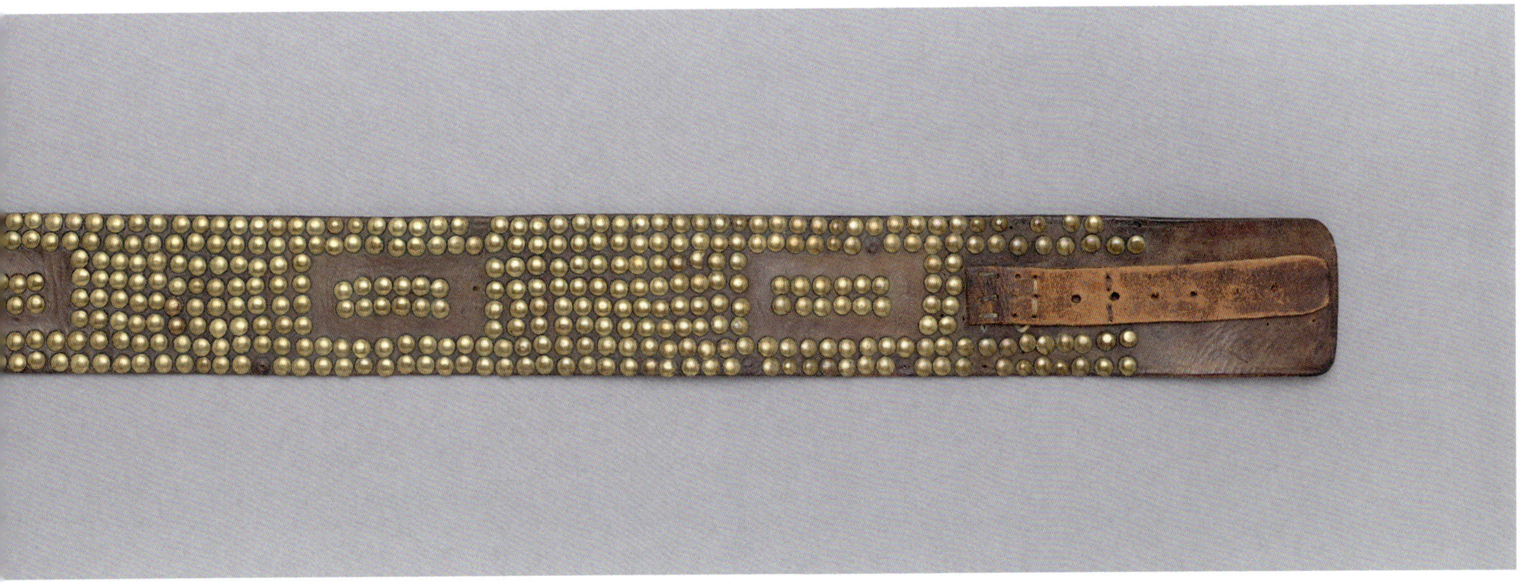

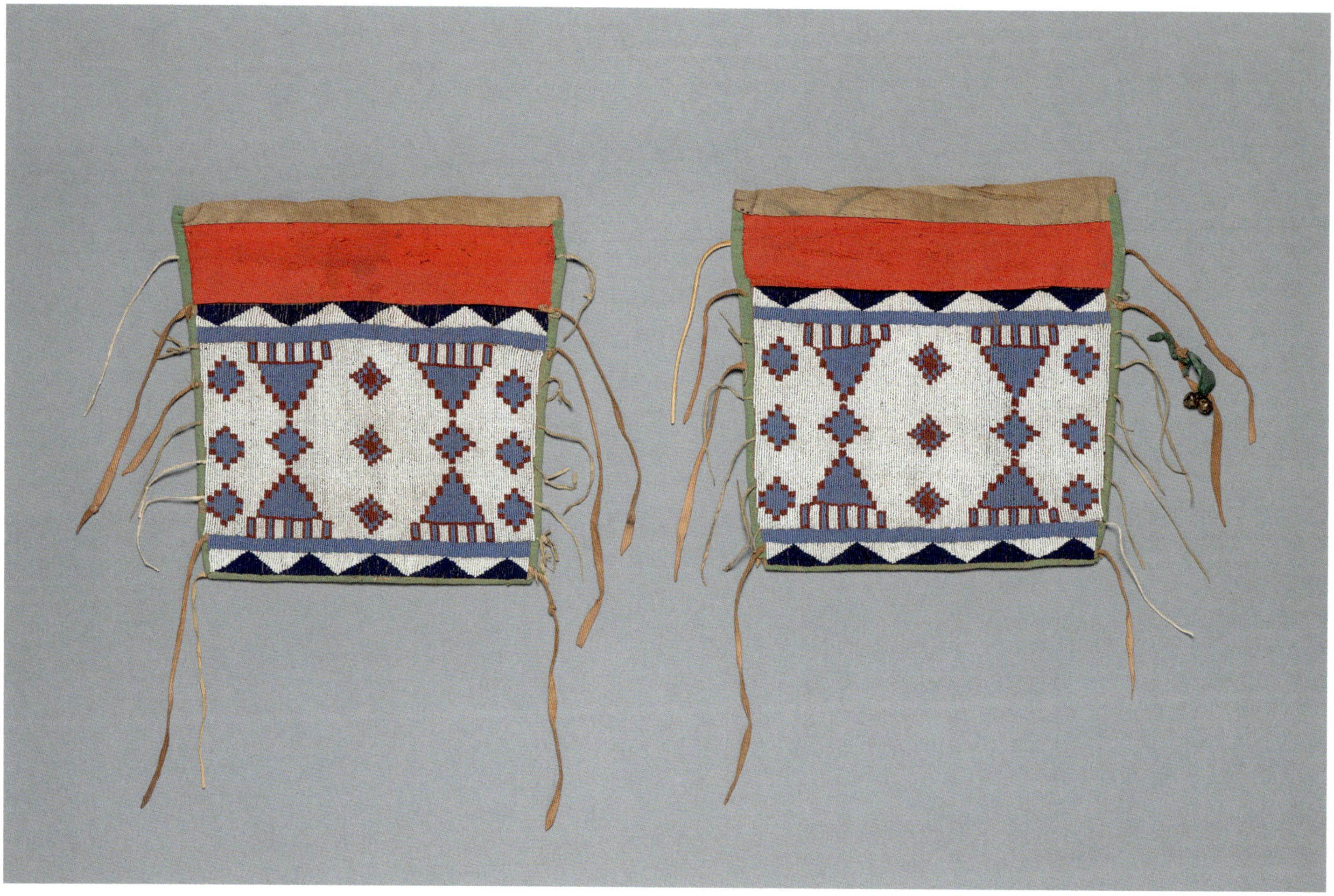

Beaded leggings like these would have been wrapped and tied around the shin, as seen on the standing female figure in Russell's painting *The Silk Robe* (cat. 52).

The intricate azure beading on the surface of these woman's leggings disguises their humble backing: a flour bag. This mundane material tells both a story of struggle and of resourcefulness. Following the brutal annihilation of the buffalo, the US government leveraged rations as a tool to suppress Indigenous culture and force restrictive and abusive treaties upon the once self-sufficient Indigenous nations. These policies, in conjunction with various nationwide scarcities, including later the Great Depression, left communities without traditional materials. They made use of what they had—in this case, a flour sack. The Nitsitapii had incorporated materials available through intertribal trade for centuries, so resourcefulness was not a byproduct of colonization but rather a persistent core value of their culture.

These leggings are also rife with symbolism: The diamond flanked with triangles represents an open-mouthed crow, and the bordering triangles invoke mountains with red-diamond stars shining above them. One of two bells remains attached, and its ringing would have signaled the presence of a spirit.

Cat. 29

Amskaapii Pikanii artist
Woman's Leggings
Late 1800s
Beads, canvas, muslin, and wool
Each approx. 12½ × 13 × ½ in.
Denver Art Museum: Gift of Dr. Charles J. Norton, 1982.90

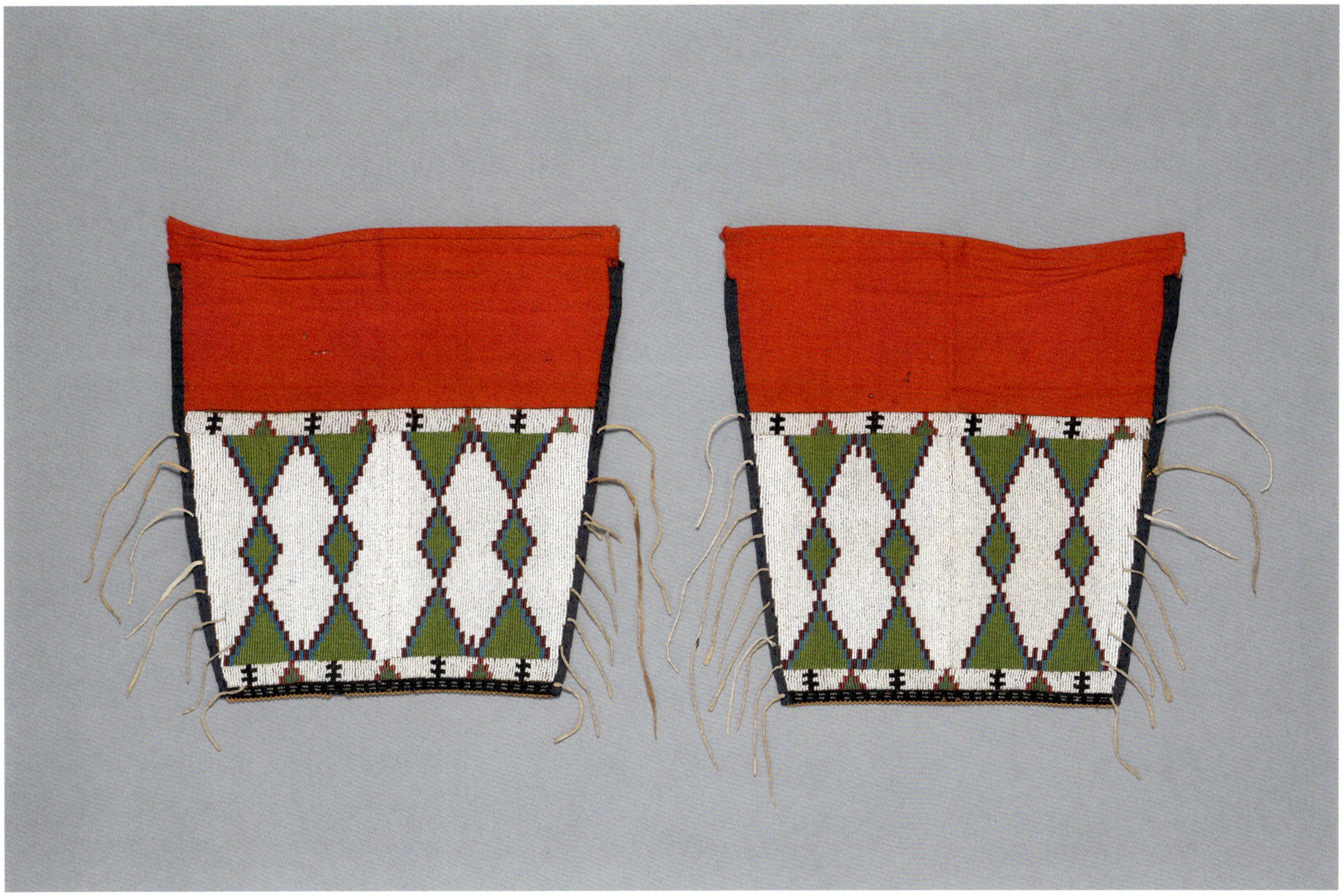

Cat. 30

Nitsitapii artist
Woman's Leggings
Late 1800s
Calico cloth, metal, flannel, silk ribbon, and beads
Each approx. 15 × 14¼ × ¼ in.
Denver Art Museum: Gift of Dr. Charles J. Norton, 1982.88

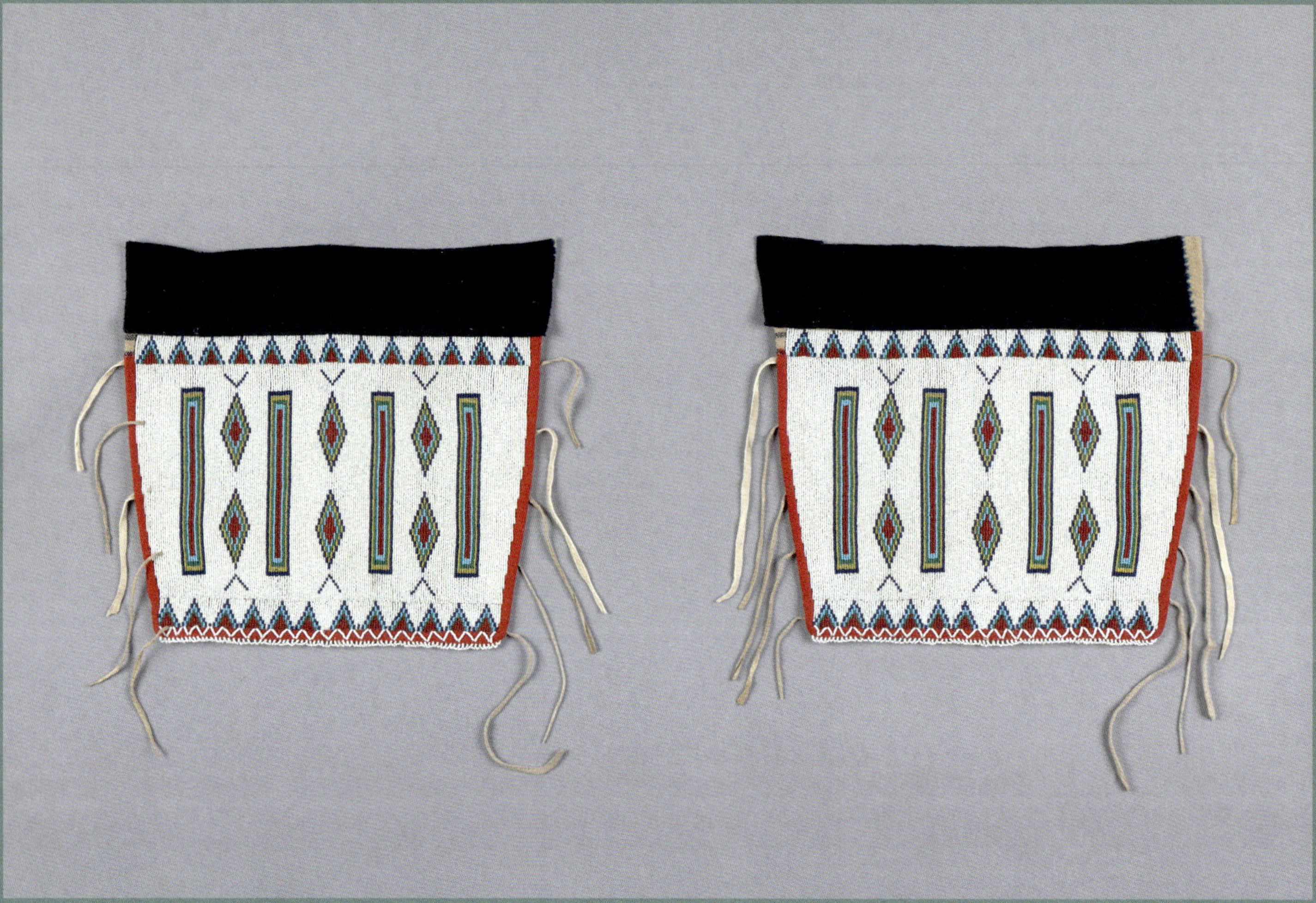

Cat. 31

Amskaapii Pikanii artist
Woman's Leggings
c. 1945
Cloth, hide, and beads
Each approx. 13 × 14¾ × ⅜ in.
Denver Art Museum: Native Arts acquisition funds, 1947.84

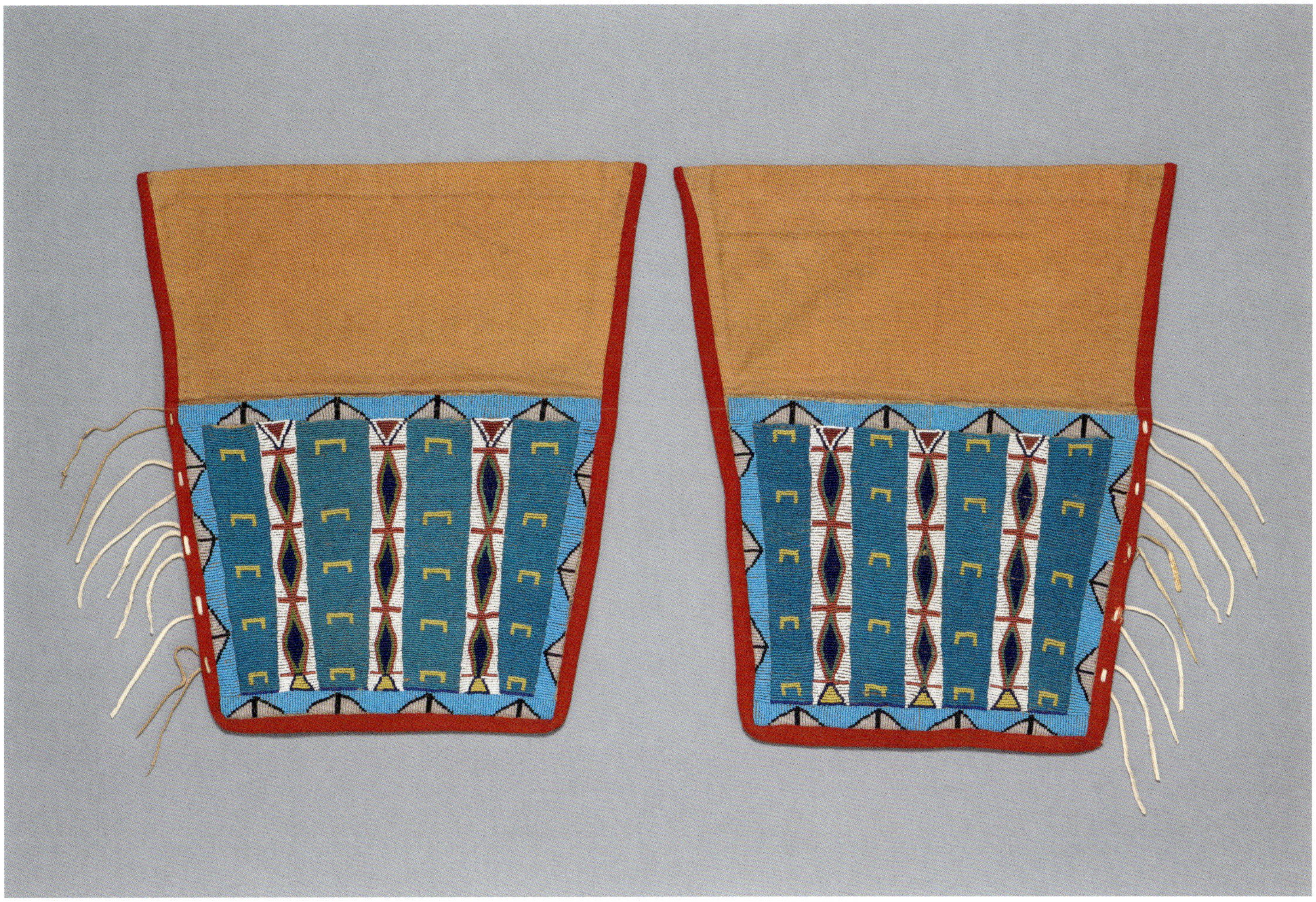

Cat. 32

Amskaapii Pikanii artist
Woman's Leggings
Before 1946
Beads, flannel, and trade cloth
Each approx. 18¼ × 11¾ × ⅜ in.
Denver Art Museum: Gift of Sarah Coolidge Vance, 1946.77

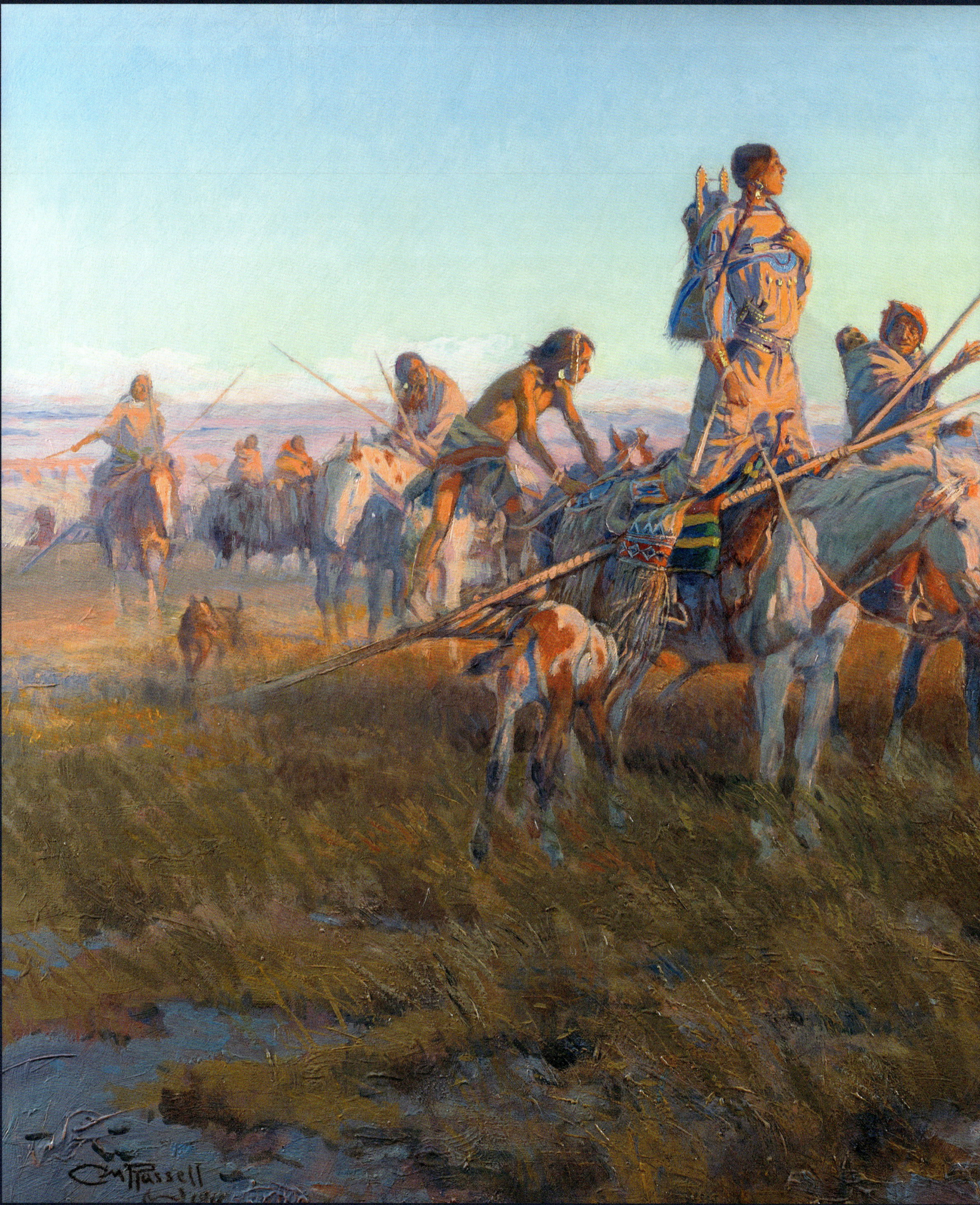
CM Russell

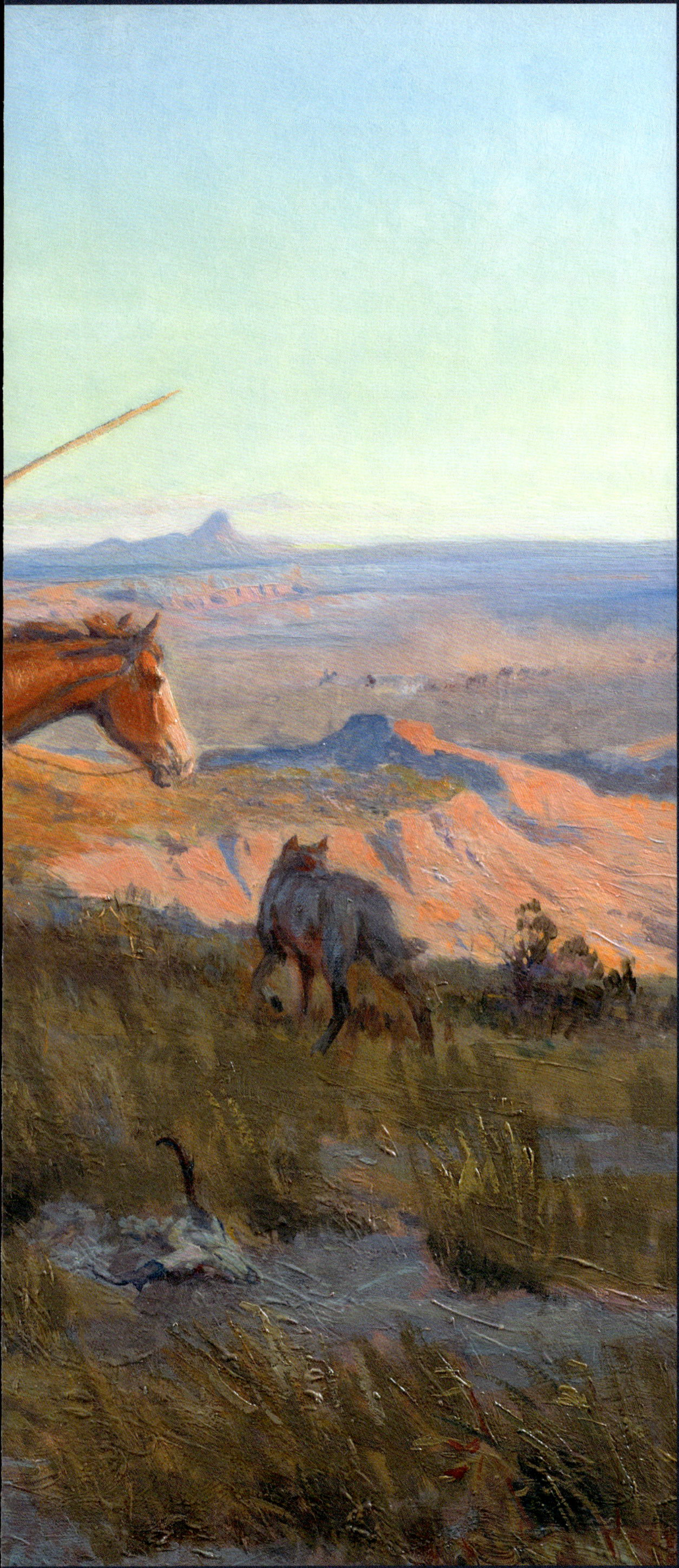

Cat. 33

Charles Marion Russell
In the Wake of the Buffalo Runners
1911
Oil on canvas
Framed: 39½ × 45½ × 3½ in.
Private collection

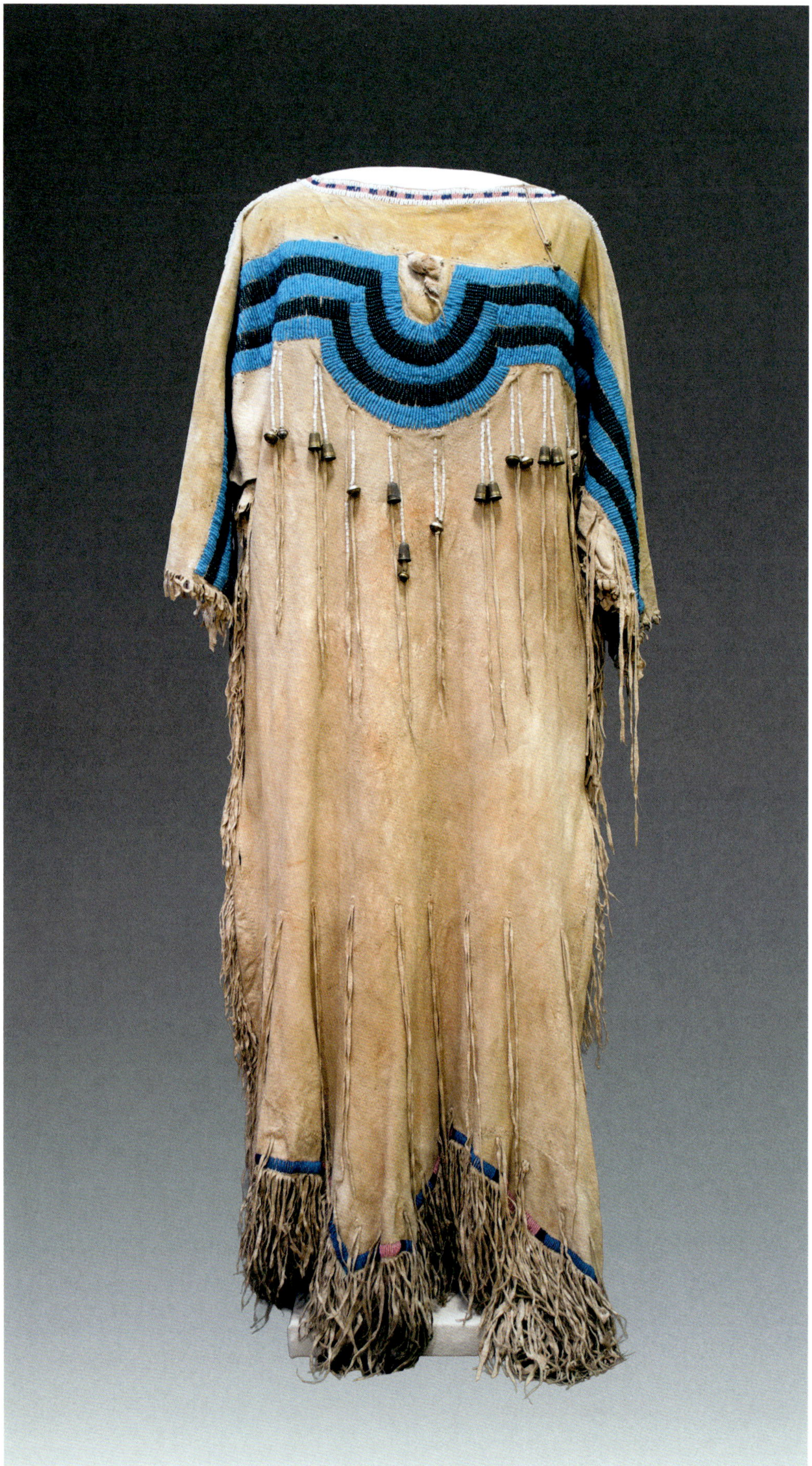

Cat. 34

Amskaapii Pikanii artist
Dress
Deer skin and tail, beads, flannel, and sinew
55 × 33 × 44 in.
C. M. Russell Museum, Great Falls, Montana

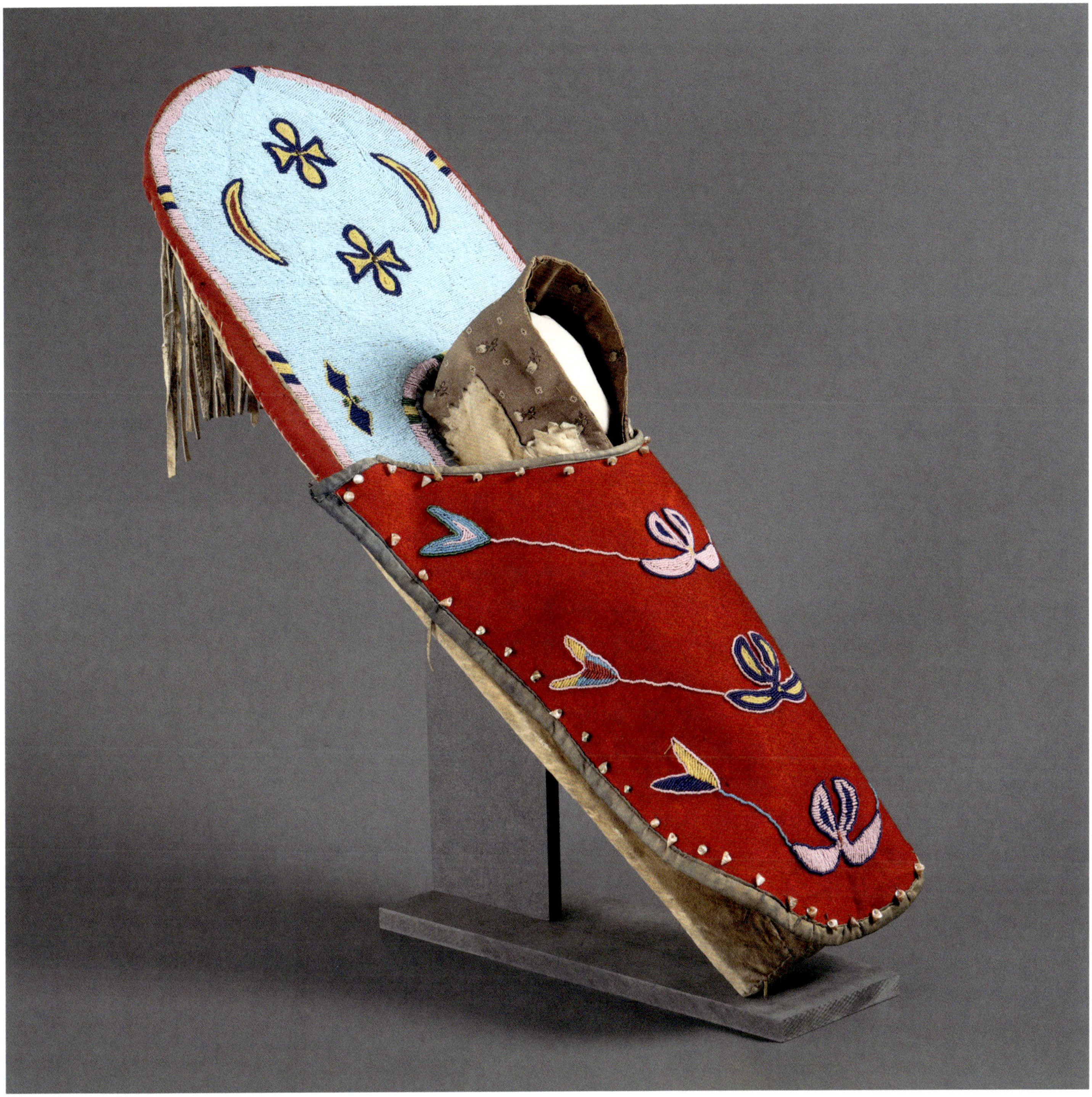

Cat. 35

Amskaapii Pikanii artist
Cradleboard
Early 1900s
Wood, hide, glass beads, thread, fabric, shells, and metal tacks
36 × 15 in.
The Crane Collection at the Denver Museum of Nature and Science

Cradleboards allowed a baby to be gently swaddled while carried on a mother's back, attached to the back of the horse, or safely hung from a tree branch. The protection bar, which is missing from this cradleboard, provided critical security and development for Amskaapii Pikanii babies. If the board tipped over, the bar would stand between the child and the ground to prevent injury. Beads hanging from the bar would stimulate the child, helping them practice hand-eye coordination, dexterity, and muscle memory, while hanging amulets containing umbilical cords reinforced maternal connection. Within the cradleboard, plant material such as dry moss padded the bottom like a diaper. The beautiful designs spanning the exterior can typically be attributed to women relatives celebrating the new life that blessed the family.

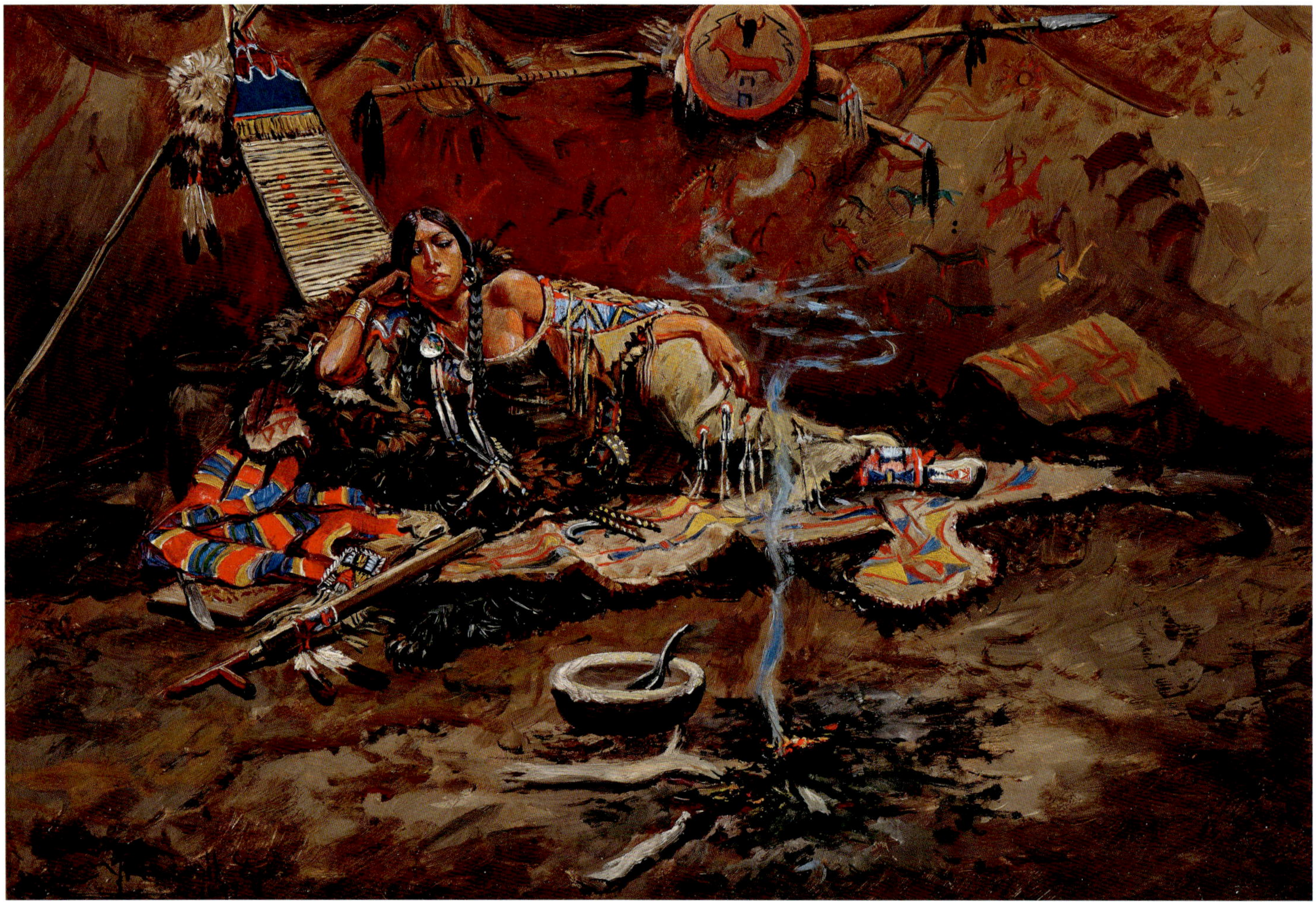

Russell's imaginative takes on Nitsitapii life have had lasting, sometimes harmful, impacts on the community and on broader perceptions of Indigenous people. *Waiting and Mad* is part of a series of paintings about a fictional Native woman named Keeoma. Created by William Bleasdell Cameron, the fictional Keeoma first appeared in "Keeoma's Wooing," a short story published in the July 1897 issue of *Western Field and Stream*. Based on existing photos and scholarship, it seems that both Nancy Russell and Josephine Wright may have posed for the Keeoma paintings (see Emily Burns's essay in this volume).

Waiting and Mad presents inaccuracies that, even if unintentional, disrespect Amskaapii Pikanii women and culture. Though it might seem a small detail, the pipe in the painting is a man's pipe, not a woman's pipe, and traditionally, the Nitsitapii used blackstone pipes. This one appears to be a Očhéthi Šakówiŋ redstone pipe, which might have been available through trade.

More troubling, though, is the way Russell depicted the woman. Bears are sacred in Amskaapii Pikanii culture, and only those with the proper rights can be close to them. Russell transgressed this strict protocol by placing the figure on a bear rug. The woman is posed like an odalisque, a visual trope borrowed from nineteenth-century Euro-American Orientalism of a reclining harem woman available to the male gaze and desire. Her pose, her immodesty (with her dress falling off her shoulder), and the idea that a woman—responsible for all aspects of camp, lodge, and family care—would be lying around waiting for her husband are not only unrealistic but also feed harmful stereotypes that contribute to the ongoing crisis of violence against Indigenous women. For these reasons, representations like this cannot be taken lightly and should be seriously interrogated.

Cat. 36

Charles Marion Russell
Waiting and Mad
1899
Oil on canvas
Framed: 21⅜ × 27⅛ × 2 in.
Indianapolis Museum of Art at Newfields, Gift of Harrison Eiteljorg Gallery of Western Art, 73.104.5

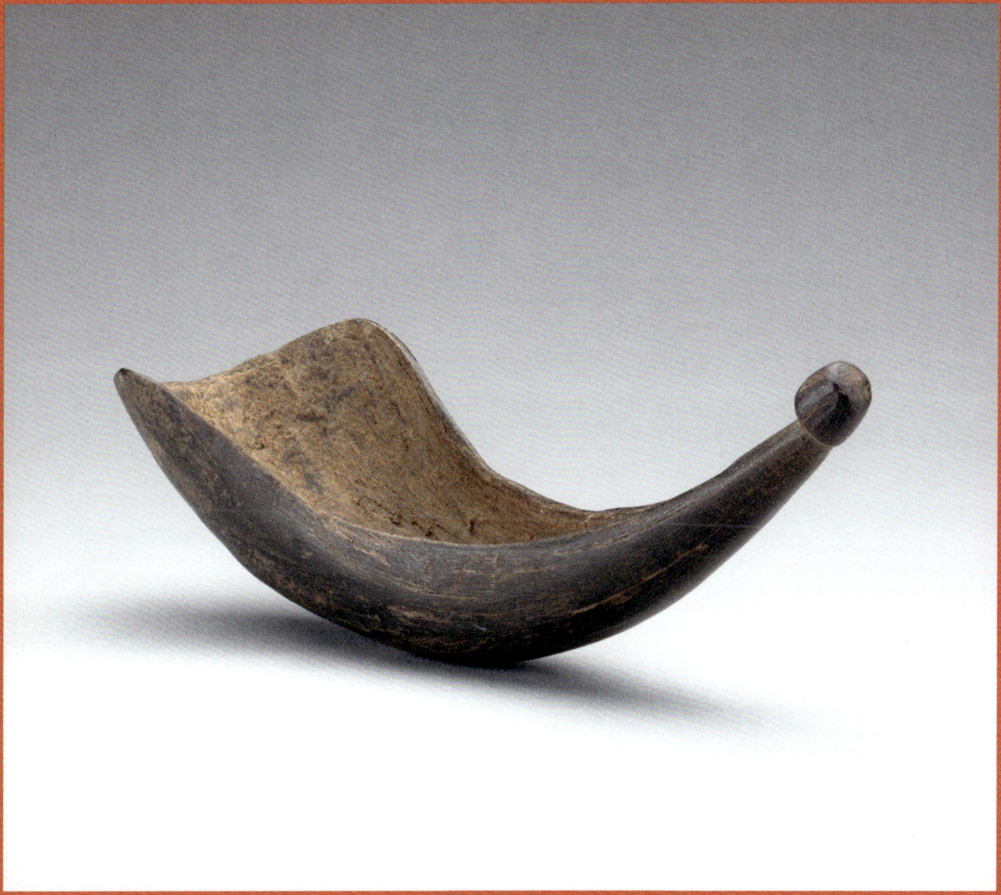

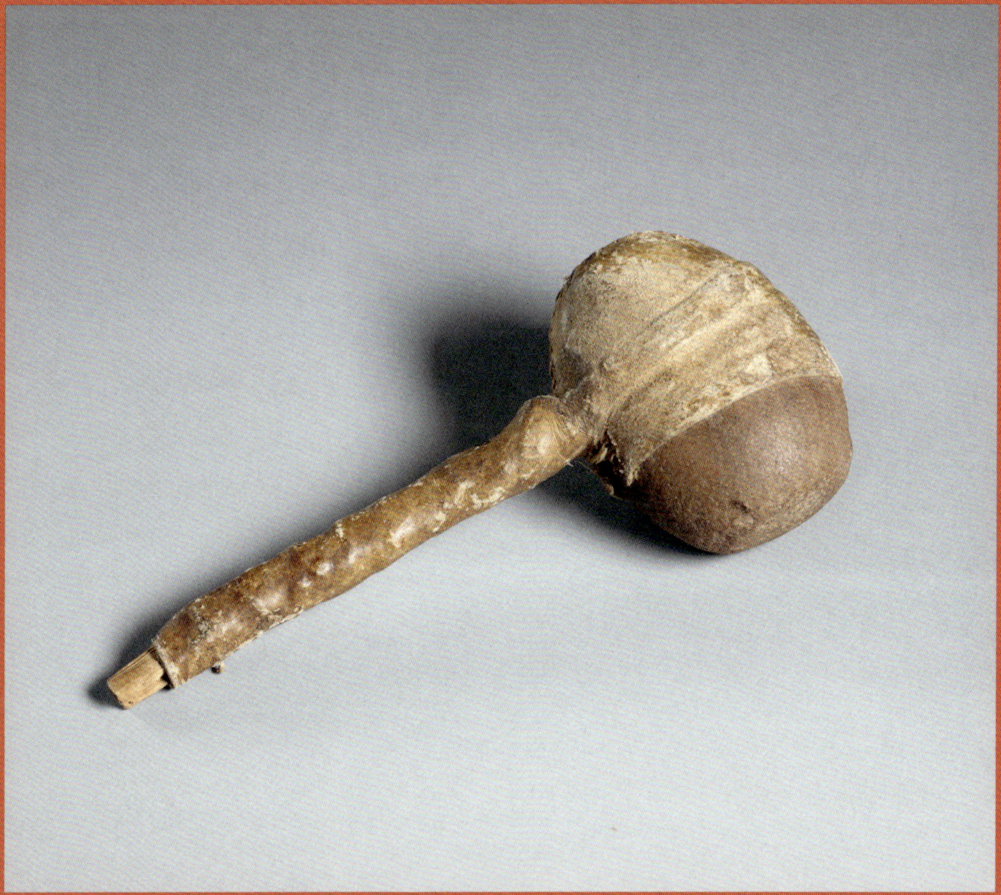

Cat. 37

Nitsitapii artist
Spoon
c. 1890
Buffalo horn
4¼ × 8⅞ × 2¾ in.
Denver Art Museum: Native Arts acquisition funds, 1938.316

Cat. 38

Kainai artist
Maul
Before 1939
Stone, rawhide, sinew, and paint
12¾ × 5⅜ × 3 in.
Denver Art Museum: Native Arts acquisition funds, 1939.309

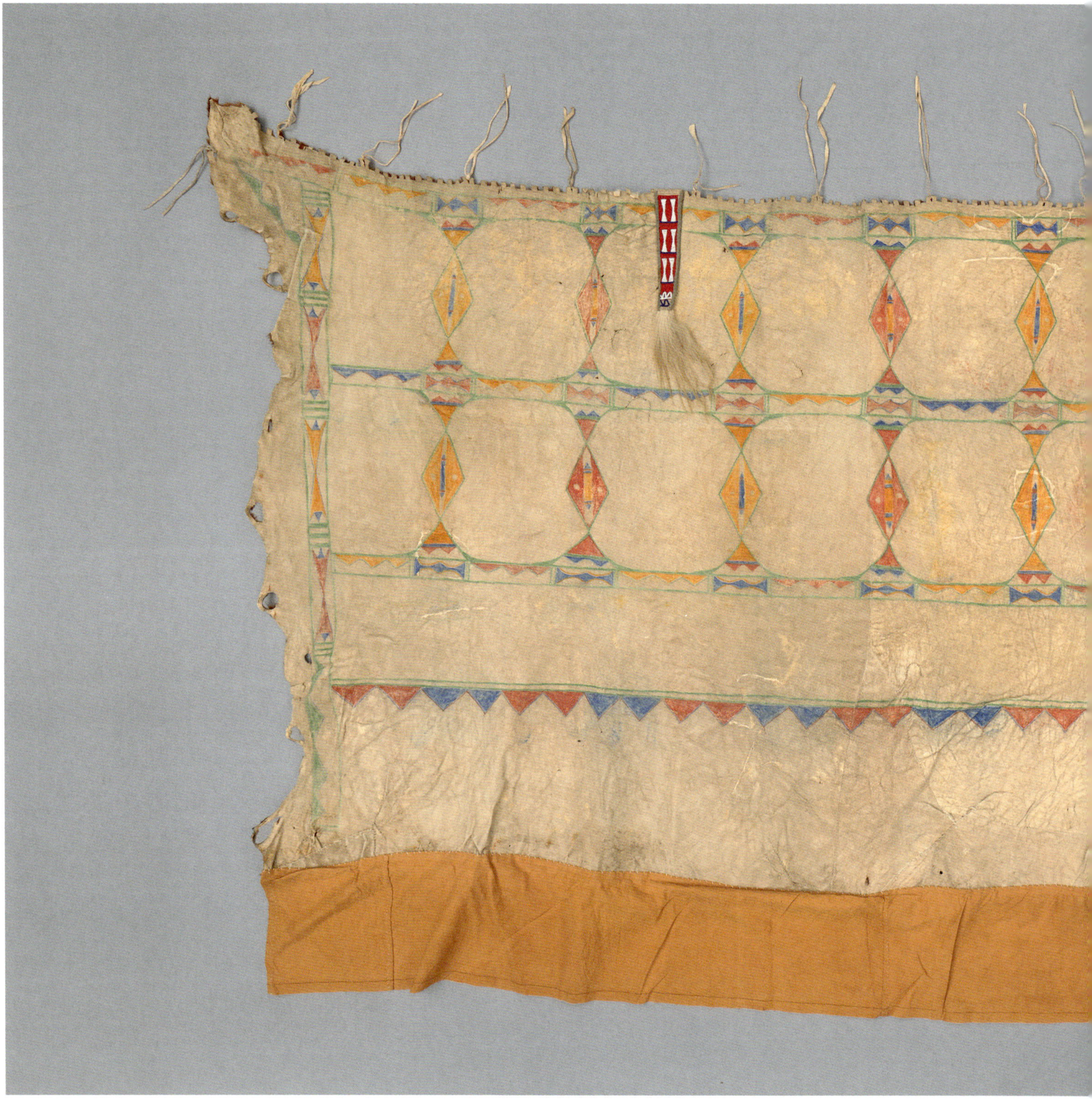

Cat. 39

Amskaapii Pikanii artist
Lodge Liner
c. 1920
Cowhide, paint, beads, and hair
82 × 174 in.
The L. D. and Ruth Bax Collection at the Denver Art Museum, 1985.259

This painted liner, made of three cowhides sewn together, would have hung along the bottom interior of a lodge. It would have been flanked by two additional liners on either side to span the lodge's internal circumference. As the central liner, it was the *paaniikataanssii*, the chief's liner. Lodge liners helped control air, temperature, and privacy. Depending on the weather, the bottom fabric could be tucked behind and weighed down to create a more insulated interior. Or, on a warmer day, the liner could be rolled up so air could pass underneath.

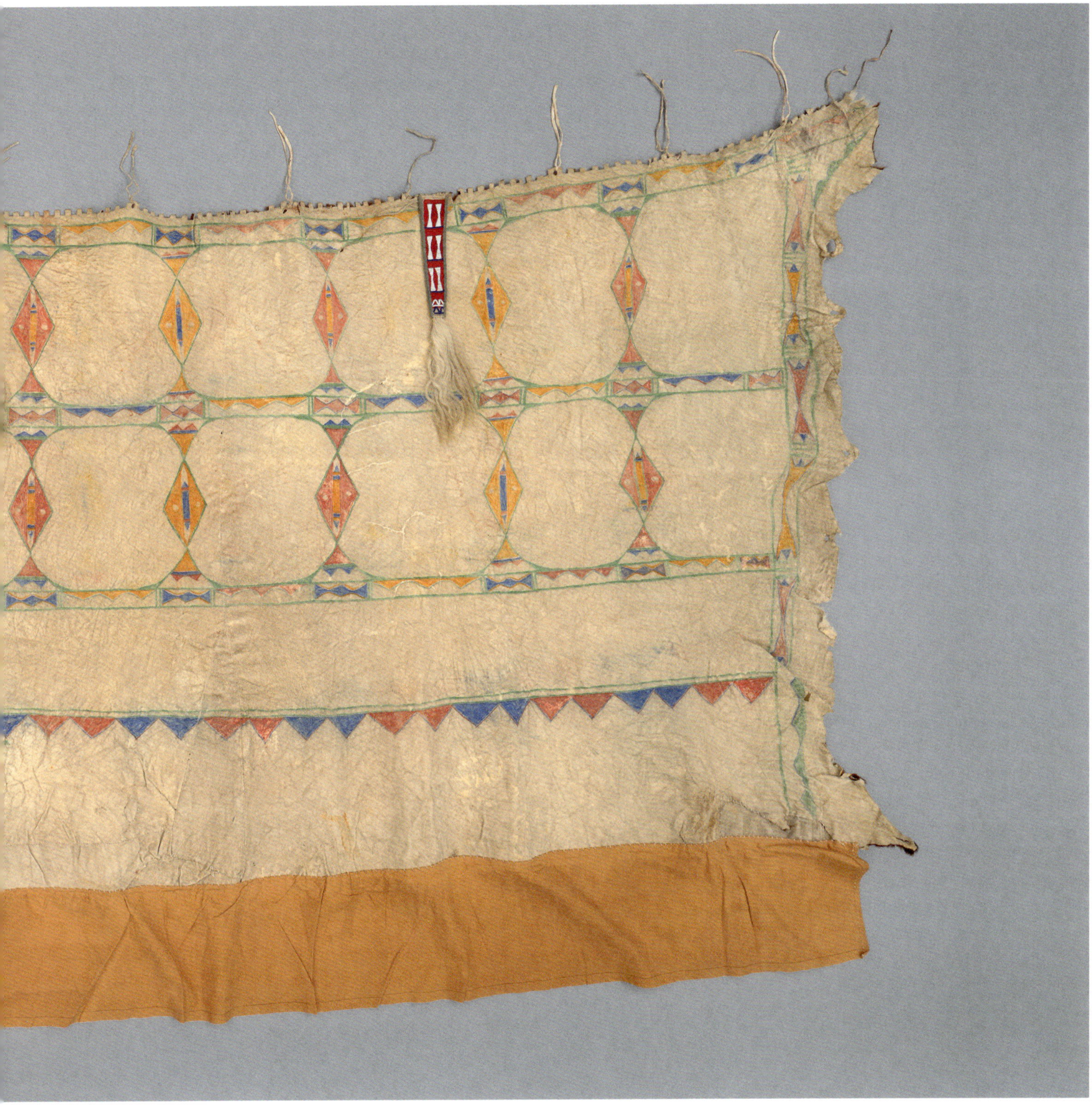

The designs painted on liners often reflect personal stories of the owner. While we do not know the meaning of this design, the quality, condition, and date of the liner suggest it may have been made for show. For many years, Amskaapii Pikanii families camped at the entrance of Glacier National Park at East Glacier where they met tourists and dignitaries arriving on the Great Northern Railway. Perhaps it was used in a context like this.

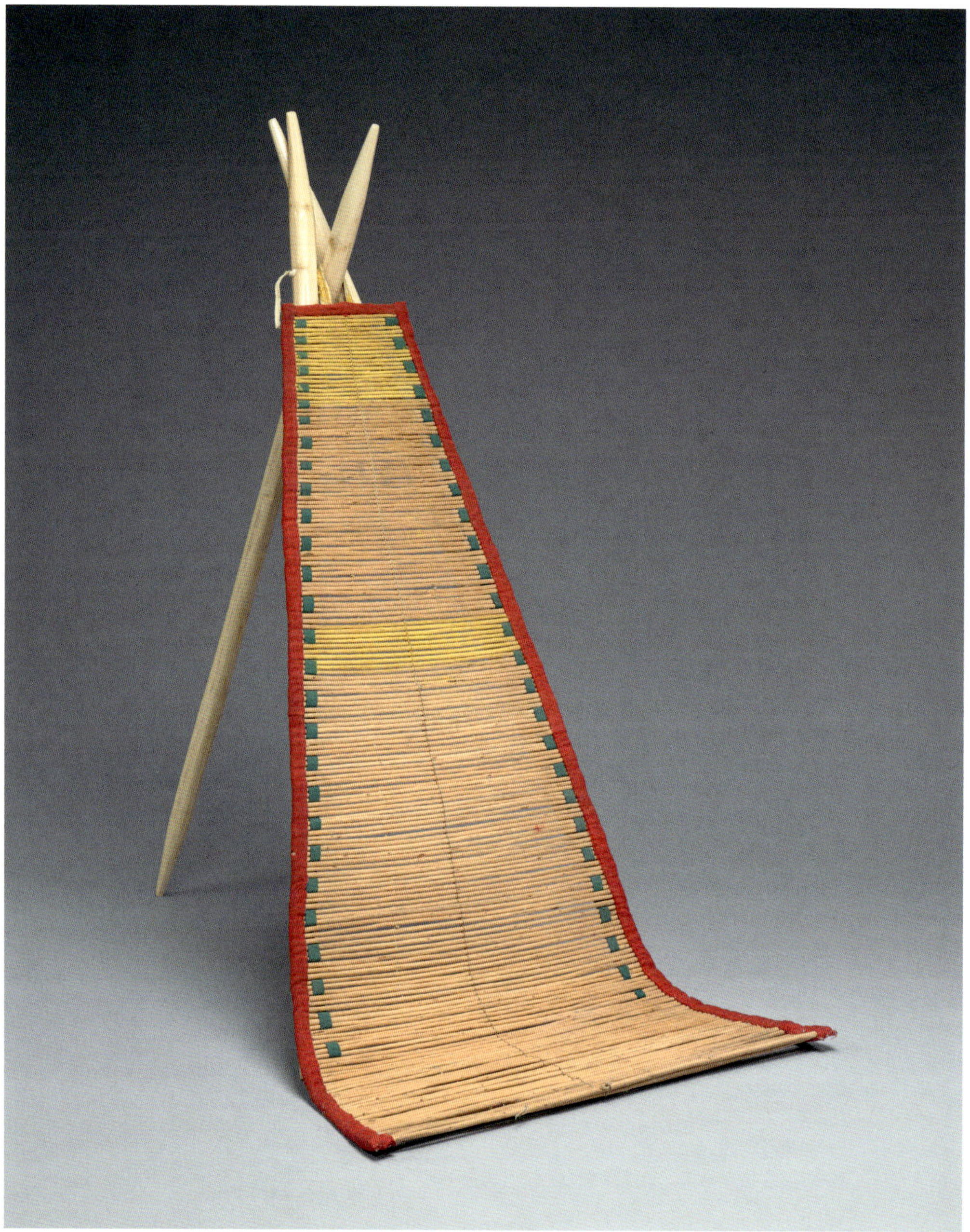

Both willow backrests in this exhibition exhibition probably date to the mid- to late 1800s. A loop at the top of the backrest hooks around the peak of a sturdy tripod, and the backrest flows to the ground for ease of sitting and resting. Such backrests were quickly dismantled, rolled up, and easily transported. Typically, two backrests were set up at the back of a lodge, in front of the *paaniikataanssii* (chief's liner; see cat. 39) and across from the lodge door, which always faced east. The husband and his *oopiitaam* ("sits beside woman," or first wife) each had a backrest. The husband's faced north and the first wife's south. In the Nitsitapii worldview, women and men share equal status and thus sit beside each other to reflect a balance of power and mutual respect.

Traditionally, men often had more than one wife, and marriages were arranged strategically for prestige and social stability. The first wife was the manager of the other wives and had to ensure that all work was done well. Women owned, designed, created, moved, and set up the lodge. If a woman became dissatisfied with her husband and wished to separate, she set his moccasins outside the door of her lodge—a sign that he should find a new home.

Cat. 40

Kainai artist
Backrest
1800s
Wood, cloth, and pigment
54¾ × 31½ in.
Denver Art Museum: Native Arts acquisition funds, 1936.251

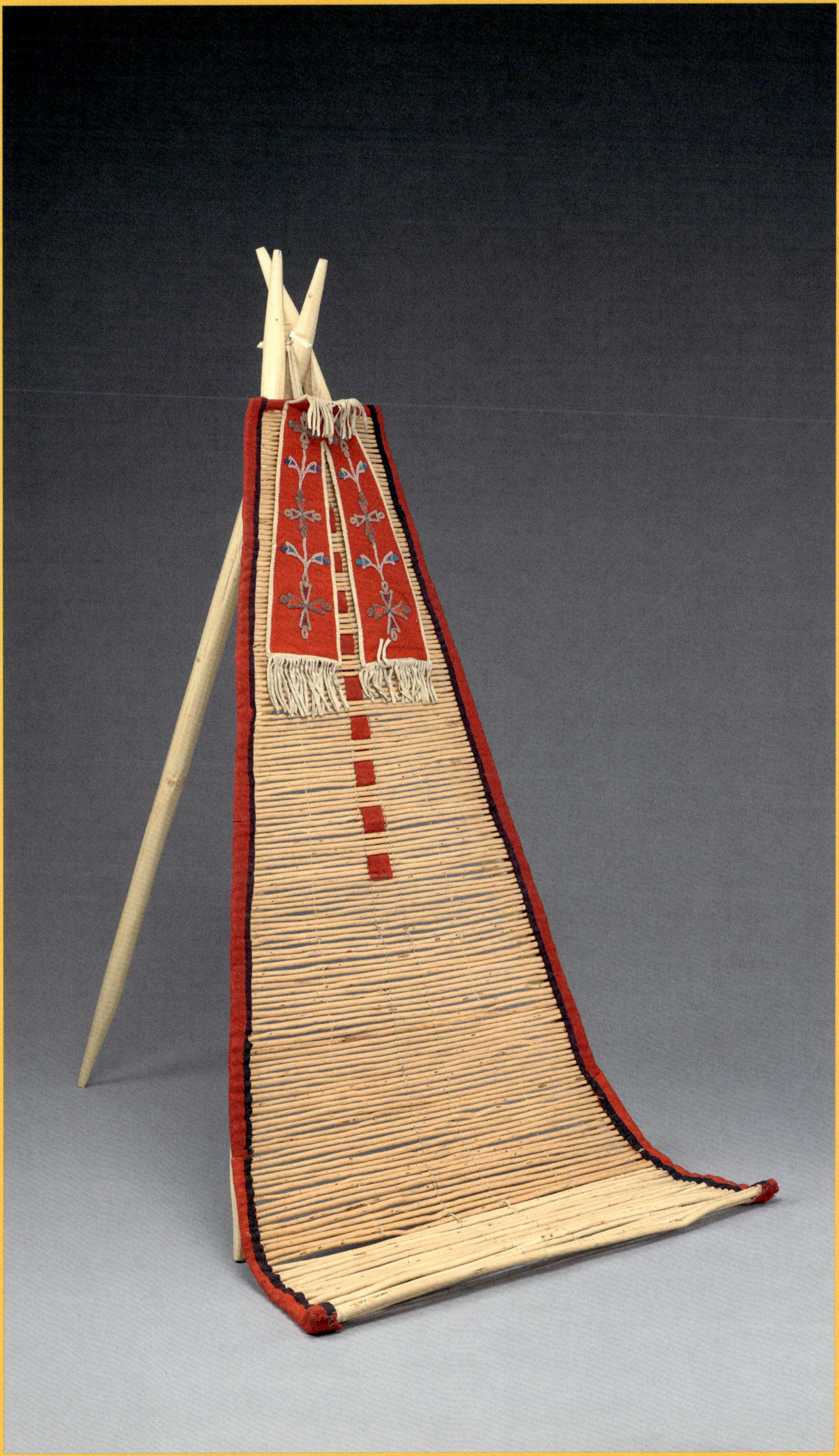

Cat. 41

Amskaapii Pikanii artist
Backrest
1885
Salix willow rods, paint, wool, cotton, real and artificial sinew, and beads
57¾ × 33¾ in.
Denver Art Museum: Native Arts acquisition funds, 1938.321

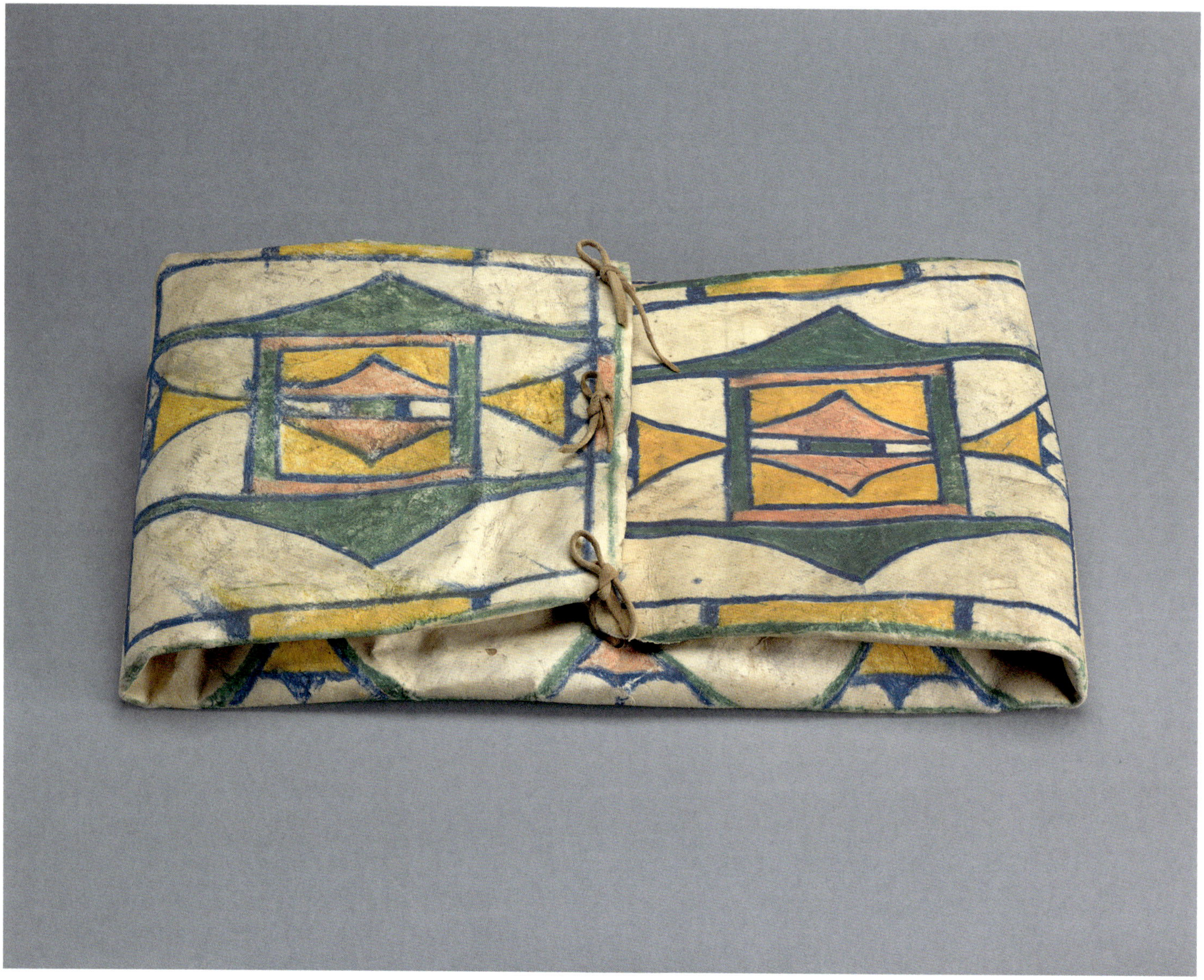

Cat. 42

Amskaapii Pikanii artist
Parfleche
1885
Processed rawhide and paint
22¼ × 12½ × 3½ in.
Denver Art Museum: Native Arts acquisition funds, 1937.200

These folded, rawhide containers often stored clothing, dried meat, roots, berries, or medicine bundles of sacred objects and made traveling easier as the Amskaapii Pikanii moved camp over the course of the year. Select women skillfully decorated parfleches. To seal the pigments onto the hide, women painted it when it was wet and finished it with a glue-like substance derived from the yellow inside of a prickly pear cactus. Parfleches were valuable presents at intertribal gift exchanges. They quickly spread across Plains cultures and inspired stylistic exchange. The painted interior, uniform outlines, and symmetrical isosceles triangles identify this parfleche as Nitsitapii.

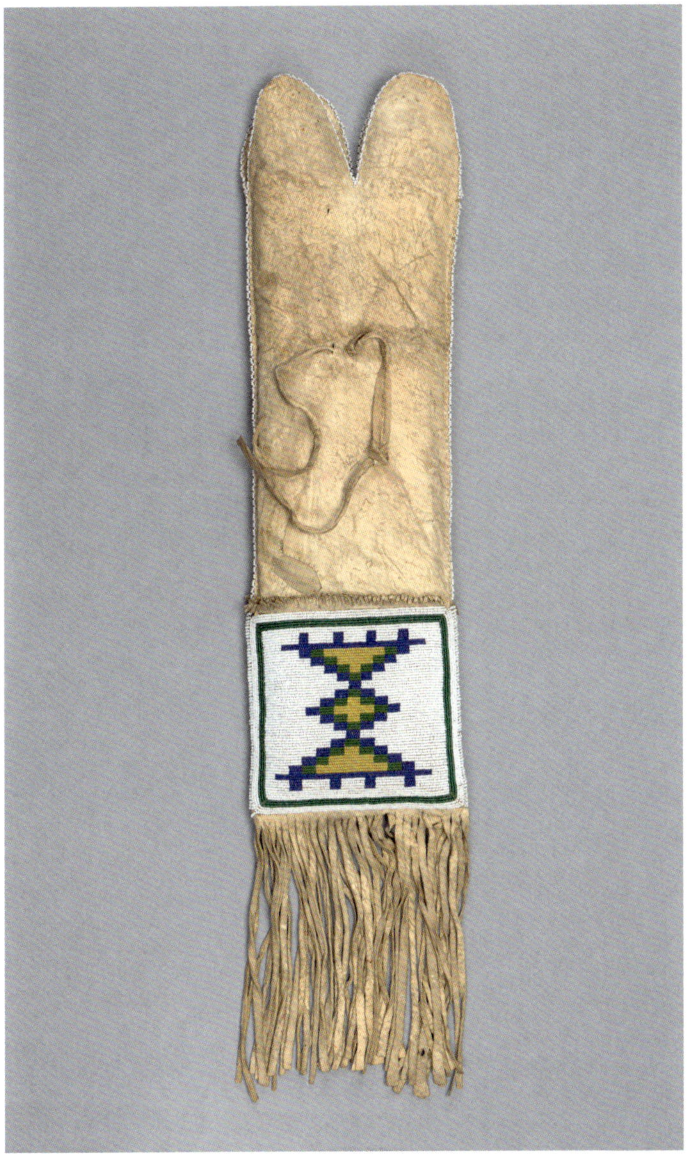

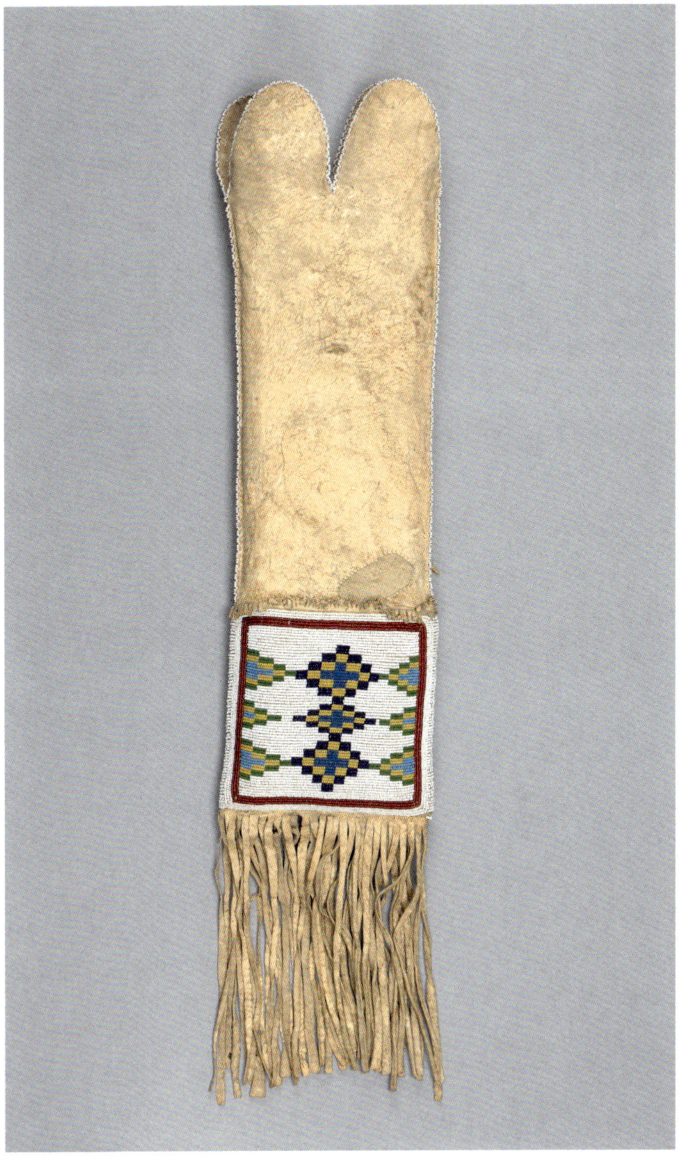

Cat. 43

Amskaapii Pikanii artist
Ah'kooyiinimaatsis (Pipe Bag)
(front and back)
Late 1800s
Leather and beads
27½ × 6½ × 1½ in.
Denver Art Museum: Gift of Dr.
Charles J. Norton, 1982.86

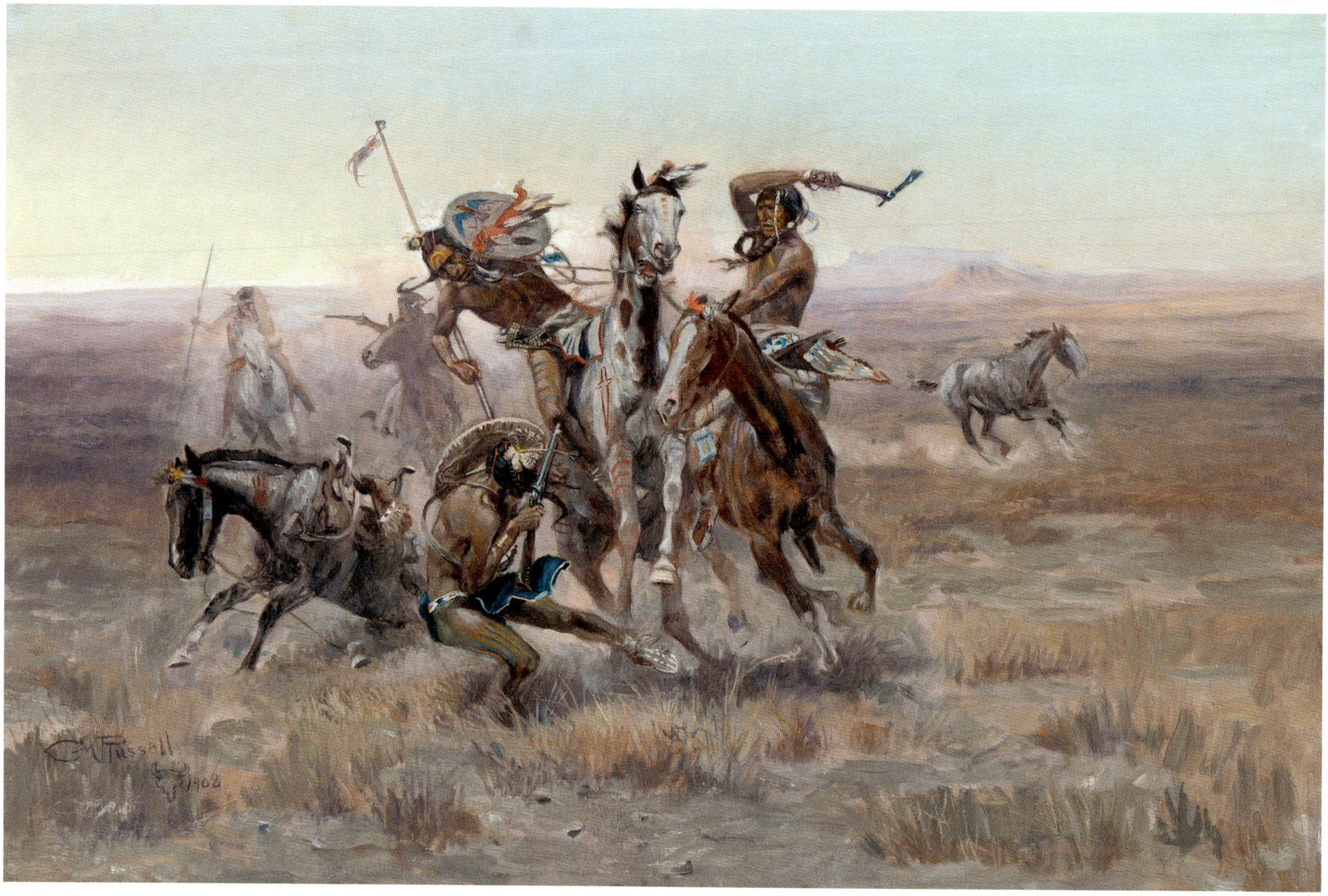

Russell worked out the composition for *When Blackfeet and Sioux Meet* in clay when he modeled *Counting Coup* in 1905 (cat. 45). In both works, he focused the drama on a tight composition of men and horses exploding out from the central focus: a Nitsitapii man counting coup on the Očhéthi Šakówiŋ man below him. Counting coup—here, touching an enemy with a coup stick—reflected masculine values of courage, bravery, strength, and honor. The subject might have been inspired by stories Russell heard among the Kainai (Blood Tribe) in Canada during his 1888 visit, perhaps from Apskinas (born Kainai, adopted and raised Siksikaa, enrolled with Tsuut'ina Nation).

Cat. 44

Charles Marion Russell
When Blackfeet and Sioux Meet
1908
Oil on canvas
Framed: 27½ × 37¼ × 3¼ in.
Sid Richardson Museum

While Russell seemed aware of some details of Indigenous life and experience, he frequently painted women's saddles on men's horses, as seen on the riderless horse on the left. Women's saddles had high pommels and cantles to hold travois, parfleches, and other family items. Men typically rode on small pad saddles. The structure of a woman's saddle in a situation like this would have caused more harm than good. Russell repeated this quirk throughout many compositions, which may be due to artistic preference at the expense of accuracy.

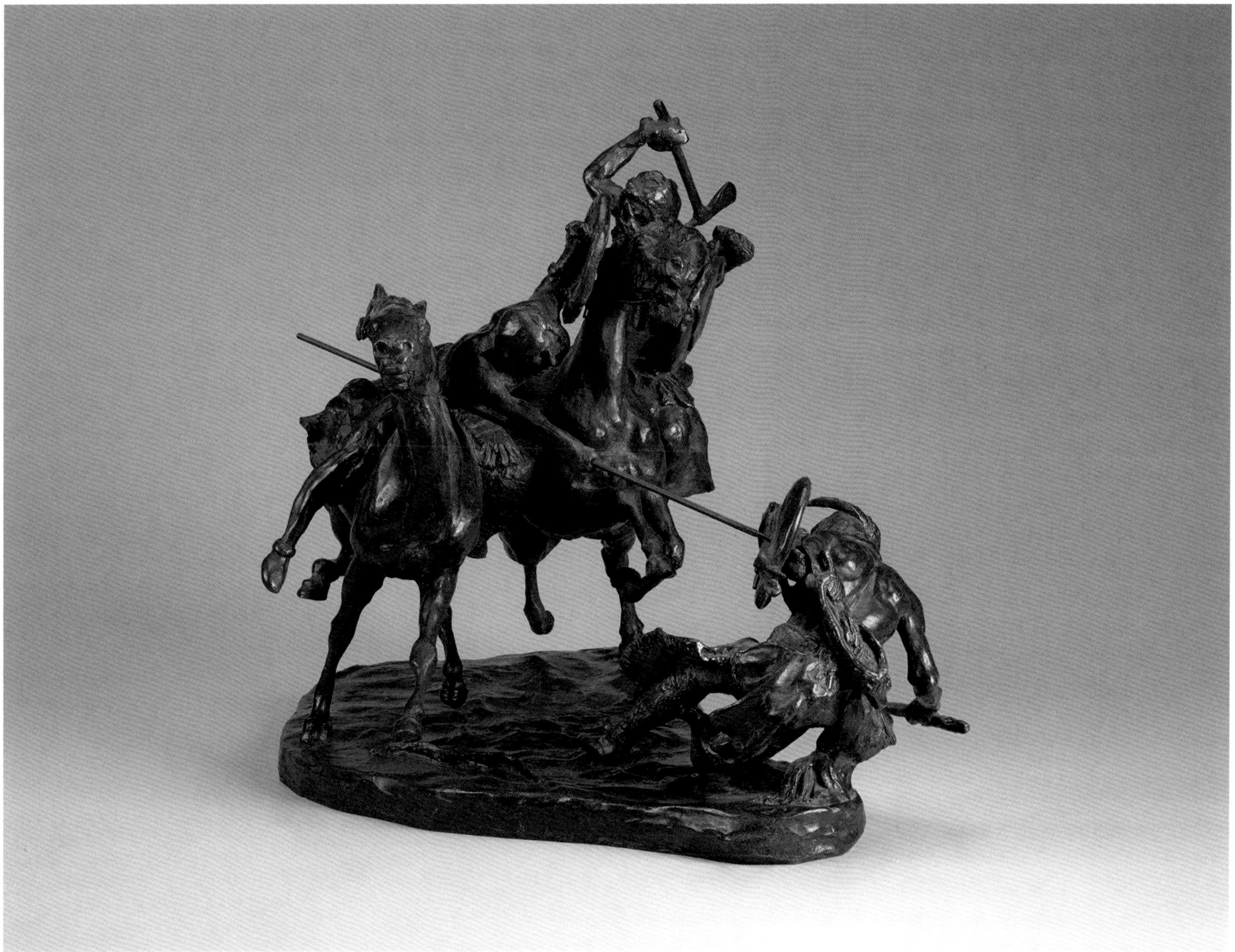

Cat. 45

Charles Marion Russell
Counting Coup
1905
Bronze
13¼ × 17 × 14 in.
Petrie Collection, Denver, Colorado

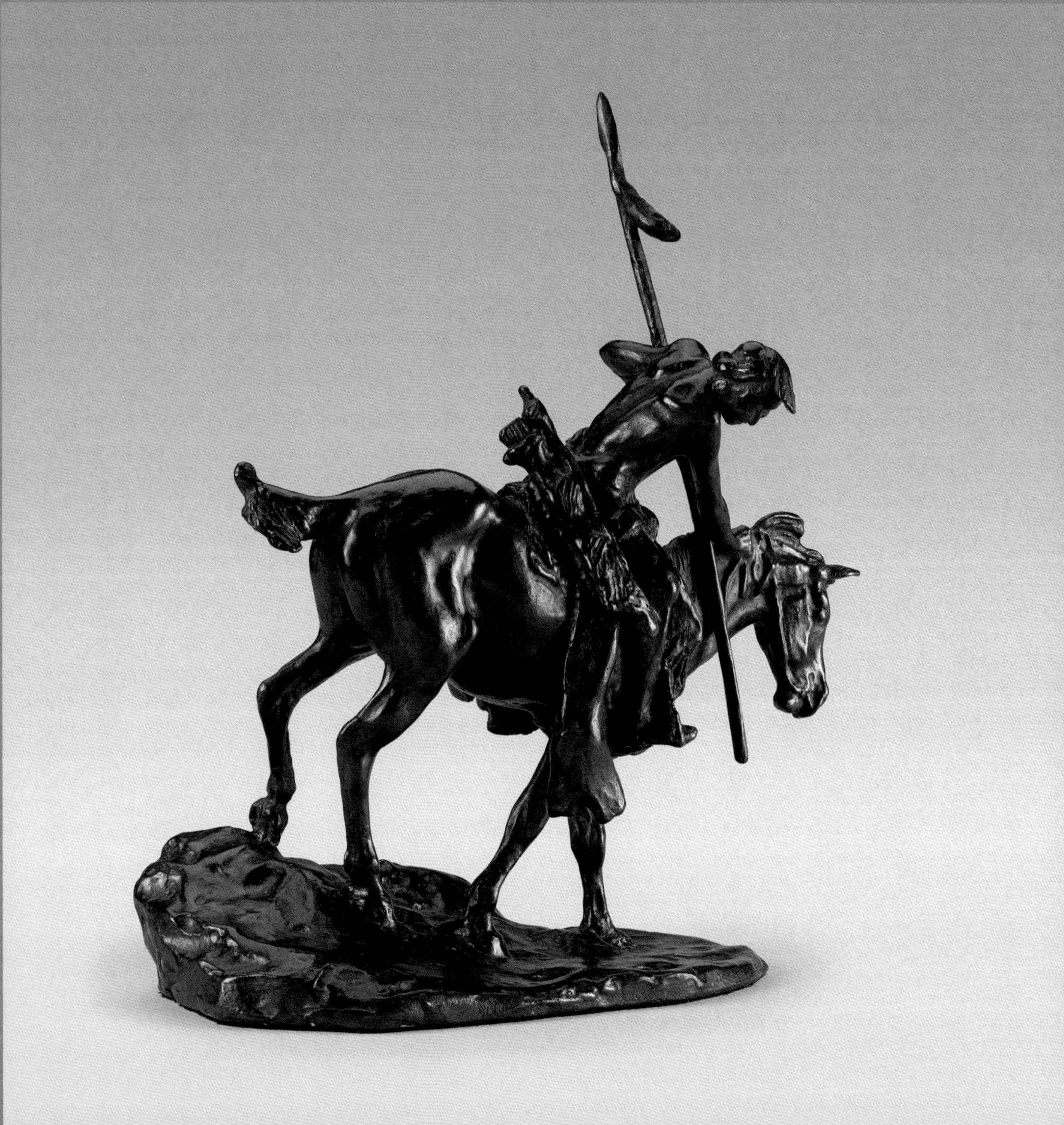

Cat. 46

Charles Marion Russell
The Enemy's Tracks
1920
Bronze
11¾ × 10¾ × 5½ in.
Petrie Collection, Denver, Colorado

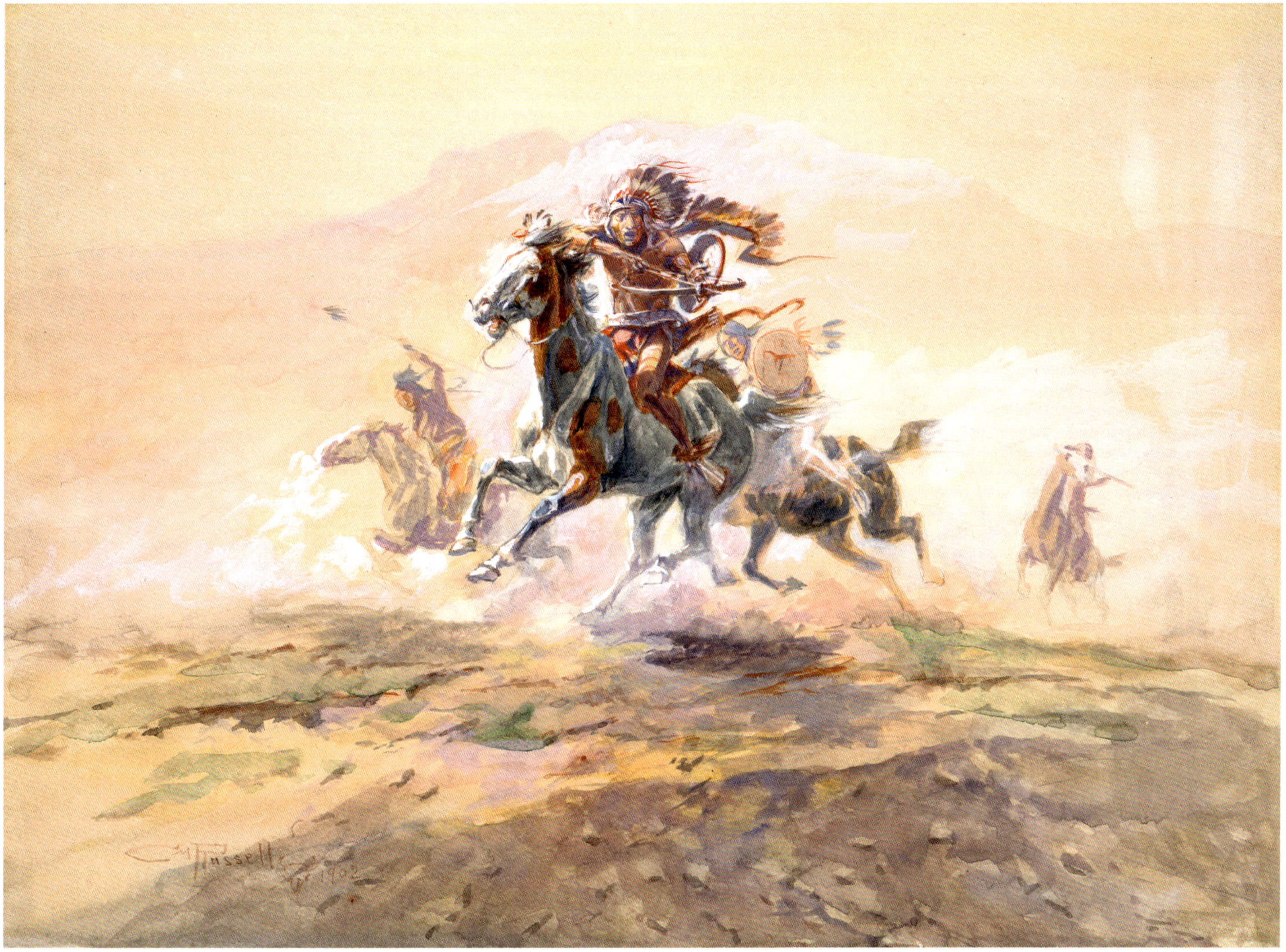

Cat. 47

Charles Marion Russell
When Arrows Spelled Death
1902
Watercolor on paper
Framed: 21 × 26¾ in.
Buffalo Bill Center of the West, Cody, Wyoming. Gift of Charles Ulrick and Josephine Bay Foundation, Inc. 97.60

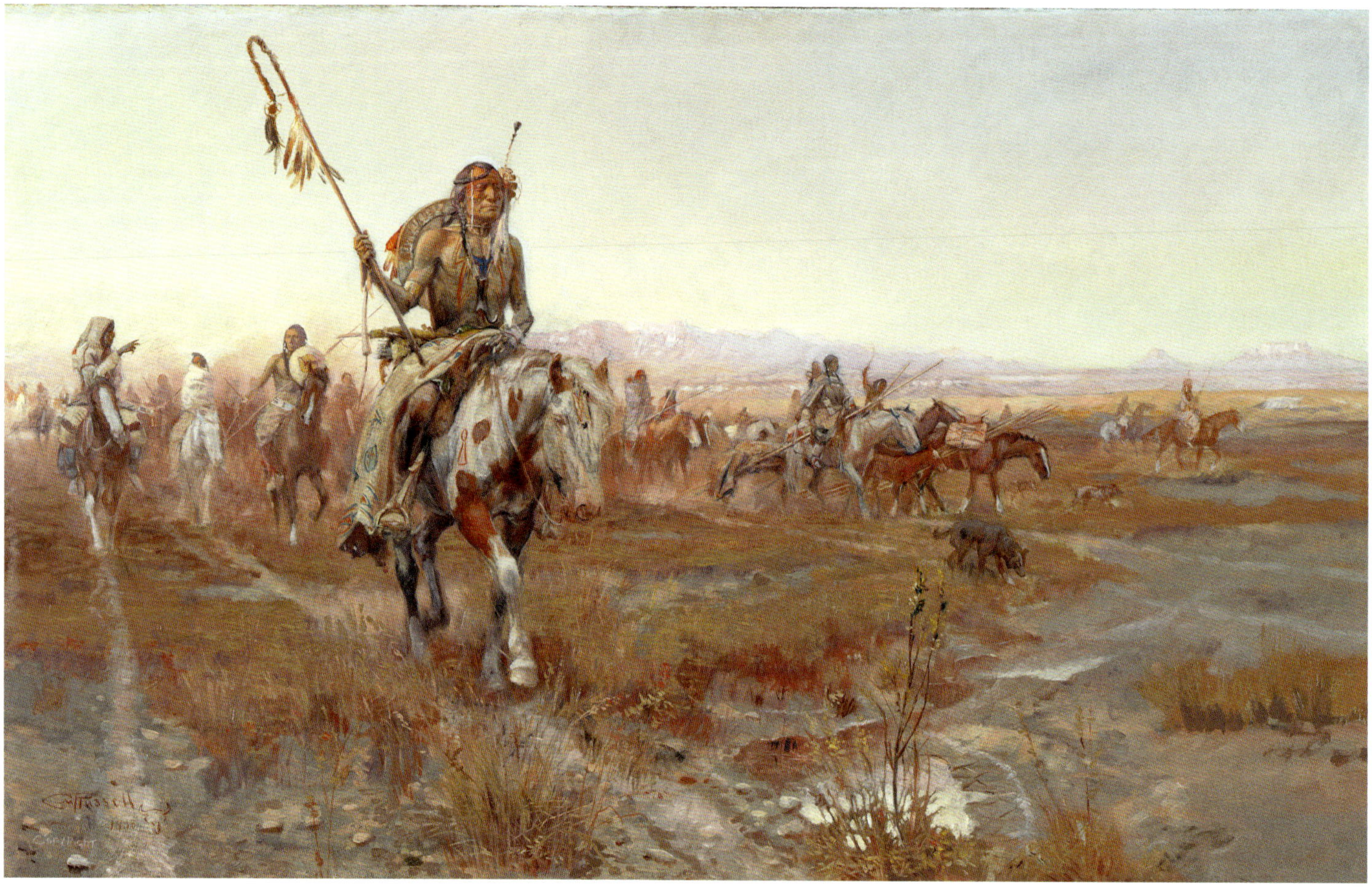

In a 1911 letter, Russell explained that, here, he depicted a Blackfeet group led by a medicine man (*natoowaapinaa* in Nitsiipowah'sin, the Blackfoot language), who speaks with spirits and animals and is responsible for directing the movement of his people. Russell identified the landscape as the Judith River Basin with the Highwood Mountains and Haystack and Steamboat Buttes in the distance. Given the autumnal hue of the painting, Russell could be depicting the journey to fall hunting grounds. Scouts would ride ahead, with warriors at the flanks and rear of the main group led by the natoowaapinaa. The man's face and body paint and accoutrements would have signified the societies to which he belonged. On the left of the composition, a man wearing a capote (see cat. 8) speaks in Plains Indian Sign Language. On the right, a woman on a white horse wears a dress similar to the one worn and modeled by Josephine Wright (cat. 34) in the painting *In the Wake of the Buffalo Runners* (cat. 33; see Emily Burns's essay in this volume).

For the Nitsitapii, the visible world is only a small dimension of the universe, which includes the parallel realms of the Above world, Below world, and Water world. Humans seek out supernatural allies to change and control natural elements, such as the weather. "Medicine man" is a general phrase used by English speakers to refer to an individual knowledgeable about supernatural relationships and power. Within Nitsitapii culture, a natoowaapinaa is identified by these relationships and his sacred bundles and pipes. He is a healer but much more than a medical doctor, as his medicine is both natural and supernatural. While the phrase "medicine man" is useful for outsiders, it glosses over the complexity of Nitsitapii spirituality and cultural protocol.

Cat. 48

Charles Marion Russell
The Medicine Man
1908
Oil on canvas
30 × 48⅛ in.
Amon Carter Museum of American Art, Fort Worth, Texas, Amon G. Carter Collection, 1961.171

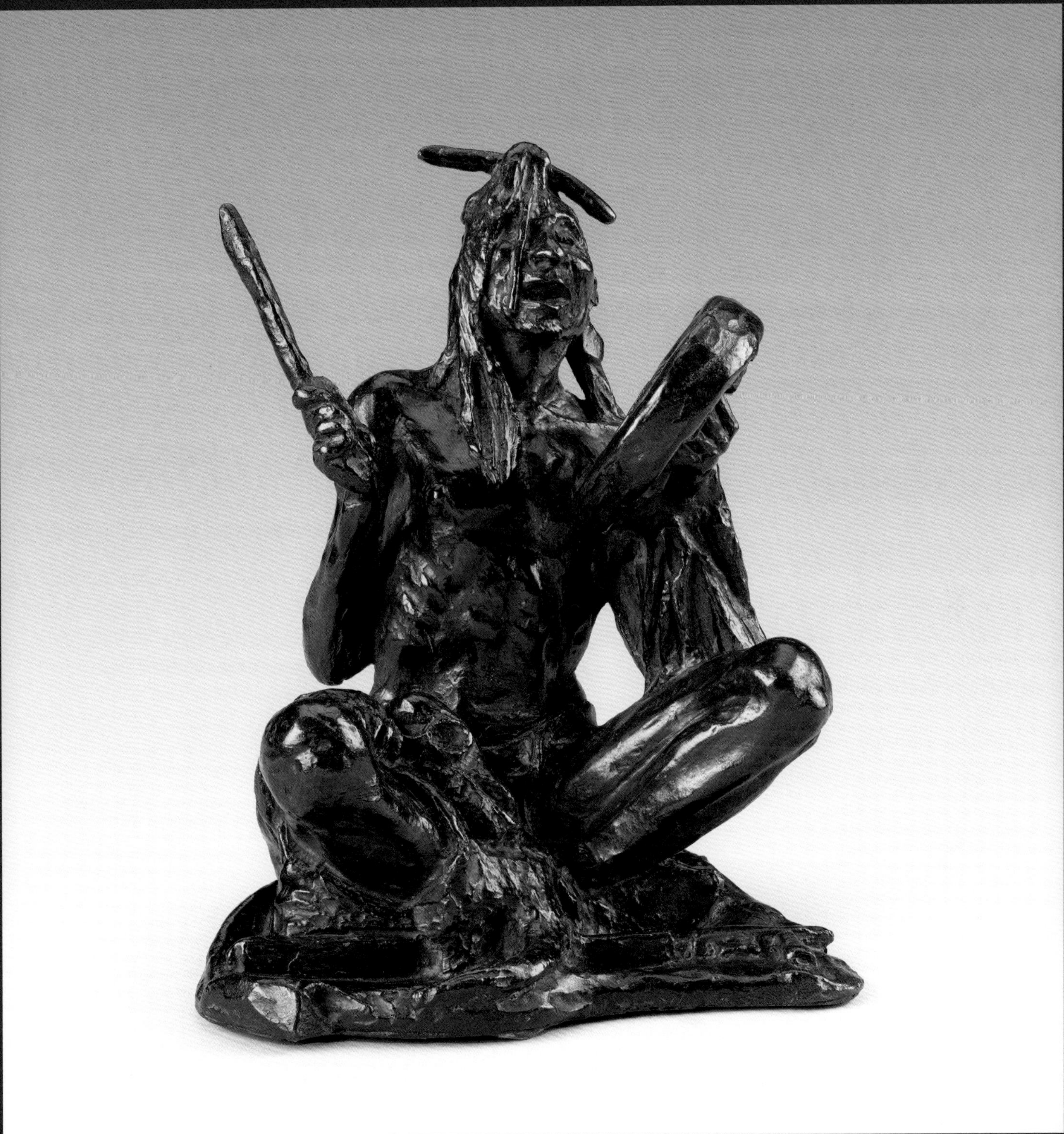

Cat. 49

Charles Marion Russell
The Medicine Man
1920
Bronze
7 × 6 × 5 in.
Petrie Collection, Denver, Colorado

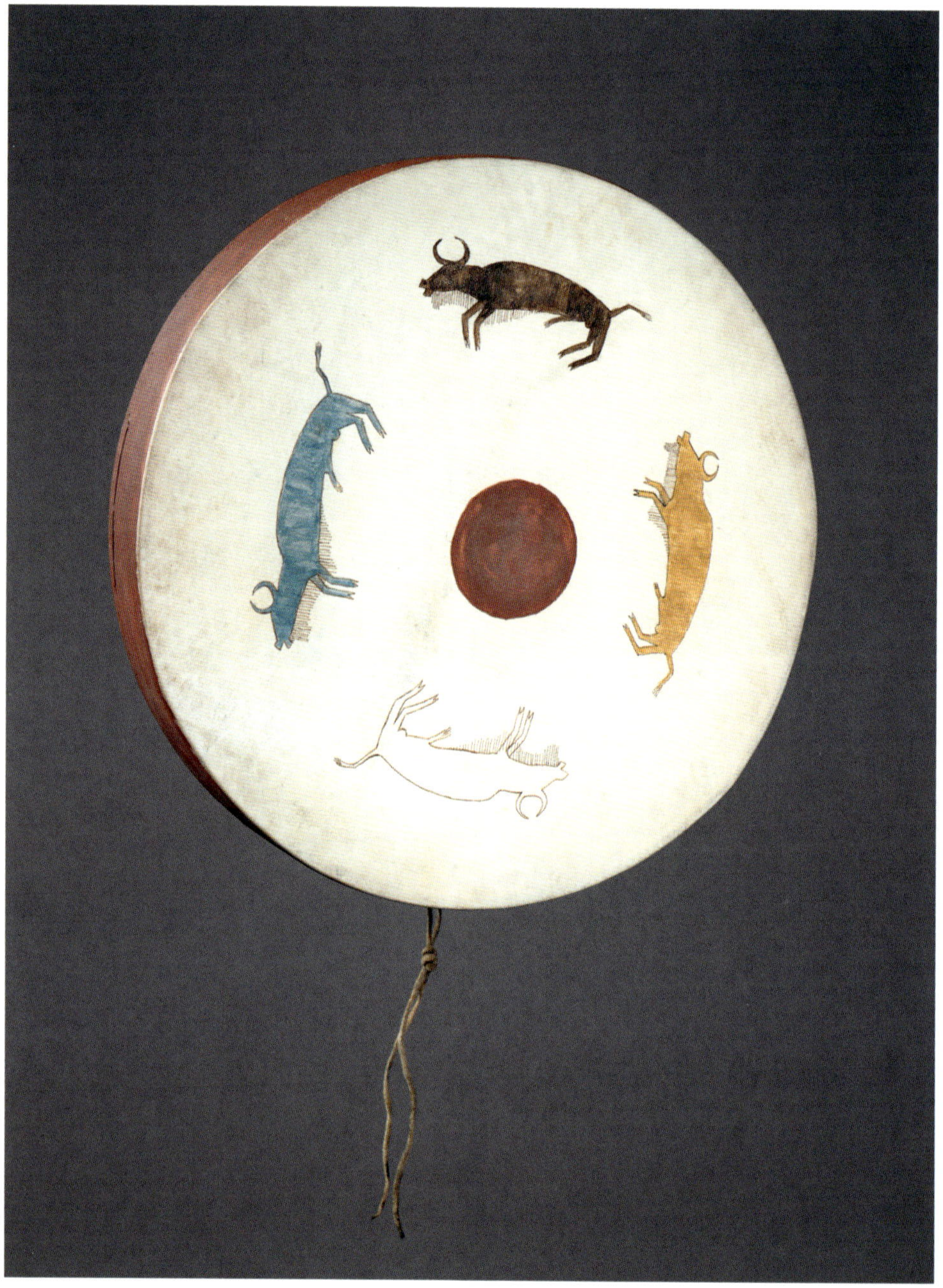

Cat. 50

Amskaapii Pikanii artist
Aistookiimaaksi (Hand Drum)
Before 1860
Leather, paint, wood, and ink
30¼ × 40¾ × 2 in. dia.
The L. D. and Ruth Bax Collection at the Denver Art Museum, 1985.245

Aistookiimaaksi (hand drums) provide a rhythmic foundation that unites songs and rituals performed in ceremonial, social, and personal contexts. Drums externalize a universal heartbeat which begins in the womb and connects all forms of life. The designs painted on them are personal to the maker, leading to a diversity of styles and subjects across instruments. This one centers a dark red sun flanked by four silhouetted buffalo—images that may have come to the maker in a dream. The dramatic contrast between the stark white, dusky yellow, earthy brown, and stormy blue of the buffalo reflects traditional Nitsitapii teachings about seasonal change.

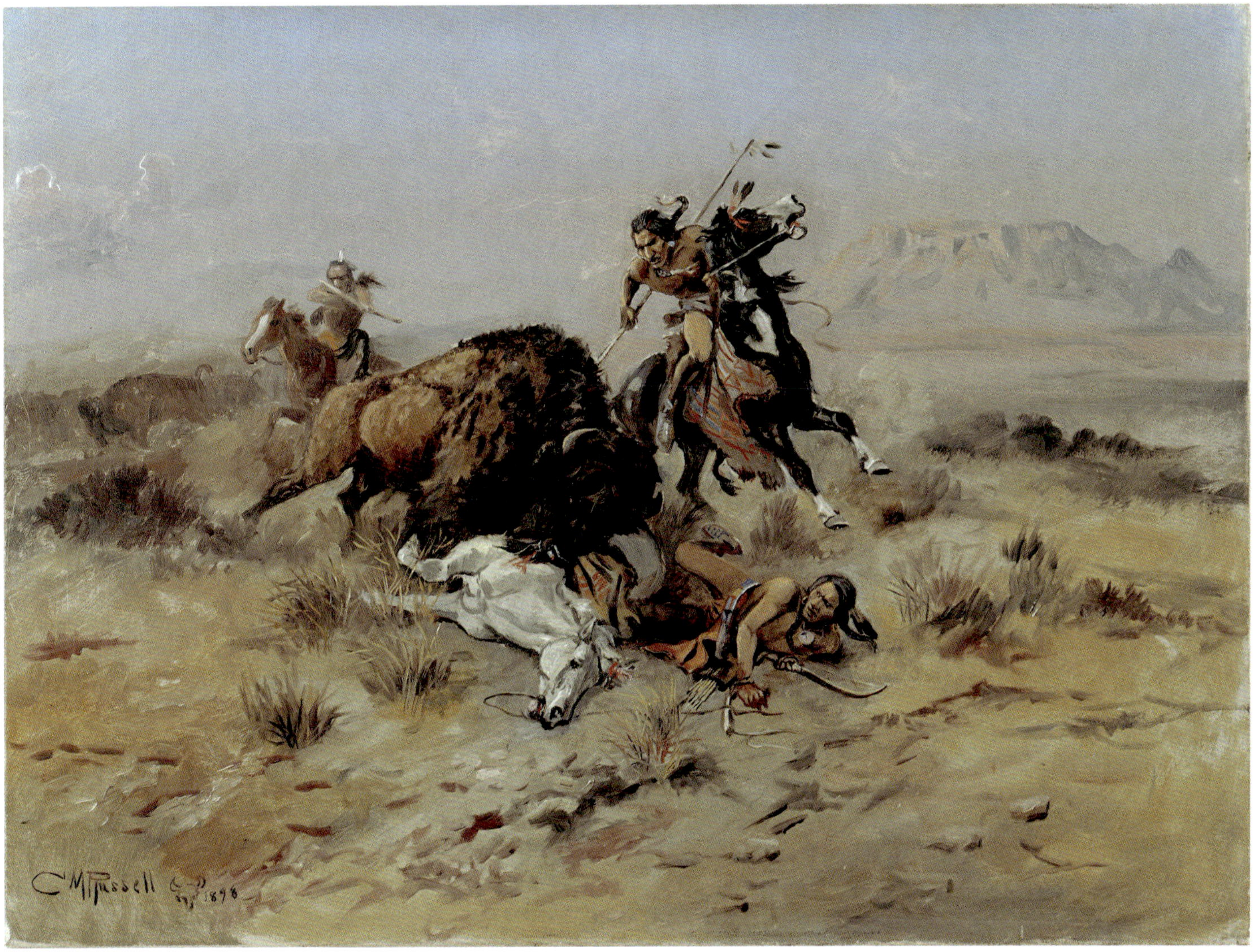

Cat. 51

Charles Marion Russell
Buffalo Hunt
1898
Oil on canvas
18⅛ × 25⅜ in.
Denver Art Museum: Gift of Sharon Magness, 1997.517

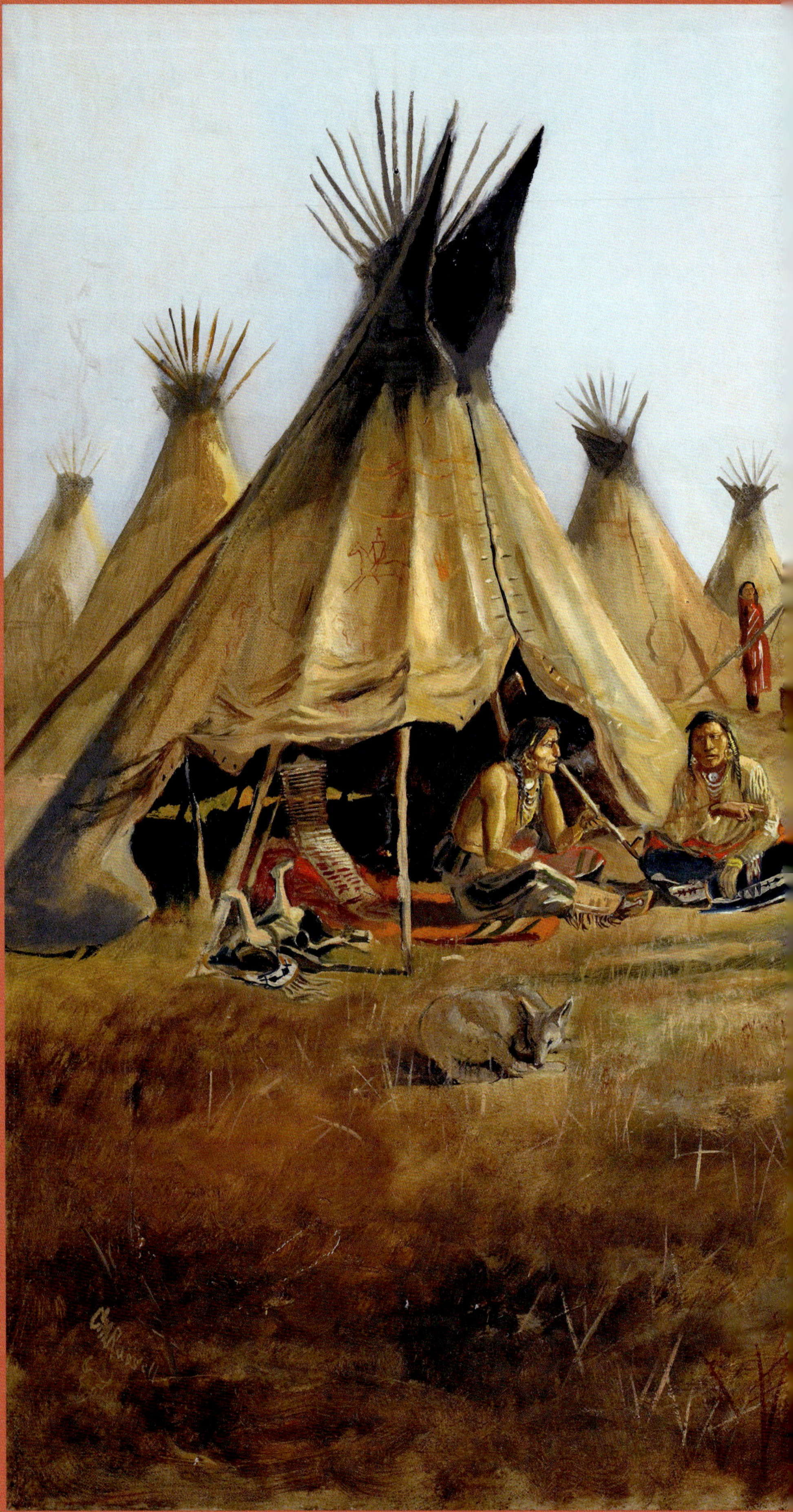

Cat. 52

Charles Marion Russell
The Silk Robe
1890
Oil on canvas
Framed: 34¾ × 46¼ × 2½ in.
Amon Carter Museum of American Art, Fort Worth, Texas, Amon G. Carter Collection, 1961.135

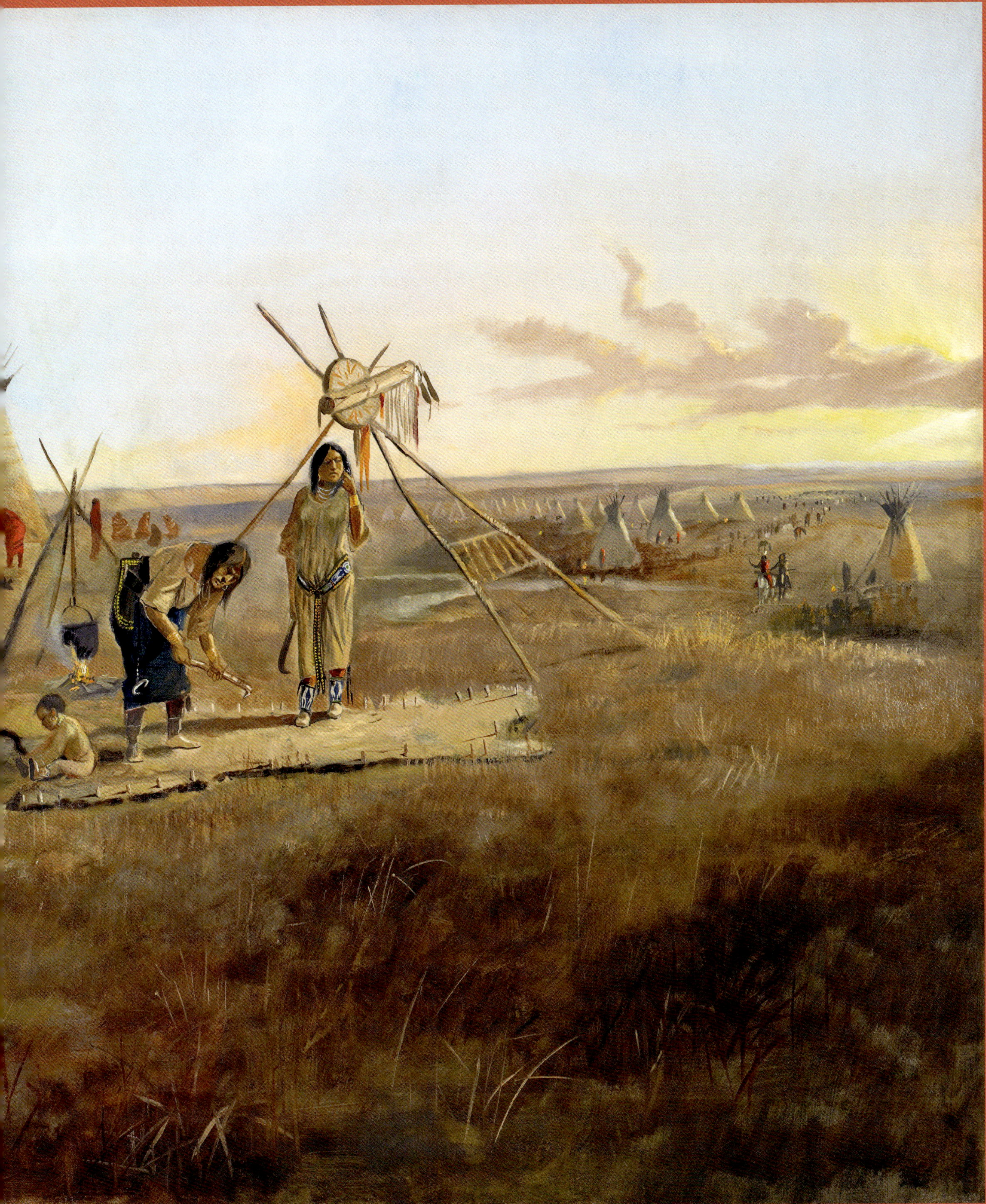

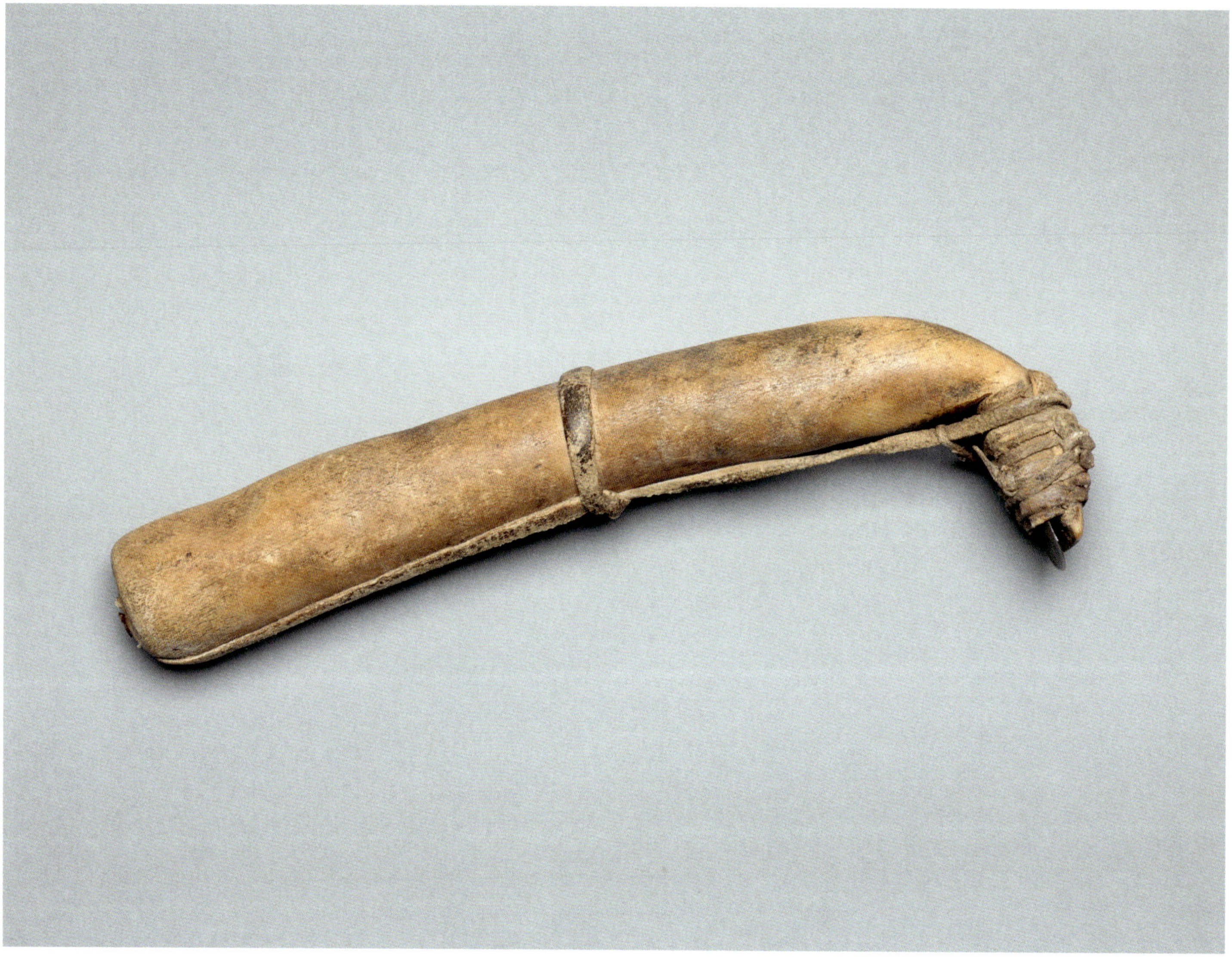

Turning buffalo hides into soft, pliable robes was arduous work undertaken by Nitsitapii women. First, the tanner removed scraps of meat and fat from a rawhide using a fleshing tool (cats. 54 and 55). Next, she laced the hide into a lodgepole frame, which held it taught until it dried. Then, she stood on the smooth (hairless) side of the hide and, with a steel-bladed elk-antler scraper like this one, chipped the hide to around half of its original thickness. She then rubbed the hide with grease, followed by a mixture of boiled liver and brains. Folded and rolled up, the hide rested for a few days as the liver and brain mixture neutralized any remaining natural glue. Finally, she firmly rubbed the hide against an upright, stretched rawhide thong until it became soft, pliable, and saleable.

Often passed down from mother to daughter, hide processing tools had to be well made, highly durable, and well-kept to stand up to years of such labor. This scraper's elk-antler handle may be much older than its metal blade acquired through trade. The serrated-edged fleshing tools in this exhibition also feature signs of age and human modification. One is made of a long bone with joint at the end, which is wrapped with a rawhide handle (cat. 54). A metal flesher might be made from a railroad spike, its sharp end flattened (cat. 55). Wrapped tightly in cloth, it also features an attached cloth suspender that may have added leverage and served as a hanging device.

Cat. 53

Amskaapii Pikanii artist
Scraper
1800s
Antler, metal, rawhide, and a screw
13⅜ × 4¼ × 2⅛ in.
Denver Art Museum: Native Arts acquisition funds, 1938.326

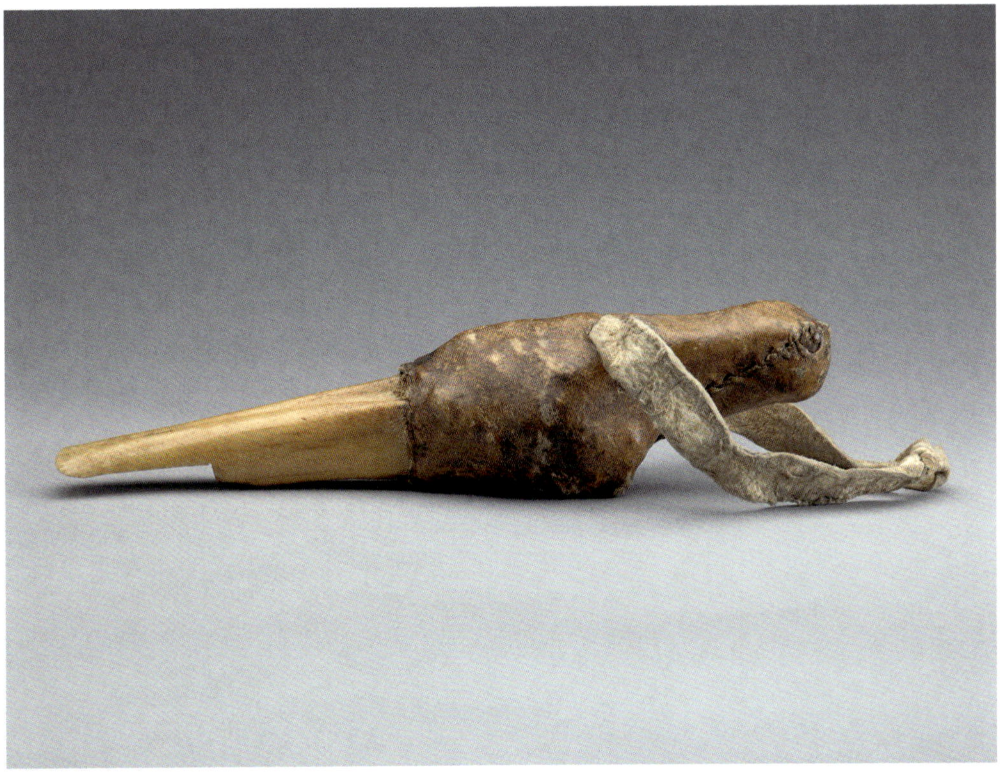

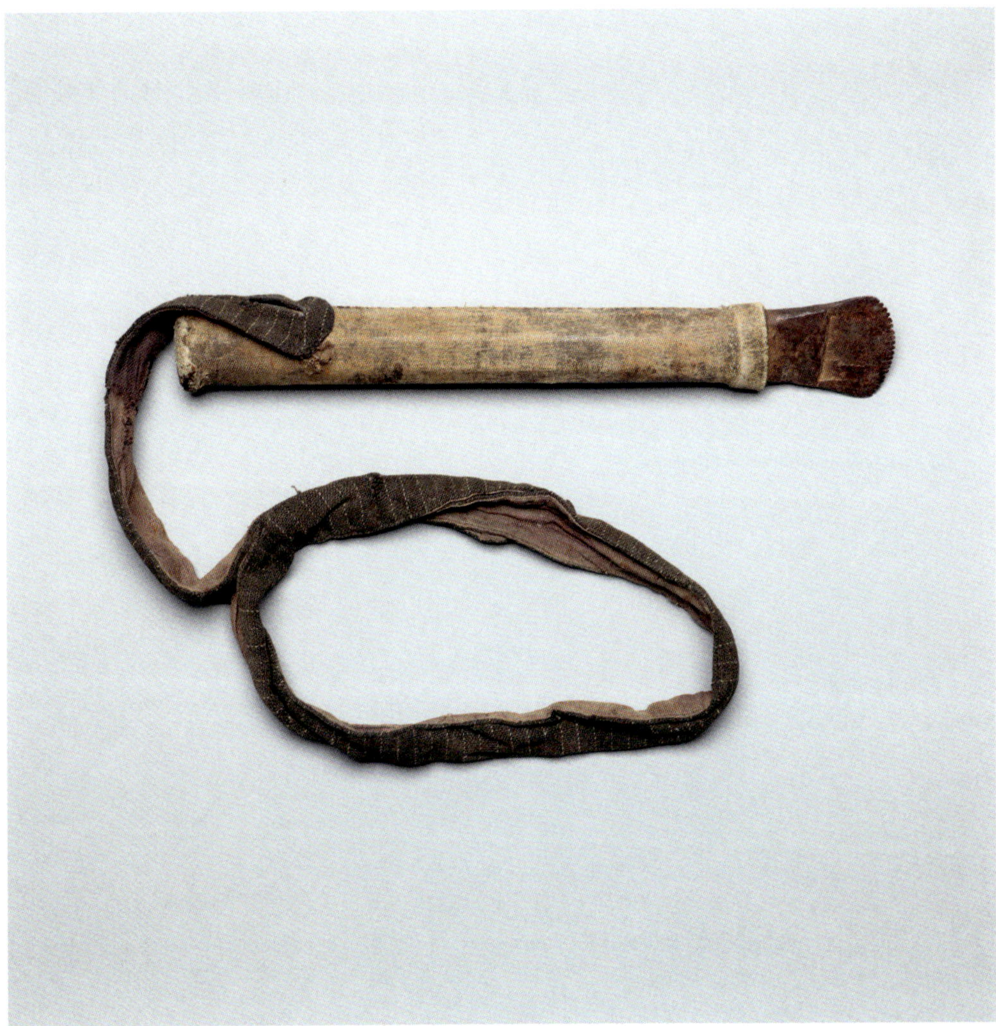

Cat. 54

Amskaapii Pikanii artist
Hide Fleshing Tool
Before 1860
Bone, rawhide, fabric, sinew, and thread
30¼ × 40¾ × 2 in.
Denver Art Museum: Native Arts acquisition funds, 1938.301

Cat. 55

Amskaapii Pikanii artist
Hide Fleshing Tool
Mid-1800s
Hide, iron, and cloth
11⅝ × 1½ × 1⅞ in.
Denver Art Museum: Gift of Dr. Charles J. Norton, 1984.624

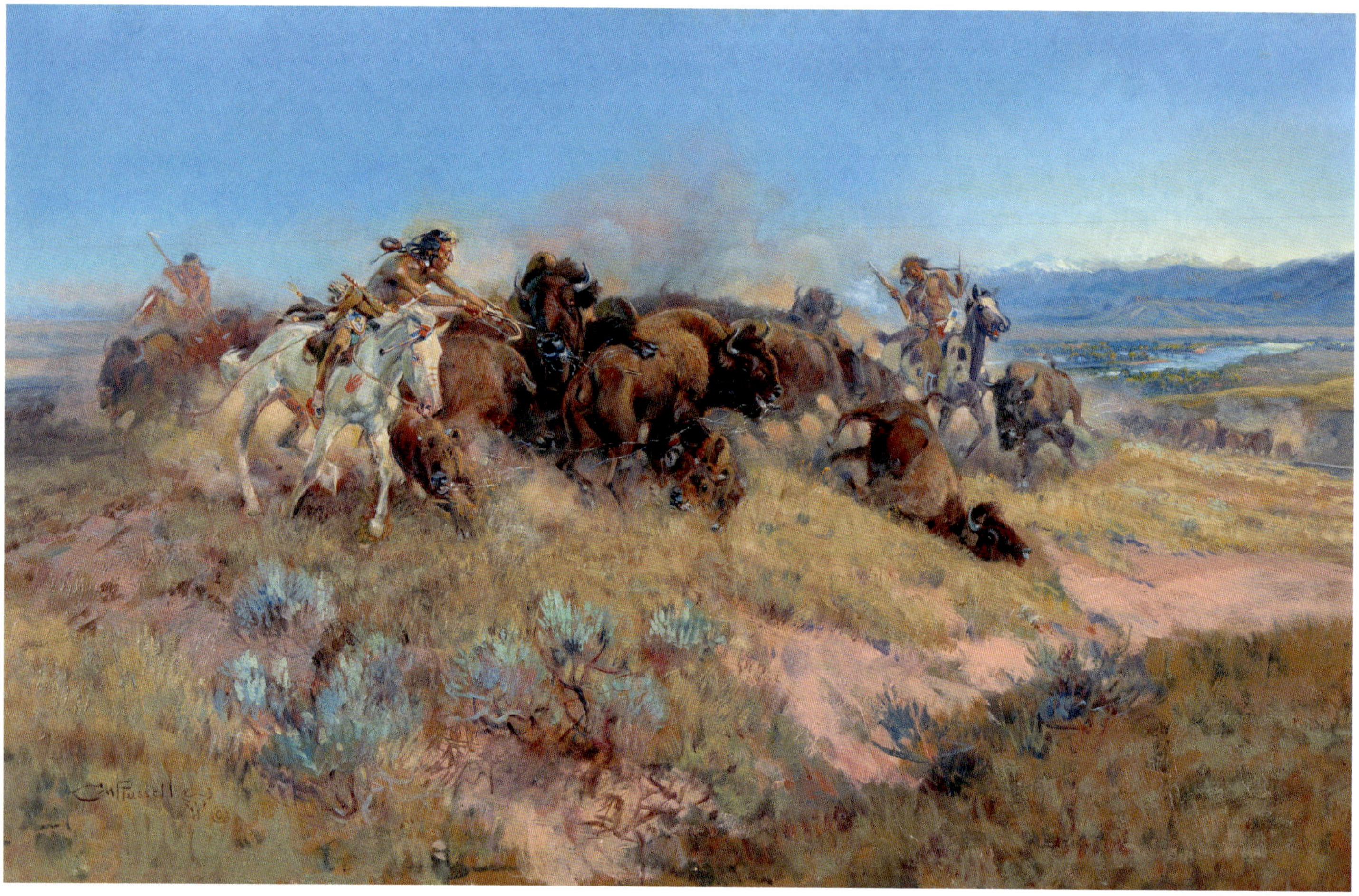

Cat. 56

Charles Marion Russell
Buffalo Hunt, Number 40
1919
Oil on canvas
Framed: 39 × 57¼ × 3½ in.
Petrie Collection, Denver, Colorado

While oral histories account for ancient horses among the Nitsitapii, the acquisition of horses in recent centuries transformed Nitsitapii society, allowing for territorial expansion and increased mobility. Most importantly, they revolutionized buffalo hunting. Horses were highly specialized, and *iinyookskasiiksi* (buffalo runners) were favored for hunting due to their superior speed. To augment their abilities, warriors painted personalized markings on their equine companions. Here, Russell painted a rosy circle around the white horse's eye, a design thought to enhance its vision amid rising dust and the chaos of hooves. Harmony between horse and warrior enabled successful buffalo hunts. To honor the buffalo's sacrifice, the Nitsitapii wasted no part of its body, which provided food, clothing, tools, and shelter.

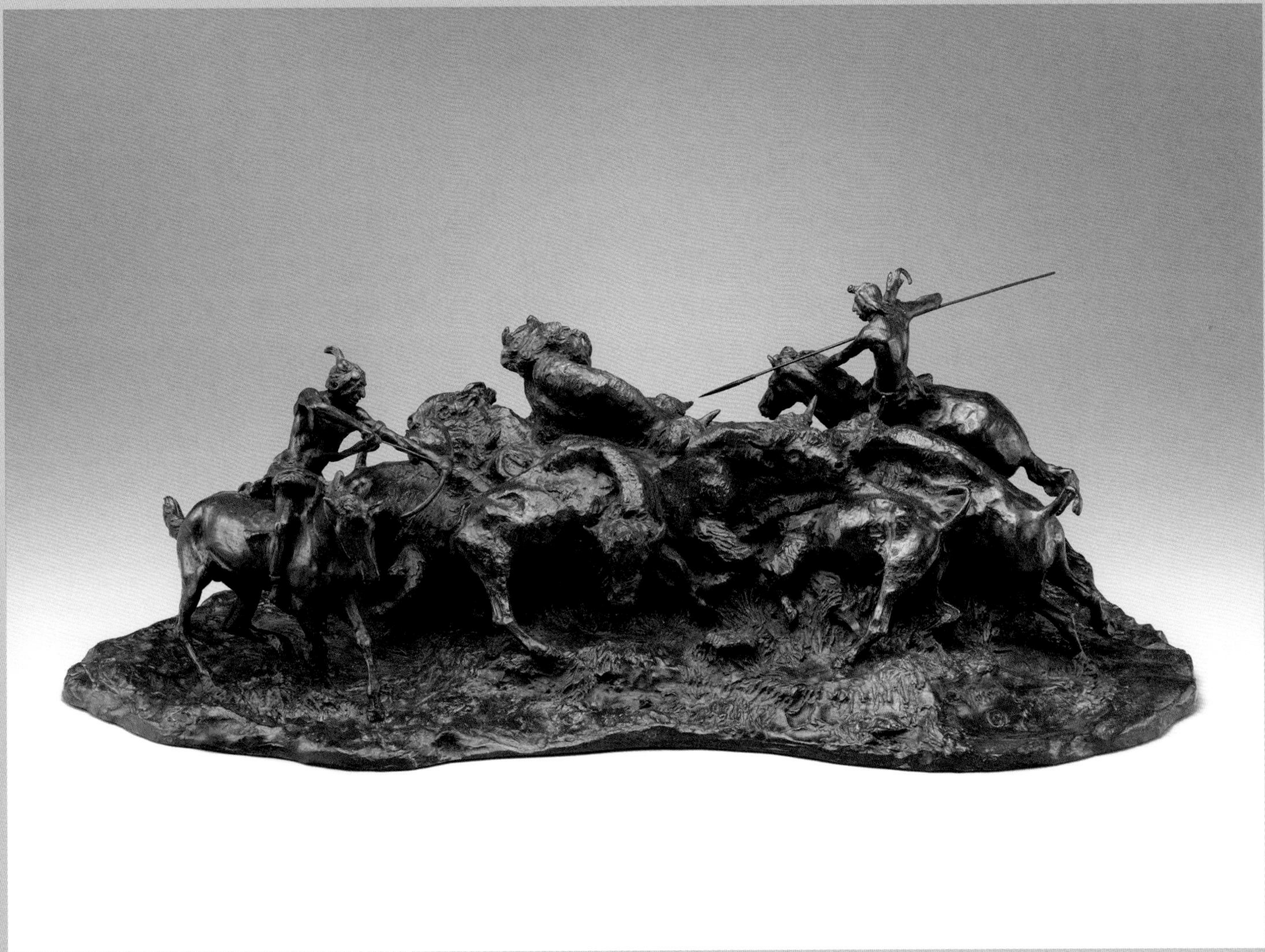

Cat. 57

Charles Marion Russell
Meat for Wild Men
1924
Bronze
11½ × 38½ × 23 in.
Petrie Collection, Denver, Colorado

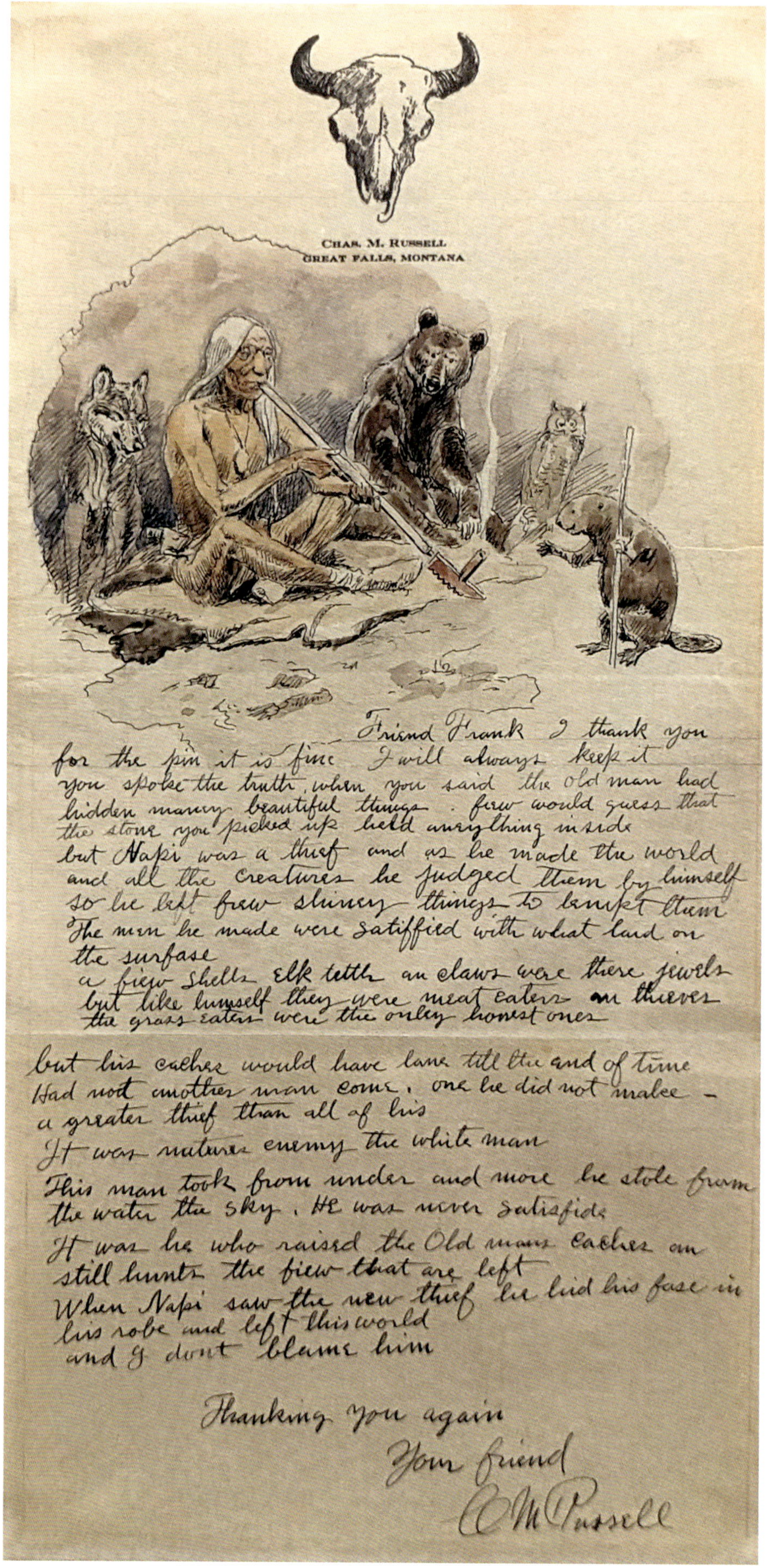

CHAS. M. RUSSELL
GREAT FALLS, MONTANA

Friend Frank I thank you
for the pin it is fine I will always keep it
you spoke the truth when you said the Old man had
hidden many beautiful things. fiew would guess that
the stone you picked up held anything inside
but Napi was a thief and as he made the world
and all the creatures he judged them by himself
so he left fiew shiney things to tempt them
The men he made were satiffied with what laid on
the surfase
a fiew shells Elk teeth an claws were there jewels
but like himself they were meat eaters an thieves
the grass eaters were the onley honest ones

but his caches would have lane till the end of time
Had not another man come. one he did not make -
a greater thief than all of his
It was natures enemy the white man
This man took from under and more he stole from
the water the sky. HE was never satisfide
It was he who raised the Old mans caches an
still hunts the fiew that are left
When Napi saw the new thief he hid his fase in
his robe and left this world
and I dont blame him

Thanking you again
Your friend
CMRussell

Cat. 58

Charles Marion Russell
Friend Frank
1914
Watercolor and ink on paper
12¼ × 6 in.
Petrie Collection, Denver, Colorado

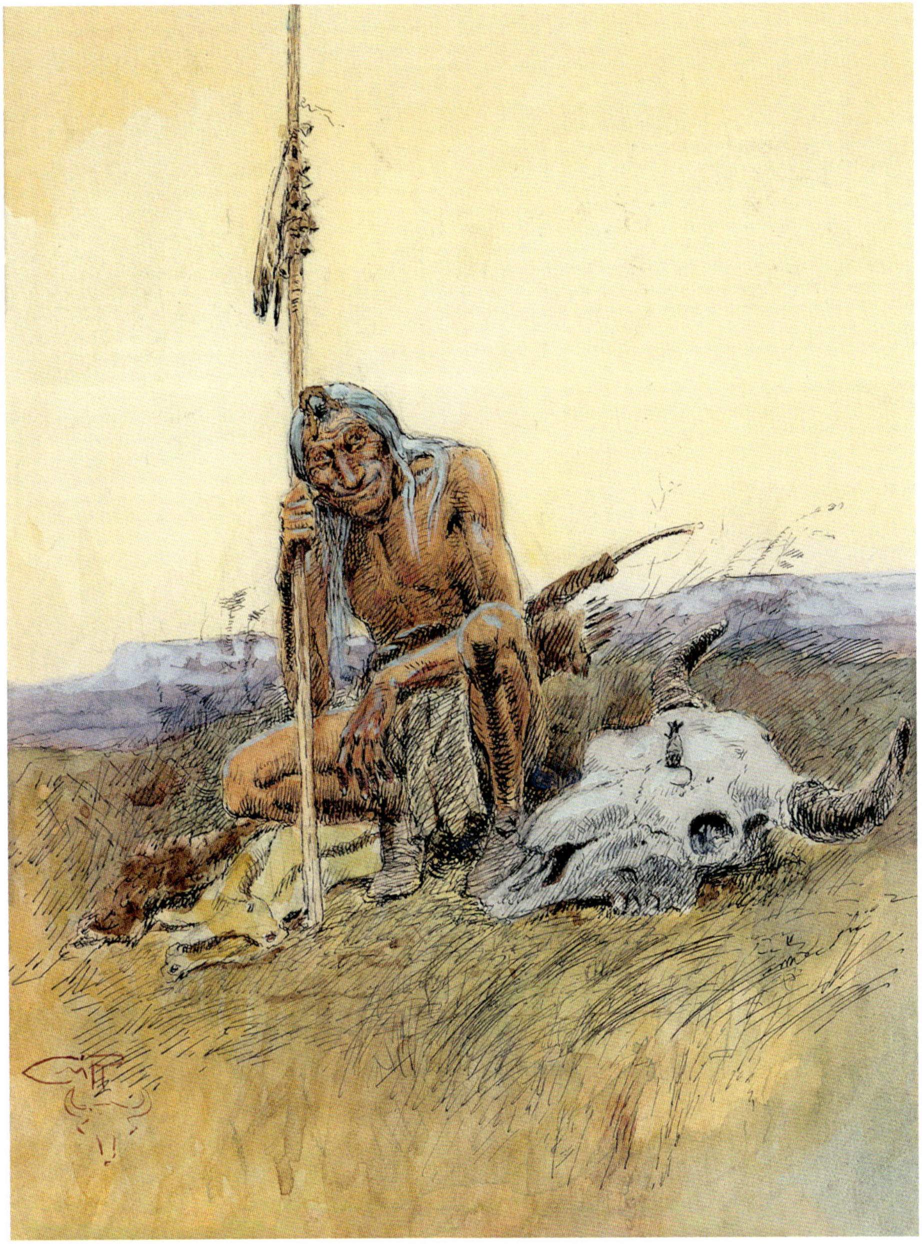

These watercolor paintings and the sculpture *Secrets of the Night* (cat. 60) feature Napi, or Old Man, a supernatural creator and prankster figure. In the letter to author Frank Bird Linderman, Russell painted Napi smoking with bird and animal people and lamented the White man's greed. In the other painting, Napi regards the *kaniskinaitapiiksi* (Mice-people) who make their homes in the skulls of *iinii* (buffalo). In the sculpture, an owl—a messenger from the Sand Hills, a sacred place where the Nitsitapii believe spirits go after death—alights on Napi's shoulder to whisper in his ear. Napi stories, told since time immemorial among the Nitsitapii, entertain and educate.

Linderman published these in his 1915 book *Indian Why Stories: Sparks from War Eagle's Lodge-Fire*. Russell's watercolor in his letter to Linderman appears on the book's title page, while *Napi and the Mice People* correlates with the story "Why Blackfeet Never Kill Mice." In this story, the animals cannot agree who should be chief, so Napi encourages them to play a bone game. Ultimately, the mouse wins the game, beating all the other animals. But, recognizing his limitation in stature and his interest in peace, he defers his leadership to humans. Since that time, mice have made homes in buffalo skulls, and the Nitsitapii have been directed not to kill the kaniskinaitapiiksi.

Cat. 59

Charles Marion Russell
Napi and the Mice People
1915
Watercolor and ink on paper
8½ × 6⅓ in.
Petrie Collection, Denver, Colorado

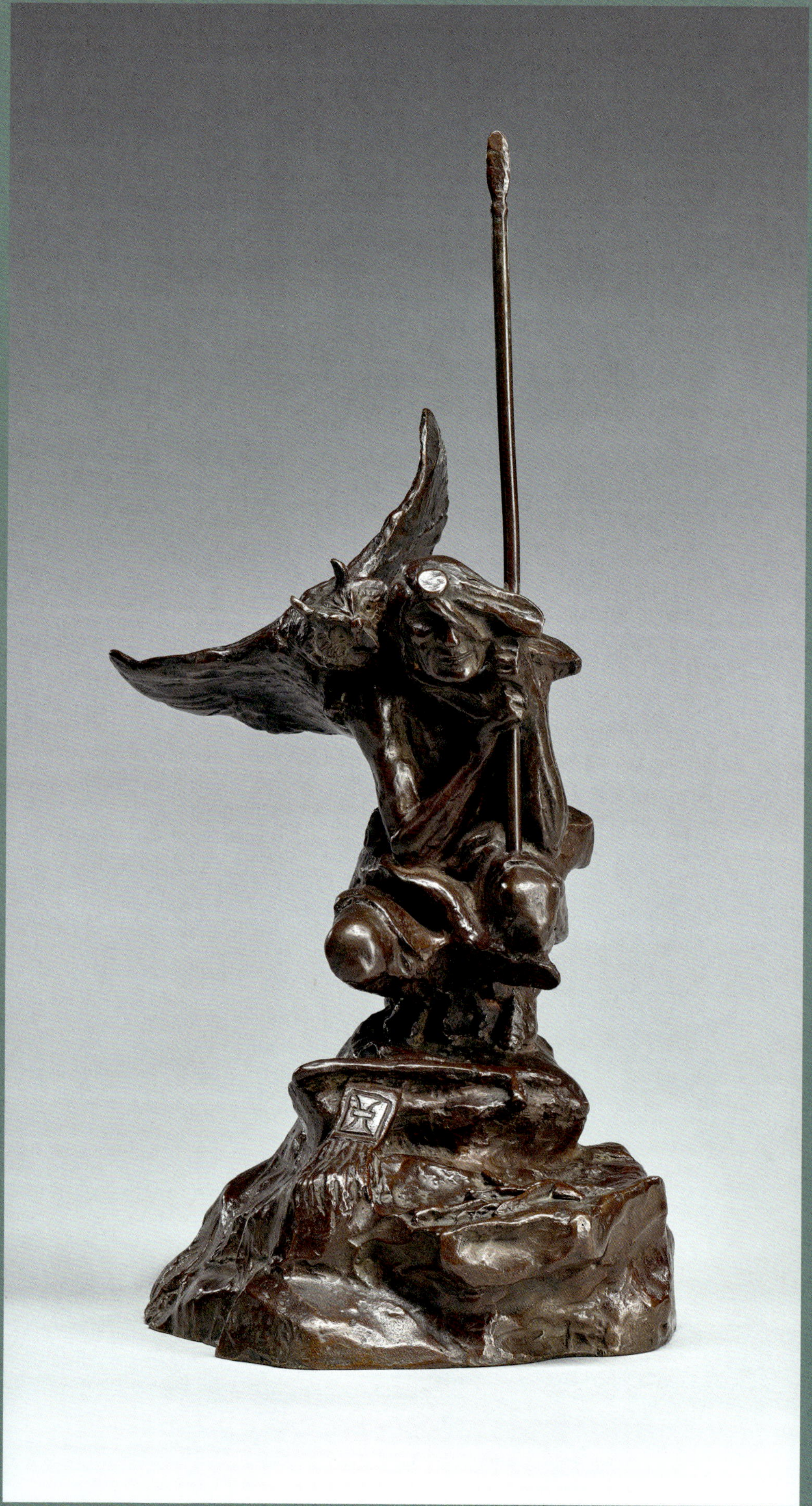

Cat. 60

Charles Marion Russell
Secrets of the Night
1926
Bronze
13½ × 6¾ × 6¼ in.
Denver Art Museum: Gift of Sharon Magness, 1997.516

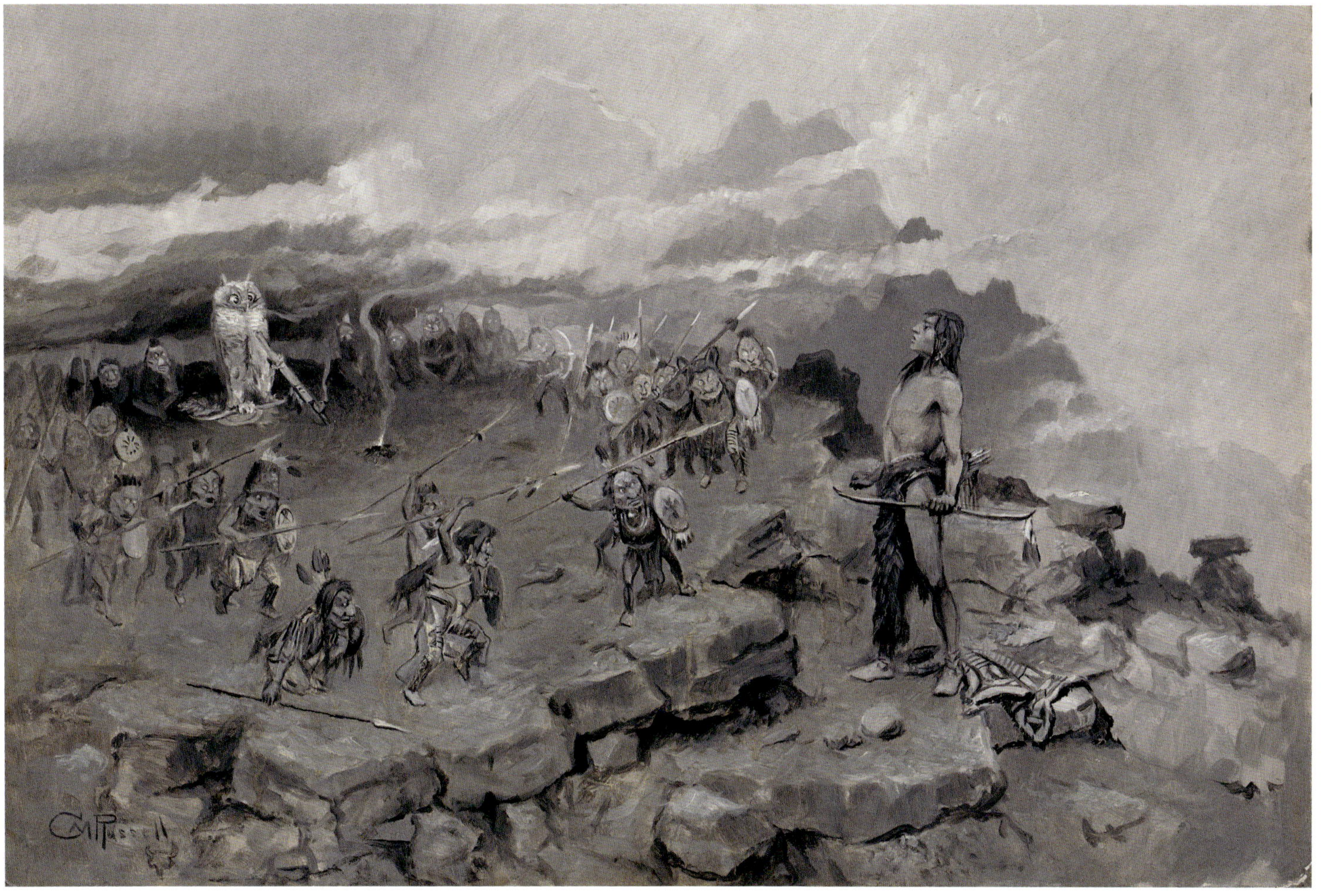

Cat. 61

Charles Marion Russell
Standing Fearlessly, His Arms Thrown Downward Exposing His Breast
c. 1898
Oil on board
Framed: 20 × 25¾ × 1⅛ in.
Denver Art Museum: Gift of Fred Rosenstock in memory of his wife, Frances, 1973.32

Painted in *grisaille*, or a gray monochrome palette, Russell created *Standing Fearlessly* as an illustration to accompany Anna P. Nelson's fictional story "The Medicine Arrow," published in *Sports Afield* in January 1898. The story tells of an unlucky Indigenous youth who seeks supernatural help to improve his life. Here, Russell appears to depict the *pookitapiiksi* ("the little people"). He must have been told of these supernatural beings who measure only a foot tall. As is the case for any outsider, Russell would not have fully understood the complex relationship between the pookitapiiksi and the Nitsitapii. Traditionally, the pookitapiiksi helped protect and grow the sacred tobacco planted in the spring and harvested in the fall. While traveling throughout their lands during the summer, the Nitsitapii sang, drummed, and prayed to the supernatural beings to help them with the tobacco crop. Women made miniature moccasins, shirts, and digging sticks for them. The pookitapiiksi are still seen today, especially by children, and some Nitsitapii community members are working to bring back the tobacco planting ceremony.

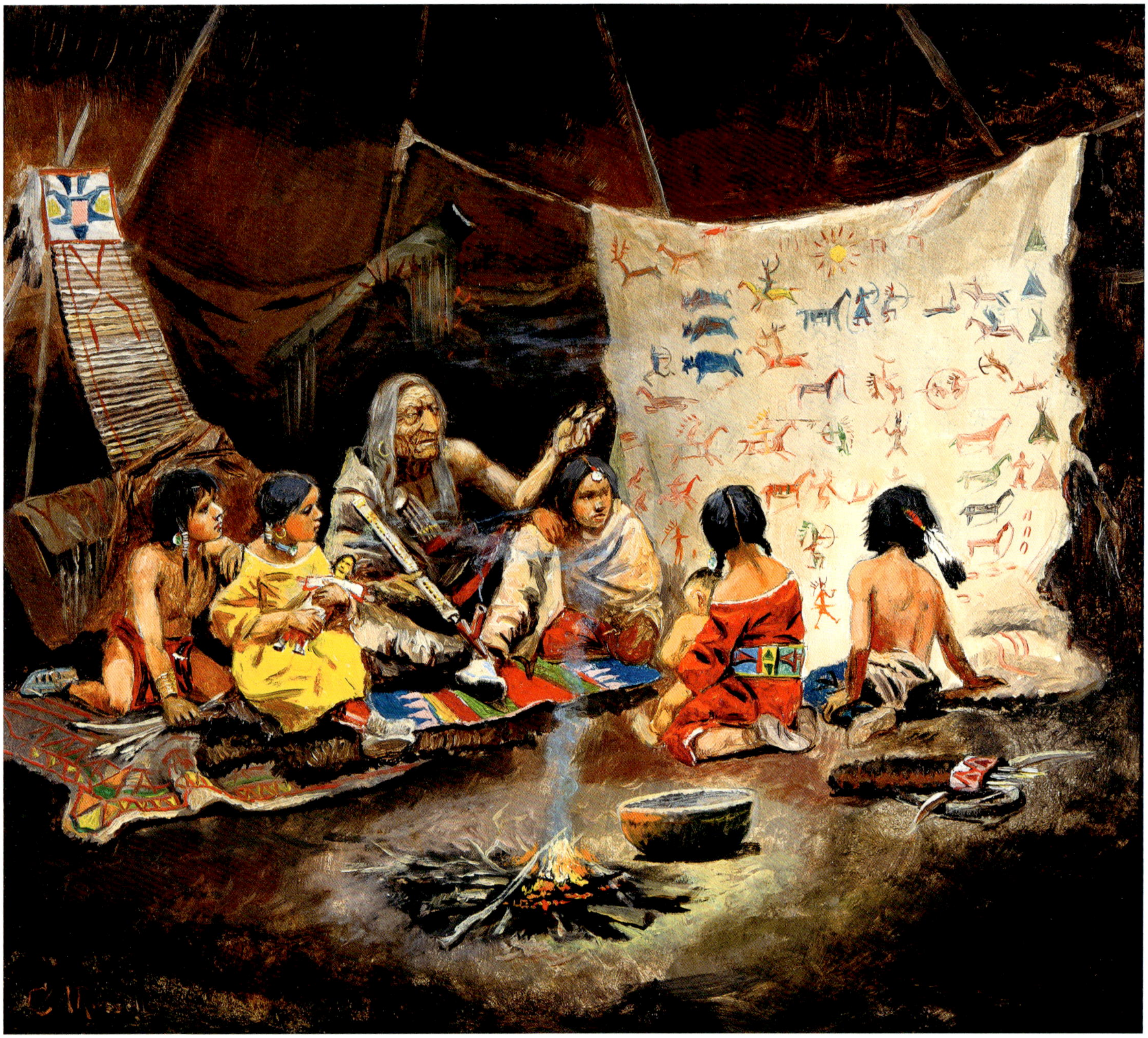

Cat. 62

Charles Marion Russell
The Kindergarten
1890
Oil on board
10½ × 12¼ in.
Petrie Collection, Denver, Colorado

The soft glow of dying embers illuminates the cozy interior of this intimate, intergenerational learning space. Commanding the room with the flick of a hand, an Elder directs attention toward a painted robe bisecting the lodge. In Nitsitapii culture, oral tradition grounds the lifelong process of learning. Stories convey how to behave in, understand, and relate to the world, centering core values of community and generosity. Pictographs, one of three traditional forms of communication in addition to sign and spoken language, tell stories, record histories, and teach communication skills. Here, and in *The Story Teller* on the facing page (cat. 63), Russell captured the intergenerational connection of Elders teaching children and children supporting each other. At the same time, his incorrect details can offend Nitsitapii values, such as modesty. In both, Russell presents girls whose dresses slip off their shoulders, even though their mothers would never have made dresses so loose.

In both paintings, children play with *atapiimiiksi* ("real dolls") like the ones in this exhibition (cats. 64 and 65).

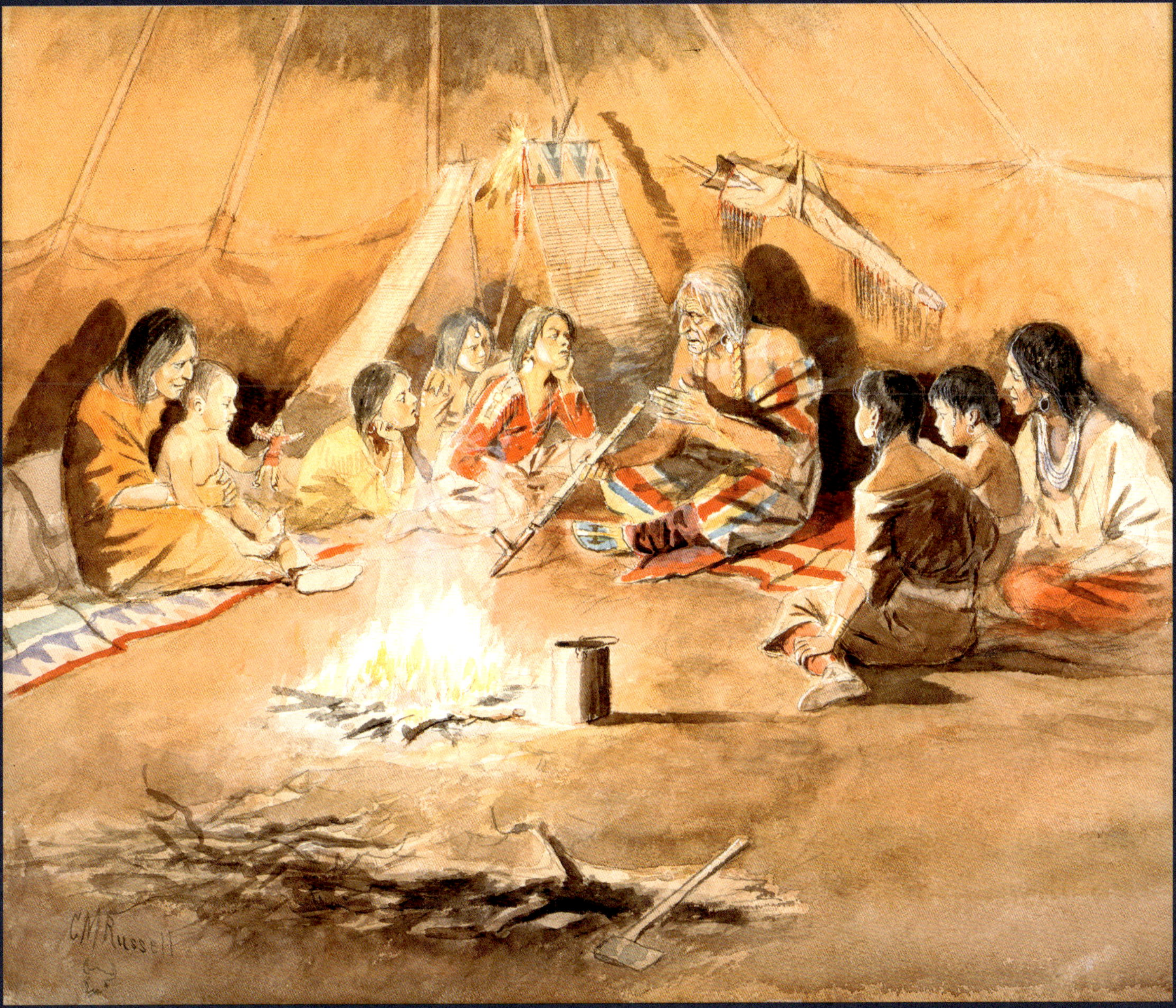

Cat. 63

Charles Marion Russell
The Story Teller
1893–95
Watercolor on paper
Framed: 24¼ × 27¾ × 1⅞ in.
Buffalo Bill Center of the West,
Cody, Wyoming. Gift of William E.
Weiss. 11.74

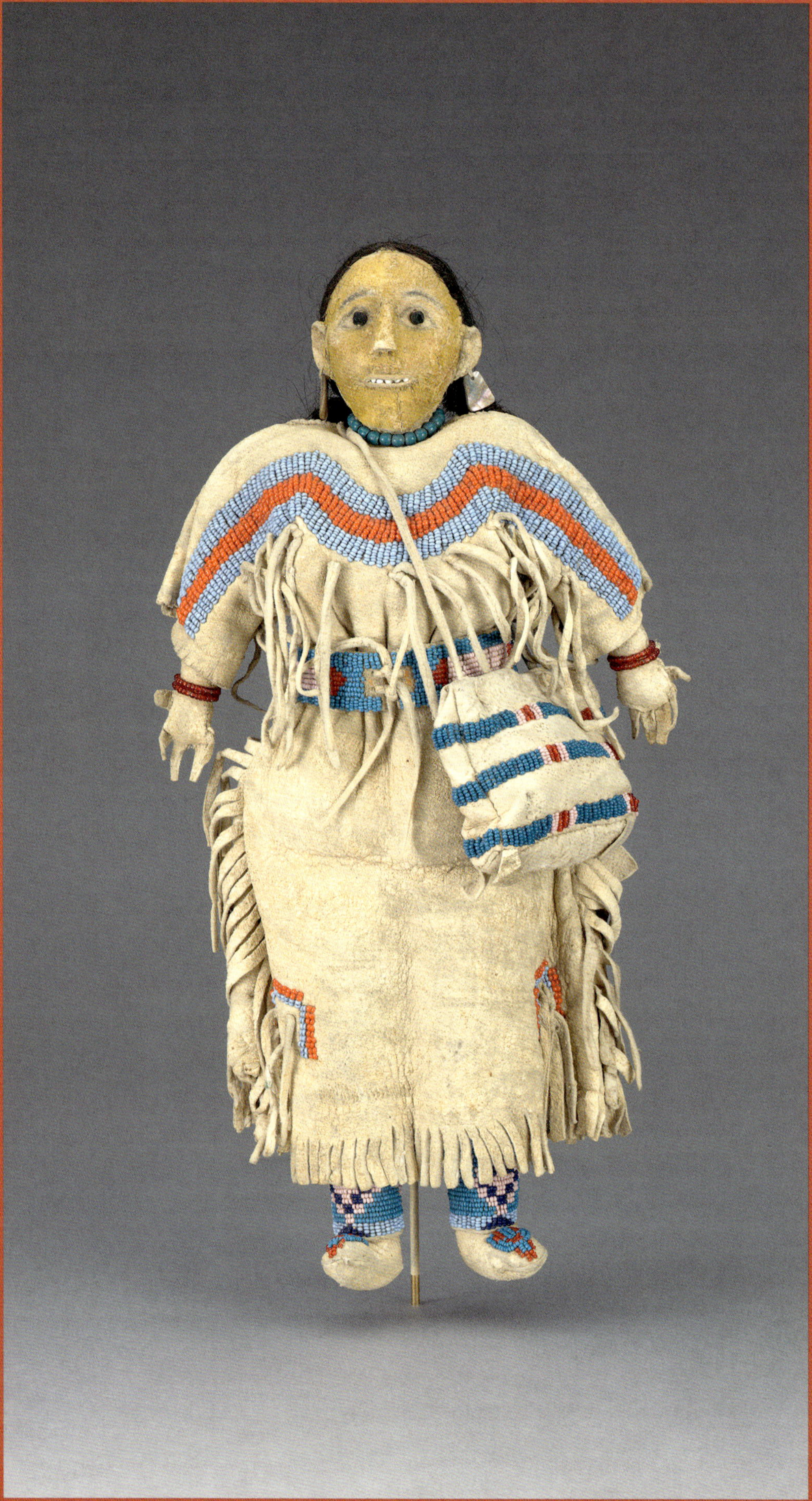

Cat. 64

Kate Red Crow
(Kainai, c. 1884–1950)
Doll
1935
Cloth, leather, beads, and human hair
13¾ × 7 × 2½ in.
Denver Art Museum: Native Arts acquisition funds, 1946.313

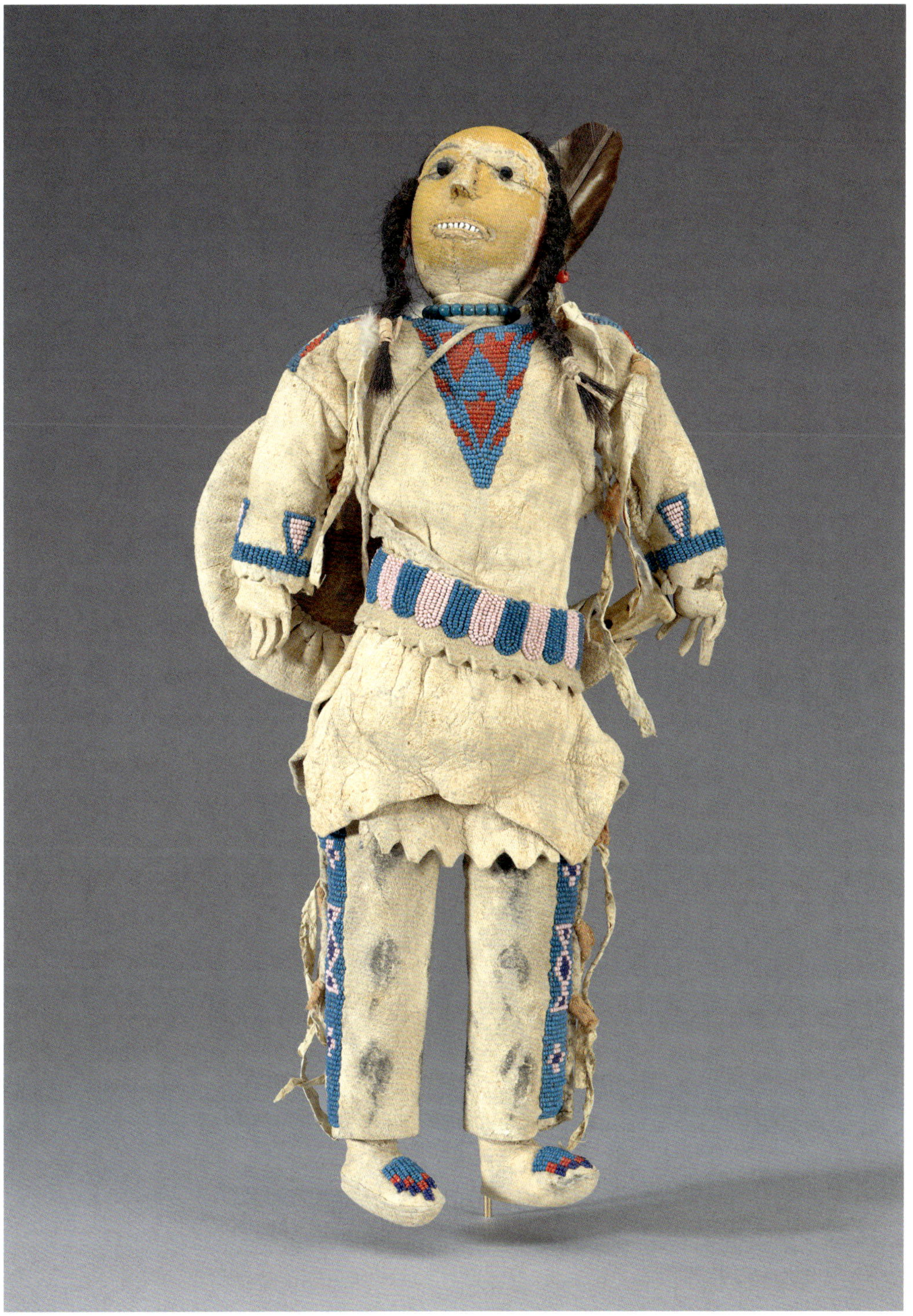

Cat. 65

Kate Red Crow
(Kainai, c. 1884–1950)
Doll
1935
Cloth, hide, beads, ermine, human hair, rawhide, and feather
15¾ × 6½ × 2¾ in.
Denver Art Museum: Native Arts acquisition funds, 1946.311

Atapiimiiksi ("real dolls") such as these functioned to entertain and, more importantly, to teach children to prepare for the responsibilities of adulthood. The female doll carries a striped pouch containing diatomaceous earth used to clean and soften leather, and the male doll holds a shield with a removable cover and a sheath encasing a bone and steel knife. Some makers would have also created miniature lodges and furnishings for the dolls. While girls were gifted dolls to learn domestic skills, boys played with arrows and figures made of bone or stick to prepare for their futures as warriors. Such exquisitely crafted dolls are given the title "real dolls," a sign of the esteem for the Kipiitapooka—the favored grandchild—to whom they were given.

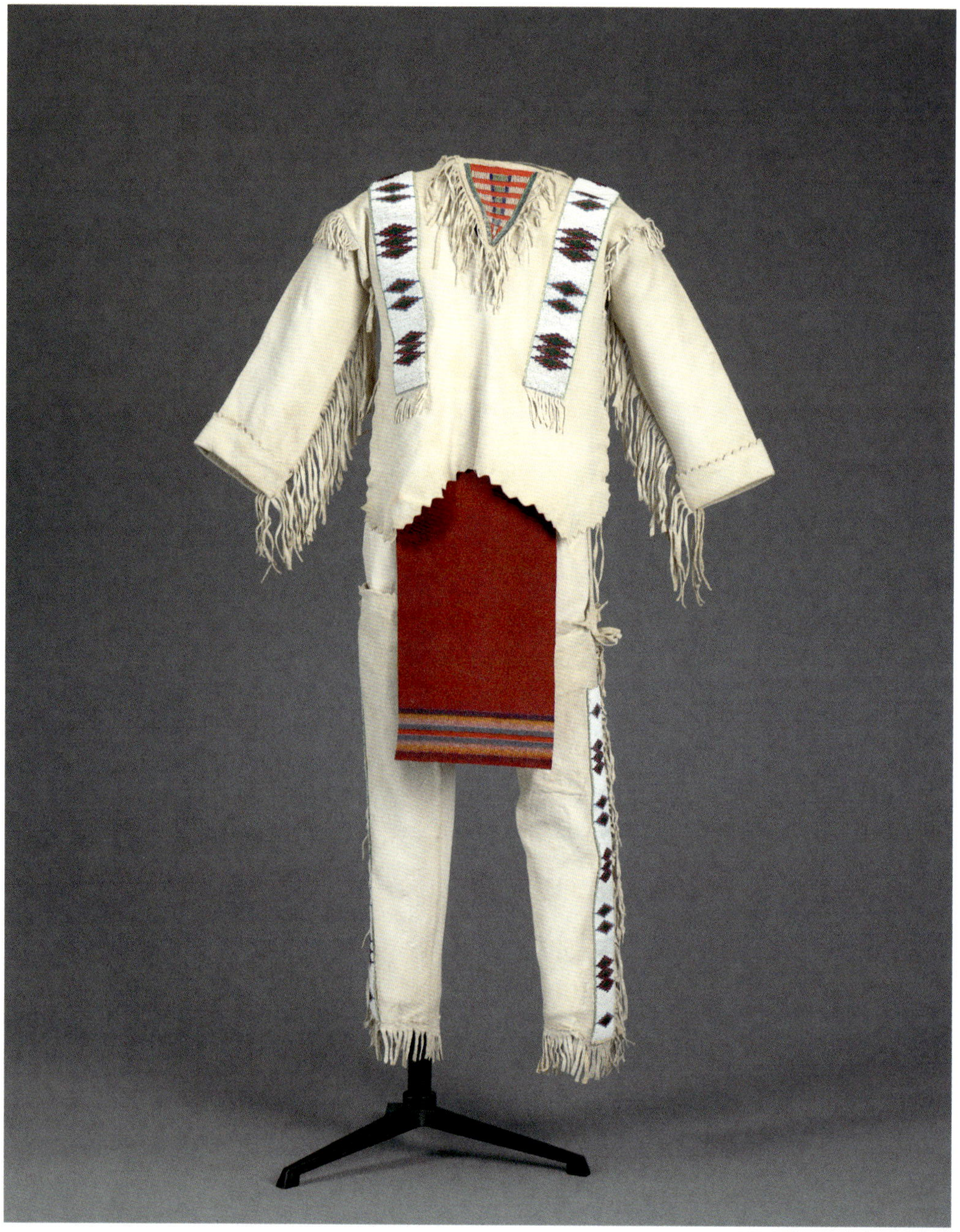

Sstaániiniki made this boy's outfit from soft tanned hide rubbed with white clay, which cleaned and whitened the hide, and beaded it with alternating diamond motifs. This ensemble won a blue ribbon at the Gallup Inter-Tribal Indian Ceremonial in Gallup, New Mexico, in 1965.

Cat. 66

Sstaániiniki (or Cecile Last Star)
(Amskaapii Pikanii, 1895–1966)
Boy's Suit
Mid-1900s
Buckskin, beads, and wool
Shirt: 21½ × 44 × 1⅝ in.;
Leggings: each approx. 23½ × 9 × 1 in.
Denver Art Museum: Native Arts acquisition funds, 1965.254

An exceptional beadwork artist, Sstaániiniki (also known as Cecile Boy, Cecile Black Boy, and Cecile Last Star) is remembered as a loving person and source of knowledge, as well as an ambassador and educator. During the 1930s and early 1940s, she collected and translated Amskaapii Pikanii stories under the Federal Writers' Project, a Depression-era program that was part of the Works Progress (later Projects) Administration. She also painted traditional lodge designs. These, and some of the stories she recorded, were later published in *Painted Tipis by Contemporary Plains Indian Artists* (1973) and *Blackfeet Indian Tipi Legends* (nd). Sstaániiniki supported ethnologist John C. Ewers's research during and after his tenure as curator of the Museum of the Plains Indian in Browning, Montana. In research undertaken by Ewers and anthropologist Clark Wissler on the Denver Art Museum's Nitsitapii collection, Sstaániiniki regularly appears as a primary source.

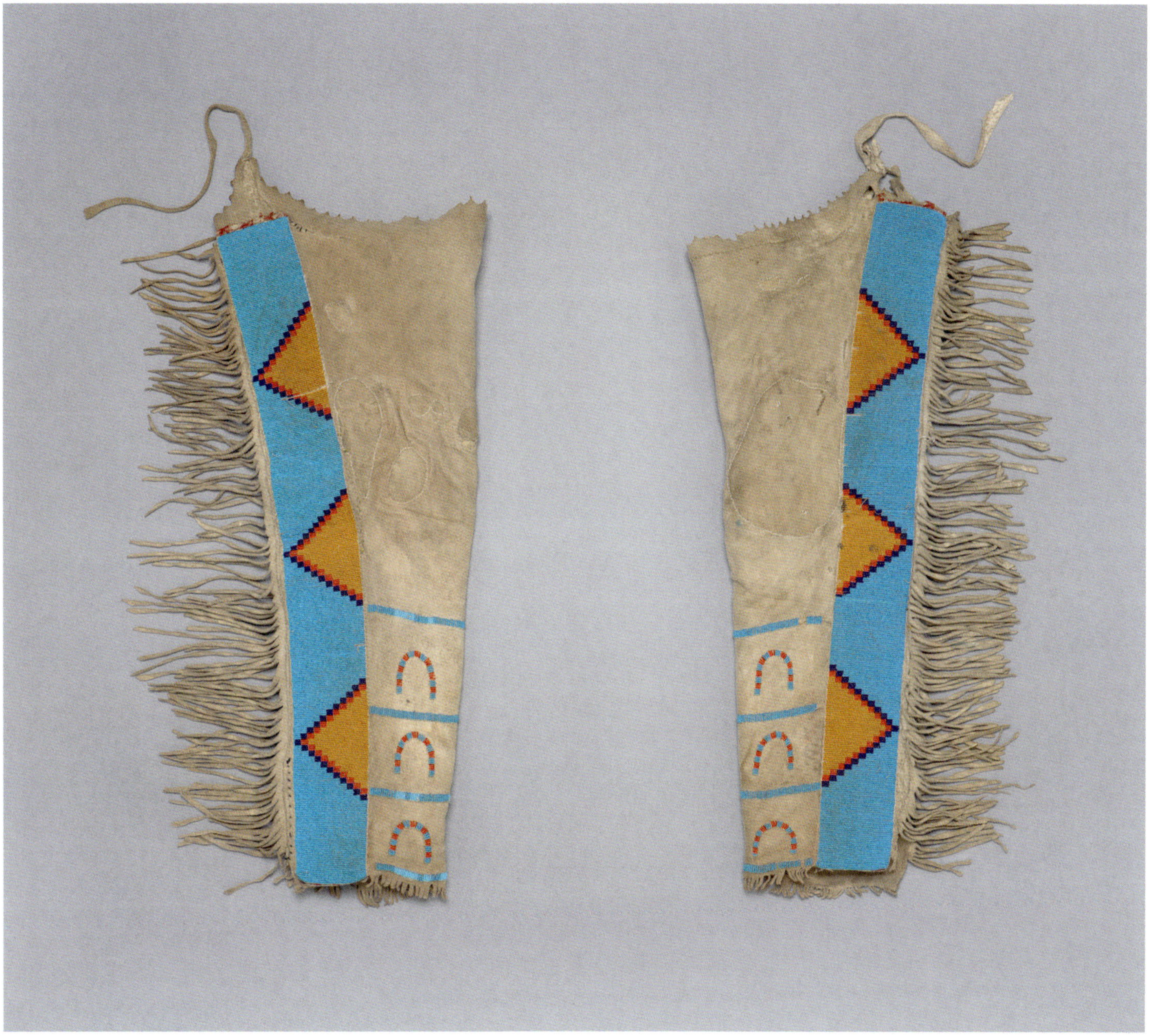

Cat. 67

Amskaapii Pikanii artist
Boy's Leggings
c. 1920
Leather and beads
Each approx. 31½ × 15 × 1⅝ in.
Denver Art Museum: Gift of Dr. Charles J. Norton, 1982.95

Considerable mending around the knees of these boy's leggings signals extensive use and demonstrates the care taken to sustain everyday aspects of Amskaapii Pikanii life. Blue-and-red striped horseshoe designs likely represent the coups or successful horse thefts of a male relative and signal masculine valor. Vibrant blue beads against the lighter hide demonstrate Nitsitapii preference for contrast in beadwork. These carefully beaded designs evolved from earlier porcupine-quill embroidery techniques, which favored shapes comprised of small rectilinear figures. The crisp outline of the triangular mountain design and the pixelation of the horseshoes are markers of this material evolution.

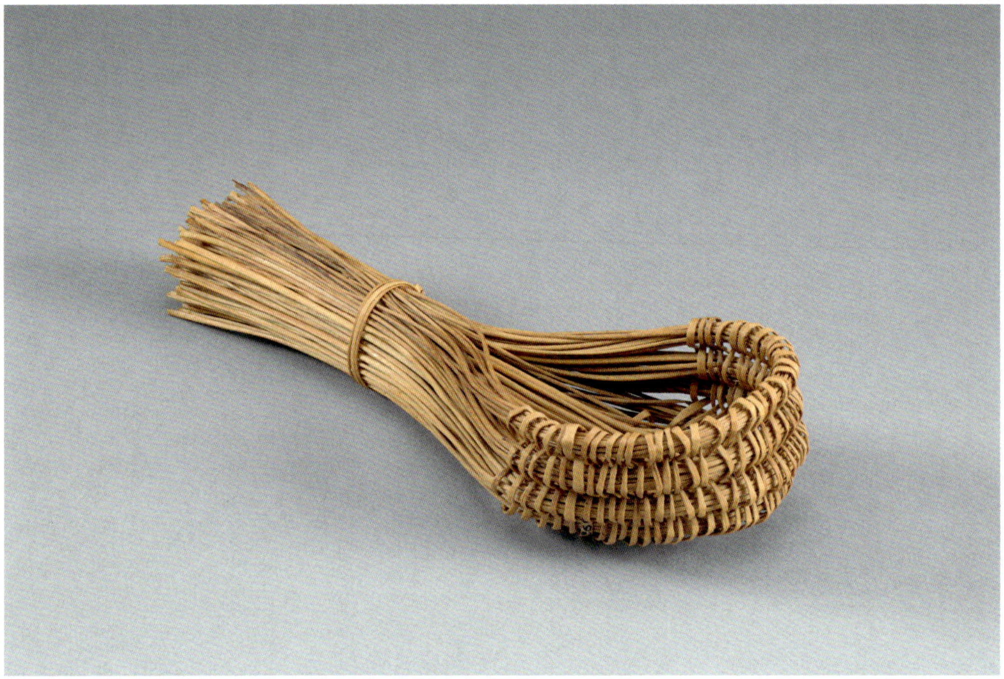

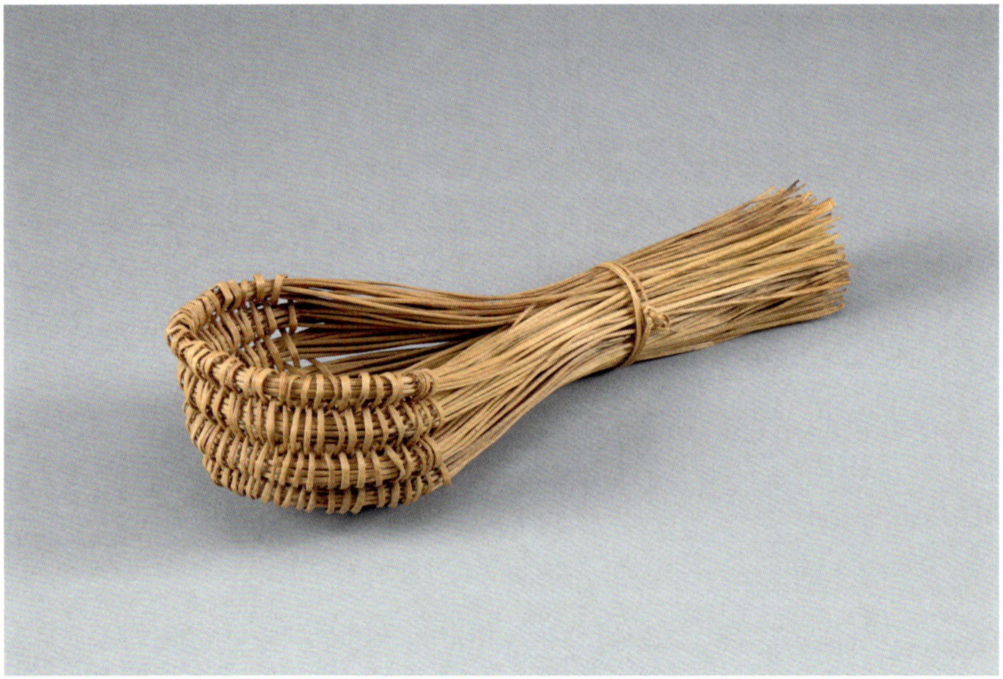

Cat. 68

Cecile Theresa Yellow Kidney
(Amskaapii Pikanii, 1866–1951)
Toy Spoon
c. 1938
Grass
6 × 2¾ × 1 in.
Denver Art Museum: Gift of
Kenneth Disher, 1938.569

Cat. 69

Cecile Theresa Yellow Kidney
(Amskaapii Pikanii, 1866–1951)
Toy Spoon
c. 1938
Grass
7⅛ × 2¾ × 1⅜ in.
Denver Art Museum: Gift of
Kenneth Disher, 1938.568

These two spoons are made from wire grass or earring grass, general terms for grasses with long slender stems and leaves. Children made such spoons as playthings. Toys for Nitsitapii children simultaneously entertained and educated. Many were smaller versions of items they would use as adults and so helped prepare them for adult tasks. The pliable nature of the grass allowed for easy manipulation and creation, fostering creativity and the development of fine motor skills. The rarity of such spoons in institutional collections suggests that they were well used, most likely played with until they fell apart.

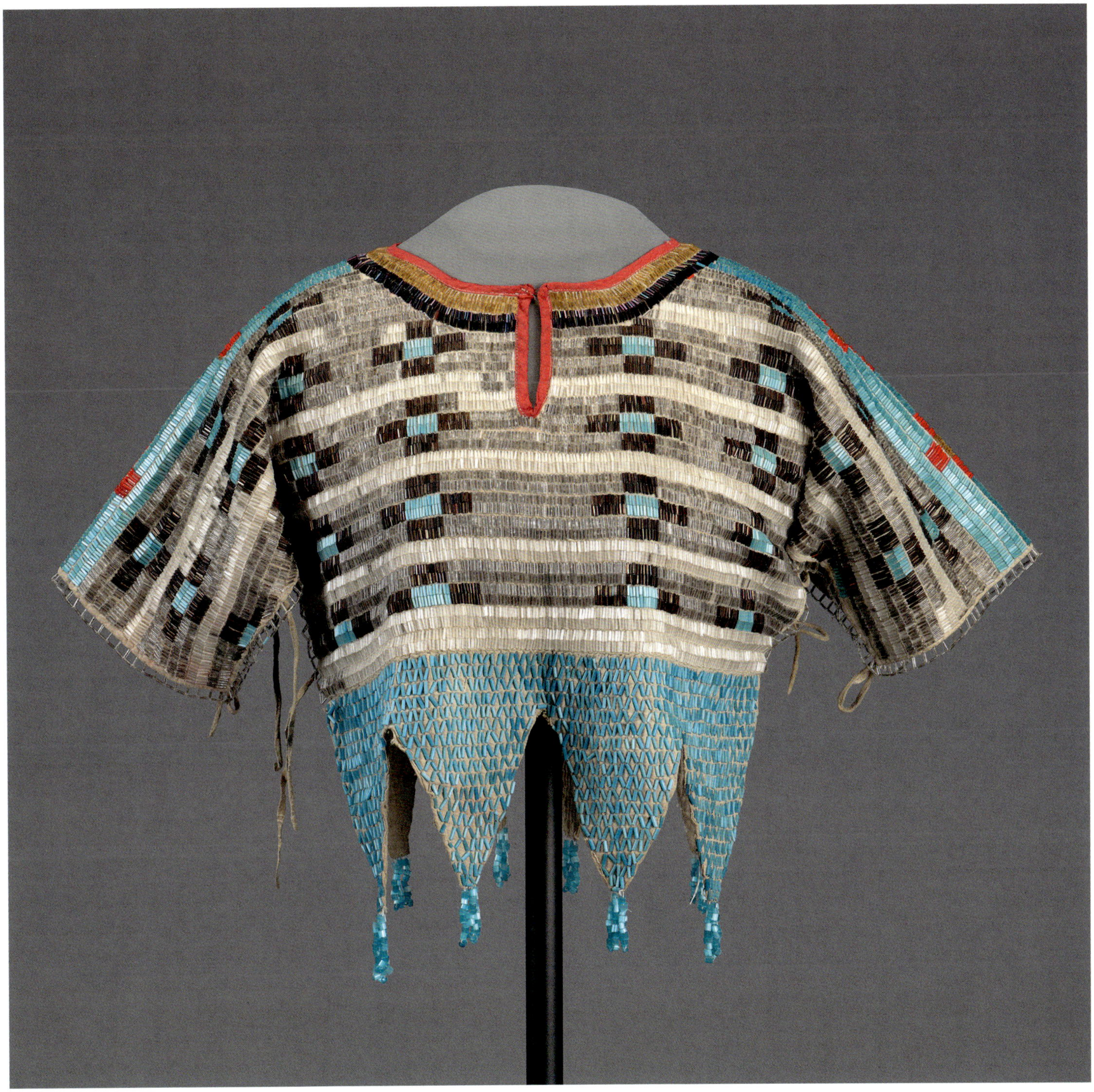

Cat. 70

Amskaapii Pikanii artist
Dress Yoke
c. 1900
Hide, beads, muslin, and flour sack
22 × 34 × 11 in.
Denver Art Museum: Gift of Dr. Charles J. Norton, 1980.214

To celebrate special ceremonies or gatherings, girls would wear their finest outfits, comprised of matching moccasins, leggings, a cloth dress, and a shawl-like shirt, or yoke. Typical Blackfeet design utilized horizontal registers that spanned the length of the garment. In this yoke, blue-and-brown cross-like designs represent the stars that form the Makoyi moosah'koo ("wolf's tail," or the Milky Way). A fiery red Morning Star design dazzles along the shoulders. The shimmering beading is backed by a Monarch flour sack from government rations. The elongated bugle beads, sourced from trade, date to the turn of the twentieth century.

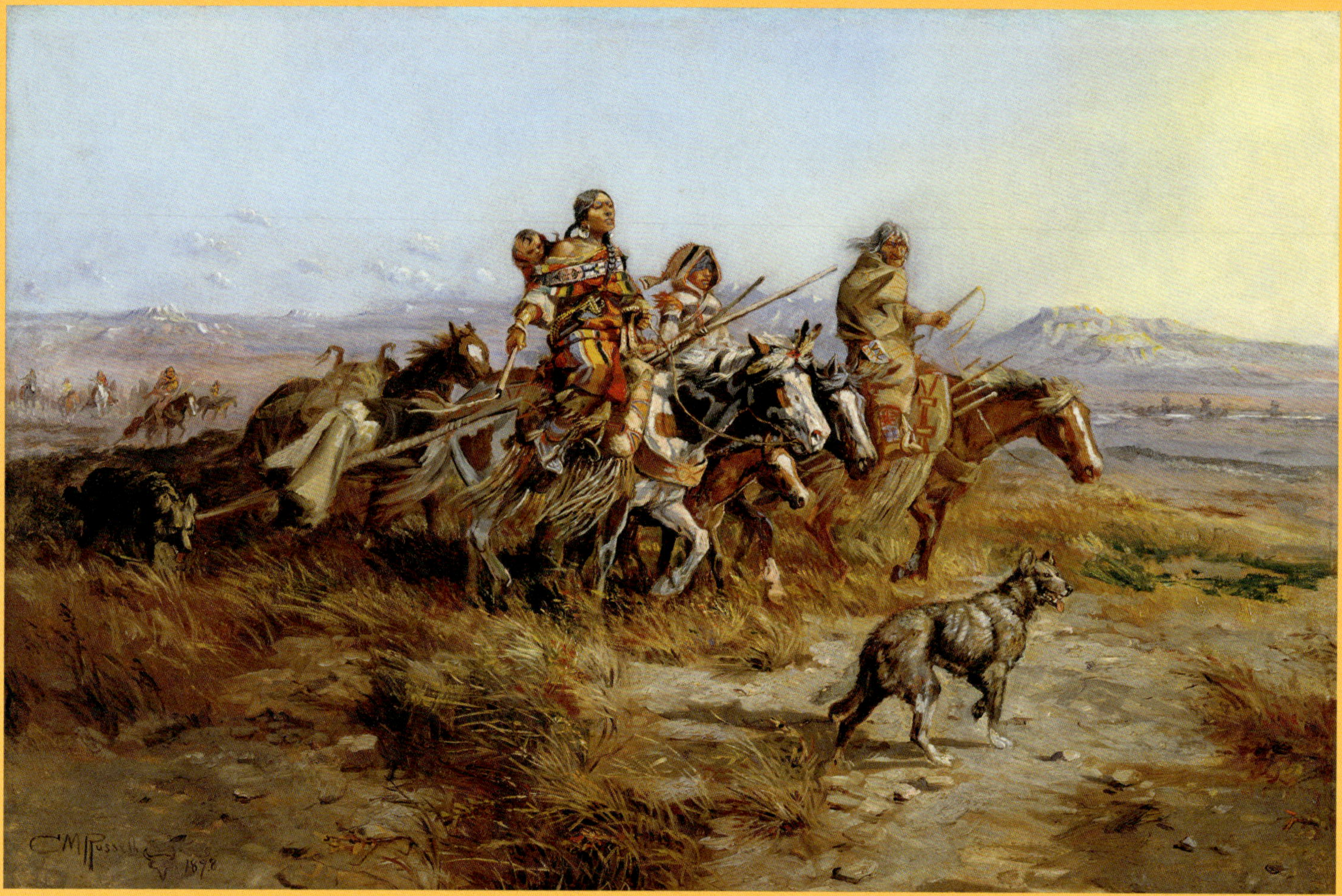

Cat. 71

Charles Marion Russell
Indian Women Moving
1898
Oil on canvas
24¼ × 36 in.
Amon Carter Museum of American Art, Fort Worth, Texas, Amon G. Carter Collection, 1961.147

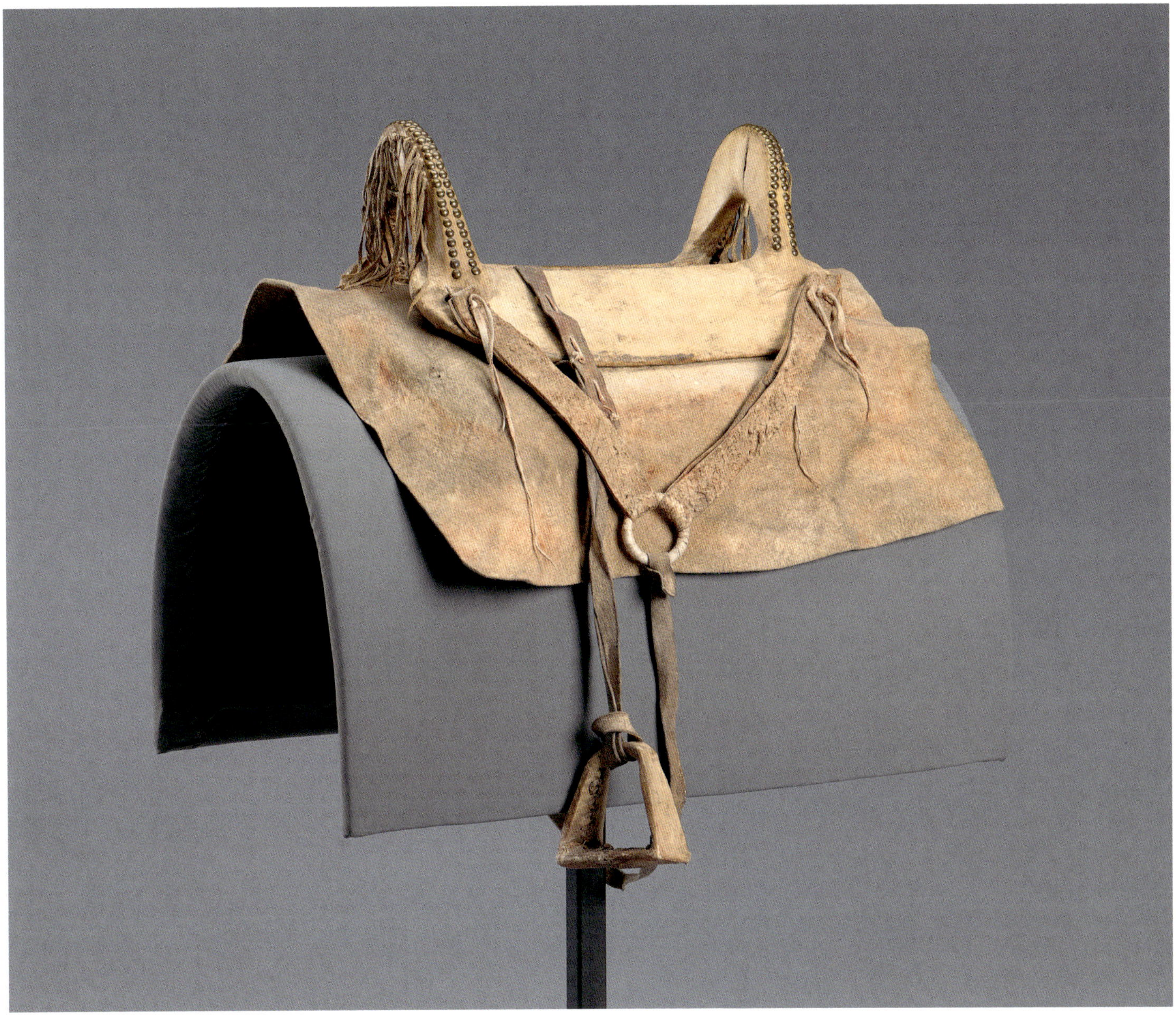

Cat. 72

Amskaapii Pikanii artist
Saddle
1870s
Wood, buffalo hide, paint, tack, copper, rawhide, and steel
25 × 22¾ × 25 in.
Denver Art Museum: Native Arts acquisition funds, 1939.312

Horses, reintroduced to North America by the Spanish in the 1500s, revolutionized Plains Indian life. After horses reached the Oomah'sisaatáa (Big River, or Missouri River) around the 1730s, the Nitsitapii quickly integrated them into their lifeways, developing extraordinarily close bonds so that, in the words of one Amskaapii Pikanii adviser, "the heart of the horse and the person become one." As the Nitsitapii trained their horses for specialized roles, they also refined their horse gear. This saddle is an example of a prairie chicken snare saddle. Primarily used as a pack saddle to bring home meat after a hunt, saddles of this style were multipurpose and used by older men, children, and some women. Typically, the pommel and cantle were made from deer or elk antlers. Here, however, they are made of wood, as is the entire saddle frame, and decorated with brass tacks and leather fringe. The stirrups and the metal ring were probably added later. In Nitsitapii culture, women were the primary saddle makers.

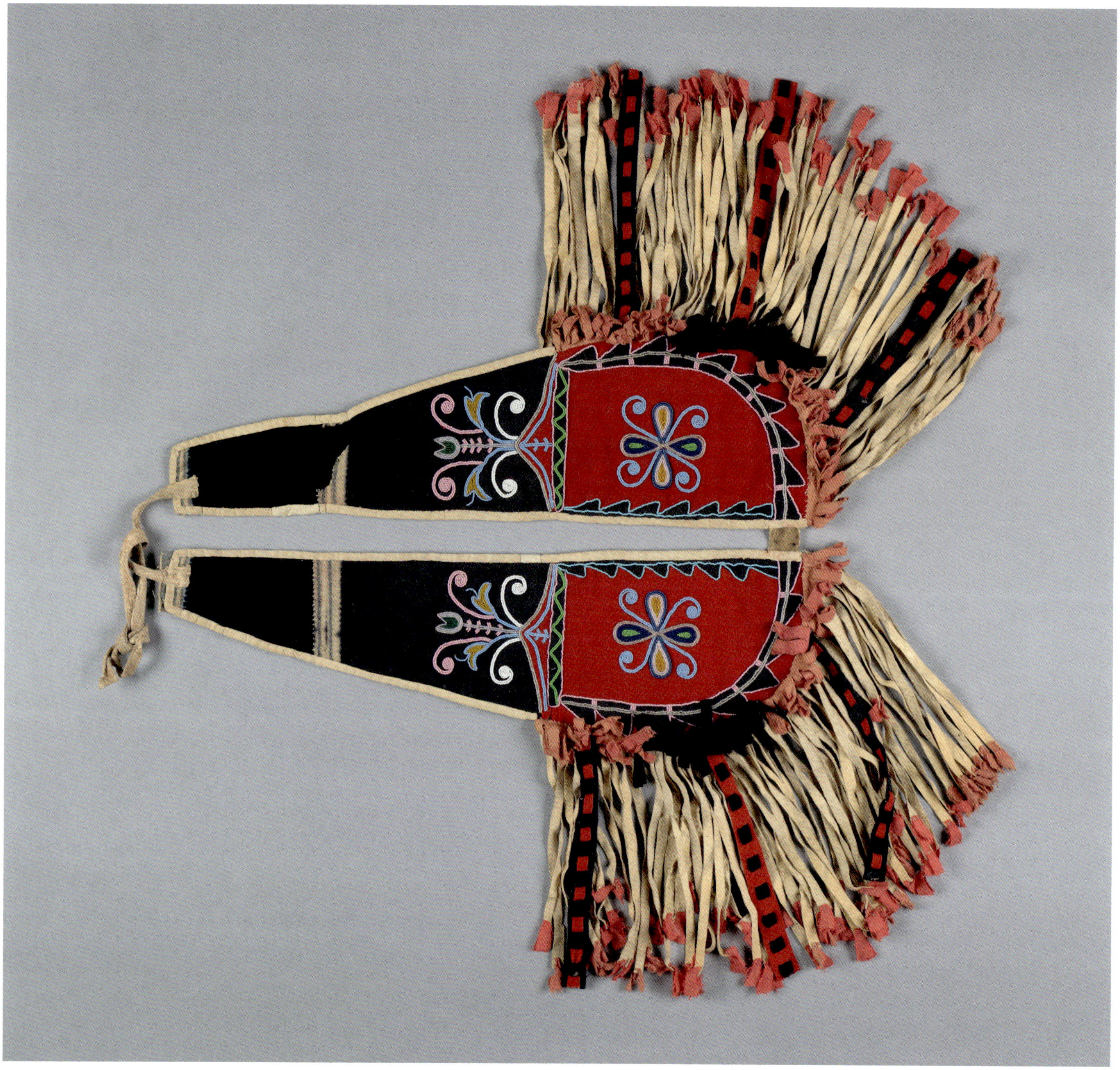

Cat. 73

Amskaapii Pikanii artist
Crupper
1885
Hide, beads, wool, cloth, canvas, and cotton
39 × 22 × 2¾ in.
Denver Art Museum: Native Arts acquisition funds, 1938.41

Cruppers and martingales serve the practical purpose of keeping a saddle and pack from slipping off a horse. Cruppers attach to the back of the saddle and sit under the horse's tail, while martingales attach to the front of the saddle and span the horse's chest. Traditionally, decorated horse gear proclaimed wealth and status. During the Reservation Era, beautifully beaded martingales and cruppers became more prevalent and were used in annual celebrations and gatherings. The martingale in this exhibition features strands of pony beads that end with thimbles, which would have jingled as the horse moved (cat. 74).

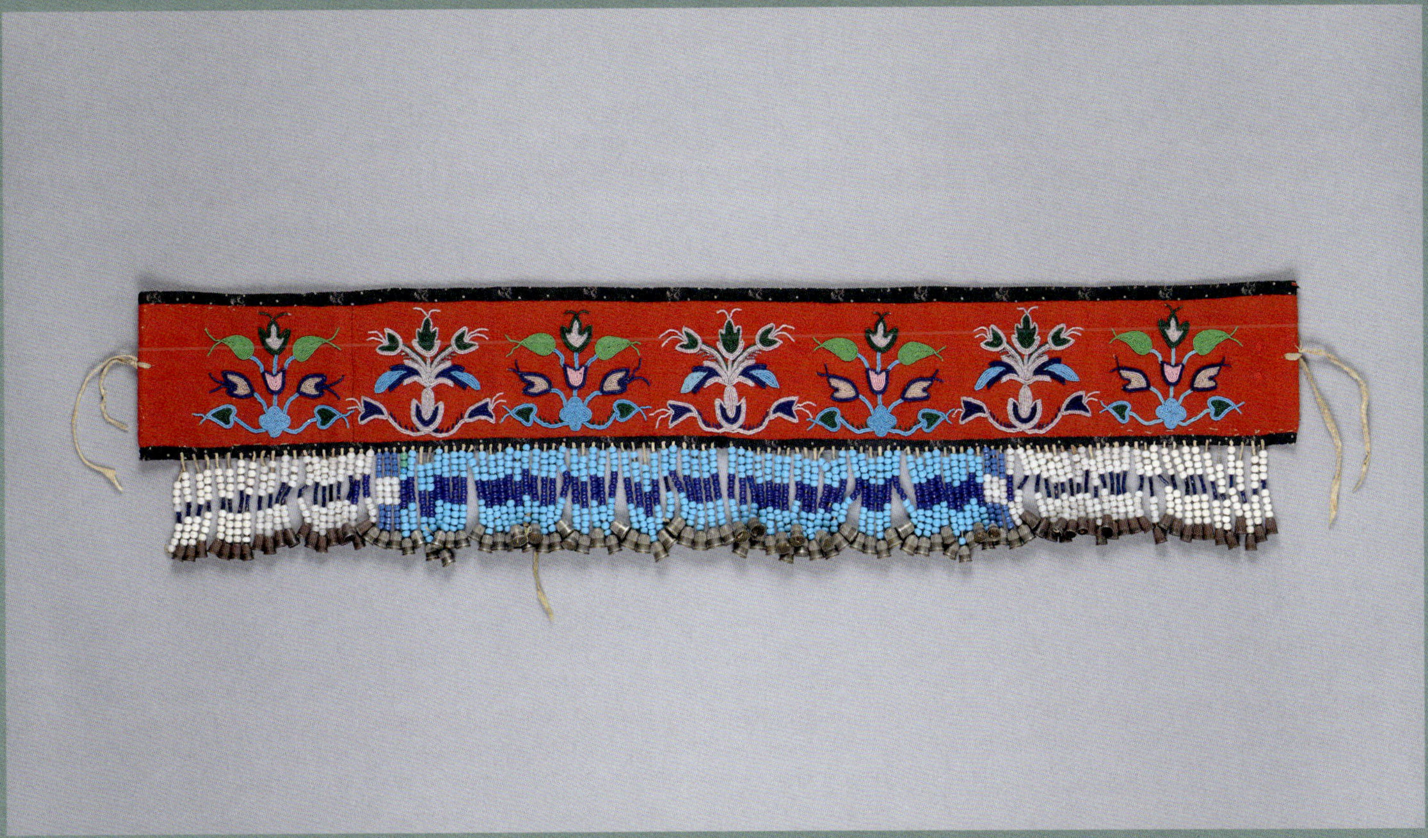

Cat. 74

Amskaapii Pikanii artist
Martingale
Late 1800s
Cloth, beads, leather, and thimbles
53½ × 12¼ × ⅞ in.
The L. D. and Ruth Bax Collection at the Denver Art Museum, 1985.111

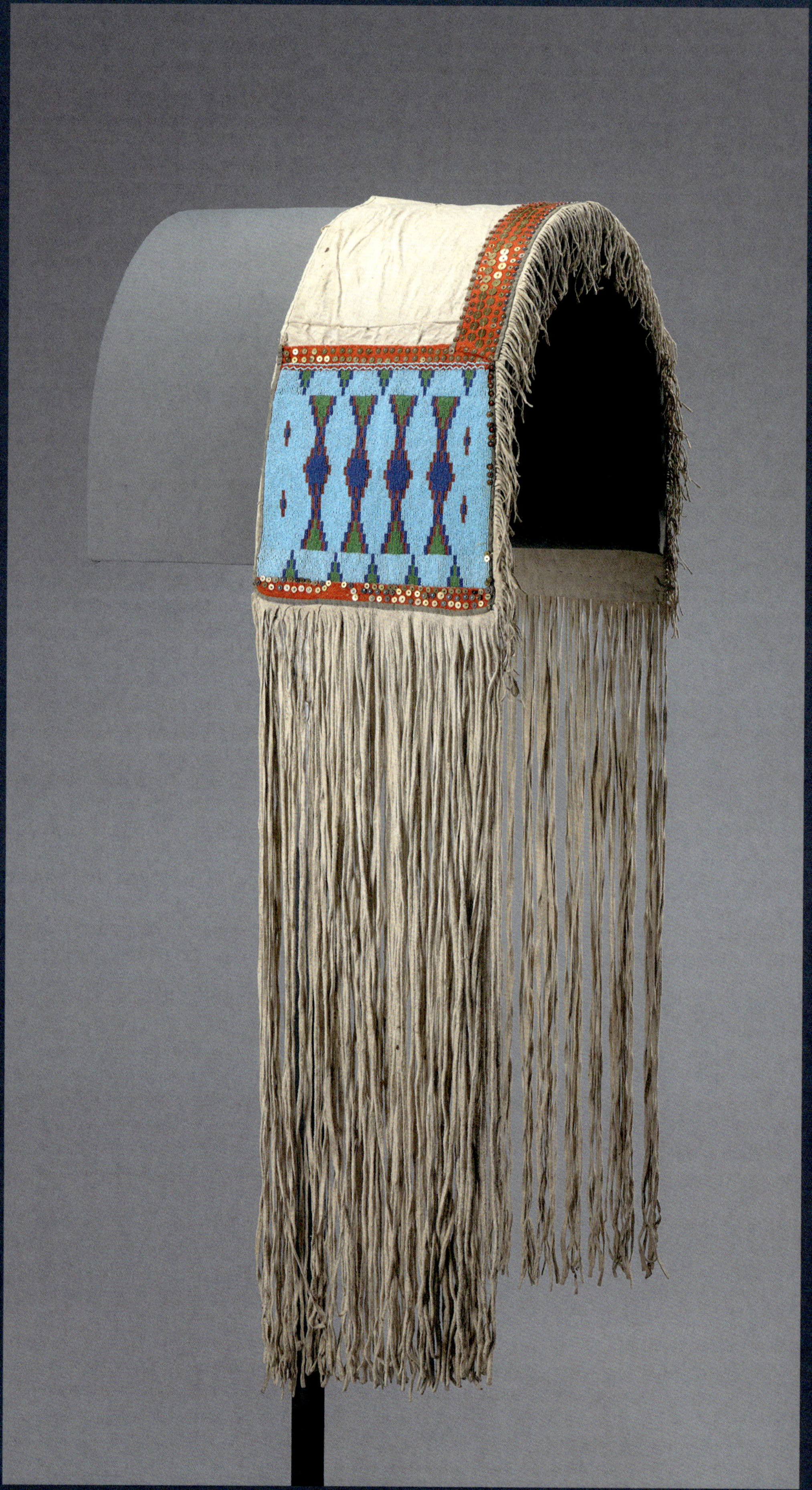

Cat. 75

Amskaapii Pikanii artist
Double Saddle Bag
c. 1930s
Buckskin, beads, sequins, and cloth
57 × 15 × 3 in.
Denver Art Museum: Native Arts acquisition funds, 1947.85

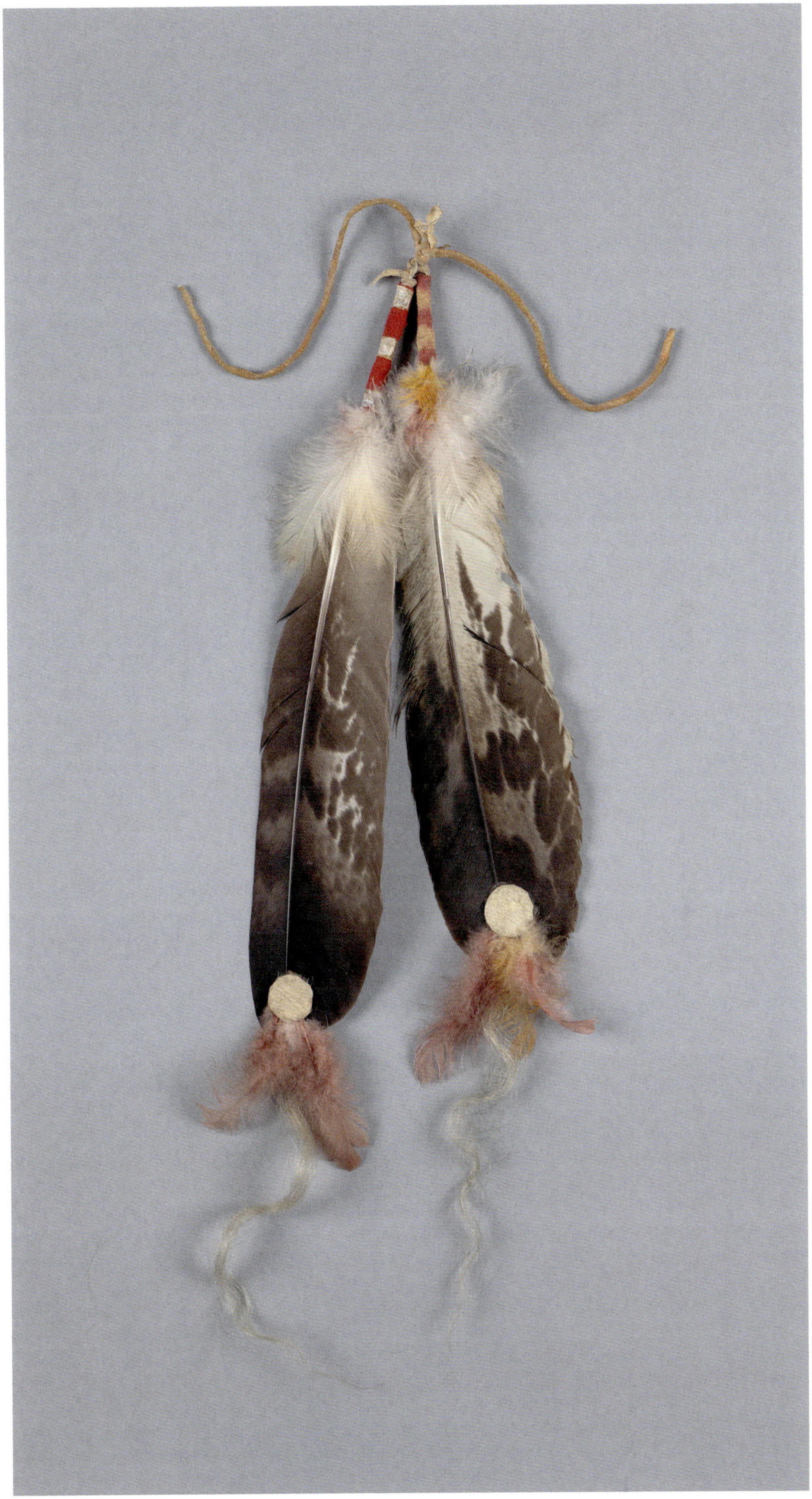

Cat. 76

Reuben Black Boy (Amskaapii Pikanii, 1883–1967)
Horse Tail Ornament
1942
Golden eagle feathers, horse hair, cloth, and hide
24 × 7½ × 1½ in.
Denver Art Museum: Gift of artist, 1942.101

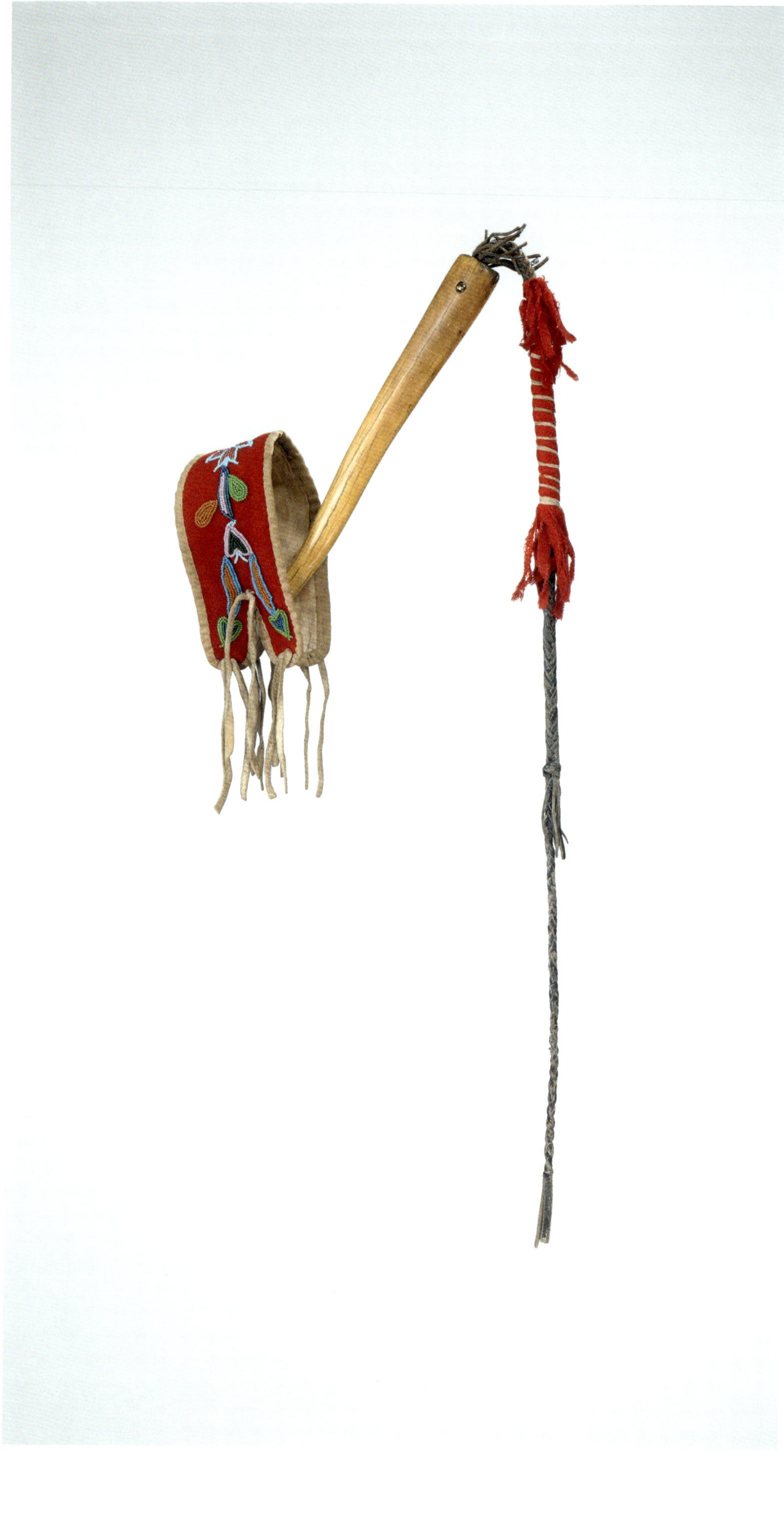

Cat. 77

Amskaapii Pikanii artist
Riding Quirt and Cuff
1900s
Bone, beads, and cloth
Quirt: 43¼ × 1½ × 1 ⅛ in.;
Cuff: 3½ × 11¼ × 1¼ in.
The L. D. and Ruth Bax Collection at
the Denver Art Museum, 1985.85

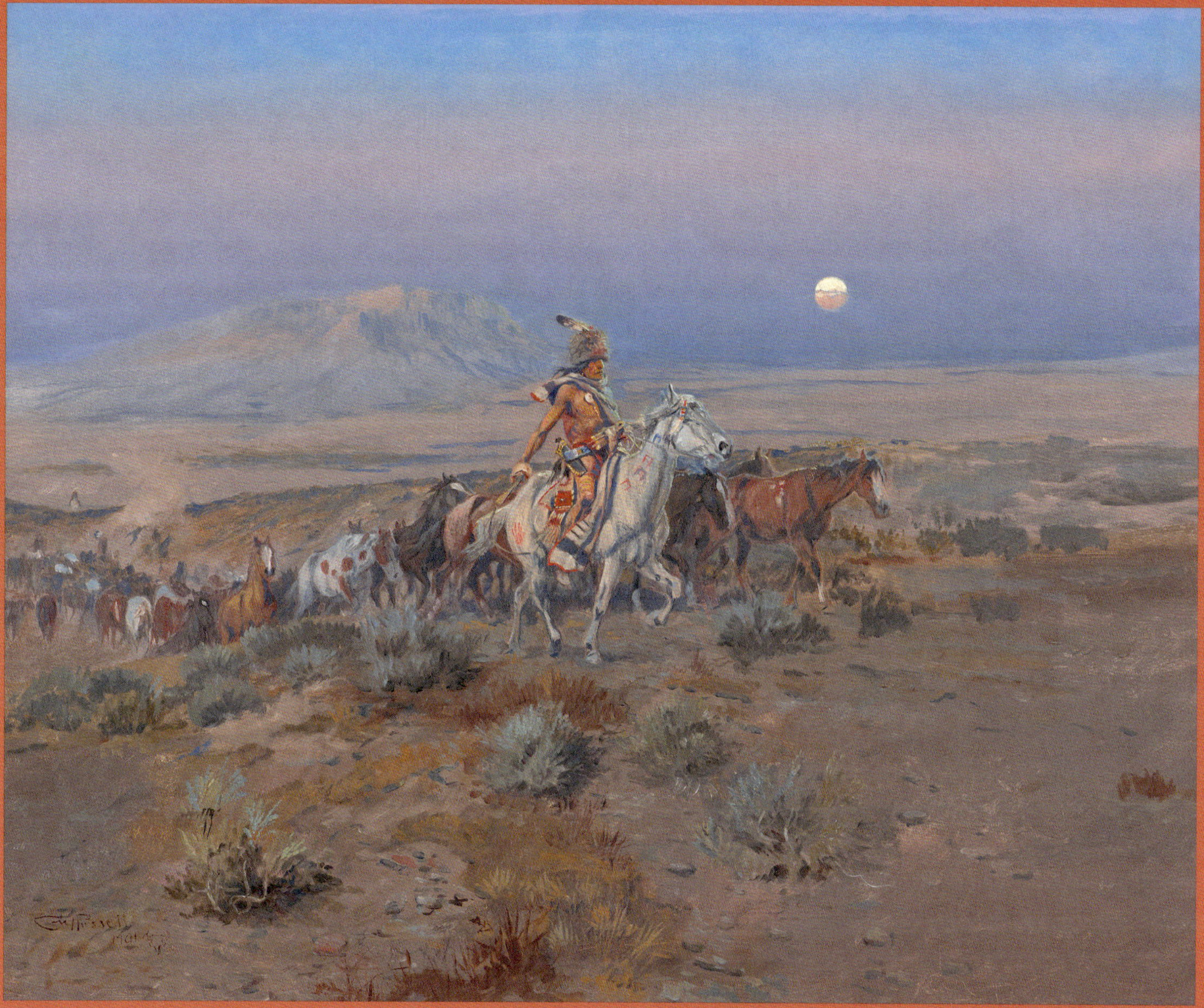

Cat. 78

Charles Marion Russell
The Horse Thieves
1901
Oil on canvas
Framed: 33¼ × 39½ × 2¾ in.
Petrie Collection, Denver, Colorado

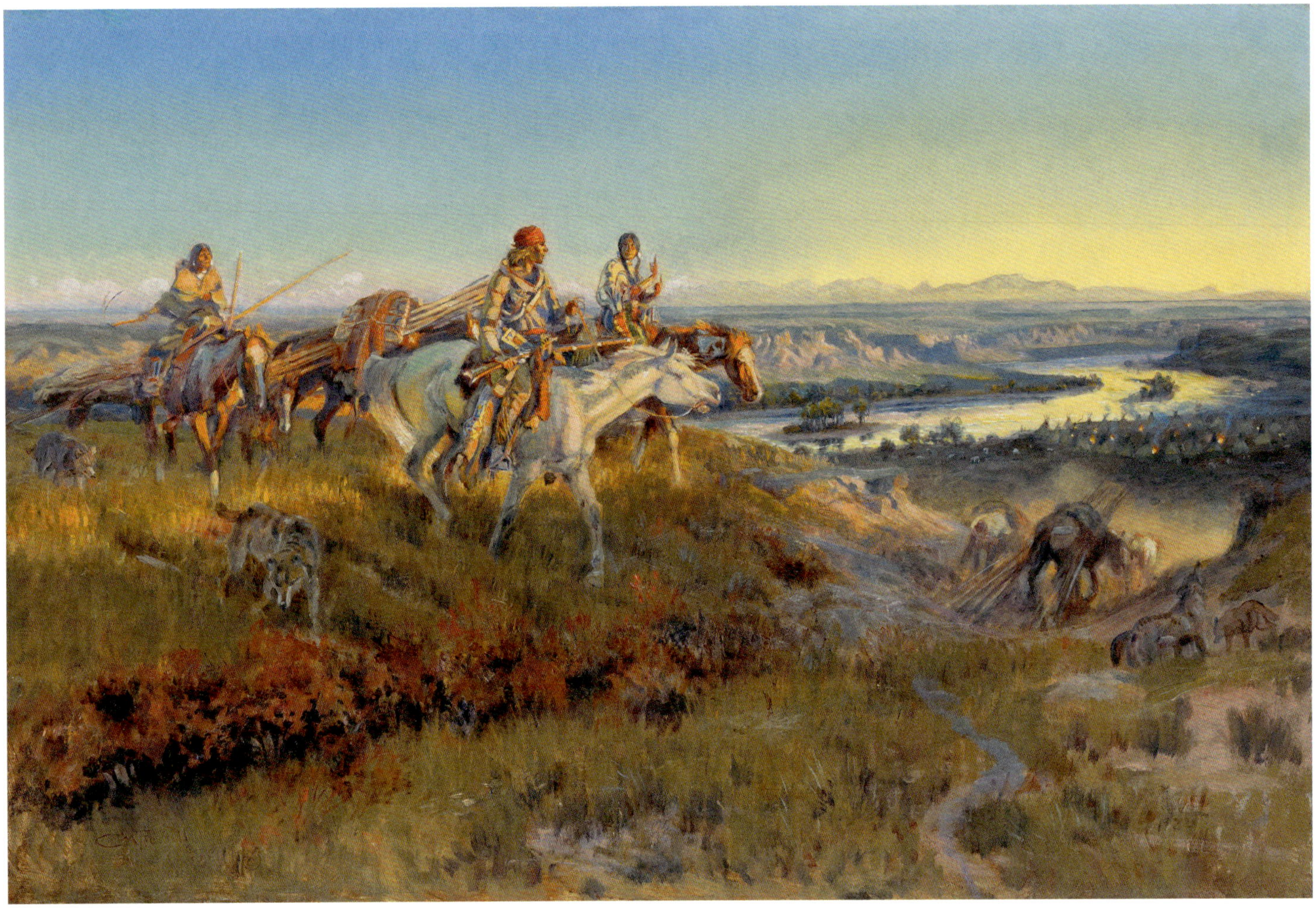

When White Men Turn Red is a fine example of Russell's later bright palette. His expressive color, initially inspired by artists including Maxfield Parrish (1870–1966) and Thomas Moran (1837–1926), grew increasingly saturated and may have underscored his heightened nostalgic romanticism as he neared the end of his life. Here, the gold hues of a setting sun reflect off the surface of a peaceful river and warm three riders moving toward the glowing fires of a camp in the distance. The title, however, reveals that this painting is about more than atmospheric color and light. Having married into an Indigenous family, the White man in the foreground has adopted the clothing and lifestyle of his new relatives. To his side, a Native woman, presumably his wife, makes the sign for "people," or perhaps "my people," implying that they are nearly home.

Russell regularly depicted Plains Indian Sign Language (PISL) in his paintings. PISL is a regional dialect of North American Indian Sign Language, also called "hand talk," one of the oldest languages on the continent. This universal language allowed communication between cultural groups, including between Europeans and Indigenous peoples. In boarding schools, Indigenous students were punished for speaking their traditional languages, including sign, even though at the same time hand talk likely influenced the creation of American Sign Language (ASL). Today, institutions such as the Piegan Institute in Browning, Montana, provide immersive language learning that includes both spoken and sign languages and pictographs.

Cat. 79

Charles Marion Russell
When White Men Turn Red
1922
Oil on canvas
36½ × 24 in.
Sid Richardson Museum

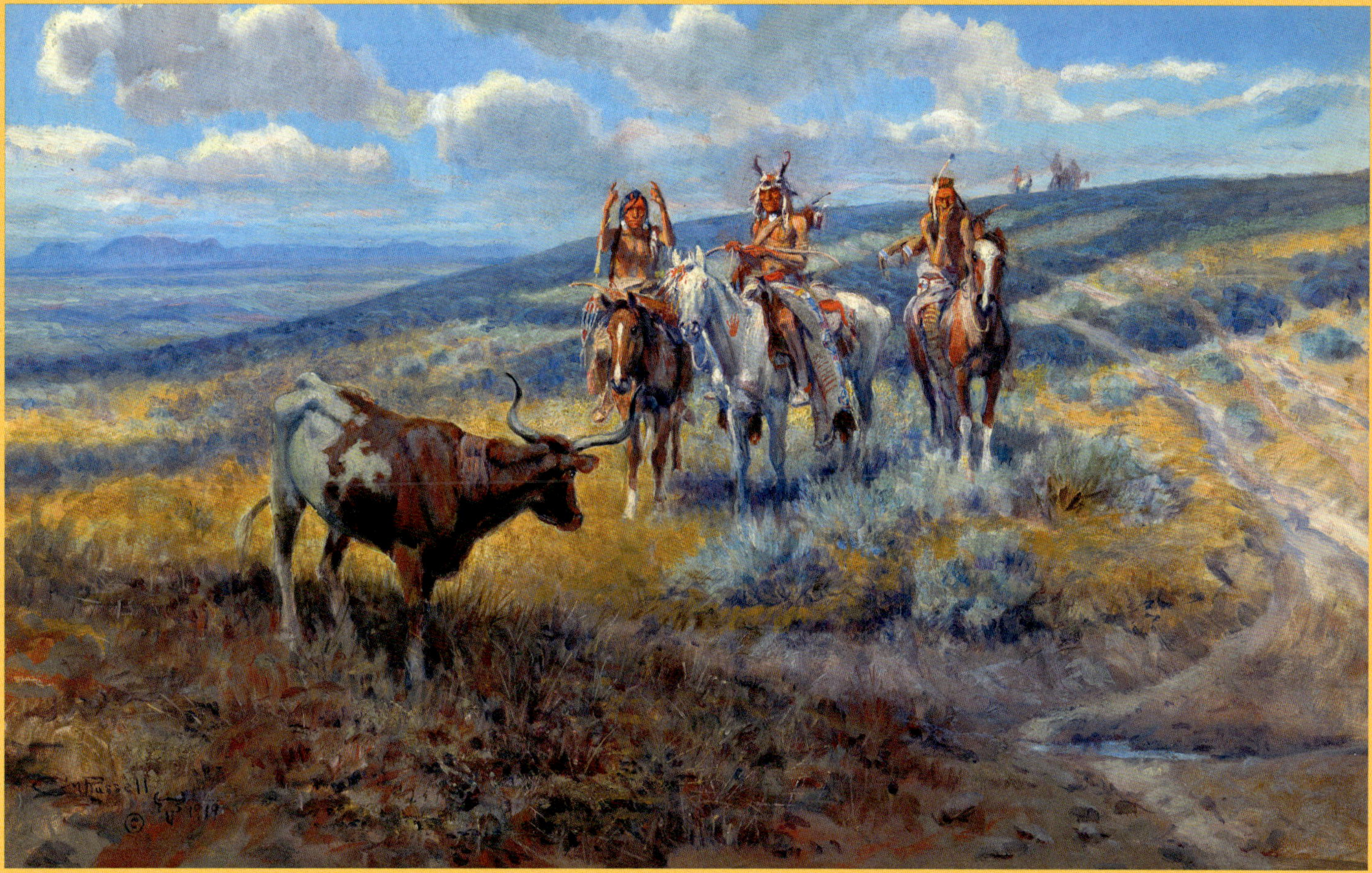

Cat. 80

Charles Marion Russell
White Man's Buffalo
1919
Oil on canvas
Framed: 20½ × 29½ in.
Gilcrease Museum, Tulsa, Oklahoma

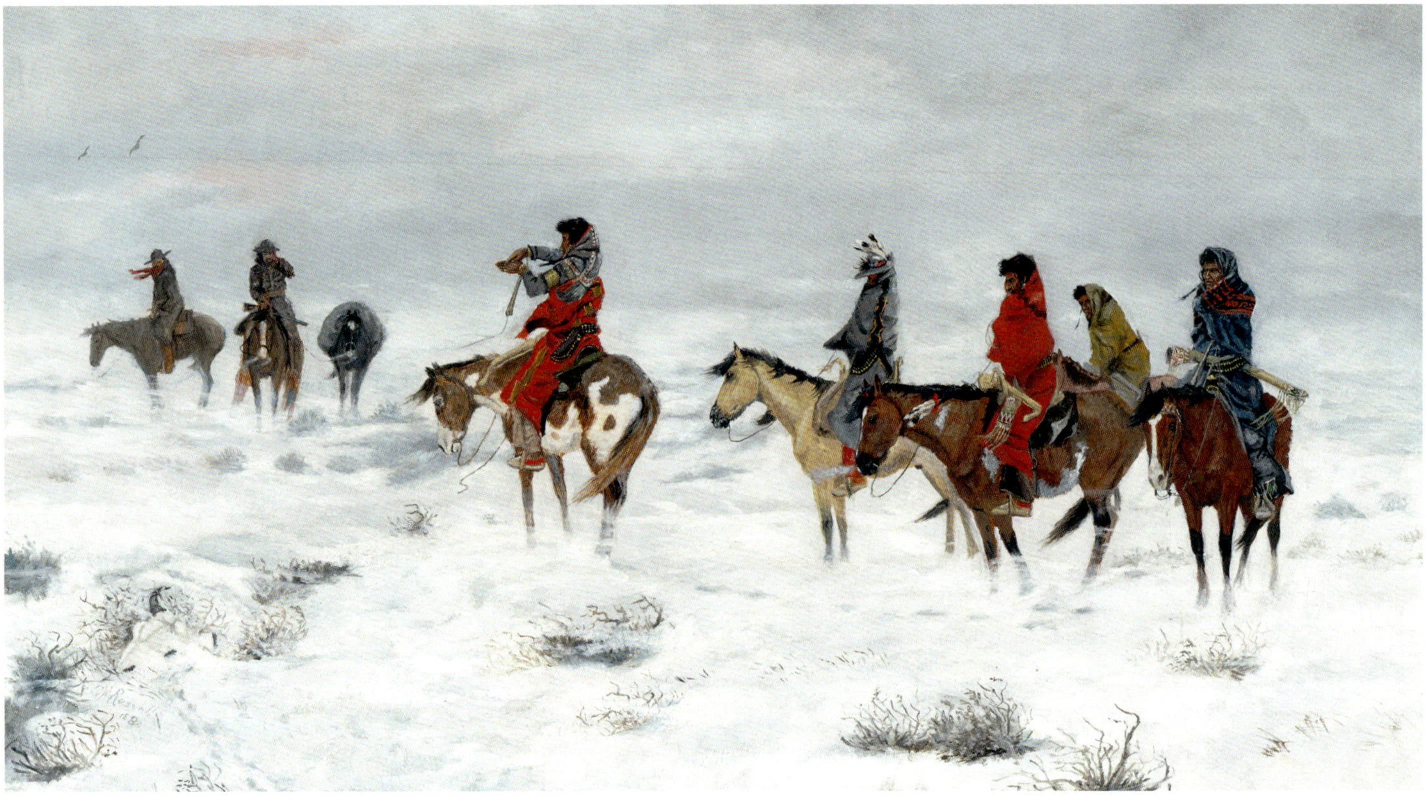

Cat. 81

Charles Marion Russell
Lost in a Snowstorm—We Are Friends
1888
Oil on canvas
24 × 43⅛ in.
Amon Carter Museum of American Art, Fort Worth, Texas, Amon G. Carter Collection, 1961.144

Russell became interested in Plains Indian Sign Language (PISL), or "hand talk," during his earliest days in Montana Territory. Over time, he learned basic signs, some of which he incorporated into his paintings. Here, the central mounted figure makes the sign for "horse." However, because signs require movement and context to fully understand, it is hard to know what, exactly, this figure is trying to communicate. Perhaps, given the painting's title, they are giving directions to cowboys lost in a snowstorm.

Lost in a Snowstorm—We Are Friends was reproduced in a variety of publications, including in Emerson Hough's *The Story of the Cowboy*, illustrated on the facing page, in which it is given the alternative description "A meeting in a blizzard (talking in sign language)" (cat. 82).

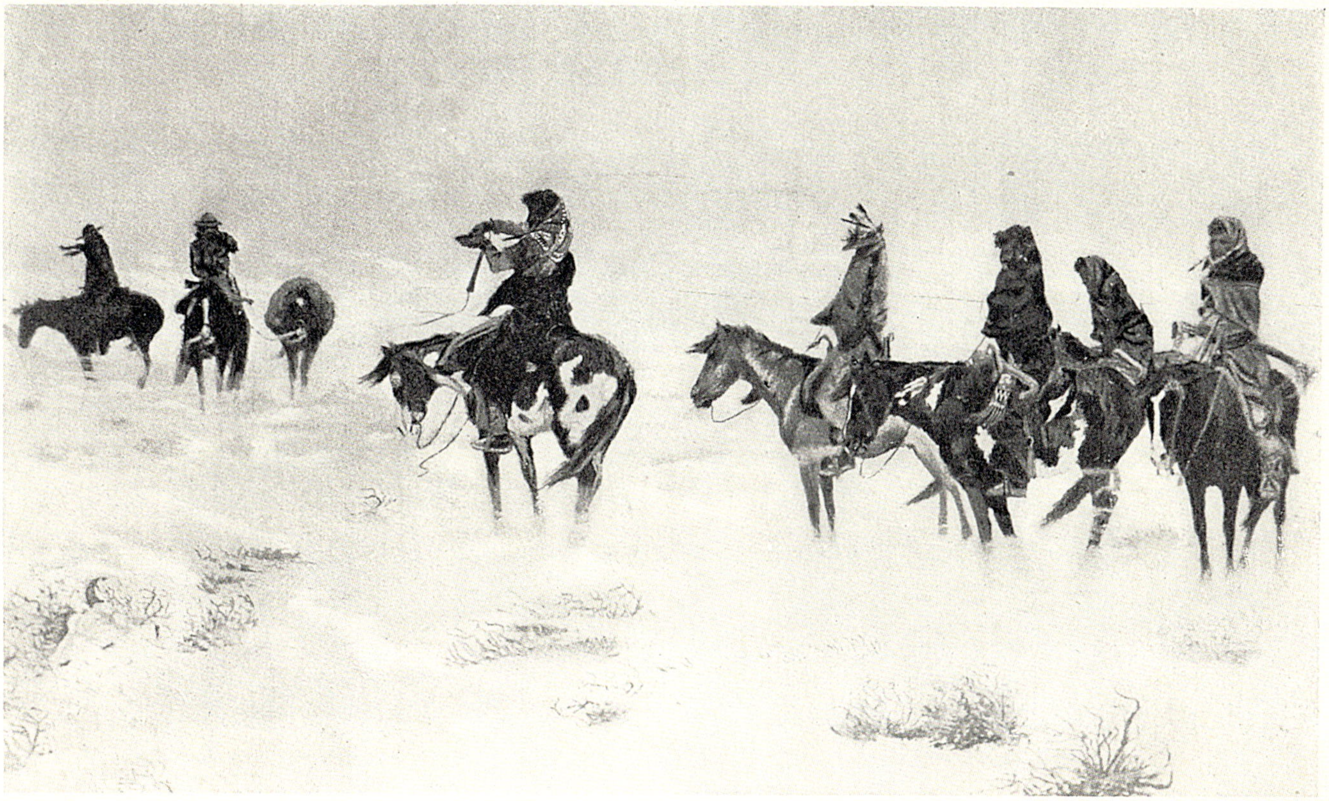

A meeting in a blizzard (talking in sign language).

Cat. 82

Charles Marion Russell
A Meeting in a Blizzard (Talking in Sign Language), in Emerson Hough, *The Story of the Cowboy*
1898
Ink on paper
8 × 5½ × 2 in.
Collection of the Craig Harrison family

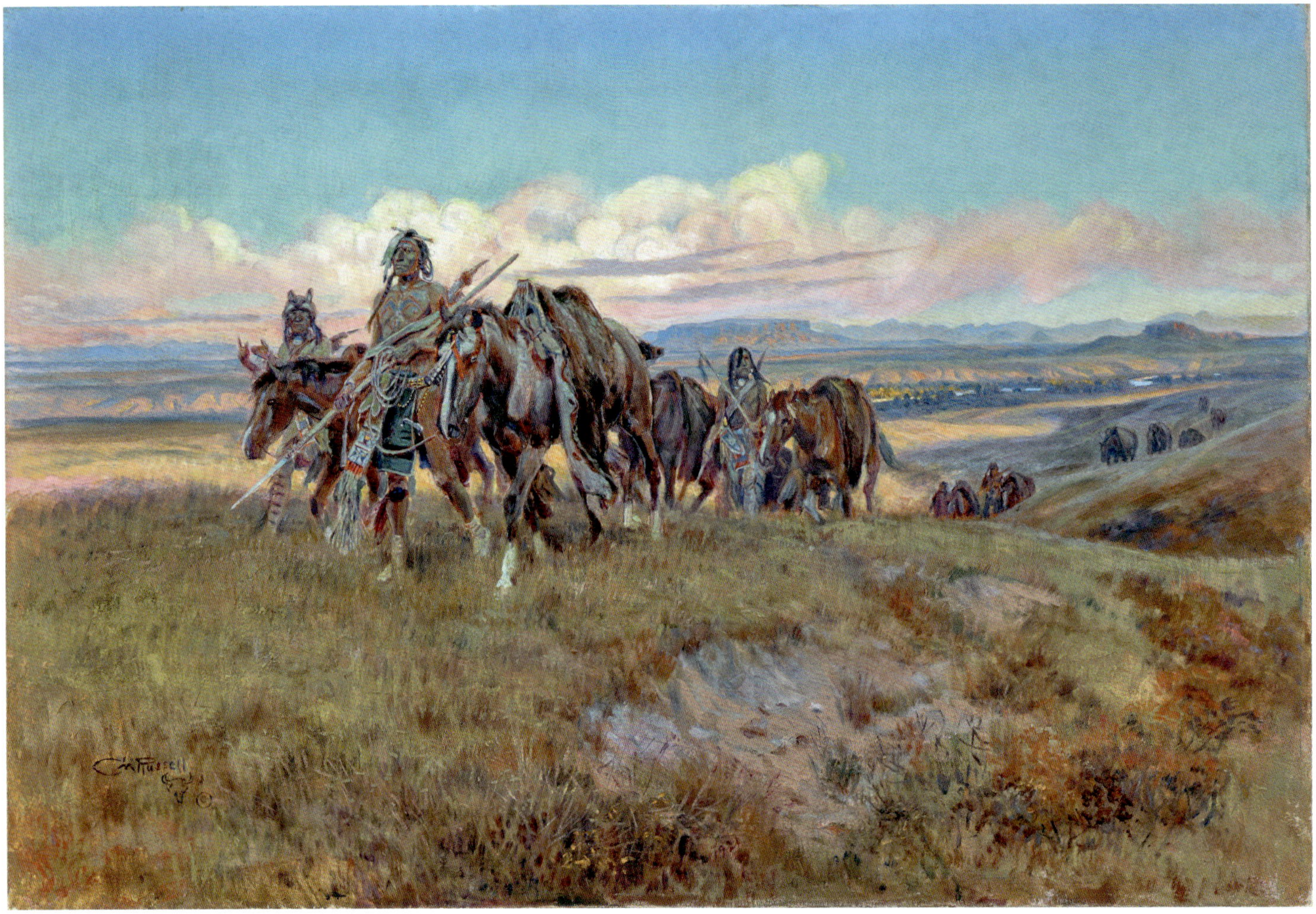

Cat. 83

Charles Marion Russell
In the Enemy's Country
1921
Oil on canvas
24 × 36 in.
Denver Art Museum: Gift of the Magness family in memory of Betsy Magness, 1991.751

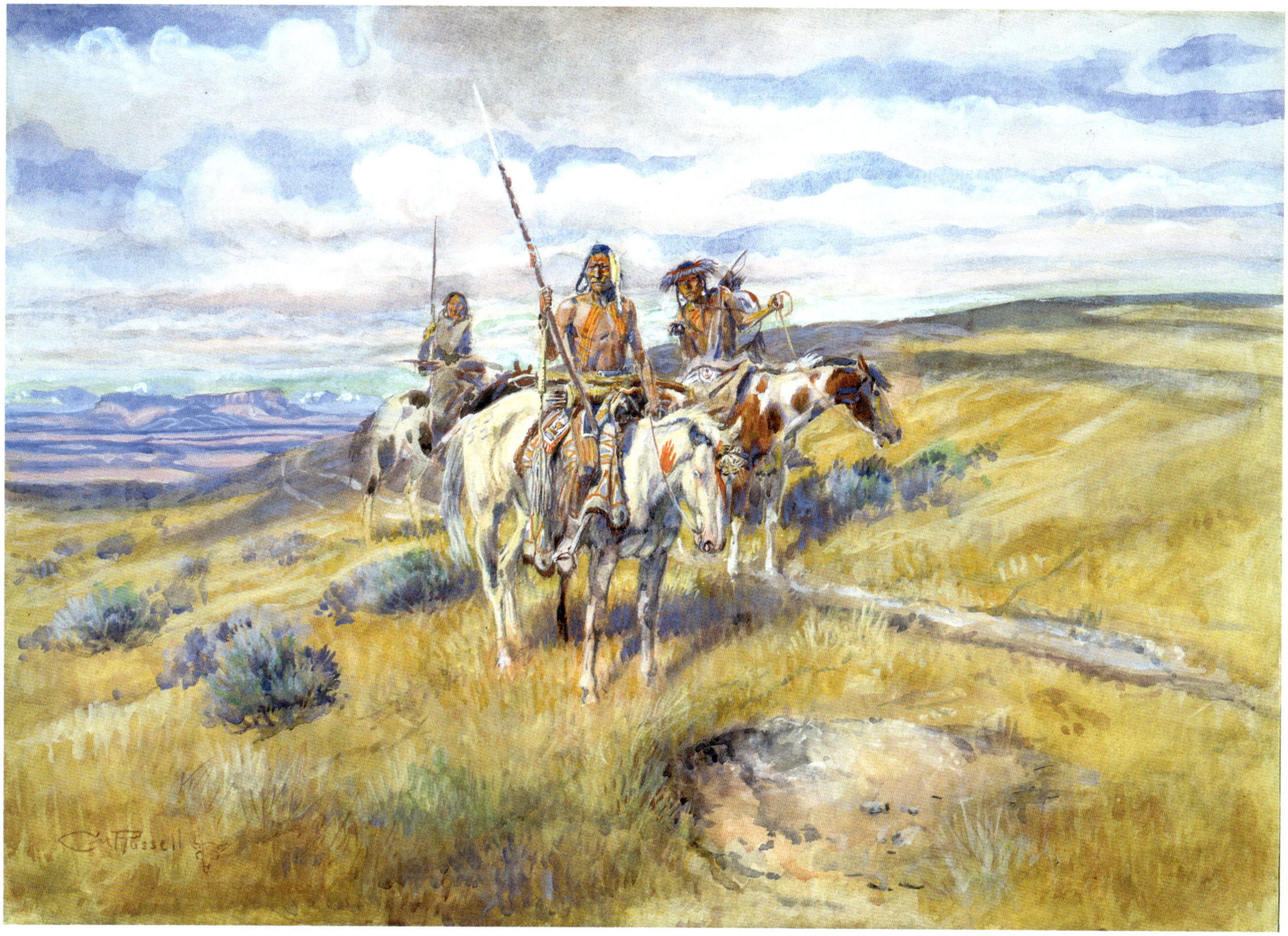

Cat. 84

Charles Marion Russell
Watching the Enemy—Blackfeet Indians, MT
c. 1918–20
Watercolor on paper
Framed: 26¼ × 33 × 2⅝ in.
Buffalo Bill Center of the West, Cody, Wyoming. Gift of William E. Weiss. 27.73

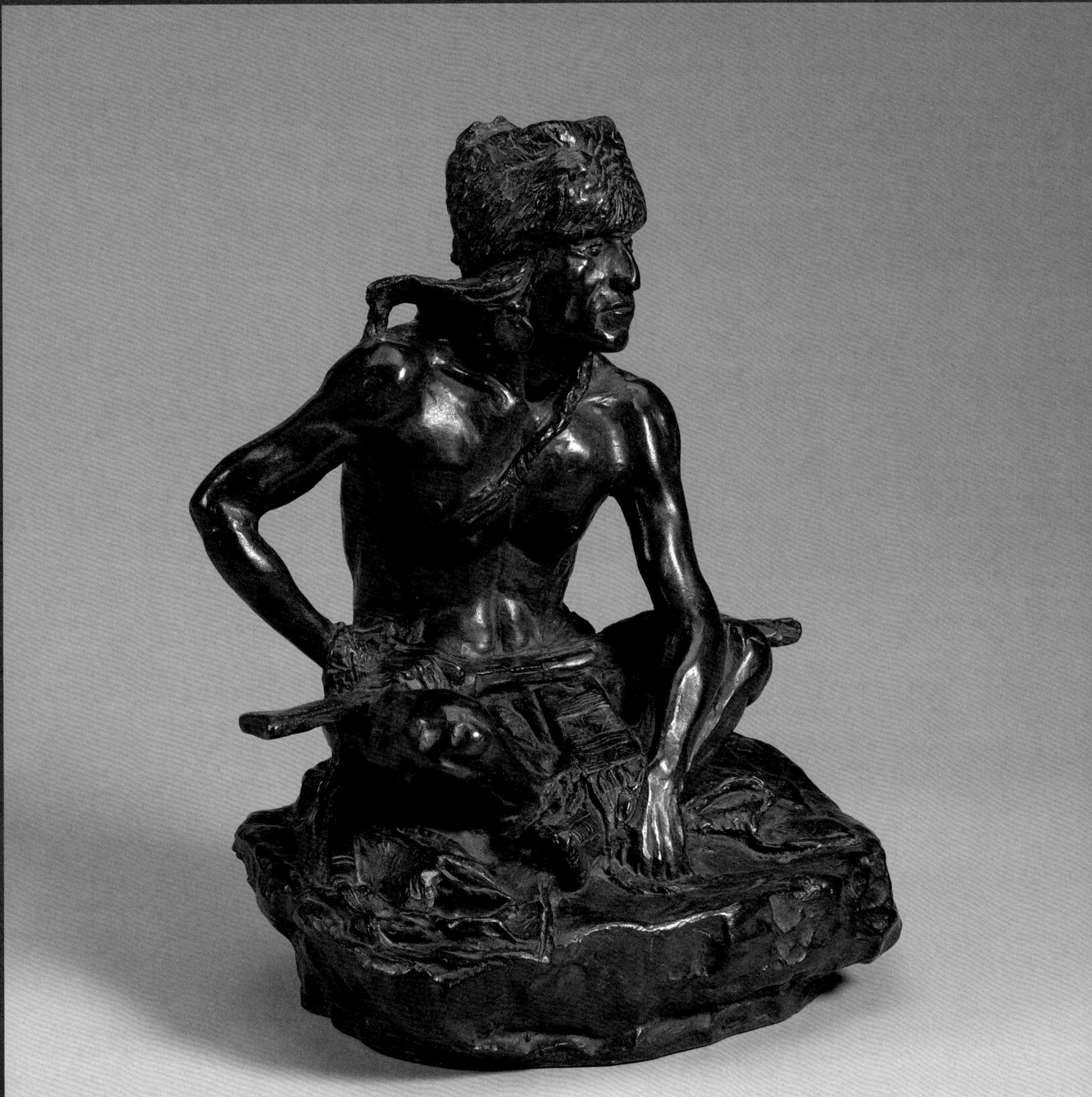

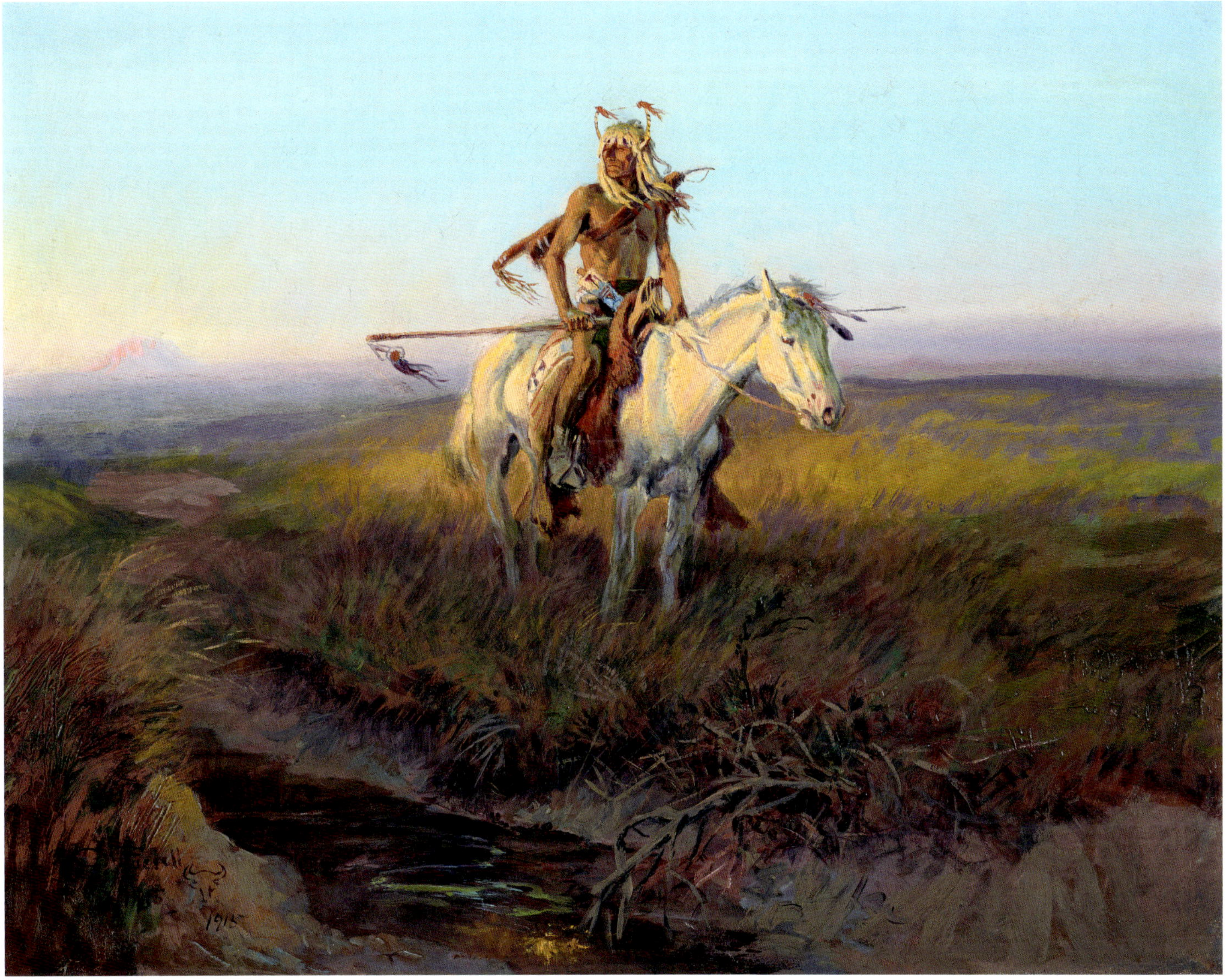

Cat. 86

Charles Marion Russell
The Scout
1915
Oil on canvas
21 × 26 in.
Petrie Collection, Denver, Colorado

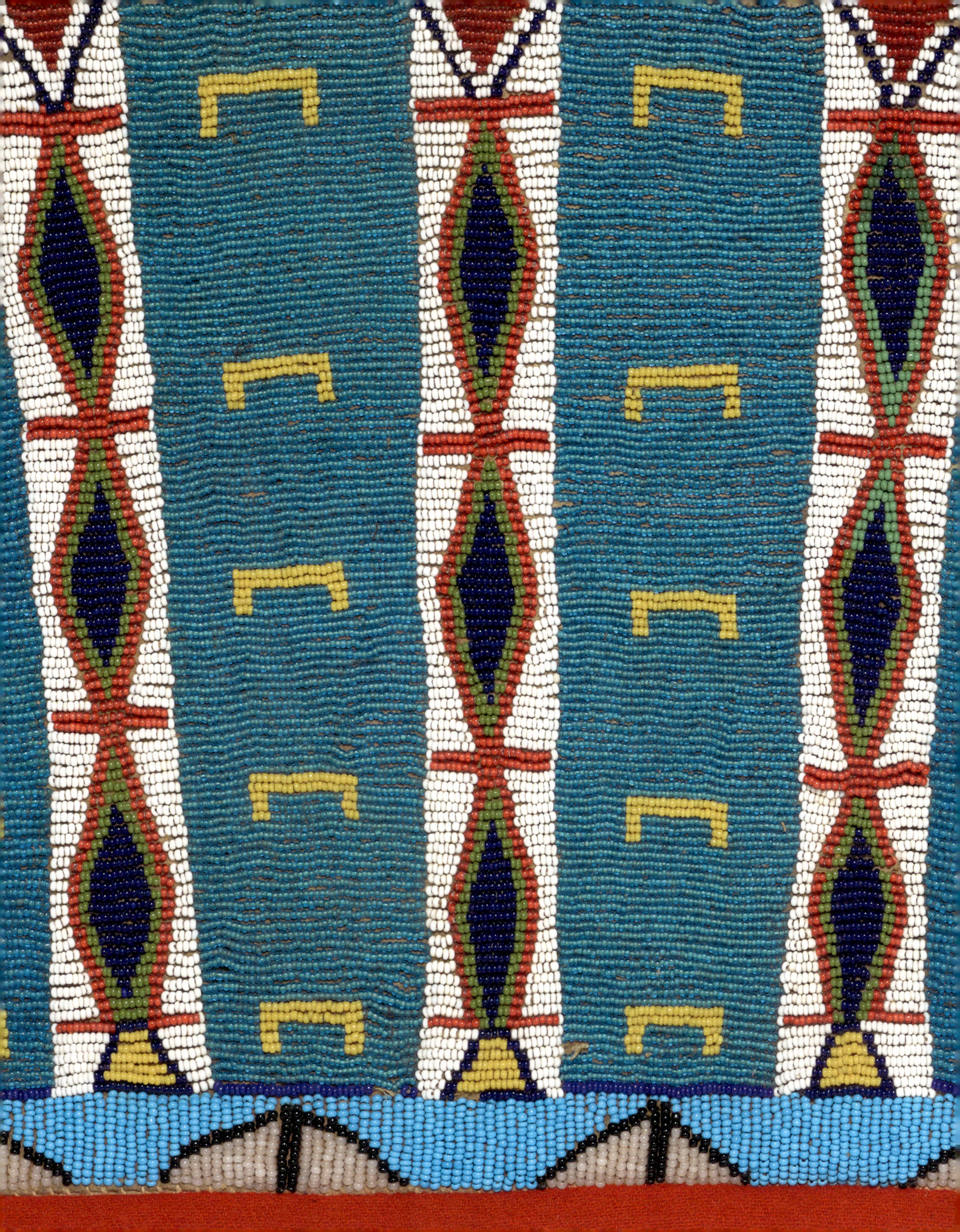

Exhibition Checklist

Provenance information as of date of publication (2026)

Cat. 1
Charles Marion Russell (1864–1926)
Piegans
1918
Oil on canvas
Framed: 34 × 46 × 2¼ in.
Petrie Collection, Denver, Colorado
Provenance: J. A. Cooper, MT; estate of Nancy Cooper Russell [1879–1940], MT and CA; collection of Cyrus Rowlett Smith [1899–1990], NY; collection of Homer E. Britzman [1901–1953], Pasadena, CA; Daniel C. Gainey [1897–1979], Owatonna, MN; William A. Findlay, Chicago, IL [d. 1976]; George A. Bates [1903–1989], Cary, IL; collection of William Foxley, CA and CO; (Coeur d' Alene Art Auction), Hayden, ID, no. 116, 2005; collection of Thomas A. Petrie, Denver, CO

Cat. 2
Amskaapii Pikanii artist
Ah'kooyiinimaatsis (Pipe Bag)
Before 1925
Beads, hide, thread, and sinew
25⅜ × 4¾ × 1¾ in.
Denver Art Museum: Source unknown, 1925.1
Provenance: Blackfeet tribe, possibly Montana or Canada, before 1925. Denver Art Museum, 1925

Cat. 3
Attributed to Percy (Two Gun) Plain Woman (Kainai, 1895–1961)
Ninaipistsii (War Robe)
c. 1930s
Painted hide
56 × 45 × 1½ in.
Denver Art Museum: Native Arts acquisition funds, 1938.26
Provenance: Scratching Chief, Southern Alberta, about 1930–38; purchased, Madge Hardin Walters [1870–1958], San Diego, CA, 1938; purchased, Denver Art Museum 1938

Cat. 4
Charles Marion Russell
Indian Hunters' Return
1900
Oil on canvas
33⅝ × 45½ in.
Montana Historical Society, Mackay Collection, x1954.02.01
Provenance: McKay Collection. Montana Historical Society, Helena, MT

Cat. 5
Kainai artist
Headdress
c. 1880
Ermine fur, golden eagle feathers, leather, fabric, bells, pigment, horsehair, resin, and rawhide
23½ × 12½ × 6 in.
Denver Art Museum: Native Arts acquisition funds, 1939.125.2
Provenance: One Spot; Stripe Bear [d.1926]. Big Sorrel Horse, Alberta, Canada; Madge Hardin Walters [1870–1958], San Diego, CA, by 1939; purchase, Denver Art Museum, 1939

Cat. 6
Amskaapii Pikanii artist
Roach
Early 1900s
Porcupine and deer hair
17 × 4 × 6 in.
The L. D. and Ruth Bax Collection at the Denver Art Museum, 1985.146
Provenance: Lionel Drewyer Bax [1898–1984] and Ruth Bax (née Schomburg) [1899–1986], Morrison, CO, by 1985; gift, Denver Art Museum, 1985

Cat. 7
Charles Marion Russell
Single-Handed
1912
Oil on canvas
Framed: 40½ × 43½ × 3 in.
Petrie Collection, Denver, Colorado
Provenance: Sale, Calgary "Victory" Stampede, 1919, Alberta, Canada; purchase, private collection, Canada, 1919; Walston C. Findlay Jr. [1903–1996], KS and NY; (Findlay Galleries), Chicago; purchase, William Whitridge, Stephenson, Maryland, ca. 1960s; (Kennedy Galleries, Inc), NY; collection of William Erhardt Weiss [1913–1985], NY and Cody, WY; Mr. and Mrs. William D. Weiss, Jackson, WY; collection of Thomas A. Petrie, Denver, CO

Cat. 8
Nitsitapii artist
Blanket Capote
1860s
Wool, beads, and brass
71¼ × 67½ × 12 in.
Denver Art Museum: Museum exchange with Jon Holstein, 1970.557
Provenance: Jon Holstein, NY, by 1970; exchange, Denver Art Museum, 1970

Cat. 9
Amskaapii Pikanii artist
Man's Leggings
c. 1890
Wool and leather
Each approx. 32 × 15 × 2 in.
Denver Art Museum: Native Arts acquisition funds, 1948.426A-B
Provenance: Lionel Drewyer Bax [1898–1984], Morrison, CO, by 1948; purchase, Denver Art Museum, 1948

Cat. 10
Charles Marion Russell
Joe Kipp's Trading Post
1898
Watercolor on paper
Framed: 20¼ × 26¼ × 2 in.
Buffalo Bill Center of the West, Cody, Wyoming. Gift of Charles Ulrick and Josephine Bay Foundation, Inc. 1.85
Provenance: Private collection, MT; private collection, MT; private collection; (Settlers West Galleries), AZ, 1980; private collection, 1980; Charles Ulrick and Josephine Bay Foundation, Inc., NY; gift, Buffalo Bill Historical Center (now, Buffalo Bill Center of the West), Cody, WY, 1984

Cat. 11
Charles Marion Russell
Robe Traders of Fort Benton
1901
Watercolor on paper
Framed: 27¾ × 37¾ × 1¼ in.
Gilcrease Museum, Tulsa, Oklahoma
Provenance: Private collection, MT; private collection, MT; private collection; (Settlers West Galleries), AZ, 1980; private collection, 1980; Charles Ulrick and Josephine Bay Foundation, Inc., NY; gift, Buffalo Bill Historical Center (now, Buffalo Bill Center of the West), Cody, WY, 1984

Cat. 12
Amskaapii Pikanii artist
Man's Shirt
Late 1800s
Leather, quills, horse hair, and commercial dye
34¼ × 55½ × 12 in.
The L. D. and Ruth Bax Collection at the Denver Art Museum, 1985.71
Provenance: Running Crane [1822–1902]; Lionel Drewyer Bax [1898–1984] and Ruth Bax (née Schomburg) [1899–1986], Morrison, CO, by 1985; gift, Denver Art Museum, 1985

Cat. 13
Charles Marion Russell
Red Man's Wireless
1916
Oil on canvas
42 × 72 in.
National Cowboy & Western Heritage Museum, Charles S. Jones Collection, museum purchase with funding provided by Joel McCrea
Provenance: Estate of Nancy Cooper Russell [1879–1940], MT and CA; purchase, Cyrus Rowlett Smith [1899–1990], NY, 1941; purchase, Homer E. Britzman [1901–1953], Pasadena, CA, 1941; purchase, Charles S. Jones [1895–1970], Los Angeles, 1941; gift, National Cowboy & Western Heritage Museum, Oklahoma City, OK

Cat. 14
Amskaapii Pikanii artist
Gun Case
Late 1800s
Beads and leather
80 × 6¾ × 1½ in.
The L. D. and Ruth Bax Collection at the Denver Art Museum, 1985.88
Provenance: Lionel Drewyer Bax [1898–1984] and Ruth Bax (née Schomburg) [1899–1986], Morrison, CO, by 1985; gift, Denver Art Museum, 1985

Cat. 15
Charles Marion Russell
Trouble Hunters
1910
Oil on canvas
Framed: 48 × 42 × 2½ in.
Petrie Collection, Denver, Colorado
Provenance: Private collection, Canada; private collection, Canada; private collection, Canada; collection of Thomas A. Petrie, Denver, CO

Cat. 16
Nitsitapii artist
Knife Case
Before 1964
Leather, cloth, wood, and beads
24 × 4½ × 1½ in.
Denver Art Museum: Museum exchange with George Terasaki, 1964.123A-B
Provenance: George Terasaki [1931–2010], New York, NY, by 1964; exchange, Denver Art Museum, 1964

Cat. 17
Charles Marion Russell
The Fireboat
1918
Oil on board
Framed: 23 × 32 × 2½ in.
C. M. Russell Museum, Great Falls, Montana
Provenance: Wade Hampton George [1877–1955], Great Falls, MT; by inheritance, Susan (née Kline) George [1872–1965], Great Falls, MT; gift, C. M. Russell Museum, Great Falls, MT

Cat. 18
Amskaapii Pikanii artist
Loop Necklace
After 1880
Leather, beads, and abalone shells
18¼ × 15½ × 1 in.
Denver Art Museum: Gift of Dr. Charles J. Norton, 1981.344
Provenance: Dr. Charles J. Norton [1929–1996], Denver, CO, by 1981; gift, Denver Art Museum, 1981

Cat. 19
Nora Spanish (Amskaapii Pikanii, 1898–1990)
Gloves
1940s
Leather and beads
Each approx. 18 × 8⅛ × 4¼ in.
Denver Art Museum: Bequest of the Estate of Gerald E. Welsh, 1981.240A-B
Provenance: Collection of the Artist; purchase, Gerald Eugene Welsh [1894–1981], Denver, CO, ca. 1940s; gift, Denver Art Museum, 1981

Cat. 20
Amskaapii Pikanii artist
Hard-Sole Moccasins
Late 1800s
Leather and beads
Each approx. 4⅝ ×4¾ × 10 in.
Denver Art Museum: Native Arts acquisition funds, 1947.91A-B
Provenance: Charles Wiegel [1873–1947], Denver, CO, before 1947; acquired, (Kohlberg's), Denver, CO, 1947; purchase, Denver Art Museum, 1947

Cat. 21
Nitsitapii artist
Moccasins
c. 1930
Hide and beads
Each approx. 4½ × 5 × 10 in.
Denver Art Museum: Native Arts acquisition funds, 1937.18A-B
Provenance: W. Grant Mackay, Banff, Canada, by 1937; purchase, Denver Art Museum, 1937

Cat. 22
Nitsitapii artist
Moccasins
Before 1938
Hide, beads, cloth, thread, and sinew
Each approx. 4½ × 4⅛ × 10½ in.
Denver Art Museum: Native Arts acquisition funds, 1938.38A-B
Provenance: Little Dog; acquired, Madge Hardin Walters [1870–1958], San Diego, CA, by 1938; purchase, Denver Art Museum, 1938

Cat. 23
Nitsitapii artist
Child's Moccasins
Before 1890
Hide and beads
Each approx. 3⅛ × 3⅛ × 5¾ in.
Denver Art Museum: Gift of Maude Steidley, 1935.27A-B
Provenance: Maude Steidley [1878–1958], Denver, CO, by 1890; gift, Denver Art Museum, 1935

Cat. 24
Nitsitapii artist
Moccasins
Before 1942
Leather, beads, and silk
Each approx. 3¼ × 3 × 6½ in.
Denver Art Museum: Gift of Mrs. J. P. Dowden, 1942.47A-B
Provenance: S. N. Wood [died 1942]; by inheritance, J. P. Dowden, Denver, CO; gift, Denver Art Museum, 1942

Cat. 25
Nitsitapii artist
Moccasins
Before 1846
Rawhide, beads, thread, and sinew
Each approx. 3¼ × 3⅞ ×10¼ in.
Denver Art Museum: Native Arts acquisition funds, 1934.16A-B
Provenance: Hazel O. Bennett, before 1934; purchase, Denver Art Museum, 1934

Cat. 26
Nitsitapii artist
Belt
c. 1900
Leather, beads, and silk
39 × 3 × ½ in.
Denver Art Museum: Bequest of Charles J. Norton, 1999.251
Provenance: Dr. Charles J. Norton [1929–1996], Denver, CO, by 1999; by bequest, Denver Art Museum, 1999

Cat. 27
Amskaapii Pikanii artist
Belt
Before 1936
Leather, beads, and cotton thread
43¼ × 2½ × ⅝ in.
Denver Art Museum: Gift of Thomas Dines, Quigg Newton Sr., and John Burnett, 1949.54
Provenance: Joseph R. Kettle [d. 1939], Denver, before 1936; purchase (Indian Crafts Association) 1936; gift, Denver Art Museum, 1947

Cat. 28
Nitsitapii artist
Belt
c. 1875
Leather, brass, steel, sinew, and thread
40 × 3½ × ¾ in.
Denver Art Museum: Native Arts acquisition funds, 1939.98
Provenance: Frank Red Crow [1880–1970], Blood Reserve, Cardston, Alberta, Canada; collection of Madge Hardin Walters [1870–1958], San Diego, CA, by 1939; purchase, Denver Art Museum, 1939

Cat. 29
Amskaapii Pikanii artist
Woman's Leggings
Late 1800s
Beads, canvas, muslin, and wool
Each approx. 12½ × 13 × ½ in.
Denver Art Museum: Gift of Dr. Charles J. Norton, 1982.90A-B
Provenance: Dr. Charles J. Norton [1929–1996], Denver, CO, by 1982; gift, Denver Art Museum, 1982

Cat. 30
Nitsitapii artist
Woman's Leggings
Late 1800s
Calico cloth, metal, flannel, silk ribbon, and beads
Each approx. 15 × 14¼ × ¼ in.
Denver Art Museum: Gift of Dr. Charles J. Norton, 1982.88A-B
Provenance: Dr. Charles J. Norton [1929–1996], Denver, CO, by 1982; gift, Denver Art Museum, 1982

Cat. 31
Amskaapii Pikanii artist
Woman's Leggings
c. 1945
Cloth, hide, and beads
Each approx. 13 × 14¾ × ⅜ in.
Denver Art Museum: Native Arts acquisition funds, 1947.84A-B
Provenance: (Private Dealer), Cody, WY, until 1945; purchase, collection of Lionel Drewyer Bax [1898–1984], Denver, 1945; purchase, Denver Art Museum, 1947

Cat. 32
Amskaapii Pikanii artist
Woman's Leggings
Before 1946
Beads, flannel, and trade cloth
Each approx. 18¼ × 11¾ × ⅜ in.
Denver Art Museum: Gift of Sarah Coolidge Vance, 1946.77A-B
Provenance: Sarah Coolidge Vance [1907–1953], Denver, CO, by 1946; gift, Denver Art Museum, 1946

Cat. 33
Charles Marion Russell
In the Wake of the Buffalo Runners
1911
Oil on canvas
Framed: 39½ × 45½ × 3½ in.
Private Collection
Provenance: Collection of artist; private collection, MT; private collection, MN, 1954; current owner, 1996

Cat. 34
Amskaapii Pikanii artist
Dress
Deer skin and tail, beads, flannel, and sinew
55 × 33 × 44 in.
C. M. Russell Museum, Great Falls, Montana
Provenance: City of Great Falls, MT; purchase, C. M. Russell Museum, Great Falls, MT, 1991

Cat. 35
Amskaapii Pikanii artist
Cradleboard
Early 1900s
Wood, hide, glass beads, thread, fabric, shells, and metal tacks
36 × 15 in.
The Crane Collection at the Denver Museum of Nature and Science
Provenance: Blackfeet, Canada. Crane Collections. Mary Crane. (EM Daniels Trading Post), Fontana, CA. Denver Museum of Nature and Science

Cat. 36
Charles Marion Russell
Waiting and Mad
1899
Oil on canvas
Framed: 21⅜ × 27⅛ × 2 in.
Indianapolis Museum of Art at Newfields, Gift of Harrison Eiteljorg Gallery of Western Art, 73.104.5
Provenance: (Kennedy Galleries), NY; purchase, Harrison Eiteljorg (Harrison Eiteljorg Gallery of Western Art), IN; gift, Indianapolis Museum of Art , IN, 1973

Cat. 37
Nitsitapii artist
Spoon
c. 1890
Buffalo horn
4¼ × 8⅞ × 2¾ in.
Denver Art Museum: Native Arts acquisition funds, 1938.316
Provenance: Collection of Madge Hardin Walters [1870–1958], San Diego, CA, by 1938; purchase, Denver Art Museum, 1938

Cat. 38
Kainai artist
Maul
Before 1939
Stone, rawhide, sinew, and paint
12¾ × 5⅜ × 3 in.
Denver Art Museum: Native Arts acquisition funds, 1939.309
Provenance: Frank Red Crow [1880–1970], Blood Reserve, Cardston, Alberta, Canada, by 1939; purchase, collection of Madge Hardin Walters [1870–1958], San Diego, CA, by 1939; purchase, Denver Art Museum, 1939

Cat. 39
Amskaapii Pikanii artist
Lodge Liner
c. 1920
Cowhide, paint, beads, and hair
82 × 174 in.
The L. D. and Ruth Bax Collection at the Denver Art Museum, 1985.259
Provenance: Lionel Drewyer [1898–1984] and Ruth Bax (née Schomburg) [1899–1986], Morrison, CO, by 1985; gift, Denver Art Museum, 1985

Cat. 40
Kainai artist
Backrest
1800s
Wood, cloth, and pigment
54¾ × 31½ in.
Denver Art Museum: Native Arts acquisition funds, 1936.251
Provenance: Frank Red Crow [1880–1970], Blood Reserve, Cardston, Alberta, Canada, by 1939; purchase, collection of Madge Hardin Walters [1870–1958], San Diego, CA, by 1939; purchase, Denver Art Museum, 1939

Cat. 41
Amskaapii Pikanii artist
Backrest
1885
Salix willow rods, paint, wool, cotton, real and artificial sinew, and beads
57¾ × 33¾ in.
Denver Art Museum: Native Arts acquisition funds, 1938.321
Provenance: Frank Red Crow [1880–1970], Blood Reserve, Cardston, Alberta, Canada, by 1936; purchase, Madge Hardin Walters [1870–1958], San Diego, CA, 1936; purchase, Denver Art Museum, 1936

Cat. 42
Amskaapii Pikanii artist
Parfleche
1885
Processed rawhide and paint
22¼ × 12½ × 3½ in.
Denver Art Museum: Native Arts acquisition funds, 1937.200
Provenance: Madge Hardin Walters [1870–1958], San Diego, CA, by 1937; purchased, Denver Art Museum, 1937

Cat. 43
Amskaapii Pikanii artist
Ah'kooyiinimaatsis (Pipe Bag)
Late 1800s
Leather and beads
27½ × 6½ × 1½ in.
Denver Art Museum: Gift of Dr. Charles J. Norton, 1982.86
Provenance: Dr. Charles J. Norton [1929–1996], Denver, CO, by 1982; gift, Denver Art Museum, 1982

Cat. 44
Charles Marion Russell
When Blackfeet and Sioux Meet
1908
Oil on canvas
Framed: 27½ × 37¼ × 3¼ in.
Sid Richardson Museum
Provenance: Estate of Nancy Cooper Russell [1879–1940], MT and CA; Alex Simpson Jr., PA; T. Carson Simpson, PA; (Newhouse Galleries), NYC; Sid W. Richardson [1891–1959], Ft. Worth, TX, 1949; Sid Richardson Museum, Ft. Worth, TX

Cat. 45
Charles Marion Russell
Counting Coup
1905
Bronze
13¼ × 17 × 14 in.
Petrie Collection, Denver, Colorado
Provenance: John Miller; purchase, collection of Thomas A. Petrie, Denver, CO

Cat. 46
Charles Marion Russell
The Enemy's Tracks
1920
Bronze
11¾ × 10¾ × 5½ in.
Petrie Collection, Denver, Colorado
Provenance: Estate of Nancy Cooper Russell [1879–1940], MT and CA. Collection of Thomas A. Petrie, Denver, CO

Cat. 47
Charles Marion Russell
When Arrows Spelled Death
1902
Watercolor on paper
Framed: 21 × 26¾ in.
Buffalo Bill Center of the West, Cody, Wyoming. Gift of Charles Ulrick and Josephine Bay Foundation, Inc. 97.60
Provenance: Estate of Nancy Cooper Russell [1879–1940], MT and CA; private collection, CA; (Hammer Gallery), NY; purchase, Charles Ulrick and Josephine Bay Foundation, Inc., NY; gift, Buffalo Bill Historical Center (now, Buffalo Bill Center of the West), Cody, WY, 1960

Cat. 48
Charles Marion Russell
The Medicine Man
1908
Oil on canvas
30 × 48⅛ in.
Amon Carter Museum of American Art, Fort Worth, Texas, Amon G. Carter Collection, 1961.171
Provenance: Private collection; Kilmer estate; private collection, PA; Amon G. Carter Sr. [1879–1955], Ft. Worth, TX; Amon Carter Museum of American Art, Ft. Worth, TX

Cat. 49
Charles Marion Russell
The Medicine Man
1920
Bronze
7 × 6 × 5 in.
Petrie Collection, Denver, Colorado
Provenance: Estate of Nancy Cooper Russell [1879–1940], MT and CA. Collection of Thomas A. Petrie, Denver, CO

Cat. 50
Amskaapii Pikanii artist
Aistookiimaaksi (Hand Drum)
Before 1860
Leather, paint, wood, and ink
30¼ × 40¾ × 2 in. dia.
The L. D. and Ruth Bax Collection at the Denver Art Museum, 1985.245
Provenance: Lionel Drewyer Bax [1898–1984] and Ruth Bax (née Schomburg) [1899–1986], Morrison, CO, by 1985; gift, Denver Art Museum, 1985

Cat. 51
Charles Marion Russell
Buffalo Hunt
1898
Oil on canvas
18⅛ × 25⅜ in.
Denver Art Museum: Gift of Sharon Magness, 1997.517
Provenance: Sharon Magness, Denver, CO; gift, Denver Art Museum, 1997

Cat. 52
Charles Marion Russell
The Silk Robe
1890
Oil on canvas
Framed: 34¾ × 46¼ × 2½ in.
Amon Carter Museum of American Art, Fort Worth, Texas, Amon G. Carter Collection, 1961.135
Provenance: Private collection, MT; private collection, MT; private collection, MT; Amon G. Carter Sr. [1879–1955], Ft. Worth, TX; Amon Carter Museum of American Art, Ft. Worth, TX

Cat. 53
Amskaapii Pikanii artist
Scraper
1800s
Antler, metal, rawhide, and a screw
13⅜ × 4¼ × 2⅛ in.
Denver Art Museum: Native Arts acquisition funds, 1938.326
Provenance: Otter Woman Morning Gun [1874–1962], Blackfeet Indian Reservation, Browning, MT, until 1937; purchase, (Blackfeet Indian Craft Shop), Browning, MT, 1937; purchase, Madge Hardin Walters [1870–1958], San Diego, CA, 1937; purchase, Denver Art Museum, 1938

Cat. 54
Amskaapii Pikanii artist
Hide Fleshing Tool
Before 1860
Bone, rawhide, fabric, sinew, and thread
30¼ × 40¾ × 2 in.
Denver Art Museum: Native Arts acquisition funds, 1938.301
Provenance: Probably collection of William G. Conrad [1848–1914], Fort Benton, MT, after 1868; by descent, private collection. Purchase, collection of Madge Hardin Walters [1870–1958], San Diego, CA, probably 1936; purchase, Denver Art Museum, 1938

Cat. 55
Amskaapii Pikanii artist
Hide Fleshing Tool
Mid-1800s
Hide, iron, and cloth
11⅝ × 1½ × 1⅞ in.
Denver Art Museum: Gift of Dr. Charles J. Norton, 1984.624
Provenance: (Blackfeet Craft Shop), Browning, MT, by 1970; purchase, Dr. Charles J. Norton [1929–1996], Denver, 1970; gift, Denver Art Museum, 1984

Cat. 56
Charles Marion Russell
Buffalo Hunt, Number 40
1919
Oil on canvas
Framed: 39 × 57¼ × 3½ in.
Petrie Collection, Denver, Colorado
Provenance: Private collection, PA; Amon Carter Museum of American Art, Ft. Worth, TX; collection of Thomas A. Petrie, Denver, CO

Cat. 57
Charles Marion Russell
Meat for Wild Men
1924
Bronze
11½ × 38½ × 23 in.
Petrie Collection, Denver, Colorado
Provenance: Charles [1864–1926] and Nancy Cooper [1879–1940] Russell, MT; William W. Armstrong, 1924; Charles M. Cotton [1884–1951], Los Angeles, CA, ca. 1930s; by descent, Cotton family, 1951; private collection; (Coeur d'Alene Art Auction), Hayden, ID, no. 80, 2008; purchase, collection of Thomas A. Petrie, Denver, CO, 2008

Cat. 58
Charles Marion Russell
Friend Frank
1914
Watercolor and ink on paper
12¼ × 6 in.
Petrie Collection, Denver, Colorado
Provenance: Private collection, MT, 1914; private collection, NH, 1941–1980. Private collection, 1981; private collection, MT, 1989. Collection of Thomas A. Petrie, Denver, CO

Cat. 59
Charles Marion Russell
Napi and the Mice People
1915
Watercolor and ink on paper
8½ × 6⅓ in.
Petrie Collection, Denver, Colorado
Provenance: Private collection, MT; collection of Thomas A. Petrie, Denver, CO

Cat. 60
Charles Marion Russell
Secrets of the Night
1926
Bronze
13½ × 6¾ × 6¼ in.
Denver Art Museum: Gift of Sharon Magness, 1997.516
Provenance: Sharon Magness, Denver, CO; gift, Denver Art Museum, 1997

Cat. 61
Charles Marion Russell
Standing Fearlessly, His Arms Thrown Downward Exposing His Breast
c. 1898
Oil on board
Framed: 20 × 25¾ × 1⅛ in.
Denver Art Museum: Gift of Fred Rosenstock in memory of his wife, Frances, 1973.32
Provenance: Fred A. Rosenstock [1895–1986], Denver, CO; gift, Denver Art Museum, 1973

Cat. 62
Charles Marion Russell
The Kindergarten
1890
Oil on board
10½ × 12¼ in.
Petrie Collection, Denver, Colorado
Provenance: (Kennedy Galleries, Inc), NY. Collection of William Erhardt Weiss [1913–1985], NY and Cody, WY, 1971; Mr. and Mrs. William D. Weiss, Jackson, WY; (Coeur d'Alene Art Auction), Reno, NV, July 26, 2003, no. 83; purchase, collection of Carl W. Knobloch Jr. [1930–2016], WY; (Christie's), New York, Stewards of the West: The Knobloch Collection, May 17, 2022, no. 45; purchase, collection of Thomas A. Petrie, Denver, CO

Cat. 63
Charles Marion Russell
The Story Teller
1893–95
Watercolor on paper
Framed: 24¼ × 27¾ × 1⅞ in.
Buffalo Bill Center of the West, Cody, Wyoming. Gift of William E. Weiss. 11.74
Provenance: Collection of artist; Andrew Jackson Davis Jr., Butte, MT. Possibly, (M. Knoedler & Co.), NY, by 1956. Collection of William Erhardt Weiss [1913–1985], NY, and Cody, WY, by 1959; gift, Buffalo Bill Historical Center (now, Buffalo Bill Center of the West), Cody, WY, 1974

Cat. 64
Kate Red Crow (Kainai, c. 1884–1950)
Doll
1935
Cloth, leather, beads, and human hair
13¾ × 7 × 2½ in.
Denver Art Museum: Native Arts acquisition funds, 1946.313
Provenance: Collection of artist. Collection of Madge Hardin Walters [1870–1958], San Diego, CA, 1935; purchase, Denver Art Museum, 1946

Cat. 65
Kate Red Crow (Kainai, c. 1884–1950)
Doll
1935
Cloth, hide, beads, ermine, human hair, rawhide, and feather
15¾ × 6½ × 2¾ in.
Denver Art Museum: Native Arts acquisition funds, 1946.311
Provenance: Collection of artist. Collection of Madge Hardin Walters [1870–1958], San Diego, CA, 1935; purchase, Denver Art Museum, 1946

Cat. 66
Sstaániiniki (or Cecile Last Star) (Amskaapii Pikanii, 1895–1966)
Boy's Suit
Mid-1900s
Buckskin, beads, and wool
Shirt: 21½ × 44 × 1⅝ in.;
Leggings: each approx. 23½ × 9 × 1 in.
Denver Art Museum: Native Arts acquisition funds, 1965.254.1-2
Provenance: Delbert Jennings Orr [1937–2020], Denver, by 1965; purchase, Denver Art Museum, 1965

Cat. 67
Amskaapii Pikanii artist
Boy's Leggings
c. 1920
Leather and beads
Each approx. 31½ × 15 × 1⅝ in.
Denver Art Museum: Gift of Dr. Charles J. Norton, 1982.95A-B
Provenance: (Private dealer), Oklahoma, by 1962; purchase, Dr. Charles J. Norton [1929–1996], Denver, 1962; gift, Denver Art Museum, 1982

Cat. 68
Cecile Theresa Yellow Kidney (Amskaapii Pikanii, 1866–1951)
Toy Spoon
c. 1938
Grass
6 × 2¾ × 1 in.
Denver Art Museum: Gift of Kenneth Disher, 1938.569
Provenance: Collection of artist; acquired, Kenneth Disher, Washington, DC, by 1938; gift, Denver Art Museum, 1938

Cat. 69
Cecile Theresa Yellow Kidney (Amskaapii Pikanii, 1866–1951)
Toy Spoon
c. 1938
Grass
7⅛ × 2¾ × 1⅜ in.
Denver Art Museum: Gift of Kenneth Disher, 1938.568
Provenance: Collection of artist; acquired, Kenneth Disher, Washington, DC, by 1938; gift, Denver Art Museum, 1938

Cat. 70
Amskaapii Pikanii artist
Dress Yoke
c. 1900
Hide, beads, muslin, and flour sack
22 × 34 × 11 in.
Denver Art Museum: Gift of Dr. Charles J. Norton, 1980.214
Provenance: (Private dealer), 1960; purchase, Dr. Charles J. Norton [1929–1996], Denver, by 1980; gift, Denver Art Museum, 1980

Cat. 71
Charles Marion Russell
Indian Women Moving
1898
Oil on canvas
24¼ × 36 in.
Amon Carter Museum of American Art, Fort Worth, Texas, Amon G. Carter Collection, 1961.147
Provenance: Private collection, MT; The Mint Corporation, MT; Amon G. Carter Sr. [1879–1955], Ft. Worth, TX; Amon Carter Museum of American Art, Ft. Worth, TX

Cat. 72
Amskaapii Pikanii artist
Saddle
1870s
Wood, buffalo hide, paint, tack, copper, rawhide, and steel
25 × 22¾ × 25 in.
Denver Art Museum: Native Arts acquisition funds, 1939.312
Provenance: Madge Hardin Walters [1870–1958], San Diego, CA, by 1938; purchase, Denver Art Museum, 1939

Cat. 73
Amskaapii Pikanni artist
Crupper
1885
Hide, beads, wool, cloth, canvas, and cotton
39 × 22 × 2¾ in.
Denver Art Museum: Purchase from Madge Hardin Walters, 1938.41
Provenance: Jeanette Calf Robe Day Rider, Blackfeet Indian Reservation, Browning, MT, until 1937; (Blackfeet Indian Craft Shop), Browning, MT, 1937; purchase, collection of Madge Hardin Walters [1870–1958], San Diego, CA, 1937; purchase, Denver Art Museum, 1938

Cat. 74
Amskaapii Pikanii artist
Martingale
Late 1800s
Cloth, beads, leather, and thimbles
53½ × 12¼ × ⅞ in.
The L. D. and Ruth Bax Collection at the Denver Art Museum, 1985.111
Provenance: Lionel Drewyer Bax [1898–1984] and Ruth Bax (née Schomburg) [1899–1986], Morrison, CO, by 1985; gift, Denver Art Museum, 1985

Cat. 75
Amskaapii Pikanii artist
Double Saddle Bag
c. 1930s
Buckskin, beads, sequins, and cloth
57 × 15 × 3 in.
Denver Art Museum: Native Arts acquisition funds, 1947.85
Provenance: Katherine Lindsey Perkins [1887–1965], Allenspark, CO; purchase, Denver Art Museum, 1947

Cat. 76
Reuben Black Boy (Amskaapii Pikanii, 1883–1967)
Horse Tail Ornament
1942
Golden eagle feathers, horse hair, cloth, and hide
24 × 7½ × 1½ in.
Denver Art Museum: Gift of Reuben Black Boy, 1942.101
Provenance: Collection of artist, Browning, MT; gift, Denver Art Museum, 1942

Cat. 77
Amskaapii Pikanii artist
Riding Quirt and Cuff
1900s
Bone, beads, and cloth
Quirt: 43¼ × 1½ × 1⅛ in.;
Cuff: 3½ × 11¼ × 1¼ in.
The L. D. and Ruth Bax Collection at the Denver Art Museum, 1985.85A-B
Provenance: Theodore Last Star [1890–1960], Blackfeet Indian Reservation, Browning, MT. Collection of Lionel Drewyer Bax [1898–1984] and Ruth Bax (née Schomburg) [1899–1986], Morrison, CO, by 1984; gift, Denver Art Museum, 1985

Cat. 78
Charles Marion Russell
The Horse Thieves
1901
Oil on canvas
Framed: 33¼ × 39½ × 2¾ in.
Petrie Collection, Denver, Colorado
Provenance: Private collection, MT; Moody Estate, TX; Amon G. Carter [1879–1955], Ft. Worth, TX; Amon Carter Museum of American Art, Ft. Worth, TX; private collection; collection of Thomas A. Petrie, Denver, CO

Cat. 79
Charles Marion Russell
When White Men Turn Red
1922
Oil on canvas
36½ × 24 in.
Sid Richardson Museum
Provenance: (Stendahl Galleries), Los Angeles; Howard M. Vanderslice [1853–1929], Kansas City and Los Angeles; Kansas City Art Institute, MO; Burr McGaughen, St. Louis, MO; (Newhouse Galleries), NYC; Sid W. Richardson [1891–1959], Ft. Worth, TX, 1946; Sid Richardson Museum, Ft. Worth, TX

Cat. 80
Charles Marion Russell
White Man's Buffalo
1919
Oil on canvas
Framed: 20½ × 29½ in.
Gilcrease Museum, Tulsa, Oklahoma
Provenance: Private collection, NY; collection of Thomas Gilcrease [1890–1962], Gilcrease Museum, Tulsa, OK

Cat. 81
Charles Marion Russell
Lost in a Snowstorm—We Are Friends
1888
Oil on canvas
24 × 43⅛ in.
Amon Carter Museum of American Art, Fort Worth, Texas, Amon G. Carter Collection, 1961.144
Provenance: Private collection, MT; private collection, NY; Amon G. Carter Sr. [1879–1955], Ft. Worth, TX; Amon Carter Museum of American Art, Ft. Worth, TX

Cat. 82
Charles Marion Russell
A Meeting in a Blizzard (Talking in Sign Language), in Emerson Hough, *The Story of the Cowboy*
1898
Ink on paper
8 × 5½ in.
Collection of the Craig Harrison family

Cat. 83
Charles Marion Russell
In the Enemy's Country
1921
Oil on canvas
24 × 36 in.
Denver Art Museum: Gift of the Magness family in memory of Betsy Magness, 1991.751
Provenance: (Morgan Wunderlich Galleries), Chicago, IL; George A. Bates, Cary, IL; private collection, Scottsdale, AZ, 1989; (Findlay Galleries), Chicago, IL; purchase, Sharon Magness; gift, Denver Art Museum, 1991

Cat. 84
Charles Marion Russell
Watching the Enemy—Blackfeet Indians, MT
c. 1918–20
Watercolor on paper
Framed: 26¼ × 33 × 2⅝ in.
Buffalo Bill Center of the West, Cody, Wyoming. Gift of William E. Weiss. 27.73
Provenance: Estate of Nancy Cooper Russell [1879–1940], MT and CA; collection of Frederic George Renner [ca. 1897–1987], AZ, by 1957; collection of William Erhardt Weiss [1913–1985], NY, and Cody, WY; gift, Buffalo Bill Historical Center (now, Buffalo Bill Center of the West), Cody, WY, 1973

Cat. 85
Charles Marion Russell
Watcher of the Plains
1901
Bronze
10¾ × 8½ × 8 in.
Petrie Collection, Denver, Colorado
Provenance: Charles [1864–1926] and Nancy Cooper [1879–1940] Russell, MT; Ernest E. Quantrell [1882–1962], NY; by descent, Quantrell family. (Questroyal Fine Art), NY; purchase, collection of Thomas A. Petrie, Denver, CO

Cat. 86
Charles Marion Russell
The Scout
1915
Oil on canvas
21 × 26 in.
Petrie Collection, Denver, Colorado
Provenance: Private collection; private collection, MO; Woodcock Foundation for the Appreciation of the Arts, MO; collection of Thomas A. Petrie, Denver, CO

Selected Readings

Adams, David Wallace. *Education for Extinction: American Indians and the Boarding School Experience, 1875–1928*. 2nd ed. University Press of Kansas, 2020.

Adams, Ramon F., and Homer E. Britzman. *Charles M. Russell: The Cowboy Artist, a Biography*. Trail's End Publishing Co., 1948.

Ahlberg Yohe, Jill, and Teri Greeves, ed. *Hearts of Our People: Native Women Artists*. Minneapolis Institute of Art and University of Washington Press, 2019.

Archibald, Jo-Ann. *Indigenous Storywork: Educating the Heart, Mind, Body and Spirit*. University of British Columbia Press, 2008.

Bastien, Betty. *Blackfoot Ways of Knowing: The Worldview of the Siksikaaitsitapi*. University of Calgary Press, 2004.

Bell, Gloria. "Competing Sovereignties: Indigeneity and the Visual Culture of Catholic Colonization at the 1925 Pontifical Missionary Exhibition," *Journal of Global Catholicism* 3, no. 2 (2019): 18–41.

Bell, Gloria Jane. *Eternal Sovereigns: Indigenous Artists, Activists, and Travelers Reframing Rome*. Duke University Press, 2024.

Binnema, Theodore. *Common and Contested Ground: A Human and Environmental History of the Northwestern Plains*. University of Oklahoma Press, 2001.

Blackhawk, Ned. *The Rediscovery of America: Native Peoples and the Unmaking of U.S. History*. Yale University Press, 2023.

Bol, Marsha C. *The Art and Tradition of Beadwork*. Gibbs Smith, 2018.

Bordeaux, Clementine. "Wówayupike: Relational Practices Between Art, Land, and Culture." PhD diss., University of California, Los Angeles, 2024.

Bottomly-O'Looney, Jennifer, and Kirby Lambert, *Montana's Charlie Russell: Art in the Collection of the Montana Historical Society*. Montana Historical Society Press Press, 2014.

Brasser, Ted J. *Native American Clothing: An Illustrated History*. Firefly Books, 2009.

Brink, Jack. *Imagining Head-Smashed-In: Aboriginal Buffalo Hunting on the Northern Plains*. Athabasca University Press, 2008.

Broughton, Deanna Tidwell. *Hide, Wood, and Willow: Cradles of the Great Plains Indians*. University of Oklahoma Press, 2019.

Bruyneel, Kevin. *Settler Memory: The Disavowal of Indigeneity and the Politics of Race in the United States*. University of North Carolina Press, 2021.

Buchanan, Meghan E., and B. Jacob Skousen, ed. *Tracing the Relational: The Archaeology of Worlds, Spirits, and Temporalities*. The University of Utah Press, 2015.

Cannon, Aubrey, ed. *Structured Worlds: The Archaeology of Hunter-Gatherer Thought and Action*. Equinox Pub., 2011.

Carlos, Ann M., and Frank D. Lewis. *Commerce on a Frozen Sea: Native Americans and the European Fur Trade*. University of Pennsylvania Press, 2010.

Carter Bulletin: Vol. 1 (Charles M. Russell: New Perspectives). Amon Carter Museum of American Art, 2025. https://bulletin-v1.cartermuseum.org/.

Caverhill, Heather. "Mutable Modernisms: An Art Colony in Nitsitapii Territory and the Lives of Its Works." PhD diss., University of British Columbia, 2024.

"Charles M. Russell—A Special Issue." *Montana The Magazine of Western History* 34, no. 3 (1984).

Clark, Ronald H. *Charles M. Russell Legacies: Amazing Tales of Charles and Nancy Russell, Josephine Wright, and Nancy Josephine Clark*. Published by the author, 2025.

Conn, Richard. *A Persistent Vision: Art of the Reservation Days: The L. D. and Ruth Bax Collection of the Denver Art Museum*. Denver Art Museum, 1986.

Conn, Richard. *Circles of the World: Traditional Art of the Plains Indians*. Denver Art Museum, 1982.

Conn, Richard. *Native American Art in the Denver Art Museum*. Denver Art Museum, 1979.

Conn, Richard. *Robes of White Shell and Sunrise: Personal Decorative Arts of the Native American*. Denver Art Museum, 1974.

"Connections: The Blackfeet and Winold Reiss." Museum of the Plains Indian. Accessed January 6, 2026. https://iacbmuseums-viewingroom.exhibit-e.art/viewing-room/connections-the-blackfeet-and-winold-reiss#tab:slideshow;tab-1:thumbnails.

Craig, David R., Laurie Yung, and William T. Borrie, "'Blackfeet Belong to the Mountains': Hope, Loss, and Blackfeet Claims to Glacier National Park, Montana," *Conservation and Society* 10, no. 3 (2012): 232–42.

Dear, Elizabeth A. *C. M. Russell's Log Studio*. C. M. Russell Museum, 1995.

Deleary, Mary. "A Place for Us to Sit: Making and Remembering Visual and Material Histories of Deshkan Ziibiing." PhD diss., University of Oklahoma, 2023.

Dempsey, Hugh A. "Tracking C. M. Russell in Canada, 1888–1889." *Montana The Magazine of Western History* 39, no. 3 (1989): 2–15.

Dempsey, L. James. *Blackfoot War Art: Pictographs of the Reservation Period, 1880–2000*. University of Oklahoma Press, 2016.

Dippie, Brian W., ed. *Charlie Russell Roundup: Essays on America's Favorite Cowboy Artist*. Montana Historical Society Press, 1999.

Dippie, Brian W. *Looking at Russell*. Amon Carter Museum, 1987.

Dippie, Brian W., ed. *"Paper Talk": Charlie Russell's American West*. Alfred A. Knopf Inc., 1979.

Dunbar-Ortiz, Roxanne. *An Indigenous Peoples' History of the United States*. Beacon Press, 2014.

Duncan, Dayton, and Ken Burns. *Blood Memory: The Tragic Decline and Improbable Resurrection of the American Bison*. Alfred A. Knopf, 2023.

Dyck, Paul. "Lone Wolf Returns to That Long Ago Time," *Montana The Magazine of Western History* 22, no. 1 (1972): 18–41.

Eggermont-Molenaar, Mary, ed. and trans., *Montana 1911: A Professor and His Wife Among the Blackfeet.* University of Calgary Press, 2005.

Ewers, John C. *The Blackfeet: Raiders on the Northwestern Plains*. University of Oklahoma Press, 1958.

Ewers, John C. "Charlie Russell's Indians." *Montana The Magazine of Western History* 37, no. 3 (1987): 36–53.

Ewers, John C. *The Horse in Blackfoot Culture, With Comparative Material from Other Western Tribes.* Smithsonian Institution Bureau of American Ethnology Bulletin 159, 1955.

Farrell-Racette, Sherry. "My Grandmothers Loved to Trade: The Indigenization of European Trade Goods in Historic and Contemporary Canada." *Journal of Museum Ethnography*, no. 20 (March 2008): 69–81.

Farrell-Racette, Sherry, Michelle LaVallee, and Cathy Mathes. *Radical Stitch*. National Gallery of Canada, 2024.

Graybill, Andrew R. *The Red and the White: A Family Saga of the American West*. Liveright Publishing Corporation, 2013.

Grinnell, George Bird. *Blackfoot Lodge Tales: The Story of a Prairie People*, 1892. Reprint, University of Nebraska Press, 1962.

Growing Thunder, Jessa Rae. "Hi-Line Treasures: Bold Colors and Geometric Designs Exemplify Beadwork from Montana's Northern Plains." *Native American Art*, no. 38 (April/May 2022): 92–97.

Guoladdle Parker, MaryAnn. "Vessels that Carried Us: Kiowa Cradleboards." First Americans Museum. Accessed January 13, 2025. https://tinyurl.com/ydv2fd3f.

Hall, Ryan. *Beneath the Backbone of the World: Blackfoot People and the North American Borderlands, 1720–1877*. The University of North Carolina Press, 2020.

Hassrick, Peter H. *Charles M. Russell*. Harry N. Abrams Inc. and National Museum of American Art, Smithsonian Institution, 1989.

Henderson, Roger C. "The Pikanii and the U.S. Army's Piegan Expedition: Competing Narratives of the 1870 Massacre on the Marias River." *Montana The Magazine of Western History* 68, no. 1 (2018): 48–70.

Her Many Horses, Emil, ed. *Identity by Design: Tradition, Change, and Celebration in Native Women's Dresses*. Smithsonian Institution Press, 2007.

Hernandez, Nimachia. "Mokakssini: A Blackfoot Theory of Knowledge." PhD diss., Harvard University, 1999.

Horse Capture, Joseph D., and George P. Horse Capture. *Beauty, Honor, and Tradition: The Legacy of Plains Indians Shirts*. National Museum of the American Indian, Smithsonian Institution, and Minneapolis Institute of Art, 2001.

Hughes, Bethany. *Redface: Race, Indigeneity, Performance*. New York University Press, 2024.

Hungry-Wolf, Adolf. *Pikunni Biographies*. The Blackfoot Papers, vol. 4. The Good Medicine Cultural Foundation, 2006.

Hungry Wolf, Beverly. *The Ways of My Grandmothers*. Quill, 1982.

Hutchinson, Elizabeth. *The Indian Craze: Primitivism, Modernism, and Transculturation in American Art, 1890–1915*. Duke University Press, 2009.

Hyman, Colette A. *Dakota Women's Work: Creativity, Culture and Exile*. Minnesota Historical Society Press, 2012.

Igloliorte, Heather, and Carla Taunton. *The Routledge Companion to Indigenous Art Histories in the United States and Canada*. Routledge, Taylor & Francis Group, 2022.

Indian Arts and Crafts Board. *Contemporary Indian Artists: Montana, Wyoming, Idaho*. Tipi Shop, 1972.

Joyce, Rosemary A., and Susan D. Gillespie. *Things in Motion: Object Itineraries in Anthropological Practice*. School for Advanced Research Press, 2015.

Kapoun, Robert W., and Charles J. Lohrmann. *Language of the Robe: American Indian Trade Blankets.* Gibbs Smith, 1997.

Knowlton, Christopher. *Cattle Kingdom: The Hidden History of the Cowboy West*. Houghton Mifflin Harcourt, 2017.

Koch, Ronald P. *Dress Clothing of the Plains Indians.* University of Oklahoma Press, 1977.

LaPier, Rosalyn R. *Invisible Reality: Storytellers, Storytakers, and the Supernatural World of the Blackfeet*. University of Nebraska Press and the American Philosophical Society, 2017.

LaPier, Rosalyn R. "Land as Text." *Environmental History* 28, no. 1 (2023): 40–46.

Linderman, Frank Bird. *Recollections of Charley Russell*. University of Oklahoma Press, 1988.

Matthews, Maureen. *Naamiwan's Drum: The Story of a Contested Repatriation of Anishnaabe Artefacts*. University of Toronto Press, 2016.

McClintock, Walter. *The Old North Trail: Or, Life, Legends and Religion of the Blackfeet Indian*. Macmillan and Co., 1910.

Mize, Ramey. "Battle Grounds: Painting, War, and Witness in the Americas, 1861–1902." PhD diss., University of Pennsylvania, 2023.

Mt. Pleasant, Alyssa, Caroline Wigginton, and Kelly Wisecup. "Materials and Methods in Native American and Indigenous Studies: Completing the Turn." *William & Mary Quarterly* 75, no. 2 (2018): 207–36.

Nítsitaipoyaaki (Only Girl; Cheryle "Cookie" Cobell Zwang), Ponokaakii (Elk Woman, Marjie Crop Eared Wolf), and Heather Caverhill, "'We Know Who They Are': Connecting with the Nitsitapii in the Portraits of Winold Reiss," in *The BNSF Railway Art Collection* (forthcoming).

Nitsitapiisini: The Story of the Blackfoot People. Glenbow Museum, 2001. https://www.glenbow.org/blackfoot/EN/html/index.htm.

Oral History Interview with Lone Wolf (audio recording). 1956. Arizona Historical Society, Library and Archives.

Peavy, Linda, and Ursula Smith. *Full-Court Quest: The Girls from Fort Shaw Indian School, Basketball Champions of the World*. University of Oklahoma Press, 2008.

Peers, Laura. *Playing Ourselves: Interpreting Native Histories at Historic Reconstructions*. Altamira Press, 2007.

Peers, Laura, and Alison K. Brown. *Visiting with the Ancestors: Blackfoot Shirts in Museum Spaces*. AU Press, Athabasca University, 2015.

Peterson, Larry Len. *Charles M. Russell: Photographing the Legend: A Biography in Words and Pictures*. University of Oklahoma Press, 2014.

Price, B. Byron, ed. *Charles M. Russell: A Catalogue Raisonné*. University of Oklahoma Press, 2007.

Renner, Frederic G. *Charles M. Russell: Paintings, Drawings, and Sculpture in the Amon Carter Museum*, 1974. Reprint, Abradale Press/Harry N. Abrams, Inc., 1984.

Robertson, Carmen, Judy Anderson, and Katherine Boyer, ed. *Bead Talk: Indigenous Knowledge and Aesthetics from the Flatlands*. University of Manitoba Press, 2024.

Robertson, Carmen. "Beading Back and Forth: Upending Temporality Through Knowledge Transmission." *21: Inquiries into Art, History and the Visual* 5, no. 1 (2024): 49–70.

Robertson, Carmen. "Land and Beaded Identity: Shaping Art Histories of Indigenous Women of the Flatland." *RACAR: Revue d'art Canadienne/Canadian Art Review* 42, no. 2 (2017): 13–29.

Russell, Nancy Cooper. *Back-Tracking in Memory: The Life of Charles M. Russell, Artist; Recollections, Reflections and Personal Perspectives*. Edited by Thomas A. Petrie and Brian W. Dippie. C. M. Russell Museum, 2021.

Sayet, Madeline. *Where We Belong*. Methuen Drama, Bloomsbury Publishing, Plc., 2022.

Schultz, James Willard. *Blackfeet and Buffalo: Memories of Life Among the Indians*. University of Oklahoma Press, 1962.

Schultz, James Willard. *Friends of My Life as an Indian*. Houghton Mifflin Co., 1923.

Schultz, James Willard. *My Life as an Indian: The Story of a Red Woman and a White Man in the Lodges of the Blackfeet*. Doubleday, Page & Co., 1907.

Scott, Sara A. "Ties That Bind on the Northwestern Plains: Contexts for Prehistoric Trade and Travel." PhD diss., University of Montana, 2014.

Scott, Tristan. "Remembering the Marias Massacre." *Flathead Beacon*. January 15, 2020. https://flatheadbeacon.com/2020/01/15/remembering-marias-massacre/.

Smetzer, Meagan A. *Painful Beauty: Tlingit Women, Beadwork, and the Art of Resilience*. University of Washington Press, 2021.

Spears, Lorén, and Amanda Thompson. "'As We Have Always Done': Decolonizing the Tomaquag Museum's Collection Management Policy." *Collections: A Journal for Museum and Archives Professionals* 18, no. 1 (2022): 31–41.

Spence, Mark David. "Crown of the Continent, Backbone of the World: The American Wilderness Ideal and Blackfeet Exclusion from Glacier National Park." *Environmental History* 1, no. 3 (1996): 29–49.

Stauffer, Joan. *Behind Every Man: The Story of Nancy Cooper Russell*. Daljo Publishing, 1990.

Stewart, Rick. *Charles M. Russell: Sculptor*. Amon Carter Museum, 1994.

Taliaferro, John. *Charles M. Russell: The Life and Legend of America's Cowboy Artist*. Little, Brown & Co., 1996.

Thompson, Sally, Kootenai Culture Committee, and Pikunni Traditional Association. *People Before the Park: The Kootenai and Blackfeet Before Glacier National Park*. Montana Historical Society Press, 2015.

Tomkins, William. *Universal Indian Sign Language of the Plains Indians of North America*. W. Tomkins, 1926.

Tone-Pah-Hote, Jenny. *Crafting an Indigenous Nation: Kiowa Expressive Culture in the Progressive Era*. The University of North Carolina Press, 2019.

Tovías, Blanca. *Colonialism on the Prairies: Blackfoot Settlement and Cultural Transformation, 1870–1920*. Sussex Academic Press, 2011.

Troccoli, Joan Carpenter, ed. *Charles M. Russell: The Women in His Life and Art*. C. M. Russell Museum, 2018.

Troccoli, Joan Caprenter, ed. *The Masterworks of Charles M. Russell: A Retrospective of Paintings and Sculpture*. University of Oklahoma Press in cooperation with the Denver Art Museum, 2009.

Truettner, William H., ed. *The West as America: Reinterpreting Images of the Frontier*. Smithsonian Institution Press, 1991.

Weasel Traveller, Audrey. "A Shining Trail to the Sun's Lodge: Renewal Through Blackfoot Ways of Knowing." Master's thesis, University of Lethbridge, 1997.

Wigginton, Caroline. *Indigenuity: Native Craftwork and the Art of American Literature*. The University of North Carolina Press, 2022.

Wissler, Clark. "Material Culture of Blackfoot Indians." *Anthropological Papers of the American Museum of Natural History* 5, pt. 1 (1910).

Wissler, Clark, and D. C. Duvall, ed. and trans. *Mythology of the Blackfoot Indians*. University of Nebraska Press, 2007.

Wylie, Paul R. *Blood on the Marias: The Baker Massacre*. University of Oklahoma Press, 2016.

Zedeño, María Nieves. "Bison Hunters and the Rocky Mountains: An Evolving Partnership." *Quaternary International* 461 (2017): 80–101.

Zedeno, María Nieves, Jesse A. M. Ballenger, and John R. Murray, "Landscape Engineering and Organizational Complexity Among Late Prehistoric Bison Hunters of the Northwest Plains." *Current Anthropology* 55, no. 1 (2014): 23–58.

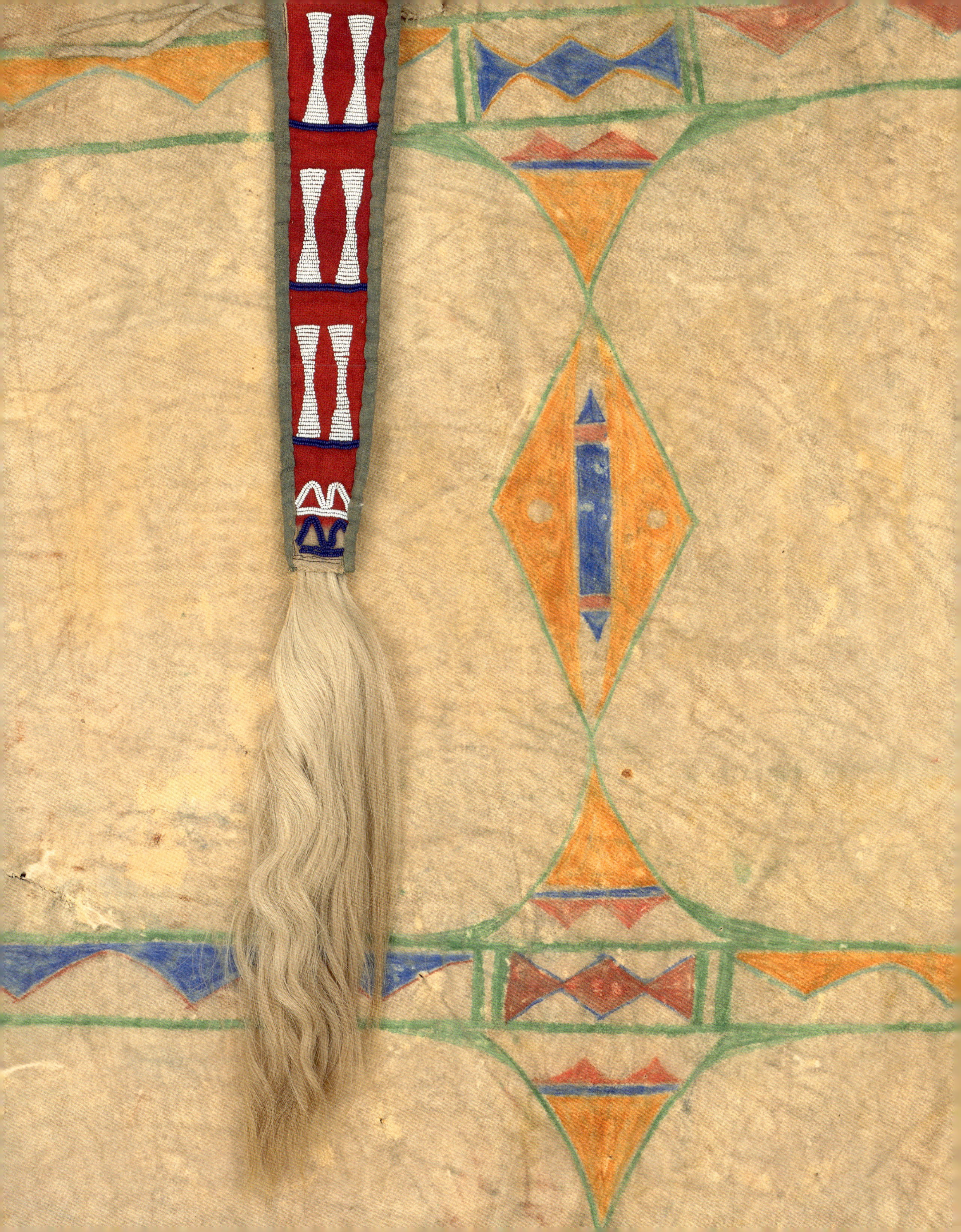

Index

Page numbers in italics indicate an illustration. All italicized titles are artworks by Charles Russell unless otherwise indicated.

Published on the occasion of the exhibition *Storytellers: The Blackfeet Nation and Charles M. Russell*

Organized by the Denver Art Museum
September 6, 2026–January 25, 2027

It is presented by Jane and Thomas Petrie. Additional support is provided by Mary Pat and Richard McCormick, the Wyeth Foundation for American Art, the donors to the Annual Fund Leadership Campaign, and the residents who support the Scientific and Cultural Facilities District (SCFD).

Denver Art Museum
100 West 14th Avenue Parkway
Denver, CO 80204
denverartmuseum.org

The Denver Art Museum is located on the homeland of the Arapaho, Cheyenne, and Ute people, along with many people from other Indigenous nations that call this place home. Learn more about our commitments to better represent, elevate, and support Indigenous cultures and people, past and present, on our website.

Distributed by University of Oklahoma Press, Norman, Oklahoma
ISBN 978-1-945483-23-3

Library of Congress Control Number: 2026937130

Managing Editor and Project Manager: Valerie Hellstein
Editor and Indexer: Leslie Murrell
Senior Curatorial Assistant: Meg Selig
Manager of Rights and Reproductions: Renée B. Miller
Photography: Unless otherwise indicated, Christina Jackson, Eric Stephenson, and Bruce Fernandez © Denver Art Museum

Book design by Kevin Coochwytewa

IMAGE CREDITS:

Front Cover: Unknown photographer, Russell and men from the Blackfoot tribe. Courtesy C. M. Russell Museum, Great Falls, Montana; cat. 26, photograph by Bruce Fernandez, courtesy Denver Art Museum.

p. 3: Charles Marion Russell, *Buffalo Hunt, Number 40* (detail), 1919. Oil on canvas; 39 × 57 in. Petrie Collection, Denver, Colorado. Photograph by Christina Jackson, courtesy Denver Art Museum.

p. 4: Attributed to Percy (Two Gun) Plain Woman (Kainai, 1895–1961), *Ninaipistsii (War Robe)* (detail), about 1930s. Deer hide and commercial pigment; 58¼ × 48½ in. Denver Art Museum: Native Arts acquisition funds, 1938.260. Photograph by Eric Stephenson, courtesy Denver Art Museum.

p. 34; p. 51, fig. 10; cat. 33; cat. 44; cat. 79: Photographs courtesy Sid Richardson Museum, Fort Worth, TX

p. 44, fig. 5; cats. 17, 58, 59, and 62: Courtesy C. M. Russell Museum, Great Falls, Montana

p. 47, fig. 8: © American Museum of Natural History, Division of Anthropology

p. 52, fig. 11: Artwork © and image courtesy Nancy Josephine Clark

p. 59, fig. 2; pp. 72–73; cat. 3; cat. 7; cat. 15; cat. 42; cat. 56; cat. 60; cat. 78; cats. 82–83: Photographs by Christina Jackson, courtesy of Denver Art Museum

pp. 62–68: Excerpts reproduced with permission from Paul Dyck, "Lone Wolf Returns to That Long Ago Time," *Montana the Magazine of Western History* 22, no. 1 (1972): 18–41.

p. 70: Amskaapii Pikanii artist, *Woman's Leggings* (detail), late 1800s. Cloth, beads, muslin, canvas, and wool; 12 ½ × 13 ¼ in. Denver Art Museum: Gift of Dr. Charles J. Norton, 1982.90A-B. Photograph by Eric Stephenson, courtesy Denver Art Museum.

cat. 2; cats. 5–6; cats. 8–9; cat. 12; cat. 13; cat. 16; cat. 18; cats. 20–25; cats. 29–30; cat. 32; cats. 37–39; cat. 43; cat. 45; cat. 50; cats. 53–55; cats. 66–70; cat. 77; cat. 85: Photographs by Eric Stephenson, courtesy Denver Art Museum

cat. 13: Courtesy Montana Historical Society

cat. 19; cats. 26–28; cat. 31; cats. 40–41; cat. 46; cat. 49; cat. 61; cats. 72–76; back cover: Photographs by Bruce Fernandez, courtesy Denver Art Museum

cat. 36: Courtesy of the Indianapolis Museum of Art at Newfields

cat. 51; cat. 86; p. 169 (detail): Photographs by Jeff Wells, courtesy Denver Art Museum

cat. 57: Photo © Metropolitan Museum of Art

cats. 64–65: Photographs by Lilly Wright, courtesy Denver Art Museum

p. 163: Amskaapii Pikanii artist, *Woman's Leggings* (detail), before 1946. Beads, flannel, and trade cloth, each approx. 18¼ × 11¾ × ⅜ in. Denver Art Museum: Gift of Sarah Coolidge Vance, 1946.77A-B. Photograph by Eric Stephenson, courtesy Denver Art Museum.

p. 171: Amskaapii Pikanii artist, *Lodge Liner*, c. 1920. Cowhide, paint, beads, and hair, 82 × 174 in. The L. D. and Ruth Bax Collection at the Denver Art Museum, 1985.259. Photograph by Eric Stephenson, courtesy Denver Art Museum.

Printed by Graphius in Belgium

The manufacturer's authorized representative in the EU for product safety is Mare Nostrum Group B.V., Mauritskade 21D, 1091 GC Amsterdam, The Netherlands, email: gpsr@mare-nostrum.co.uk